A RICH LAND, A POOR PEOPLE

Ill fares the land, to hastening ills a prey,
Where wealth accumulates, and men decay.

Oliver Goldsmith
The Deserted Village

A RICH LAND
A POOR PEOPLE

POLITICS AND SOCIETY IN
MODERN CHIAPAS

REVISED EDITION
WITH A FOREWORD BY LORENZO MEYER

THOMAS BENJAMIN

UNIVERSITY OF NEW MEXICO PRESS
Albuquerque

Library of Congress Cataloguing-in-Publication Data

Benjamin, Thomas, 1952–
A rich land, a poor people: politics and society in modern Chiapas/
Thomas Benjamin.—1st paper ed.
p.   cm.
Bibliography: p.
Includes index.
ISBN 0-8263-1713-8
1. Chiapas (Mexico)—Economic conditions.   2. Chiapas (Mexico)—
Social conditions.   3. Chiapas (Mexico)—Economic policy   4. Elite
(Social sciences)—Mexico—Chiapas—Political activity—History.
5. Peasantry—Mexico—Chiapas—History.   6. Agricultural industries—
Mexico—Chiapas—History.   7. Chiapas (Mexico)—Politics and
government.   I. Title
CIP

Frontispiece and Part openings:
Drawings by Alberto Beltrán reproduced from Ricardo Pozas Arciniega,
Chamula (México, D.F.: Instituto Nacional Indigenista, 1977).
Reproduced by permission of the publisher.

FOR MY MOTHER
AND IN REMEMBRANCE OF MY FATHER

CONTENTS

TABLES

FIGURES

MAPS

Foreword

Lorenzo Meyer[1]

THE VIOLENCE THAT RECENTLY ERUPTED IN SOUTHERN MEXICO, AS A result of extreme conditions of misery and injustice, is not the best path for the country; but neither is authoritarian neoliberalism, which has been followed up until now. A new national political covenant is necessary, one without tricks and one that responds to the needs of Mexico the way it really is and not the government's image of Mexico. It should be a covenant that does not repeat the pattern in which the Institutional Revolutionary Party (PRI)–government obtained 97.7 percent of the vote in 1976, 90.2 percent in 1982, 89.9 percent in 1988—and an armed rebellion in 1994!

Today, as at few other times, the Mexican political class, in its broadest sense, has been united: the PRI and the Party of the Democratic Revolution, the bishops and the Ministry of Government, business leaders and public opinion makers. All have declared that the political violence that erupted in the highlands of Chiapas is not the right response to the old and obvious problems of misgovernment and extreme social injustice which have accumulated there. The motives—fears—which explain why each group rejects violence are different but essentially correct: as a national project, the declaration of war by the Zapatista Army of National Liberation (EZLN) against the national army for the purpose of overthrowing the government of Carlos Salinas and establishing social justice is untenable and suicidal given national and international conditions in the aftermath of the collapse of communism.

We must do more than condemn the violence of a few rebels (which has profound and historic causes) and reject State violence as an acceptable response. We do not need another 1968 in 1994.[2] If violence is not

xi

the solution, what is? No one, being completely honest, would suggest that Mexico's existing political institutions and current leaders are satisfactory. Today the electoral system and the political parties do not work and, as a result, are more illegitimate than legitimate. The aberration in Yucatán has just demonstrated this clearly: the loser is the official winner and vice versa, giving elections in Mexico an Alice-in-Wonderland quality. The state legislatures and the national congress are perfect examples of total and absolute political uselessness since the majority of their members represent no one except themselves and their only purpose is to serve the president. Finally, the judiciary is neither powerful nor dedicated to the provision of justice (indeed, the opposite is true); anyone in Mexico seeking justice before a prosecutor or a court who finds it has only luck to thank.

Given these circumstances—which everyone, the people and the politicians, has understood for a long time—how can one give a clear and credible response to the question regarding the best way to resolve the profound injustice which Chiapanecos, and many more Mexicans throughout the country, suffer? A new political system has to be designed and rapidly put into place: the current authoritarian system has to be brought to an end, not only because it is extremely unfair but also because it is dysfunctional and obsolete, and it should be replaced by a modern, genuinely representative system, in which the marginalized in society have a voice and an effective vote. In short, what has to be done is what has been announced a thousand times in official pronouncements and negated a thousand times in practice—the development of a state of law, one that is democratic, fair and just, and one that gives primacy to votes rather than bullets. The basic political problem that confronts a poor and premodern Mexico—whose leaders try to fool themselves and foreigners alike that the country has achieved First World status (the Mexican government's petition that it be considered equal to the other members of the OECD in this respect seems like a cruel joke)—became tragically evident twenty-five years ago, in Tlatelolco. Nevertheless the powers-that-be then and now have sidestepped seeking any fundamental solutions. The problem can be summed up like this: while Mexican society has grown and matured, the political system has remained the same as it was in the 1940s. For this reason our institutions as well as those who direct them have been overwhelmed by circumstances. The result is an accelerating failure of the political process. Now the chain has shattered at its weakest link: in Chiapas, land of the poorest of the poor.

According to the pamphlet published in 1990 by the Consultative Council of Solidarity[3]: "If the share of wealth generated by petroleum (which does not remain in the state anyway, same as the electricity produced by the hydroelectric dams at Malpaso, Chicoasen, Angostura, and Penitas) is eliminated from the economic statistics of Chiapas, its per capita gross internal product is substantially reduced and that state is then placed among the poorest in the country," which is to say, alongside Oaxaca and Guerrero. The problem of Chiapas is, as the manifesto of the EZLN indicates, a hundred years old. Anyone who wishes to better understand this problem today would do well to read the book by Thomas Benjamin, *A Rich Land, A Poor People*. Professor Benjamin's thesis is stated in the title: Chiapas is a rich land with a poor people as a result of a political process burdened by violence, and a society profoundly divided ethnically and, above all, economically.

Violence has been a constant element in Chiapanecan society; in the nineteenth century and the Mexican Revolution of 1910, it had particularly destructive effects on native communities. Revolutionary factions— "Mapaches" and Carrancistas—although mutual enemies, both plundered native communities during the Revolution. The postrevolutionary era did not bring an end to the violence because disputes over land—the key to wealth in every rural society, such as Chiapas—were not settled by agrarian reform; indeed, with the growth of the cattle industry, the violence became worse. The "cattle-ization" of the state, beginning around 1950, was fast, as fast as the ecological destruction it generated. Between that year and 1985, land under cultivation and population growth increased at the same rate—quadrupling—but the number of cattle increased even faster: it septupled. As a result, cattle ranchers and native communities found themselves in conflict, fighting for the same fundamental but scarce resource: land.

The distribution of wealth in Chiapas today, Professor Benjamin writes, is not very different from that which prevailed at the end of the Porfiriato (1910). The general standard of living has improved, but the profound sense of injustice and the insecurity these communities feel about the future have not changed. In 1960, landowners with properties of one thousand hectares and larger constituted 2.4 percent of all private landowners in Chiapas but they controlled 60 percent of all privately owned land. On the other hand, ejidos—there are more than a thousand—possess lands valued at less than one third of the value of privately owned lands. In Chiapas, according to General Absalón Castellanos in 1982, then at the beginning of his gubernatorial term, "there is no middle class," the rich are very rich and the poor are extremely poor. Recognizing that fact and doing something about it, however, is not the same thing; in 1987 the Mexican Academy of Human Rights published a report ("Chiapas: cronología de un etnocidio reciente") which characterized the administration of General Castellanos as one of the most repressive and corrupt in the country.

In the 1970s, as social polarization became worse, a movement of agrarian and native community organizations developed, which was generally independent of the traditional control of the PRI: the First Native Congress of Chiapas (1974) organized by Bishop Samuel Ruiz was followed by the 10th of April Campesino Alliance (1976). Then came the Campesino Bloc of Chiapas, the Union of Ejidal Unions and Marginalized Groups, the Miguel de la Cruz Agricultural Workers' Union, and the Emiliano Zapata Campesino Organization. The aggressiveness of peasant communities in the defense of their interests is apparent in certain figures: during the 1970s there were 115 agrarian conflicts characterized as serious, among these were 87 disputes between native ejidatarios and ranchers for control of communal and ejidal lands. The use of the army and the police to regulate conflict between landowners and ejidatarios became all too common. Hamlets and villages were frequently burned and destroyed; the murder of campesinos also became common, and the murder of landowners by campesinos should not be ignored. After the state of Veracruz, Chiapas reported the greatest number of violent incidents. In 1983, for example, the community of Monte Libano in Ocosingo sent a letter to the President complaining that in 1976, 1979, and again in 1982 the state police had burned down their hamlet. The letter concluded with a warning: if we have to, we will fight to recover our lands because we know that no one else will help us struggle against bosses and land barons. A similar warning was made the same year by the Tzeltales of the Organization of Indigenous Peoples of Southeastern Mexico in a proclamation: "We have learned from the study of the history of man and the history of Mexico that only by struggling in an organized form can we achieve a new and better way of life."

In 1989 Professor Benjamin concluded that Chiapas was under a "state of siege" and that politics in the state was a matter of force. By 1987 the national army had four thousand soldiers in the state, today the number is said to be twelve thousand and this will surely increase.

The drama now occurring in Chiapas took many of us by surprise although it shouldn't have: the coming of violence had been announced long before. Guillermo Correa, (echoing the concern of the Catholic Church) writing in *Proceso* in 1983, warned that Chiapas was "one step away from guerrilla war." That was ten years ago, just about the time when the Zapatista movement, according to one of its leaders, was becoming organized. What did regional politicians and the national authorities do at this time? What did the current Minister of Government do when he was governor of the state? As far as anyone can tell, not very much, at least not enough.

Now is not the time to grumble about lost time but to make proposals and do something. There has to be decisive, intelligent, sensible, and rapid action. The challenge facing Mexico and its political class is more serious and profound than that faced by the government when it negotiated the Free Trade Agreement with the United States. A new political covenant between the governing elite and the majority of the people has to be negotiated, one which recognizes the people as citizens, one that redistributes the burden of economic development in a fairer and more equitable manner, and one without the corruption, chicanery, pretense, and the irresponsibility that have made the Mexican political class world famous ("the perfect dictatorship"). Is the government and the political opposition up to the challenge? For their own sakes as well as that of all Mexicans, I hope so.

NOTES

1. Originally published as "Fallaron las Instituciones" ("The Institutions Failed"), on the front page of Mexico's newspaper of record, *Excelsior*, January 6, 1994. Lorenzo Meyer is a historian and the coordinator of the Program of Mexican–U.S. Studies at the Colegio de Mexico in Mexico City. He is the coauthor of *In the Shadow of the Mexican Revolution: Contemporary Mexican History, 1910–1989* (1993).

2. In 1968 the Mexican government used the national army to violently repress a civic movement for democracy and social justice in the Plaza of Three Cultures, Tlatelolco, Mexico City.

3. Solidarity, the shorthand name given to the National Solidarity Program, was an anti-poverty program established by President Carlos Salinas de Gortari.

PREFACE

DESPITE THE FERTILITY OF THIS PROVINCE, IT IS EXTREMELY POOR. . . ."[1] This description of Chiapas, written in 1823, has been repeated time and again over the past century and half. In 1985 President Miguel de la Madrid rendered it into the language of modern technocrats: "The natural wealth of the state of Chiapas contrasts with the imbalances in its development."[2] A rich land, a poor people. It is the unhappy byword of Chiapas.

Distant, provincial, and underdeveloped, Chiapas has generally kept to itself and is largely unknown even to most Mexicans except by reputation. A political cartoon in one of the Mexico City newspapers represented Chiapas in 1982 as a medieval castle surrounded by a hostile jungle. In the 1980s, as in the 1880s, the news from Chiapas is bad. Reports of endemic poverty and repression occasionally make their way into the newspapers and magazines of Mexico City. In the public mind the state is representative of the worst conditions of rural Mexico.

Chiapas is rich, in fact—rich in fertile farmlands, pastures, and forests: in coffee, cattle, cacao, and petroleum; and in productive enterprises owned by a few families. Yet most Chiapanecos remain very poor despite the wealth of the land, the reforms of the Mexican Revolution, and the modernization policies of successive state and federal governments. Natural plenty, of course, does not necessarily create social plenty. Modernization and reform need not lead to progress for all. That is the paradox of Chiapas, a rich land of poor people.

Beginning in the 1890s commercial farmers and ranchers, primarily those of the Central Valley, and their mercantile and professional allies initiated a sustained effort to use government to make Chiapas a pro-

Campesinos, recipients of a land reform grant, in Colonia F. I. Madero, in the municipality of Cintalapa, 1930. From: Archivo "seis de enero de 1915" de la Secretaría de Reforma Agraria, Mexico City.

ductive agricultural region integrated into national and international markets. Across sixty turbulent years—spanning intraregional conflicts, revolution from without and popular pressure within, and national political centralization—the landowners of Chiapas successfully adapted to changing circumstances within the region and the nation and carefully transformed their state. This book is about those landowners, the so-called *familia chiapaneca*—their governments and political struggles, efforts to modernize and reform Chiapas, and efforts to preserve and advance their power and wealth. It is also about the large majority of Chiapanecos whose toil (and, at one time, village lands) has made Chiapas a rich region but who have themselves been kept poor. What follows is a regional history of power and interests, that is, a study of the social and economic basis of politics and the socioeconomic impact of government.

The persistence of mass poverty admittedly is a topic of great complexity. Any one effort to unravel this problem, particularly one based on primary sources, can only suggest answers for one place. My investigation of the history of Chiapas since Independence has brought me repeatedly to an understanding of the great importance of government as the essential shaping force of wealth and poverty in the region. The power of the familia chiapaneca, an economic group and not a social class, was often translated into an ability to use government to promote its interests. The connection between power and interests was never simple, but a pattern is discernible over the course of decades. The way the familia chiapaneca has used government to modernize and reform Chiapas could have had no other result but narrow economic growth without broad-based social development. The greatest challenge to this program was the Mexican Revolution, which intruded into Chiapas with its momentum for economic redistribution and social justice.

Historians of regional Mexico during the last two decades have been drawn to the Mexican Revolution. While undermining the traditional "populist" interpretation of the Revolution as a triumphant peasant movement, they too often view it as the fundamental watershed initiating modern Mexico. Historian John Womack, Jr., in this regard, suggests that the Revolution has become a fetish for historians and that in the larger sense "we have resisted comprehending what the Revolution meant."[3] Hans Werner Tobler poses the right question by asking "whether the revolution is to be understood as a profound and radical reorientation of Mexico's political, social and economic systems or rather—for all the surface change in politics—as the expression of a basic continuity in the country's development since the Porfiriato."[4]

Most students of the Mexican Revolution have difficulty answering this question in detail because of the limited chronological focus of their monographs. "It would be much more invigorating and perhaps more fruitful," writes Paul J. Vanderwood, "to think of [the Revolution] over the *longue durée* as advocated by the Annalist school of historical thought."[5] The primary value of this study of Chiapas is its extended temporal perspective—the entire modern period, with particular emphasis on the period 1890 to 1950. The answer to Tobler's question for Chiapas is clear and unequivocal: continuity reigns. The great historical project of Chiapas since the 1890s has been the modernization of commercial agriculture. The Mexican Revolution, which intervened from without in Chiapas, interfered with and in time contributed in an important way to this development. In the final analysis, however, in

Chiapas the Revolution was but a chapter in the longer historical process of elite-directed modernization and reform.

This is a regional history that explores, in the words of Stuart Voss, "the character and evolution of a region in its own right."[6] The Prologue tells of the development of an intense regional rivalry within Chiapas from Independence to the 1880s. During this period the farmers and ranchers of the Central Valley politically and economically eclipsed the colonial oligarchy of the Central Highlands, to become the political constituency of "modernizing" state governments during the latter Porfiriato.

The three chapters in Part One chronicle the efforts of energetic governors, the so-called enlightened caciquismo, to develop the state economically in the 1890s and 1900s. Their program of modernization (implemented during a favorable time for national and international markets) appeared at the time to be remarkably successful in promoting commercial agriculture; what the prospering elites of Chiapas did not see were the high costs of their "progress" paid by Indian and mestizo villagers, migrant laborers, and indebted servants.

Part Two, composed of two chapters, is an account of the Mexican Revolution in Chiapas, or rather, the decidedly unrevolutionary political-military regional movements sparked by the national revolutions. The convulsions in Chiapas between 1910 and 1920 were affairs of the familia chiapaneca (and intruding outsiders); "the people" did not rebel for land and liberty, but the long years of disorder and war did fracture the tight system of social control and open the door to their participation in regional politics.

The three chapters in Part Three consider the popular challenge to the familia chiapaneca, and the response and survival of landowners, from 1920 to 1950. Landless villagers and agricultural workers were mobilized into agrarian leagues, labor unions, and political parties to secure land, just wages and working conditions, and power. Popular mobilization, however, also served the cause of factional political struggle within the state and, in time, the interests of landowner-politicians.

The Epilogue follows the success story of the familia chiapaneca from the 1950s to the 1980s and describes the agrarian rebellion, so long delayed, which erupted throughout the Chiapas countryside in the 1970s and continues to this day.

From the 1890s to the 1950s and beyond, the governments of Chiapas sought the modernization of the regional economy and society by means of roads and schools, developmental projects, and social reforms. If we accept their statements and promises at face value, they wanted to create a productive and prosperous regional economy that would in time benefit all social classes. If mass poverty persisted, as it did, it was understood to be the result of too few roads, insufficient federal investment, low market prices for crops—but also the "backwardness" or traditionalism of Indians and the complacency, laziness, alcoholism, and corruption of villagers, farm workers, peasant farmers, and ejidatarios. The model of modernization, although often adjusted and reinvigorated, was never doubted. And the intimate protection government provided private property against "bandits," "agitators," and "communists" never faltered. This institutionalized protection—extended in the name of free enterprise but actually reinforcing a narrow monopolization of land, resources, and opportunity—was never acknowledged as destructive of truly free enterprise, economic opportunity, and regional prosperity more widely shared. In short, the familia chiapaneca attempted to purchase regional growth and development cheaply, unwilling to forego their de facto monopoly privileges for genuine regional development and widespread prosperity, to say nothing of social justice. Unknowingly, Charles Darwin was speaking to them: "If the misery of the poor be caused not by the laws of nature, but by our institutions, great is our sin."

I have been most fortunate in the personal and institutional support given me in the research and writing of this book. Archival research was undertaken in Mexico and the United States during the years 1978 to 1981 and the summers of 1982, 1983, and 1984. Financial support for travel and residence was generously provided through fellowships by the College of Arts and Letters at Michigan State University, the Henry L. and Grace Doherty Charitable Foundation, and the Faculty Research and Creative Endeavors Committee of Central Michigan University. Research leads, suggestions, and assistance were given by M. Favio Gálvez, Natalio Fuentes, Gary Gossen, Alfonso López, Prudencio Moscoso Pastrana, Thomas Neihaus, Peter Reich, Gloria Sarmiento, Daniela Spenser, Ángeles Suárez, Lawrence Taylor, and John Taylor. I would also like to thank the staffs of the archives listed in the bibliography; without their friendly cooperation and assistance, I would long ago have given up.

Several friends read and criticized various drafts. The advice (and just as important, encouragement) of David C. Bailey, Friedl Baumann, Leslie Rout, Jan Rus, Paul Vanderwood, and Allen Wells has been invaluable and is gratefully acknowledged. Daniela Spenser, my Chiapaneca soulmate, read each draft and pointed me in the right direction countless times. Despite the best advice, of course, errors of fact and interpretation are mine alone.

Finally, the support of my family through the lengthy and rocky course of research and writing proved vital. Christina Johns patiently put up with Tuxtla Gutiérrez, San Cristóbal de Las Casas, Mexico City, and my Mexican obsession, and gave me the confidence to do more than I thought I could. Christine Mattley helped me put my life in order enough to finish writing and rewriting. My parents, even under trying circumstances, provided unswerving encouragement and support. To my father who did not live to see the fruit of those efforts but who lives in me, and to my mother, this book is dedicated.

POLITICAL ABBREVIATIONS

CCCR   Comité Chiapaneco de la Confederación Revolucionaria
CCM   Confederación Campesina Mexicana
CCOC   Confederación Campesino y Obrera de Chiapas
CGOCM   Confederación General de Obreros y Campesinos de México
CLA   Comisión Local Agraria
CNA   Comisión Nacional Agraria
CNC   Confederación Nacional Campesino
CROM   Confederación Regional Obrera Mexicana
CTM   Confederación de Trabajadores Mexicana
INI   Instituto Nacional Indigenista
LCA   Liga de Comunidades Agrarias
LNC   Liga Nacional Campesina
PCM   Partido Comunista Mexicana
PNR   Partido Nacional Revolucionario
PRI   Partido Revolucionario Institucional
PRM   Partido de la Revolución Mexicana
PSC   Partido Socialista Chiapaneco
PSS   Partido Socialista de Soconusco
STI   Sindicato de Trabajadores Indígenas
SUTICS   Sindicato Único de Trabajadores de la Industria del Café del Soconusco

A RICH LAND, A POOR PEOPLE

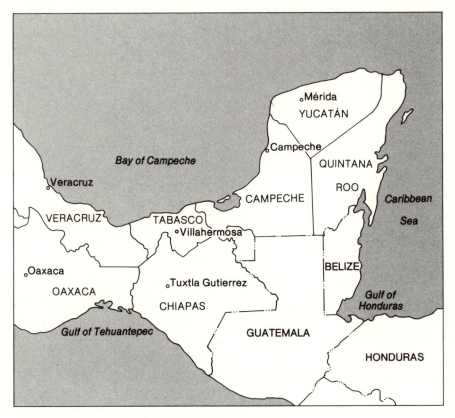

The State of Chiapas and
Southeastern Mexico

PROLOGUE

The Sentiment of Localism Is Very Deeply Rooted (1820s–80s)

POLITICS IN NINETEENTH-CENTURY CHIAPAS INVOLVED LOCAL CONFLICTS of interest within the landowning familia chiapaneca to the disadvantage of the powerless and dispossessed *pueblo chiapaneco,* whose land and labor was most often the focus of contention. In a province with an Indian majority and a history of Indian insurrection, competing elite factions in Chiapas did not seek or enlist the support of peasant villagers until the twentieth century. Politics was not a matter of class or race but of economic geography. The surviving colonial oligarchy of the province—the clergy, landowners, and merchants located in the provincial capital in the Central Highlands—subsisted on the labor and the surplus production of the large nearby Indian populations whom the elites regarded as a "natural resource" (in the phrase of one contemporary). The farmers and merchants of the less populated but more fertile Central Valley coveted Indian labor and church lands and, therefore, provincial governmental power to implement "reforms" to transfer those resources into their more productive hands.

National politics, particularly competition and conflict in the center of Mexico to control Mexico City and certain key provinces, intersected with but by no means dominated regional politics and local interests. Given the weakness of the national state until late in the century, the peripheral provinces of Mexico enjoyed considerable home rule; but they were not, however, immune from the conflicts of the center. The farmers and merchants of the Central Valley of Chiapas identified with and became loosely allied to the national Liberals in a mutually beneficial arrangement. The former colonial oligarchy of the provincial capital associated with the former colonial oligarchy of the national

I

capital, the national Conservatives, and were motivated less by the fate of the nation than the fate of their province and their predominance in it. The Liberal triumph over the Conservatives, nationally and provincially, in time favored the construction of a stable national state, which emerged near the century's close. The politics of local interests, however, still governed Chiapas even as the new century began. "The sentiment of localism," complained a governor in 1891, "is very deeply rooted in the sons of each community in this state."

That "sentiment of localism" became the target of modernizing provincial politicians beginning in the 1890s, of revolutionary proconsuls sent from the center in the 1910s, and of state and national government bureaucrats in the 1920s, 1930s, and beyond. To future reformers, localism was synonymous with backwardness, disorder, and poverty. And the cure to these maladies was strong, effective central government.

LA PROVINCIA DE CHIAPA

"Its territory is composed of beautiful valleys and magnificent mountains," wrote Brigadier General Vicente Filisola of Chiapas in 1823.[1] "La provincia de Chiapa," as it was called prior to Independence (it became Chiapas after 1821), which Filisola rediscovered on behalf of Mexico, was located to the south and east of the Mexican provinces of Oaxaca and Tabasco and northwest ("in the backyard," it was generally said) of Guatemala.[2]

Chiapas, like Mexico generally, is physically contorted by mountains interspersed among valleys. The Sierra Madre de Chiapas, a volcanic range that rises from the Isthmus of Tehuantepec, dominates the topography of the region. This range is bisected by an intermontaine basin comparable in size to the Valley of Mexico. Through this great Central Valley of Chiapas (elevation 1,500–2,500 feet), also called the Central Lowlands, the Central Depression, and *tierra caliente,* flows the Río Grande de Chiapas, which becomes the Río Grijalva farther north and flows into the Bay of Campeche on the coast of Tabasco. The Central Valley is composed of a number of wide alluvial valleys, possesses fertile soils and extensive grasslands, and is usually hot and dry. As a result of a series of epidemics during the sixteenth and seventeenth centuries, the native population of this area was severely re-

Regional Physical Features

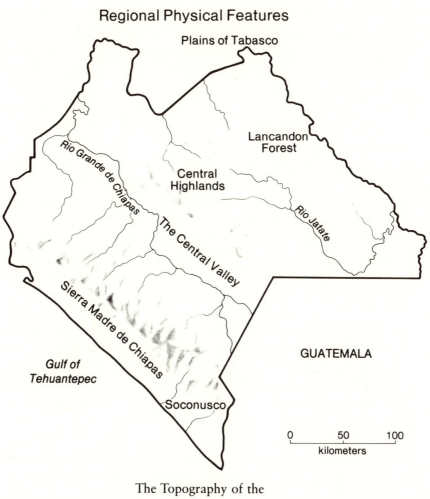

The Topography of the
State of Chiapas

duced. The Meseta Central (elevation 5,000–7,000 feet), also called the Central Highlands and *tierra fría,* rises sharply from the Valley of Chiapas and dominates the northern portion of the Sierra Madre de Chiapas. This region is an extremely rugged and heavily forested area containing several small rocky valleys and is generally cold. Here the epidemics of the early colonial period were less deadly due to the colder climate and the wider dispersion of settlements, thus making the highlands the home of the vast majority of Chiapas's native peoples, speakers of Tzotzil and Tzeltal principally and sharing the general Mayan culture of southeastern Mesoamerica. To the north and east, the Central Highlands gradually fall off and eventually disappear into the plains of Tabasco and the Lacandón tropical forest. The portion of the Sierra Madre south of the Central Valley gradually rises to a maximum elevation of 12,000 feet and runs along the Pacific coast into Guatemala. The Pacific Littoral (its southern portion is called Soconusco), bounded by the Sierra Madre and the Pacific Ocean, is a sea-level plain no more than fifteen to twenty-five miles wide. The native population along the coast was so reduced by epidemics during the sixteenth century that it came to be known as "el Despoblado," the uninhabited place. Chiapas is not a natural region; instead it's the political artifact of the Conquest and Spanish rule and contains several regions, a condition giving rise to opposing local interests and political conflict.

Chiapas in the early 1820s was and had always been a frontier. It formed the northern border of the kingdom of Guatemala. The pre-Columbian cities of Palenque and Bonampak were located on the northern periphery of classic Mayan civilization. By the end of the fifteenth century, Aztec political-military influence had advanced as far south as the towns of Zinacantan and Soconusco. Chiapas was conquered early in the sixteenth century by Spanish military expeditions proceeding from Mexico City in the north and, a few years later, from Guatemala in the south. Spanish settlements in the region, like small European islands in an Indian sea, were rustic frontier towns, "no fit place for Jesuits," commented the English Dominican monk Thomas Gage.[3] Regionalism—a striving for cultural, economic, and political autonomy—flourished on this periphery of Mexico and Guatemala.

On the eve of independence and annexation by Mexico, Chiapas possessed a population of about 130,000 inhabitants. Most of the population, wrote Filisola in his report to the Mexican government, was Indian, there were fewer mestizos ("or ladinos, as they call them") and still fewer creoles and Spaniards. The 1814 census counted more than 105,000 Indians, 21,000 mestizos, and fewer than 4,000 Spaniards. "Although those called Spaniards have in general the same culture that is common in the towns of Méjico . . . ," noted an 1822 report sent to Filisola, "the Indians remain most ignorant, and are very degraded, because in this part of America [meaning all of the Kingdom of Guatemala] they have been treated with much contempt, and they have been forced always into a very humiliating submission."[4] The province had 2 cities, Ciudad Real and Comitán; 3 towns, Tuxtla, Tonalá, and Palenque; and 157 villages. The capital of the province, Ciudad Real de Chiapa de los Españoles (also called San Cristóbal after the city's patron saint), was located in the valley of Jovel in the Central Highlands. Of the 6,000 Cristobalenses (residents of Ciudad Real) reported in 1814, fewer than 700 were American-born or European-born Spaniards. The capital was surrounded by nearly 70 Indian villages. The towns and their surrounding countryside in tierra caliente were generally described at the time as possessing fertile lands, extensive pastures, and an unhealthy climate.[5]

"Despite the fertility of this province," wrote Filisola, "it is extremely poor."[6] This was Chiapas as described two years after its independence from Spain and one year before its permanent annexation by Mexico: a rich land, a poor people. And so it had been for nearly three hundred years, an age when Chiapas was a backwater province within a bypassed corner of Spanish America, the Kingdom of Guatemala.

There was wealth to be had here, although it was insignificant compared to the fortunes made in Mexico, Peru, or even Guatemala proper. The wealth of Chiapas was squeezed from the native population in the form of tribute and tithes, forced labor, and forced sales of merchandise for the benefit of a small circle of royal officials, prominent settlers, and enterprising friars.[7] These privileged few were located for the most part in the Central Highlands and in the provincial capital Ciudad Real. Their power and wealth were derived from the privileges and prerogatives ingrained in the colonial Central American system of government. Competitors for the wealth of the region—criollo (creole or American-born Spanish) and ladino (mestizo) farmers and ranchers—were generally excluded from this system and most of its benefits. They lived more modestly from the land of the Central Valley surrounding the towns of Chiapa, Tuxtla, San Bartolomé, and—on the long grassy plateau south of Ciudad Real—Comitán. They produced sugar, cotton, maize, cattle, and horses for export to Guatemala and to parts of Mexico.[8] By the late eighteenth or early nineteenth century, two ill-defined, regionally based groups of Spanish-speaking settlers were forming in Chiapas. The rivalry between them for land, labor, and political power became increasingly bitter and violent as the decades passed. It accounts for the political turbulence of this region during the time of independence (from Spain and Guatemala) and annexation by Mexico, and was the essence of politics in nineteenth-century Chiapas.

THE ONE THAT WANTED TO BE OF MEXICO

The immediate stimulus to the movement for independence in Spanish America was the Napoleonic invasion of Spain in 1807–8. Provincial Spanish councils of resistance arose to oppose the French, while in America creoles established loyal governing councils in many cities to rule until King Ferdinand VII was restored to the Spanish throne. In 1810 the Spanish councils united, formed a central council, and summoned a national parliament—the Cortés. The Cortés, which assembled in the port city of Cádiz to write a constitution, also granted American representation. This move encouraged provincialism and separatism, which was already high, in Central America. The delegate from Chiapas, for example, introduced a slate of eight propositions outlining home rule. The Cádiz Cortés promulgated its liberal constitution in 1812; both the constitution and the governing body, however, were suppressed in 1814 upon the restoration of King Ferdinand.[9]

In January 1821 a liberal faction of the military seized power in Spain, restored the Cádiz Constitution, and reconvened the Cortés. The new government enacted measures restricting the privileges of the Catholic Church and the military, reforms that were not welcome in elite circles in America. In response, the royalist military commander of Mexico, the creole Agustín de Iturbide, published his Plan de Iguala in February 1821. In defense of the existing social order, Iturbide and his Mexico City backers made a conservative revolution for independence and established a Mexican Empire to immunize Mexico from the Spanish reforms and social revolution. By August 24, Spain's Superior Political Chief of Mexico, Juan de O'Donojú, signed the Treaty of Córdova recognizing the Mexican Empire as a sovereign and independent nation. Four days later in Chiapas, the town council of Comitán seconded the Plan de Iguala, which was soon followed by similar pronouncements by various town governments. The provincial assembly (a creation of the Cádiz Constitution) formally declared independence from Spain and Guatemala on September 26 and requested annexation by Mexico.[10]

The Spanish elite of Chiapas, particularly those of Ciudad Real, favored annexation of their province by Mexico for several reasons. The proclamation of independence maintained that "Guatemala never has proportioned to the Province, sciences, industry, or any other utility and has looked upon it with much indifference. . . . Chiapas has been under the Guatemalan government for three centuries, and in all this time has not prospered." Mexico appeared in a different light. "The Provinces of the [Mexican] Empire enrich ours by the circulation of commerce which exists one with the other."[11] And, in fact, during the first two decades of the nineteenth century, trade with Mexico greatly surpassed that with Guatemala. Chiapas had become commercially tied to Mexico.[12] Another, and more compelling, reason for favoring annexation involved the natural desire of provincial elites to escape the dominance of a capital city.[13] As one modern historian explains:

Mexico offered an alternative to the independence of the regions under the old Guatemalan hegemony, and Mexico, for being far away, for being unknown, for its imperial airs, for its similarity with the old and distant Spanish monarchy, strongly attracted the local políticos who expected more autonomy with Mexico than with Guatemala.[14]

Yet another reason was proposed at the time. One observer of political sentiments in Chiapas in 1821, Colonel Manuel Mier y Terán, a Mexican, believed that Mexico's monarchical government, and rumors of republicanism in Guatemala, compelled the elite of Ciudad Real to favor Mexico. Given Chiapas's large and exploited Indian population, furthermore, the elite of Ciudad Real believed that Mexico could and would better defend the province in case of popular insurrection.[15]

Iturbide's empire collapsed in early 1823, a victim of rebellion in central Mexico. In light of this, Chiapanecos debated whether to maintain or sever their union with Mexico. The twelve-member provincial assembly—the Junta Provisional Gubernativa—(with two members absent) was divided equally into two factions. The pro-Mexico group, essentially the oligarchy of San Cristóbal and the surrounding Central Highlands, favored continued union with Mexico for the reasons given above. The pro-Guatemala group, which represented the outlying areas of Tuxtla, Chiapa, Comitán, and Tapachula, opposed union with Mexico, fearing such union as the means of Cristobalense control over the localities of Chiapas and exclusion from the Guatemalan market. Furthermore, "a majority of people with any sense, understood the disadvantages of being united to Mexico given the great distance which separated them from the country, and the advantage of continuing united to Guatemala given the similarity of their habits and customs [and] given the commercial relations only with [Guatemala]. . . ."[16] Unable to reach a consensus, proponents of autonomy in June formed a sovereign government of Chiapas, the Suprema Junta Provisional, until a final decision could be reached regarding annexation by Mexico or Guatemala.[17]

At the same time, the other provinces of Central America, which had joined the Mexican Empire in 1822, declared their independence in July and formed the United Provinces of Central America, an ill-fated federal republic. Although invited to participate in the Central American Congress, Chiapas sent no representatives. To prevent the loss of Chiapas, the new republican government in Mexico City ordered General Vicente Filisola, then garrisoned in Guatemala, to march to Ciudad Real and dissolve the Suprema Junta Provisional, which he did on September 5. Filisola then participated in the reestablishment of the provincial assembly—which immediately requested annexation by Mexico—and returned to Guatemala, leaving Colonel Felipe Codallos and a small force in the province. The Mexican government quickly reversed its course, however, after receiving protests from proponents of Mexican annexation in Chiapas that Filisola's action was counterproductive. The province, the Mexican government pledged, was to be permitted to determine its political future without interference.[18]

Filisola's intervention outraged the leaders of the other towns of the province. Before communication of the new policy of the Mexican government reached Chiapas, the municipal councils of Tuxtla, Chiapa, Los Llanos (San Bartolomé), and Comitán proclaimed the Plan de Chiapa Libre on October 2, declaring that Chiapas would not blindly depend on any country and would remain independent of both Mexico and Guatemala until the province itself decided what to do. "The rights of this province and of each citizen," proclaimed the town council of Tuxtla, "have been violated and abused by the violence by which it has been newly united with the Mexican metropolis."[19] To avoid bloodshed and further damage to the cause of Mexican annexation, the provincial assembly requested the withdrawal of Mexican troops from Chiapas (with which Colonel Codallos complied on November 4). In consultation with the leaders of the Plan de Chiapa Libre, the provincial assembly then revived the Suprema Junta Provisional. Following the exit of Mexican troops from Ciudad Real, the armed militias of Tuxtla, Los Llanos, and Ixtacomitán—called the Tres Divisiones—entered San Cristóbal, looted the city, and imposed forced loans on its citizens. "Unfortunately," as one Cristobalense characterized the situation, "a faction rebelled to pursue its depraved private interests."[20]

Chiapas verged on civil war in late 1823. In reaction to the abuses of the occupying forces and the ascendancy of the pro-Guatemala faction, militiamen in Ciudad Real rebelled on November 16 and seized the hill of San Cristóbal. The town council of Ciudad Real, seeking to avoid a battle within the city, negotiated the surrender of the rebels and a general amnesty. The power of the pro-Guatemala faction in Chiapas now appeared absolute. The commander of the Tres Divisiones, Manuel Zebadúa, was appointed Jefe Político (governor) of Chiapas by the Suprema Junta Provisional. In January 1824 rumors circulated in Ciudad Real that Mexico had dispatched an army to Chiapas to bring an end to the "state of anarchy." At the same time, the town council of Ciudad Real requested Mexican assistance and threatened to dissolve itself and transfer its policing power to groups of armed citizens if the Tres Divisiones refused to end their occupation of the city. Faced with the possibility of Mexican intervention from without and urban guerrilla war from within Ciudad Real, Zebadúa accepted the request of the Suprema Junta Provisional to transfer his forces to Tuxtla. Zebadúa withdrew, however, only after the Junta appointed an advocate of union with Guatemala as Jefe Político.[21]

Events continued to go against the pro-Guatemala faction in early 1824 with what was essentially a coup d'état in Comitán, the second city of the province. In January the town "elected" a new municipal council that allied itself with Ciudad Real to promote annexation by Mexico. This defection for unknown reasons altered the entire political situation in the province. The Suprema Junta Provisional, now with a majority favoring union with Mexico, established a five-man commission to study the question of annexation. In March the commission sent a circular to each of the twelve districts of the province requesting plebiscites to decide the question of annexation by Mexico or Guatemala. This tactic merely lent an appearance of democracy to a decision that essentially had already been resolved. The Central Highlands and the district headed by Comitán were densely populated, but by Indians who were oblivious of the entire issue and whose votes were controlled by local landowners and clerics. The Mexican Congress, meanwhile, aware of the shift of forces in Chiapas, magnanimously declared that "Chiapas should be left in absolute liberty for pronouncing its union with Mexico or Guatemala."[22] In the spring, General Zebadúa requested the expenditure of funds by the Suprema Junta Provisional for the maintenance of the Tres Divisiones in light of rumors, speeches in the Mexican Congress, and newspaper reports that once again Mexico had ordered troops to Chiapas. Pleading insufficient funds, the Suprema Junta Provisional responded that it could not accede to the request and proposed a deal: the partial demobilization of the Tres Divisiones and assurances that Mexican troops would not intervene in Chiapas to influence the plebiscite. Zebadúa accepted the compromise, having little alternative since the towns of the lowlands apparently were unwilling or unable to support financially their own troops over an extended period of time. In less than six months the momentum in favor of annexation by Guatemala had been completely reversed.

When the documentation from each district was examined and the votes tallied in September 1824, the Suprema Junta Provisional proclaimed the union of Chiapas to Mexico based on a vote of 96,829 in favor of union with Mexico against 60,400 for union with Guatemala. The distribution of the vote was along regional lines: The Central Highlands and Comitán voted for union with Mexico while the Central Valley and Soconusco favored union with Guatemala. It is quite likely that a majority of the Spanish-speaking population of Chiapas actually opposed annexation by Mexico.[23] Referring to the voting in Indian villages, Matías Romero argued that "if by their ignorance they could not appreciate the importance of their vote, that wrong will always be less than if the result had gone the other way, that is, that the few could nullify the vote of the many, on the pretext that they were not sufficiently enlightened."[24]

One month before the vote, the municipal council of Tapachula announced that Soconusco would join the United Provinces of Central America. Mexico and Guatemala, however, to avoid war agreed that Soconusco should govern itself until a general boundary agreement was reached.[25] The "Free State of Chiapas" was formally annexed by Mexico on September 14, 1824, in spite of Guatemalan protests that the plebiscite had been rigged and was therefore meaningless. During the following week, the town councils of Tuxtla and Chiapa rebelled against the annexation and the government in Ciudad Real. Their "pronouncements" were rescinded in October when Mexican troops returned to Chiapas.[26]

"El que quiso ser de México," opined President José López Portillo referring to Chiapas in 1977, "the one that wanted to be of Mexico."[27] The myth of Chiapas's voluntary and popular aggregation to Mexico, revived every September 14, obscures—as no doubt originally was intended—a significant conclusion that should be drawn from this episode. The annexation of Chiapas by Mexico was engineered by the oligarchy of Ciudad Real for the purpose of extending its political domination within the province, maintaining its economic domination of the Indian population of the Central Highlands, and promoting the commercial and business interests of the colonial elite. San Cristóbal's eminent historian, Prudencio Moscoso Pastrana, is certainly correct in writing that "it was not possible to ask of the ayuntamiento of Ciudad Real more Mexicanism!"[28] Many farmers and ranchers living outside the Central Highlands opposed Cristobalense control of the provincial government and favored aggregation to Guatemala and to the Central

American federation. The conflict that ensued in 1823–24 was the first of a series of confrontations for provincial power in defense of local interests.

LAND, LABOR, AND POLITICS

The struggles of the independence period in Mexico unleashed the forces opposed to Spanish and Mexico City centralism and created "de facto regionalization of authority."[29] The cohesiveness of the early Mexican state, as a result, was almost completely illusory. The national government, at the mercy of its own army, lacked the capacity to impose its authority throughout the country and to suppress most rebellions. It was, writes John Tutino, "a financially weakened and increasingly divided elite that presumed to rule Mexico from Mexico City after independence."[30] Effective power was diffused among the nearly autonomous provincial and municipal regimes as well as among informal authorities—the caciques and caudillos found in every corner of Mexico. Legislation by national and provincial congresses was decided as much by force of arms as by constitutional procedure, and the enforcement of laws was not common. The civil state also confronted the more unified and powerful ecclesiastical state, a parallel system of government that was organized nationally and was not hesitant to defend its own corporate interests.

This "cannibalism of civil power," as Gilberto Argüello terms the political environment, was the result of an increasingly irreconcilable division within the small Europeanized Mexican elite.[31] The consolidation of the Mexican state was contingent upon the resolution, if not by reason then by force, of the differences between the anticlerical Liberal federalists and the proclerical Conservative centralists.[32]

The political climate in Chiapas after 1824 was no more stable and orderly than in Mexico as a whole. Rebellions against legally as well as illegally constituted governments occurred every year. They were instigated by town councils, the federal military garrison in San Cristóbal,* neighboring provincial governments, or exile groups proceeding

---

*Ciudad Real was officially renamed San Cristóbal in 1829.

from Guatemala. Personal advancement, in an age when only a hundred supporters constituted a powerful association, accounted for the rise and fall of not a few governments.[33]

From the 1830s until the civil wars of the 1850s and early 1860s two principal regional factions struggled for control of land and labor in Chiapas: the grandees of the Central Highlands, and the farmers and ranchers of the Central Valley. Within just a few years following union with Mexico, each faction had adopted the ideology of, and linked its political fortunes to, the opposing factions struggling for power and national direction in central Mexico. In Chiapas as in Mexico "those who challenged the power of the heirs to the colonial oligarchy, and who often envisioned a new structure for Mexican society, identified with liberalism."[34] The landowners of the Central Valley became Liberals, while the oligarchy of the Central Highlands, including clerics, became Conservatives. This meant that the overthrow of governments in Mexico City reverberated sooner or later in Chiapas. The struggle, from the periphery to the center, involved political alliances based on shared interests, ideological preferences, and common enemies.[35]

Time and the expansion of commercial markets favored the Liberal landowners of the Central Valley. When, in 1797, the Crown removed taxation on trade between Mexico and Guatemala, the commercial value of the largely undeveloped lands of the Grijalva river valley increased. This accelerated the movement of enterprising colonists into the valley that continued after annexation.[36] Production for the Mexican and North Atlantic markets of such crops as cotton, sugar, rice, and coffee transformed the valley over many decades into the most economically dynamic region in Chiapas. The settlement and development of new towns in the Central Valley, as well as the progress of such established towns as Chiapa and Tuxtla, increased the political weight of the Liberal faction in Chiapas.[37]

Both factions in Chiapas sought control of more land in their respective regions, although for different reasons, and agreed upon two early agrarian laws, which the provincial legislature decreed in 1826 and 1832.[38] These laws defined the maximum legal extension of village *ejidos* (village commons) according to population and opened up the *terrenos baldíos* (the "vacant lands" that surrounded Indian communities and had been held in trust by the Crown to protect Indian landholdings) to entitlement by private citizens. These laws permitted, and even encouraged, ladino (meaning non-Indian) elites to entitle what had been generally considered Indian lands both in the Central Highlands and the Central Valley.[39] While lowland landowners put the land into direct production for market, Cristobalense landowners entitled Indian milpas, forcing many to become wage laborers and renters. "By 1850," writes anthropologist Jan Rus, "virtually all the state's Indian communities had been stripped of their 'excess' lands."[40] The landowners of the Central Valley were far from satisfied by the despoilment of Indian lands. Increasingly, land-hungry *finqueros* (a Central American term for farmers or ranchers) fixed their sights on the rich haciendas of the Dominican order, which occupied some of the best lands in the Central Valley.[41]

More importantly, however, the Central Valley was starved for laborers. The Servitude Law, decreed by the government of Chiapas in 1827, was intended to resolve this problem. According to this law, vagrants (those over the age of 18 without gainful employment) could be assigned by municipal authorities to the military or to employers needing laborers.[42] This compromise measure was clearly inadequate. The overwhelming majority of potential laborers in Chiapas were Indians who lived in highland communities. Their labor was controlled by Cristobalense landowners and parish priests who oversaw the collection of native taxes. The farmers and ranchers of the Central Valley, therefore, viewed the secular and ecclesiastic elite of San Cristóbal as the most important hindrance to their economic advancement. It is not surprising, then, that lowland finqueros embraced the anticlericalism of Mexican Liberalism or that Cristobalenses were Conservatives.[43]

The struggle for the control of Indian labor, often disguised by the larger conflict over the power and privileges of the Church, was one of the central motivations of political strife in the decades following annexation. In 1830, for example, the Liberal government of Chiapas secularized the administration of Indian pueblos by giving control over all civil affairs in these communities to government appointees.[44] A few years later the bishop of Chiapas encouraged and helped finance the rebellion that deposed the Liberal government, and the offensive measure was repealed. In 1844 a Conservative government decreed an agrarian law permitting citizens to entitle terrenos baldíos already occupied by Indian settlers—a measure clearly designed to facilitate ladino control of highland Indian labor.[45] The succeeding Liberal government responded in 1849 by abolishing the practice of *baldiaje* (legal servitude in exchange for rent) and by seeking to enlarge village ejidos. This measure was repealed by a Conservative government three years later.[46] And, in the early 1850s, a Conservative government prohibited the export of cattle from Chiapas: according to Rus, this action was designed to wreck the economy of the Central Valley.[47] The central government of Antonio López de Santa Anna, furthermore, enacted a law in 1854 that threatened to despoil the lands of those elites not in accord with the politics of "his Most Serene Highness." By the mid-1850s factional and interregional antagonism in Chiapas had become very bitter. Each side viewed the other as a dangerous threat to its interests and livelihood. It is at this point that a Liberal revolution radicalized by a Conservative counterrevolution erupted in Mexico and Chiapas.

REGIONALISM, REBELLION, AND REVOLUTION

In March 1854 a group of regional caudillos and dissident army officers led by General Juan Álvarez of Guerrero withdrew their support for the dictatorship of General-President Antonio López de Santa Anna and proclaimed the Plan de Ayutla in the name of federalism, local autonomy, and weak central government. Within a year and a half Santa Anna was forced into exile, Álvarez became president, and a group of Liberal ideologues were appointed to high positions in the government. President Álvarez resigned within a few months, turning power over to the Liberals who were led first by Ignacio Commonfort and later, after 1857, by Benito Juárez. Once in power, the Liberals made a revolution and defended it successfully against Mexican and foreign enemies. They transformed Mexican society and laid the foundation for a real national government.[48]

Chiapas was drawn into the storm. In August 1855, following the resignation of Santa Anna, Governor Fernando Nicolas Maldonado, a Santanista appointee, declared support for the Plan de Ayutla. Maldonado was soon ousted by the Liberal forces of the Central Valley, and their leader Ángel Albino Corzo—colonel of the National Guard, former jefe político of the town of Chiapa, and son of a lowland sugar

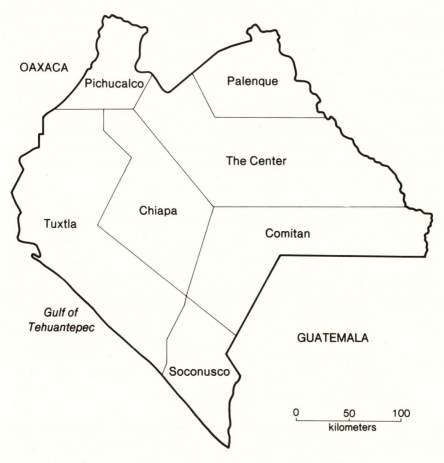

The State of Chiapas, 1855

planter—became governor. Corzo, as governor of Chiapas from 1855 until 1861, implemented the reform laws of 1855 and 1856, the Constitution of 1857, and the more radical reform laws of 1859 and 1860. By these laws and the new constitution, the military and ecclesiastical "special courts" were abolished; church and village lands were privatized; freedom of the press, of education, and freedom from compulsory service were guaranteed; all church properties were nationalized; monastic orders were outlawed; cemeteries were secularized, as was registration for births and marriages; and church and state were separated.[49]

"The revolution will have been sterile for Chiapas," wrote the editor of the Liberal newspaper *La Voz del Pueblo* in December 1855, "if it is limited to a change of personnel of the administration, if the same abuses continue under the new regime, but it will not be like that: the Government is actively employed in bandaging the wounds of the unfortunates, in promoting the welfare of the State, and in completing the job in a permanent manner."[50] The revolution was certainly not sterile for Chiapas, at least not as far as the Liberal faction was concerned. First of all, a considerable number of urban and rural properties were transferred from Indian communities, the Church, monasteries, and a nunnery into the hands of Liberals. During the first year of the nationalization of church properties in 1859, all of the claims took place in the departments of Chiapa, Tuxtla, and Comitán, benefiting well-known Liberal families. Cristobalense Conservatives generally did not take advantage of the disentail and were often hurt by it, since they expected that the abominable Liberal laws would eventually be abolished.[51]

In 1861 Corzo's government secularized the control of Indian pueblos by the appointment of ladino municipal secretaries who were responsible for the collection of the head tax and the liberation of Indians from the system of baldiaje. As priests abandoned Indian pueblos due to government explusion and war conditions generally, Indians abandoned the Church and its fees and taxes, and began—or rather continued more openly—the practice of their own folk Catholicism. Highland Indians also began to abandon the highlands to work or rent land in the lowlands.[52] The Liberal government prohibited the sale of alcohol to Indians, religious instruction to Indians, baldiaje in the Central Highlands, and certain kinds of exploitative trading practices between Cristobalense and Indians.[53] The reovlution shifted the balance of economic and political power to the Liberal towns of the Central Valley, although not without a fight.

Like their ideological compatriots in Central Mexico, highland Conservatives rebelled against the Liberal revolution and its government in Chiapas almost continually from 1856 until 1864. In September 1856 Juan Ortega and José María Chacón raised the banner of rebellion in the departments of Comitán and Soconusco. Chacón, leader of the movement in Soconusco, took the popular action of withdrawing that department from the jurisdiction of the government of Chiapas, "considering that the same Soconusco has never received any reward or favor from the Government of Chiapas."[54] The Liberal National Guard units counterattacked and drove both leaders and their followers into Guatemala. Following this first aborted Conservative counterrevolution, the bishop of Chiapas, priests, and friars began a more subtle campaign against the Liberal government. The faithful were admonished not to obey law contrary to the laws of God and the Church; priests punished those who obeyed the civil government and encouraged armed rebellion.[55] By early 1858 the highlands region was so hostile to the Liberal regime that Governor Corzo transferred the government from San Cristóbal Las Casas to Tuxtla Gutiérrez as a precaution.[56] Beginning in January 1859 and extending through most of the year, Ortega and Chacón renewed their rebellion in the state, picking up more supporters than in 1856 and causing more damage. Ortega began by attacking and looting Comitán, while Chacón revived the separatist movement in Soconusco. The counterrevolutionary forces, however, were no match for the National Guard force of 2,000 men—most recruited from the towns of the Central Valley—defending the government. During that violent year the Church in San Cristóbal published several subversive pastorals and encouraged rebellion. Citing the "obstinate resistance of the clergy" and their "threat to public tranquility," Governor Corzo expelled Bishop Colima y Rubio in October. The bishop was followed into exile to Guatemala by the friars of the Dominican and Franciscan orders.[57] By 1860 the War of the Reform was won both in Mexico and Chiapas. Ortega and Chacón were driven back into Guatemala and the government was returned to San Cristóbal in 1861.

Mexican Conservatives, however, were not finished. They conspired with the French Emperor Napoleon III for the intervention of French troops into Mexico (on the pretext of debt collection) to bring down the Liberal government and to establish in its place a Conservative government headed by a European prince. By mid-1863, the government of President Juárez was forced to evacuate Mexico City, and the French army installed a Conservative government. One year later Ferdinand Maximilian of Hapsburg arrived in the country. Although the Liberal revolution appeared to be all but defeated, Juárez, his generals, and his Liberal colleagues did not give up the fight and resorted to guerrilla warfare. Even during the darkest days of 1864 and 1865 the Liberals continued the struggle on Mexican soil. Following the end of the U.S. Civil War, the government of President Andrew Johnson provided arms and ammunition for the Liberal armies and pressured Napoleon III to remove his troops from Mexico. Napoleon, who was also under Prussian pressure in Europe, began withdrawing troops in late 1866. This rapidly led to the triumph of the Liberal armies by the spring of 1867, the execution of Emperor Maximilian, and the victory of Liberalism and republicanism in Mexico.

The struggle in Chiapas was less protracted during the War of the French Intervention. In order to help defend Mexico from the French invasion, in May 1862 the government of Chiapas organized and dispatched to central Mexico the 550-man Battalion "Chiapas," which was commanded by Lieutenant Colonel José Pantaleón Domínguez, chief of the state's National Guard. With the triumph of the interventionist forces in central Mexico by the spring of 1863, Juan Ortega returned to Chiapas. He joined forces with the friar Víctor Chanona, forced the retreat of the Liberal government once again to Tuxtla Gutiérrez, and after an unsuccessful attempt finally took possession of San Cristóbal and established a conservative government loyal to the empire of Maximilian. It was not until early 1864 that the Liberal government was able to take the offensive. Reinforced by National Guard troops from neighboring Oaxaca and by the return of Domínguez's Battalion "Chiapas," Liberal forces retook San Cristóbal by the end of January. The rest of 1864 was devoted to clearing the province of the remaining Conservative forces. Finally, in December, General Porfirio Díaz, military commander of the southern states for the Juárez government, appointed Domínguez governor and military commander of Chiapas.

He retained the office until he was overthrown during the Tuxtepec rebellion of 1875.[58]

The defeat of the Conservatives of San Cristóbal and the Central Highlands was severe at first but not completely devastating. The wars had led to much material destruction of the city and surrounding haciendas as well as to the immigration of many merchants and professionals to the towns of the Central Valley. Governor Domínguez at first treated the Cristobalenses as a conquered people. Public expenditures were severely limited in the highlands, Liberals were appointed to civil offices both in San Cristóbal and in the Indian pueblos, and the government remained in Tuxtla Gutiérrez. At the end of the interventionist war in 1867, however, the national government granted an amnesty and restored civil rights to all but the highest-ranking Conservatives and Imperialists and ordered that all state capitals displaced by the struggle be returned to their original locations. Domínguez transferred his government from Tuxtla to Chiapa and began a campaign to end all Cristobalense control over the highland Indian pueblos before returning the government to San Cristóbal.[59]

The highland elite, meanwhile, began to renew their domination of the Indians. The native communities refused to cooperate and boycotted ladino priests and businesses. Claiming that the Indians were preparing a caste war against the "civilized people" of the highlands, the leaders of San Cristóbal organized a militia to end Indian separatism and regain control of the highlands. At the end of 1868 Cristobalense militiamen met Indian resistance. So began the famous "Caste War," as it came to be called, leading to an Indian siege of San Cristóbal by early 1869. Governor Domínguez, facing political opposition in the lowlands by rival Liberal leaders, mobilized the state militia and placed it under his personal command to save San Cristóbal from a bloodbath and also to save his political career. Following the end of the fighting against ill-prepared Indians, Domínguez reached a rapprochement with the leaders of San Cristóbal to share control of the Indian communities and Indian labor and to enter into a political alliance beneficial to both sides. When Domínguez returned the government to San Cristóbal in 1872, Cristobalenses were no longer the outcasts of before. By the 1870s, the labels "Liberal" and "Conservative" began to lose their former meanings. The new leaders of San Cristóbal, like Miguel Utrilla, were now self-professed Liberals. Liberal or Conservative, however, Cristobalenses still had a powerful interest in controlling the Indians of the highlands and, to a considerable extent, still did so. Farmers and ranchers of the lowlands still had an interest in obtaining highland Indian labor and succeeded to a greater extent than before.[60]

The revolution that was called the Reform began the process of political integration in Mexico generally and in Chiapas in particular. The triumph of the Liberal faction in Chiapas curtailed the political and economic power of the "other government," the Catholic Church, and strengthened the political influence of the national government of Chiapas. Government in Chiapas, however, remained relatively weak and inefficient. With victory in 1864, the Liberal faction disintegrated. The appointment of Domínguez to head the government proved to be a divisive action. The military men who had risen to prominence and command during the previous ten years—the commanders of local militias such as Julián Grajales, Sebastián Escobar, Miguel Utrilla, José Eutimio Yañez, Pomposo Castellanos, and others—divided Chiapas among themselves and frequently rebelled against Domínguez. In 1875–76, when General Porfirio Díaz rose in rebellion against the national government of President Sebastián Lerdo de Tejada and took power in Mexico City, Domínguez was finally overthrown by a loose alliance of Liberal chieftains who then scrambled for position and power. When the cacique of Soconusco, Sebastián Escobar, finally emerged on top by mid-1877, he desperately needed Díaz's political suport to defend his position against numerous rivals. In exchange for that support, Escobar—and each succeeding Porfirian-era governor of Chiapas—became an unconditional Porfirista, eager to do the bidding of the president and fully conscious of the political risk of failure to do so.[61] In Chiapas, as in Sonora and Sinaloa according to Stuart Voss, "the promotion of local interests necessitated the forging of close, working connections with those who directed the nation's politics in Mexico City."[62] An informal but effective system of patronage brought the periphery increasingly under the influence of the center. This was how the political machine of the age of Porfirio Díaz began to work and also how the national state became a reality.

CACIQUES, PEONS, AND FARMERS

Although perhaps no more than in the past, Chiapas was ruled by caciques during the 1870s and 1880s. In this time of supposed constitutional restoration and Liberal consensus, however, their prominence seemed exaggerated and their influence especially pernicious. Soldiers of the Liberal revolution, participants in and supporters of the Porfirian Tuxtepec rebellion, wealthy landowners, and political bosses: these powerful men divided Chiapas into spheres of influence and control that have been called *cacicazgos*. Governors were, at best, first among equals. None served more than one term in office, in contrast to the open-ended tenure of the caciques. The governors were the nominal directors of a primitive governing structure designed primarily to tax and maintain order but barely managing to do either. They commanded a bureaucracy of sorts, in which many officials took their orders from the local caciques or directly from the president in Mexico City. Government in Chiapas during these years was weak, ineffective, and passive.

A remarkable report on conditions in Chiapas was sent in 1878 to Secretary of the Treasury Matías Romero, who had taken an interest in the economic development of the region. The author of this "Analysis of the General Situation of the State of Chiapas" chose to remain anonymous, although a close reading of the document seems to suggest that it was written by the administrator of customs along the Guatemalan border near Comitán. The portrait of Chiapas drawn by the author of this report is vivid, accurate, and perceptive, and therefore deserves quotation at length:

The State of Chiapas as you know is destined by its topographic situation to be for many years the last of all the states of the Republic in civilization, culture, learning, morality, and wealth. The heterogeneity of its races, the proponderance of the clergy which still possesses the most repugnant fanaticism, the lack of any familiarity with people of other parts, the complete and constant division that reigns between Indians and ladinos, the absolute insignificance of the men that have influence in politics and in the local administration, the bad faith, selfishness, and absence of patriotism that distinguish the

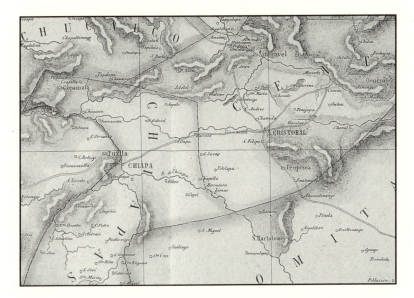

Detail of Carta XXII, State of Chiapas (Mexico), from Antonio Garcia y Cubas, *Atlas Geográfico, Estadístico e Histórico de la República Mexicana* (México, 1858). (Courtesy of the William L. Clements Library, The University of Michigan, Ann Arbor, Michigan)

men of wealth; all of these defects which are preserved in Chiapas in the masses of citizens in a latent sense, have forced me to form a very sad impression of the future which is reserved for this portion of Mexican territory that seems to be destined to retrocede always, when everywhere else feels the effects of positive advancement under the protection of the honorable and moralizing government of Porfirio Díaz.

It is said that peace is a fact in the state, but it is a peace, one that demands of me a vulgar expression, that can be called crazy, without benefit whatever for society and the country. There is peace, because here there is not one man who could serve as a popular caudillo, or better said, because there is no people that is suitable for a democratic nation such as ours. . . .

If you can penetrate the intricate labyrinth that passes for government here—the floundering of a system without foundation, without virtuous traditions, without determined objectives, and forming an indescribable chaos—you would be astonished at the meagerness of the Treasury, an impotent and odious administration of justice devoted to the spirit of faction while in criminal matters abandoned to the oppression of the law of John Lynch; while on the other hand, there is political administration without conformity and in the hands of arbitrary jefes políticos, ignorant school teachers, and corrupt priests; and to crown this work, a dreadful wretchedness, no spirit of enterprise, the most repugnant slavery, the monopolization of agricultural wealth whose exploitation is condemned to antediluvian customs, commerce destroyed by the want of consumption, until at last . . . An Intractable Malady![63]

Despite these enormous political and administrative problems, the pace of social and economic change in Chiapas began to accelerate following the disorders of the 1850s and 1860s. Economic progress in Chiapas during the 1870s and 1880s was to a great extent related to the increasingly favorable external conditions affecting the region. Chiapas's products—coffee, cacao, cotton, sugar, and mahogany—found more markets and better prices as Mexico was integrated into the expanding North Atlantic economy. Foreign investment also began to penetrate into the forests and valleys of this isolated region. The national government of Porfirio Díaz, furthermore, beginning in the 1880s initiated measures to stimulate private economic activity, such as the creation of a national banking system, financial support for the construction of railroads, tax and commercial legislation to attract foreign investment, land colonization laws designed to expand productive land use, and more.[64]

Chiapas, following the rebellions and wars of the 1850s and 1860s, began to attract immigrants, families of middling wealth, who apparently perceived Chiapas to be a frontier region abundant with opportunity. Merchants, farmers, professionals, and artisans settled in Chiapas in numbers greater than ever before. A relatively large infusion of German immigrants contributed to the development of Chiapas. Men like Guillermo Steinpreis who established a brewery in San Cristóbal; Herna Munch, who established a pharmacy; José Aggeler, who set up an electric light generator; Hublado Hess, who built a successful law practice; and many others helped create a more heterogeneous and entrepreneurial elite class in the region. The most successful Germans, immigrants from Guatemala to Soconusco, were coffee planters, exporters and financiers, and plantation managers.[65]

The population of Chiapas, which grew quite slowly from about 130,000 at the time of independence to about 200,000 by 1870, expanded rapidly during the next few decades (see figure 1). This signified an increase in the number of agricultural workers, thereby permitting an expansion of the number of rural estates. Although the accounts of landholdings in Chiapas in the nineteenth century are not completely trustworthy, the sources that are available indicate an impressive expansion in the number of farming and ranching properties during the 1870s and 1880s, as table 1 shows.[66]

Laborers, however, remained a relatively scarce resource, as the expansion of the practice of indebted servitude (labor legally bound to fincas and plantations by debts held by the landowners) in every district confirms. Debt peonage (described in the "Analysis of the General Situation of the State of Chiapas" as "the most repugnant slavery") was certainly an old system of labor utilization and control in Chiapas; it became socially and economically institutionalized in the second half of the nineteenth century. The expansion of this labor system in Chiapas, both geographically and in the number of workers bound, accompanied and facilitated the expansion of commercial agriculture.[67] It was a partial solution to the old problem of labor scarcity in the Central Valley.

Figure 1

Population Growth
Chiapas, 1828 - 1910

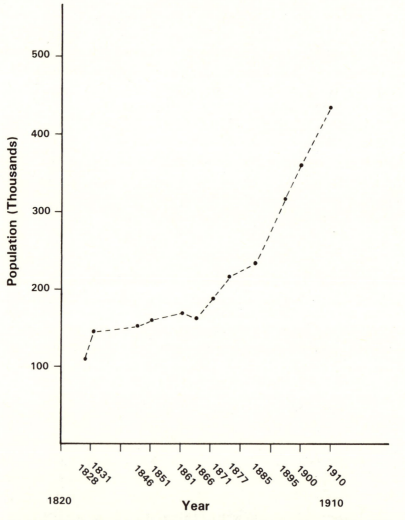

Sources: Viviane Brachet, <u>La población de los estados mexicanos (1824–1895)</u> (México: INAH, 1976), p. 54; <u>Estadísticas Historicas de México, Tomo I</u> (México: Instituto Nacional de Estadística Geografía e Informática, 1985), p. 13.

TABLE I

LANDHOLDINGS IN CHIAPAS, 1778–1889

Year	Number and Description	Source
1778	32 haciendas	Molina
1778	58 fincas and estancias	Wasserstrom
1816	145 fincas and estancias	Wasserstrom
1837	835 fincas rusticas	Memoria 1889
1855	515 haciendas and ranchos	Orozco y Berra
1862	42 haciendas and 123 ranchos	Perez Hernandez
1877	448 haciendas and 501 ranchos	Busto
1889	3159 fincas rusticas	Memoria 1889

Note: The sources do not explain the differences between haciendas, ranchos, fincas, and estancias. These names do have general meanings in Mexico and Central America: *haciendas* are larger in size than ranchos; *finca* is the Central American term for estate or farm; *estancia* refers to a cattle and/or horse ranch; and *finca rustica* is taken to mean any rural property, regardless of size or function.

Sources: Molina, *San Bartolomé de los llanos*, p. 69; Wasserstrom, *Class and Society in Central Chiapas*, p. 39; Orozco y Berra, *Apendice al diccionario universal*, Vol. 3, pp. 31–32; Pérez Hernández, *Estadística de la república mejicana*, p. 52; Busto, *Estadística de la república mexicana*, p. xviii; and Chiapas, *Memoria que presenta el ciudadano Manuel Carrascosa....* (1889).

Peonage found a friendly environment in the region, as Friedrich Katz notes: "The isolation of many southern regions, the lack of an industry which would have competed with the estate owners for scarce laborers, the strengthening of both hacienda police forces and the organs of the state made it extremely difficult for the peons to circumvent their owners. . . . On the whole, the landowners were successful in the economic as well as the social and political fields. Production soared, resistance was extremely limited, and the ensuing stability attracted new capital and investment."[68]

As early as the 1870s Chiapas was criticized in Mexico City as the "slave state" of Mexico, while in Chiapas "apologists were driven to admit, in order to defend, the fundamentals of debt servitude."[69] In 1885 the editor of the official newspaper of the state government admitted that peonage was lamentable but argued the system was justified by the existence of a labor scarcity and the "natural laziness" of the Indian. Former governor Miguel Utrilla that same year explained that peons knew their rights and received paternal treatment except in the Department of Pichucalco. There, he noted, the work was unhealthy, the debts hereditary, and workers were chained and shackled. Utrilla insisted that such conditions existed "because of the lack of education of the servants, their stern and obstinate character, the laziness which is proverbial by custom and habit, and because it is the only way of maintaining their obedience."[70] A U.S. consular report on Chiapas and Tabasco in 1886 documented pervasive peonage: "In the State of Chiapas servitude still exists, the remains, unfortunately, of slavery in the past."[71]

Indebted servitude in Chiapas was not a lingering symptom of a past illness but a spreading cancer that enriched a few but impoverished many. Servitude existed in every district; it was not an issue that divided the familia chiapaneca. This was one of the faces of the "progress" of Chiapas in the 1870s and 1880s. Later, in the 1890s, progressive landowners would condemn peonage but do little to end it. That would take a revolution imposed from the north.

Interregional rivalry and conflict within Chiapas did not disappear during the 1870s and 1880s; it was simply muted. As Rus writes, "Through resumption of their roles as merchants and civil servants the Cristobalenses were able to indebt the Indians, and so dispose of their labor. This was an arrangement apparently acceptable to the lowlanders through the 1870s and 1880s."[72] Enough Indians either traveled to the Central Valley to tend rented fields or work as agricultural laborers on a seasonal basis, or were lured into debt servitude that lowland farmers and ranchers were able to keep pace with the (rather slow) expansion of the markets for their products. Their principal concern had shifted to the nature of government in the region. When the status quo was upset by a stronger regional government in the 1890s, the deep antagonism between the Central Highlands and the Central Valley resurfaced.

Economic progress in Chiapas was seriously limited by the lethargic and chaotic system of government that persisted despite a rising chorus of complaints by members of the region's landowning and commercial class. In 1881 Federico Larrainzar echoed the sentiments of nearly every farmer and merchant when he decried the lack of even one good road in Chiapas.[73] Governor Miguel Utrilla asserted in 1884 that the laws protecting the rights of landowners and employers were the principal means for advancing the enrichment of the state, thus reaffirming the minimal role of government.[74] Government efforts to promote positive economic development were timid and largely ineffective. Tax concessions to landowners for the promotion of certain export crops had little impact since most members of that class paid little or no property taxes anyway.[75] The unit of government primarily responsible for road construction was the impoverished municipality, which was incapable of utilizing the draft labor provided by law.[76] Governor Manuel Carrascosa in 1888 gave a contract to a North American company to construct a railroad from Tonalá to Tuxtla Gutiérrez, and finally to San Cristóbal. The result of this project by 1891 was the loss of 612,000 pesos in federal and state subsidies and 1 million pesos in bonds, all of which vanished into the pockets of government officials and North American contractors.[77]

An important progressive step was taken by the government of Carrascosa in 1890 to liberate commerce. In that year the state government began to suppress the *alcabalas* (taxes on internal commerce in transit), which were collected by the municipalities and brought in the most municipal revenue. To compensate the municipalities, the governor ordered that they receive one half of the alcohol distillation tax revenues.[78] This step further impoverished the municipalities but certainly helped to spur commerce in Chiapas. This measure, however, was an exception. By 1890 Chiapas possessed a communications and transportation infrastructure that was not significantly better than that which existed at the time of independence.[79]

During the late 1870s and 1880s, landowners and merchants frequently complained about a "system of government" that many viewed as destructive to economic and social progress—the cacicazgos. Julián Grajales of Chiapa de Corzo, Sebastián Escobar of Soconusco, and Miguel Utrilla of the Central Highlands, the three most important caciques in Chiapas, headed large extended families that controlled numerous landed estates and businesses. They commanded private armies, appointed local officials, "elected" state legislators, and collected taxes. So long as provincial caciques were loyal Porfiristas, Díaz tolerated caciquismo and even encouraged rivalry among them.[80]

To operate a profitable finca, conduct business, or practice law within a cacicazgo, one had to befriend the cacique or beware of the consequences. Due to these "public men," wrote Jesús Rabasa, a rancher of the department of Tuxtla, in 1879, "there is no security, there are no guarantees, and there is no confidence. The honorable man is jailed and mistreated." He further advised Treasury Secretary Matías Romero: "Only the Federation through well-intentioned and energetic action can correct the disorder which reigns here."[81] Rigaud Keller, a Soconusense planter, informed Romero in 1880 that "it is absolutely necessary that this district obtain the protection and guarantees of both the Government of the State and principally that of the Federal Government."[82] In 1888, Teleforo Merodio complained in a letter to President Díaz that Escobar "impedes progress and improvement in order to prevent anyone from surpassing his local influence or arousing ideas of equality and true democracy."[83] To Lauro Candiani of Tapachula, Escobar appeared as an absolute despot, "master of our lives and haciendas."[84] Domaciano Gómez of Chiapa reported to Díaz in 1890 that due to caciquismo, in this case that of Julián Grajales, "it is not possible to freely [farm] in the department."[85]

These complaints, only a small sample of those found in the archives of Matías Romero and Porfirio Díaz, suggest that caciquismo appeared to encumber the regional economy of Chiapas in the eyes of local entrepreneurs. As private correspondence and newspaper articles seem to confirm, the familia chiapaneca increasingly looked for stronger government at the state and national levels to propel economic development and destroy local tyrannies.[86] Chiapas suffered from a political failure, most agreed; there was a sense of urgency in many of the demands for regeneration. As one newspaper editor asserted in 1888: "The hour for reforms nears, the capitalists are fixing their sights upon Chiapas."[87]

PART 1

"Señor Rabasa may justly be regarded as the
harbinger of progress and commercial activity."

"The campesinos are the ones who have paid the
costs, high and at times terrible,
of modernization."

First quotation from U.S. consul Albert Brickwood, October 4, 1910, NA,
Record Group 84, Tapachula; Second quotation from Octavio Paz, "Hora
cumplida," *Vuelta* IX, June 1985.

MODERNIZATION
1890–1910

(or the public career, celebrated successes, and social
costs of the "enlightened caciquismo")

"ADELANTE! ADELANTE!" PROCLAIMED THE STUDENTS OF THE NEW ESCUELA
moderna in 1893: "Forward! Forward! It is the common cry of hu-
manity." The future beckoned, promising "modernity" and "progress,"
seizing the imagination of the elite class in distant, isolated, and "backward" Chiapas in the 1890s. *Modernización,* to become modern, was
the unquestioned goal of the Central Valley elites. Making Chiapas
modern meant many things: building roads and railroads; erecting telegraph and telephone lines; establishing schools; applying scientific
methods to farming and industry; and transforming Indians into yeoman farmers, free laborers, and Mexicans. First and foremost, however,
modernization involved strengthening government to reform or dis-
mantle antiquated local and regional institutions that inhibited economic expansion and development.

The modernization initiated in Chiapas during the last decade of the
nineteenth century and the first decade of the twentieth century was
organized by, and largely benefited, only part of the regional elites, and
the landless majority not at all. The farmers and merchants of the
Central Valley in particular, and entrepreneurial elites generally, took
advantage of favorable political and economic conditions to promote
their interests under the banner of modernization. The consolidation
of the power of the national government of Porfirio Díaz by the 1890s
was accompanied not coincidentally by the establishment of a strong
state government in Chiapas. In the 1890s and 1900s, during a period
of national and international capitalist expansion, the *caciquismo ilus-
trado* (the enlightened caciquismo) of progressive governors of Chiapas,

33

such as Emilio Rabasa and his successors, became a key agent of modernization in the following ways.

First, the government of the state consolidated and extended its power within Chiapas to remove the perceived obstacles to modernity and to carry out necessary reforms and projects. The state government increased its police forces, expanded its financial resources, geographically extended its administrative control, and diminished the power of local caciques.

Second, the government of the state developed more extensive and efficient administrative capacities to perform the tasks of modern government. The beginning of a modern bureaucracy was put into place in the 1890s and 1900s to control and regulate district officials and local governments, public education and health, taxation and public expenditures, and internal improvements.

Third, the government of the state took active and sometimes effective measures to modernize the regional economy and society. The state government built roads, constructed telegraph and telephone networks, reformed land tenure, constructed and staffed schools and a hospital, and attempted to reform labor practices.

The Porfirian regime attempted a conservative "revolution from above" to modernize Mexico. The State of Chiapas, in tune with the temper of the times but also driven by the demands of provincial elites, was one of the laboratories of modernization. Political centralization and economic development, one reinforcing the other, did accomplish much of what elite Chiapanecos wanted. What they viewed as progressive change and modernization, however, in fact reinforced and aggravated the longstanding social reality of Chiapas as a rich land for a few but home to a poor people. In the words of Octavio Paz: "The campesinos are the ones that have paid the costs, high and at times terrible, of modernization."

The State of Chiapas, 1910

I

ON THE ROAD TO REAL PROGRESS

CHIAPAS SET OFF ON A NEW COURSE IN THE EARLY 1890S. COMMERCIAL farming for extraregional markets began to assume importance for the first time, entrepreneurs immigrated to the region to establish rich and productive plantations, and the state government initiated a program of political centralization and development of infrastructure. Politicians, editors, and citizens spoke of a spirit of enterprise finally energizing Chiapas. Governor Emilio Rabasa in 1892 optimistically declared that "the state is moving" and promised "more extensive and effective government action."[1] Many believed the region had embarked on the road to modernity. The gubernatorial administration of Emilio Rabasa (1891–94) coincided with and gave impetus to many of the changes that were taking place in Chiapas at the time. Rabasa took the first significant and deliberate steps toward the establishment of effective government as an agent of modernization and progress in Chiapas. The history of modern Chiapas, in a political and economic sense, begins with his reforms.

THE CAPITALIST IMPULSE

President Porfirio Díaz's program of "order and progress" began to be implemented in the 1880s and 1890s. A new commercial code, which lifted archaic restrictions on business, was decreed in 1884. A reformed mining law in 1887 and special banking legislation in 1897 helped restructure the national economy. Major railroad construction projects got under way in the 1880s, and during the 1890s the Díaz government balanced the national budget and refunded the internal and foreign

37

debt. Mexico's new liberal economic environment and political stability attracted foreign capital and entrepreneurs. United States and European capital built railroads, electric plants, and commercial plantations, and refurbished the mining industry. "Capitalist modernization," writes John Coatsworth, "had begun."[2]

In Chiapas the trickle of foreign investment and business activity of the 1870s and 1880s became a vigorous stream in the 1890s and 1900s. European, American, and Mexican entrepreneurs established plantations in the tropical regions of Chiapas, Tabasco, and Guatemala to extract hardwoods (primarily mahogany), rubber, sugar cane, coffee, and cacao. Formerly neglected and nearly deserted tropical forests became filled with dozens of plantations, which employed—almost enslaved—thousands of Indians from the Central Highlands of Chiapas.[3]

Following the border accord between Mexico and Guatemala in 1882, German planters from Guatemala began to establish coffee fincas in the Soconusco district. At a time of high coffee prices, these planters expanded into Chiapas in search of virgin and inexpensive land. Their success in Guatemala and the high coffee prices of the late 1880s and early 1890s led to a natural spillover into Mexico. The expansion of coffee cultivation—that is, the creation of the Soconusco enclave economy—provided the single most important push for economic growth in Chiapas during the Porfiriato.[4]

Most of the early purchases of land for coffee cultivation were made for only centavos per hectare. These acquistions were from survey and colonization companies, which had obtained from the federal government the right to sell and colonize more than 4 million acres of public lands in Chiapas. Louis Heller and Company, a U.S. firm, obtained the second concession in 1886. In exchange for making an accurate survey of all national lands in the state, the company was granted the right to sell one third of the total concession and colonize the remaining two thirds. Fertile coffee land in the late 1880s sold for sixty to seventy centavos per hectare and rose in value to 50 to 100 pesos by the mid-1890s and to well over 300 pesos by 1910.[5]

Coffee cultivation became an extremely profitable industry in Chiapas. In 1892 it was estimated that coffee produced for seven centavos a pound could be sold for more than twenty centavos a pound. Plantations of only 250 hectares could gross as much as $75,000 to $100,000 a year. In 1892 there were twenty-six large coffee plantations in Soconusco.[6]

The best coffee lands in Soconusco were purchased in the early 1890s, but coffee production continued to spread to other parts of Chiapas. The departments of Tuxtla, Palenque, Simojovel, and Mezcalapa became important producers, and by the end of the decade coffee production took place in nearly every municipality of the state. Coffee exports brought millions of pesos into the state each year, contributing significantly to the increase of agricultural investment and commerce. The new tax revenues that accrued to the region from coffee strengthened the state government and made possible many of the reforms and developmental projects carried out by Emilio Rabasa and his successors.[7]

The 1880s and especially the 1890s also saw the expansion of agriculture in the Central Valley as well as in the departments of Pichucalco and Tonalá. Cacao production in Pichucalco, revived by Spanish and Mexican entrepreneurs, rivaled coffee production in Soconusco in importing wealth into Chiapas. Finqueros and rancheros in Pichucalco possessed easy river transport to a ready market in San Juan Bautista, Tabasco.[8] In the Central Valley an ambitious ranchero class expanded, attracted by fertile lands at good prices and easy river transportation. The entire state reported only 501 ranchos in 1877; by 1895, however, due to the settlement of national lands and the privatization of village ejidos, the department of Chiapa alone counted 527 ranchos, Tuxtla 240, Tonalá 368, Soconusco 530, and Pichucalco 529.[9] This group of entrepreneurial rancheros and finqueros sought to end caciquismo and replace it with an active regional government that would, above all, construct a network of roads and railroads. This element in Chiapas was the constituency behind capitalist modernization and the administration of Emilio Rabasa.[10]

EMILIO RABASA ESTEBANELL

When Emilio Rabasa became governor of Chiapas in 1891, Porfirio Díaz had fully consolidated his power nationally. Díaz's presidential term from 1888 to 1892 demonstrated to allies and rivals alike that he could survive consecutive reelections. By the end of his third term in office, Díaz had become "el indispensable, el necesario."[11] In this political environment of increasing centralization—built on a firm foundation of clientelism and a skillful policy of divide and rule by Porfirio Díaz—and under the tutelage of Rabasa, Chiapas became politically integrated into the Mexican nation.

Díaz's candidate for governor of Chiapas in 1891 possessed a number of qualities that recommended him to the entrepreneurial elites of Chiapas's Central Valley and to Díaz himself. In the first place, Rabasa was a native of the Central Valley. His parents, José Antonio Rabasa and Manuela Estebanell de Rabasa, moved to Chiapas in the 1850s and purchased a modest ranch near Ocozocuautla in the department of Tuxtla. Don José was a Spanish emigrant who had lived in New Orleans and Mexico City before finally settling on the Chiapas frontier. Neither rich nor poor, he was a hardworking man who made his ranch "Jesús" a profitable enterprise. Perhaps more than anything, he was ambitious for his two sons.[12]

Emilio, José and Manuela's third child, was born on May 22, 1856. At the age of twelve Emilio was enrolled at the Institute of Arts and Sciences in Oaxaca City, the same school where Benito Juárez and Porfirio Díaz had studied as boys. His professional studies were undertaken at the School of Law, also in Oaxaca, where he received his degree in 1878 at the age of twenty-two. By all accounts he was an excellent student and possessed an outstanding intellect.

Following law school Rabasa dabbled in Chiapanecan and Oaxacan politics. In 1881 he was elected to the Chiapas state legislature and one year later appointed professor of law at the State Institute of the Sciences. During the year 1885–86 Rabasa served as private secretary to Oaxaca's governor, Luis Miér y Terán. He moved to Mexico City in 1886 to take up an appointment as federal judge and to teach law. As a result of his talent, ambition, and influential friends he was appointed to the Supreme Court of Justice and shortly thereafter became attorney general of the Federal District. During his five-year residence in Mexico City Rabasa also found time to write five novels, to collaborate with Rafael Reyes Spindola to revive the newspaper *El Universal,* and to establish (with fellow Chiapaneco Víctor Manuel Castillo) the prestigious legal journal *La Revista de Legislación y Jurisprudencia.* As a result of his early friendship with Rosendo Pineda (a close advisor to

President Díaz), Rabasa met many of the most important politicians and intellectuals in Mexico, including Porfirio Díaz himself. He also became identified with a group of influential men known some years later as *Científicos*. In 1891, at the age of thirty-five, Rabasa became the youngest governor in Mexico.[13]

Aside from his obvious talent and influential acquaintances, Rabasa received the governor's office in Chiapas for several practical reasons. The previous governor, Manuel Carrascosa, had lost his bid for a second term as a result of a financial scandal surrounding a proposed Chiapas railroad.[14] Further, during Carrascosa's tenure the state debt had ballooned from 30,000 to more than 200,000 pesos without any noticeable public improvements.[15] The governor's personal life also contributed to his unsuitability. Although Carrascosa was married, he lived with another woman and scandalized "culta sociedad" in San Cristóbal Las Casas.[16]

Having ruled out Carrascosa in mid-1891, President Díaz chose and "elected" Emilio Rabasa. Unlike the other petitioners for the post, Rabasa neither led nor belonged to any *camarilla* (political clique) in the state. He owed his political career entirely to Díaz. Rabasa returned to Chiapas as a national politician, independent of local political groupings, and possessing a broad, modern vision of the purpose of government. Finally, Rabasa's backers in Mexico City, Rosendo Pineda and other Científicos, saw Rabasa's candidacy as an important step away from outdated localism and personalism and toward the spread of scientific, intelligent, and civilian government throughout Mexico.[17]

Rabasa became governor of Chiapas at a propitious time, providing a definite direction for the farmers and merchants of the Central Valley at the beginning of the decade that witnessed Mexico's most rapid economic growth in the nineteenth century. It seemed to many of his contemporaries that the age of progress and modernization was finally at hand. "Regeneration and progress," according to *El Monitor Republicano*, summed up the Rabasa program for Chiapas.[18] The governor, wrote another supporter, "took hold of the reins of the state government at the most opportune time; all of his valor, all of his influence, all of his integrity, and all of his energy was necessary in order to put Chiapas on the road to real progress."[19]

A COMPLETELY NEW PROGRAM OF GOVERNMENT

Emilio Rabasa's program of "regeneration and progress" had a dual nature: political and developmental. The centralization of power and authority by the state government contributed largely to the success of the developmental reforms and projects. Rabasa believed that to get Chiapas moving he had to strengthen his own position and office. The governor, however, inherited a weak office and a politically fragmented state. The governor's authority did not extend very far into Escobar's Soconusco or Grajales's Chiapa. In San Cristóbal Las Casas the clergy and certain important families still possessed considerable influence over local and state politics. The situation, Rabasa believed, required strong and dramatic action.

In mid-1892 Governor Rabasa transferred the state government from San Cristóbal to Tuxtla Gutiérrez. In letters to President Díaz, Rabasa explained that the move was due to the high cost of food in the highlands, which necessitated higher salaries; to the apathy and laziness of Cristobalenses; to the undue influence of the clergy; and to the commercial importance of Tuxtla Gutiérrez.[20] The most important reasons, however, were unstated. First was the desire to establish an entirely new governing center and bureaucracy, free of the pernicious influences that plagued all governments in San Cristóbal. When the government did move to Tuxtla some Cristobalense government officials refused to follow—a result Rabasa had anticipated. Second, the move represented an important geographical reorientation of Chiapas. San Cristóbal was located on the trade route to Guatemala, and most of the important Cristobalense families maintained close ties with Guatemala, while Tuxtla Gutiérrez was the self-proclaimed gateway to Mexico City. Tuxtlecos, furthermore, were a more diverse group of immigrants, foreigners, and Mexican-educated elites. Already the commercial center of the Central Valley, Tuxtla was becoming the undisputed business, transportation, and political center of the state. For Rabasa, the transfer of the government signified nothing less than the political rebirth of Chiapas.[21]

The transfer of the government strengthened Rabasa's position within his own administration but did little to rid him of the state's chief political problems, the caciques. Given the ability of the caciques Escobar and Grajales to disrupt his administration, Rabasa approached this problem slowly and cautiously. The governor did, however, have Díaz's support and therefore the stronger position. When, for example, General Escobar sent two of his nephews to confer with Rabasa early in his term over the election of certain favored persons, Díaz informed Rabasa "to comply only with his requests of public interest."[22]

Soon after taking office Rabasa established a state rural police force, the Seguridad Pública, dependent on the governor, to reduce banditry, quiet political troublemakers, and enforce decrees in remote parts. This force eventually comprised 10 officers, more than 100 well-armed soldiers, and a captain who was originally from Oaxaca.[23] The governor replaced nearly everyone who had served in the Carrascosa administration and most departmental political officers, or jefes políticos. He staffed many of the most important posts in the state government with Oaxaqueños, individuals he knew and trusted.[24] The system by which jefes políticos were "elected" by citizens of the departments was revamped so that the officials became political appointees of the governor and served at his (and Díaz's) will. The post of *visitador de jefaturas* (inspector general) was established to examine the conduct of jefes políticos. The visitador could overrule or dismiss a jefe político.[25]

Not unexpectedly, Rabasa's new political order encountered resistance. The transfer of the government to Tuxtla Gutiérrez elicited almost universal disapproval in San Cristóbal. One Cristobalense complained anonymously to the national government that the abandonment of San Cristóbal would lead to the economic decline of the Central Highlands, a worsening of conditions for Chiapas's indigenous population, and possibly to another Caste War.[26] Former governors Miguel Utrilla and Manuel Carrascosa strongly opposed the move.[27] The transfer remained a constant source of discord within Chiapas until at least 1911, when a military effort to recover the capital for San Cristóbal was attempted.

Governor Rabasa's appointments of new jefes políticos, customs officials, judges, tax collectors, and even office workers also encountered resistance. Within two months of assuming office, Rabasa persuaded Díaz to replace customs officials and military officers in Tapachula and Tonalá who were Escobar loyalists. Rabasa's new jefe político for Soconusco, Manuel Figuerro of Oaxaca, was appointed without the traditional consultation with the Soconusense cacique. After several conflicts between Escobar's municipal president and Rabasa's jefe político, Escobar demanded that Díaz remove Figuerro. Rabasa refused to compromise, commenting: "I have confidence in [Figuerro] since he is new to Tapachula and entirely independent of the parties or bands that exist in that city."[28]

General Escobar was assassinated in a Tapachula street in 1893, most likely by his political rival Juan Félix Zepeda. Rabasa soon after informed Díaz that "I have indicated to the jefe político that now with the assassination, he will take this advantage to make sure that Soconusco will never again have caciques."[29] Jefe político Figuerro made some personnel changes in the local government and confiscated 211 rifles and more than 20 boxes of ammunition—Escobar's personal armory.[30] The Escobar cacicazgo no longer existed when Rabasa returned to Mexico City in 1894. Thereafter local merchants, Mexican cattlemen, and German coffee planters dominated local government in Soconusco, remaining fully cooperative and submissive to the government in Tuxtla Gutiérrez.[31]

Rabasa's encroachment into Julián Grajales's territory of Chiapa de Corzo was less spectacularly and definitively successful. For one reason, Grajales lived another ten years. Yet the mystique of dominion Grajales had cultivated over twenty years was shattered under Rabasa. The governor's appointment of individuals outside the Grajales camarilla to posts in the state and local governments brought cries of harassment from the old cacique. "The enemies that I have in this city," lamented Grajales in a letter to Díaz, "are now placed in the principal political posts suitable to molest me when it pleases them best."[32] Later in that year he again complained that "I do not think it is just or reasonable to be molested by those I had to fight before."[33] Although Díaz feigned sympathy for his old comrade in arms, he did not call off Rabasa.[34]

Elsewhere in the state, the extension of the authority of the governor and state government had top priority as well. In San Cristóbal Rabasa avoided difficulties with the local authorities by placing a personal friend and political supporter, Manuel J. Trejo, in the municipal presidency.[35] In 1893 the governor established the *partido* (administrative district) of Motozintla to project state authority in this remote region and to end conflicts between the departments of Comitán and Soconusco over demarcation of the boundary between them.[36]

As Rabasa prepared to leave state government early in 1894 he recalled for Díaz some of the achievements of his administration. Among those he singled out was the progress of political consolidation. "The departments of Soconusco, Chiapa, and Pichucalo," wrote Rabasa, "previously removed from the action of the government, are now entirely submissive."[37] Under Rabasa the state government became the most significant focus of political power in Chiapas. Years later, one of Chiapas's most respected revolutionary leaders, Luis Espinosa, recalled that Emilio Rabasa "developed and put into practice a completely new program of government which until then was unknown in Chiapas."[38]

MORE EXTENSIVE AND EFFECTIVE GOVERNMENT ACTION

The developmental program of the Rabasa administration—fiscal reform, road construction, agrarian reform, and educational development—although not strictly political in nature, was very important in the political modernization of Chiapas. In each area the state government took on a decidedly new and expanded role in the economic and social life of the region. In the struggle for regional prosperity, Rabasa emphasized the necessity of "more extensive and effective government actions." His Porfirian (and revolutionary and postrevolutionary) successors continued the work he began in 1891.

In the area of fiscal reform Governor Rabasa inherited an important measure from the preceding state government. Governor Carrascosa had begun the task of suppressing the municipal transit taxes on commerce. Rabasa continued and finished this campaign against the alcabalas, a policy that had profound political and economic implications for the state. As the revenues of local governments diminished, municipalities became more dependent on state government largess and as a consequence less politically independent. The suppression of the alcabalas also contributed to the expansion of trade throughout Chiapas. No longer burdened by tax collectors in each town, landowners and merchants found it profitable to market their produce and manufactures in other parts of the state and even outside of Chiapas.[39]

Following the president's instruction, Rabasa made fiscal reform his first priority. The state's financial situation demanded strong and immediate action; Rabasa had inherited a disaster. Bondholders of the Chiapas railroad scheme were demanding payment, the state debt had climbed to more than 200,000 pesos from only 30,000 pesos four years earlier, and the fiscal system of the state government was disorganized and corrupt.[40] Upon taking office, Rabasa appointed a special commission to study the state's tax structure and collection system and to recommend reforms. Acting on the commission's proposals, Rabasa increased the rural property valuations from 5 million to 17 million pesos, but leaving rural properties still undervalued, it was estimated, by half. He also reduced and prorated property and commercial taxes and tightened collection procedures.[41] The governor established the State Treasurer General's Office to coordinate tax collection and expenditures. By law this office was required to publish quarterly financial balances as well as the income of each rent collector. The rent collectors, for the first time, were regularly audited by accountants of the central office.[42] Through new appointments and closer vigilance, Rabasa attempted to reduce smuggling into Chiapas from Guatemala and off the Pacific shore.[43]

Rabasa's program of fiscal reform proved successful. State government revenues, according to Rabasa, doubled in two years, from 180,000 pesos in 1891 to 359,000 in 1894 (see figure 2). For the first time in Chiapas history, property taxes brought in more revenue than the highly regressive head tax. "This was the charge that you entrusted to me in 1891," Rabasa informed Díaz, "and I believe I have now complied with it, without coercion or violence, although with the discontent of two or three friends who previously had paid nothing."[44]

The new fiscal order provided the resources for the state government to begin an ambitious program of public works, from roads to schools. Rabasa's favorite project was the construction of a network of roads and telegraph and telephone lines. In 1891, when Rabasa began his duties, Chiapas possessed nothing that could even remotely be called a road.[45] Earlier efforts to establish a network of roads by contracting the work to private companies had come to nothing. What commerce there was in Chiapas was carried by canoe or oxcarts or on the backs of Indian carriers along centuries-old trails and paths.[46] Governor Francisco León (1895–99), the military officer in charge of road construction under Rabasa, expressed his opinion concerning the delay in constructing roads in Chiapas: "In these regions [San Cristóbal, Simojovel, Chilón, and Palenque] the capitalists raise objections to the reparation of

Figure 2

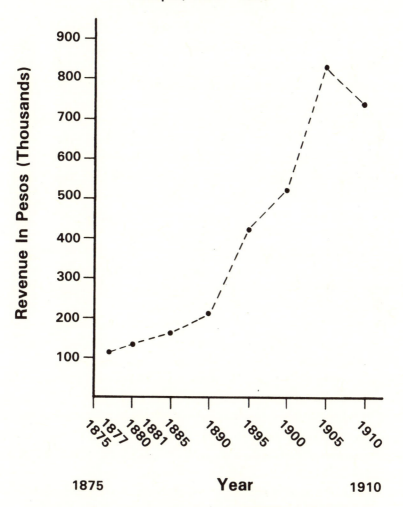

State Government Revenue
Chiapas, 1877 - 1910

Sources: Emiliano Busto, Estadística de la república mexicana México, 1880), Vol. I, p. xix: Anuario estadística de la república mexicana (México: Sria. de fomento), volumes for 1984–1912.

roads because they find it less costly to be served by *cargadores* [Indian carriers] who are paid a trifle and work like mules. . . ."[47] According to León, the highland elite perceived no pressing need for roads.

Governor Rabasa initiated construction of the first highway in Chiapas, running from the border of Oaxaca to Arriaga, Tuxtla Gutiérrez, Chiapa de Corzo, San Cristóbal, Comitán, and finally to the border with Guatemala. Earlier governments had planned for the state's first road to link San Cristóbal and San Juan Bautista, Tabasco, which was the route best suited for the Central Highlands. Rabasa dispensed with road-building concessions and subsidies and, with the approval of President Díaz, instructed the army's Tenth Battalion to do the work; materials and salaries were financed by state revenues. By the end of Rabasa's term the Oaxaca to San Cristóbal segment had been completed.[48] To Rabasa the highway's significance was "to open [Chiapas] to becoming Mexican."[49] The Rabasa administration also expanded the telegraph network, begun in 1886; constructed the first telephone lines in the state; and opened the Grijalva River above Tuxtla Gutiérrez to river boat transport from the Gulf of Mexico. Improved seaport facilities were constructed at Tonalá and San Benito (off Tapachula), thereby permitting large vessels to pick up regional commodities for export, particularly the increasing quantities of coffee.[50]

The road-building program brought incalculable benefits to Chiapas. The state highway, like the government's move to Tuxtla Gutiérrez, put Chiapas in closer contact with Mexico. This road opened the agriculturally rich Central Valley to the port at Tonalá and markets in the Central Highlands and the Isthmus of Tehuantepec, thereby giving an important impulse to commercial agriculture in that region. Since the road favored the Central Valley more than the highlands, it became part of a discriminatory pattern of development, whose effect is apparent even today.

In the liberal tradition of Juárez and Lerdo de Tejada, Emilio Rabasa strongly believed that the divison of communal village lands and the creation of a new class of yeoman farmers would promote productive capitalist agriculture and the integration of the Indian (and traditional campesino) into Mexican civilization. To advance these goals Rabasa enacted and vigorously enforced a measure (prior to the 1894 federal Ley de Ocupación y Enajenación de Terrenos Baldíos[51]) to divide all ejidos in Chiapas into private parcels. Jefes políticos were instructed to set up municipal commissions to oversee the division and the sale of plots to individuals. These commissions were required by law to apportion five-hectare plots at no cost to heads of family who could not afford the payment schedule. Well-to-do village farmers were able to purchase enough land to form respectable ranchos and accentuate the class differences in small villages. Only the most destitute received the minimum free allotments (anywhere from 10 percent to 50 percent of a village population). Many more, however, received no land at all due to corruption and residency requirements. Proceeds of the land sales were to be used for local public works and schools, with 20 percent reserved for the state treasury.[52]

Emilio Rabasa's agrarian reform, called "el reparto" and "el fraccionamiento," was an economic success and a social disaster. The number of small property owners did increase significantly in particular localities, such as in the Central Valley. Many payments were less than twenty pesos a year, an affordable sum even for some campesinos.[53] The number of ranchos in Chiapas more than doubled between 1890 and 1910.[54] Enterprising sharecroppers, renters, small merchants, and ranch foremen benefited most from this opportunity to become landowners.[55] In 1903 the average size of agricultural properties in Chiapas was only 380 hectares, compared to the national average of 5600 hectares. One in forty Chiapanecos owned land by 1910. The U.S. Consul in 1911 noted that "Chiapas is unique among the states of Mexico for the number of small holdings and peasant farmers."[56]

The effect of the reparto upon Chiapas's villages, however, was devastating; the Rabasa legislation constituted the final assault on a large number of village ejidos in the state. Between 1893 and 1909 at least sixty-seven village ejidos were affected. As the number of ranchos and haciendas increased, communities that had been independent for hundreds of years either disappeared or became hacienda rancherías. According to one report, "the ejido of Pueblo Nuevo Chiapilla was divided into lots in the year 1895 and from that date Señor Adrián Culebro, owner of the finca 'Santa Rosalía' and Señor José A. Velasco, owner of the finca 'El Castaño,' incorporated this land into their fincas."[57] Another complaint reached President Díaz early in 1895 from Chiapa de Corzo, accompanied by nine pages of signatures and thumb prints. "We are

trying to save the only source which provides us life," wrote the petitioners. "It is true that we are granted lots for free but this places us
in a worse condition of poverty."[58] There were numerous requests to
Díaz and to the state government to stop the reparto, to no avail.[59] In
1895 Governor Fausto Moguel admitted that "we have had some difficulties originating from the greed of some finqueros who, to the detriment of the poorer classes, attempt to acquire large portions of land."[60]

The reparto had two faces. As it added to the size of established fincas
and the ranchero class it also forced more villagers into more exploitative and less secure work such as migrant labor, indebted servitude,
sharecropping, and baldiaje. Many villagers, whether through fraud or
sale, never received plots or were unable to maintain possession of them.
At the time Rabasa believed that the distribution of parcels to villagers
was the best way to prevent large landowners from claiming and buying
all ejido land and leaving villagers (who could not prove ownership)
completely landless.[61] Twenty-five years later Rabasa admitted that he
had erred in permitting parcel holders to sell their plots. Too many
ended up without land, which he maintained was not his intent.[62]

Rabasa's educational program was both ambitious and realistic. After
1891 the state government took primary responsibility for public education in Chiapas. The poverty of most municipal governments forced
the state government to give direct support to rural primary education.
"When I arrived in the state," Rabasa informed Díaz, "the government
sustained one school in the pueblo of Huistán, and no more; today it
supports more than 100 primaries of first, second, and third class;
two preparatory schools; one college of superior studies for girls; and
the Industrial-Military School. All of this is under the supervision of
the General Office of Public Instruction, which previously did not exist
in the state."[63] The state's budget for education climbed from 7,000
pesos allocated by Governor Carrascosa in 1891 to 40,000 pesos under
Rabasa.[64]

In keeping with his inclination for centralization, Rabasa established
the General Office of Public Instruction to supervise the establishment
of new schools, the certification of new teachers, and the creation of
a uniform statewide curriculum. The director general was authorized
to appoint inspectors to visit schools and municipalities to enforce the
public instruction law and to encourage municipal and private edu-

cational efforts. The governor added a new head tax to be used exclusively for municipal primary schools and a law that required landowners to maintain a primary school if more than ten school-age children resided on their property. Despite this flurry of legislation, rural primary education remained entirely inadequate due to the poverty of both state and municipal governments.[65] "And still Señor Rabasa complains, and with reason," wrote *El Universal*, "that it is not possible to comply with the law of obligatory education."[66] The governor did, however, take the first steps to make education a public responsibility in modern Chiapas. He created two state-supported preparatory schools, a night school of agricultural and technical education for Indians in San Cristóbal, and two public libraries.[67]

Rabasa, unlike many of his contemporaries, did not view education as the primary means of integrating the Indian population into Mexican society. "Before teaching him to read," he insisted, "it is necessary to liberate the Indian from his misery and from the grasp of the superior class." He believed a hundred schools would not do as much as one railroad in improving the working and living conditions of the Indian population.[68]

Rabasa's new fiscal order and program of internal improvements found greater approval and support in the Central Valley than elsewhere in the state. David Castellanos and Segundo Alfonso, hacendados from Comitán, believed the high property valuations were impoverishing their department.[69] The increased property valuations of the large but generally idle haciendas around San Cristóbal, combined with the transfer of the government to Tuxtla Gutiérrez, made Rabasa most unpopular in tierra fría.[70] Although the Rabasa developmental program tended to alienate the highland elites, it was also creating a larger and more important constituency in other parts of the state. This fact perhaps best explains its continuation after Rabasa returned to Mexico City.[71]

RABASA'S LEGACY

In his writing and government service Emilio Rabasa demonstrated that he was a sincere reformer, not unlike the U.S. progressives at the turn of the century. He advocated better sanitation in the cities, an effective and honest police force, prison reform, and clean government.

In his novels he criticized the mistreatment of Indians, incompetence and corruption in government, personalism, nepotism, and sycophancy. He despised the thousands of minor despots in Mexico. Rabasa was convinced the state governments had an important role to play in the creation of modern Mexico. That role, he later wrote, was one that emphasized the power of the state government to promote modernization while at the same time curbing localism and parochialism.[72]

Like other científicos, Rabasa accepted Porfirio Díaz as the only alternative to anarchy, but he wanted to move gradually to a less personalistic system of rule and one with more democratic procedures. As a political creation of Díaz, he never failed to demonstrate his loyalty and submission to the supreme caudillo. Although Rabasa pursued his own program of reform and development in Chiapas with characteristic energy and intelligence, he never proceeded with any program, reform, or important appointment without first consulting the president. Rabasa was in many ways the model governor for modern Mexico: loyal, intelligent, and energetic.[73]

Rabasa had been more than just a good governor for just over two years; he also set a course for Chiapas continued by his successors. Like Rabasa, the next four Porfirian governors of Chiapas came from the middle strata of society. Fausto Moguel, originally a Tuxtleco but living in Oaxaca when Rabasa recruited him in 1891 for state treasurer, was appointed to finish Rabasa's elected term. Moguel informed Díaz that he would continue the Rabasa program, which "has now begun to transform the state and which will be the base of its future prosperity."[74] Lieutenant Colonel Francisco León, a native of Oaxaca, was elected governor for the period 1895-99 on Rabasa's recommendation. León had directed the road-building program under Rabasa and Moguel and was strongly committed to extending the reforms begun under Rabasa.[75] León's successor, Rafael Pimentel, another native of Oaxaca, was the only one of Rabasa's successors whom the former governor did not select. Governor León was forced to resign due to a political scandal and Pimentel, already in Chiapas as Díaz's political agent, assumed the office. However, Ramón Rabasa—Emilio's elder brother and an important politician in Chiapas in his own right—was selected state treasurer, which gave his brother some influence during Pimentel's term from 1899 to 1905. In 1905 Governor Pimentel attempted to transfer the state government back to San Cristóbal Las Casas. The Rabasa brothers blocked this move, and Pimentel resigned. Ramón assumed the office and remained in power until 1911.

Emilio Rabasa was not a powerful regional caudillo like Bernardo Reyes of Nuevo León or Teodoro Dehesa in Veracruz. He maintained an important influence in the affairs of Chiapas but he did not dictate to his successors. Rabasa intervened only in matters of some importance. His successors counted on him to be their informal representative and Chiapas's agent in Mexico City. The history of Chiapas from the early 1890s to the beginning of the Revolution was indelibly marked by this man.

Rabasa left the governor's office in February 1894 after serving a few months more than two years of his four-year term. As he told the president, he wished to return to Mexico City to take care of the education of his daughters and because of his wife's poor health.[76] Rabasa was elected senator from Sinaloa and also continued to practice, teach, and write about the law. His criticism of the Constitution of 1857, in two books published in 1906 and 1912, influenced the members of the 1917 constitution convention at Querétaro.[77] As a governor and a political thinker, Emilio Rabasa bridged the gap between what Mexico was and what it soon became. On the 100th anniversary of his birth, the editors of El Universal commented that "Rabasa represents the culmination of liberal thought in Mexico and he began something more, the neoliberalism of the twentieth century."[78]

The administration of Emilio Rabasa represented a watershed in the history of Chiapas. Building upon the ideological consensus that emerged from the Reform, the political stability Porfirio Díaz established in the nation, and the energy and expectations of a growing entrepreneurial class in Chiapas, Rabasa began the sustained process of economic development and political consolidation that was to characterize Chiapas and Mexico over the next fifty years. To Rabasa, government was a useful tool that could help transform an isolated and backward region into one more prosperous and modern. He realized, however, that before a state government could become an effective tool of modernization its authority had to be centralized and consolidated. Rabasa began this process by undermining the power of local political bosses, strengthening the fiscal base of state government, and establishing a new center of government. At the same time, he expanded the functions of state government, which began to intervene in important ways in regional society and economy—through road construction, reform of village land tenure, and support for education. "Señor Rabasa," noted the U.S. consul in 1910, "may justly be regarded as the harbinger of progress and commercial activity."[79]

ONE OF THE MOST PROGRESSIVE GOVERNORS

EMILIO RABASA RETURNED TO MEXICO CITY IN 1894, YET THE COURSE HE set for Chiapas during his brief administration endured. His personal influence in state affairs remained considerable. Fausto Moguel, selected by Rabasa to serve out his term, was little more than a caretaker governor. Moguel kept Rabasa's appointees, continued to work on the Rabasa program, and arranged the election of Francisco León. "One of the most progressive governors of the Republic," León tested the limits of Porfirian toleration of liberal social reform.[1] During the León government the regional elites of Pichucalco and Comitán became dissatisfied with the Rabasa program, and malcontents in San Cristóbal Las Casas became ever more determined to return the seat of state government to their city and rid the state of the influence of Emilio Rabasa. The experience of the León government demonstrated the political costs and the limits of provincial modernization. State government was not sufficiently independent of regional elites to enact the reforms necessary for the long-term expansion of commercial agriculture.

THE MOGUEL INTERREGNUM

Governor Fausto Moguel served the remaining nineteen months of Emilio Rabasa's term and prepared Francisco León's accession to the governor's office. Two events that were to have lingering effects for years to come took place during the interregnum of 1894–95.

A war scare during the winter of 1894 threatened to make Chiapas the battlefield in a conflict between Mexico and Guatemala. In 1892

President Justo Rufino Barrios of Guatemala had signed the final accord with Mexico regarding the boundary between Guatemala and Chiapas. Two years later, primarily for domestic political effect, Barrios moved troops and cannon to the border and threatened war. President Porfirio Díaz ordered the transfer of the 12th Battalion, then stationed in Juchitán, Oaxaca, to Tapachula and sent General Bonifacio Topete to Chiapas to report on the state's readiness for war.[2] The tension subsided by April 1895, although not as the result of Mexico's show of force. Due to the absence of a good road between Juchitán and Tapachula, the 12th Battalion reached the border only after a long delay. For reasons of national security, Díaz came to view the construction of a coastal railroad as an absolute necessity.[3] Although construction did not begin for another six years, the Panamerican Railroad was conceived during this crisis.

With Emilio Rabasa's resignation in 1894, several discreet campaigns commenced to influence Díaz's selection of the next governor of Chiapas. Most petitions to the president expressed opposition to any Rabasa appointee and support for a native son—a Cristobalense, Comiteco, or Chiapaneco.[4] In no city, however, was electioneering more intense or better organized than in San Cristóbal Las Casas, whose leading citizens adamantly opposed any continuation of "Rabacismo." During the Moguel interregnum a Cristobalense camarilla was formed, united not by a caudillo but by a cause. This clique was led by landowners and lawyers, including Jesús Martínez Rojas, José H. Ruiz, Jesús Flores, Gregorio Culebro, Clemente Robles, and Manuel Pineda. The group worked almost unceasingly over the next seventeen years to return the state government to San Cristóbal.[5]

By April 1895 the Cristobalense camarilla, known as the Iron Circle,[6] had captured the sympathy and fired the ambition of General Topete, who had assumed command of the federal garrison located in San Cristóbal. Topete became the group's candidate for governor in the July elections.[7] Díaz, however, supported León and ordered Governor Moguel to have him elected. León took office on December 1, 1895. The Iron Circle was discouraged but not defeated. Rafael Pimentel, Díaz's political agent in Chiapas, reported that "the supporters and directors of Topete" continued to meet and plot after the election.[8] Manuel Lacroix, a member of León's administration, informed President Díaz in

December 1895 that "this state seems content with the new government, with the exception of certain persons in San Cristóbal." General Topete, Lacroix continued, was slandering León, calling him a drunk and worse to discredit him.[9] Pimentel advised Díaz to transfer Topete to another state "because at the least he would create difficulties for León in the function of his government."[10] The general was transferred in January 1896 but the problem remained in San Cristóbal, as serious and dangerous as before.

THE LEÓN PROGRAM

Francisco León, perhaps even more than Emilio Rabasa, was an activist governor. He continued the road-building program, the division of ejidos, the establishment of schools, and the centralization and consolidation of state government power and authority. León enlarged the role of the state government in public health and attempted to reform labor and Indian legislation. He was surely one of the most progressive governors of his time, yet he was forced to resign from office in political disgrace.

Chiapas's need for easier communication was, according to León, "a question of life or death."[11] During his tenure the state government expended more than 200,000 pesos on road construction, which the governor accounted for personally to avoid fraud.[12] In 1896, for example, it was reported that more than 100 men were at work daily on the state highway.[13] In 1898 the state government extended the telephone network along the highway route.[14] The government finished construction of the state highway yet, as León informed Díaz, "only the departments of Tonalá, Tuxtla, Chiapa, Las Casas, and Comitán receive the benefits of this road, leaving the rich departments of Palenque, Chilón, and Simojovel without easy communication."[15] Despite this problem, the Tuxtleco periodical *El Porvenir de Chiapas* was optimistic, boasting that "one of the driving wheels of progress is now being built."[16]

Governor León, like Rabasa, invested a large percentage of the state budget in education and, again like Rabasa, was not encouraged by what he saw. The governor informed Díaz in 1896: "Even though I have invested considerable sums in this branch, the practical result has come to almost nothing, in preparatory and professional instruction and in primary instruction."[17] The principal cause of the underdeveloped state of education in Chiapas, as León saw it, was the lack of suitable professors. To correct this deficiency, León established the State Normal School.

In the area of fiscal policy the León administration increased the rate of taxation on commercial capital,[18] excepted legally constituted investment partnerships from rural property taxes to encourage joint capital ventures,[19] and attempted unsuccessfully to reduce Chiapas's contribution to the federal treasury. During most of the nineteenth century the federal states were required to forward to Mexico City between 25 and 30 percent of all taxes collected within their jurisdictions. Certain taxes—those levied on the sale of national lands and on mail and telegraph services, custom duties, and stamp taxes on official documents—were exclusively national; the central government limited states to the collection of only a few taxes, on property, alcohol, and individuals. In two studies commissioned by Governor León, the state treasurer calculated that since 1824, Chiapas had contributed some 13 million pesos to the federal treasury but had received only about 100,000 from Mexico City in the form of subsidies, emergency aid, and material improvements. The implication was clear: Chiapas deserved more help from the national government or less of a tax burden.[20]

President Díaz did have a plan for public improvements in Chiapas, although his motives had little to do with fairness. In 1896 Díaz informed León:

For some time now Guatemala has cajoled the residents of Soconusco and has established ports of deposit on the frontier, in which they charge such low taxes on coffee and the other products of Soconusco that it amounts to a free service.

They are, furthermore, bringing a railroad to the frontier and will ask permission to extend it into Mexican territory. Added to this we have no railroad or docks on the coast of Soconusco and the government of the state imposes taxes that appear to be high to the residents of Soconusco. I propose for your consideration that the government of Guatemala is skillfully and slyly breeding a spirit of separation in the heart of Soconusco.[21]

Díaz promised that the national government would construct a railroad from Tehuantepec to Tapachula, build a steel pier on the coast, and encourage a bank to open a branch in the region. He suggested that the state government "treat Soconusco with a gentle hand and relax their taxation a little, because the landowners there in their conversations with Guatemalans will assure them that Soconusco is remaining firm to the state."[22] Due to the mediation of Emilio Rabasa, a contract was signed for the construction of a railroad (although the Chicago firm later backed out) and the Bank of London proposed to establish a branch in Tapachula.[23] Certainly a bank was needed. The German moneylenders of Tapachula charged from 2 to 4 percent a month, "signifying the ruin of commerce and agriculture."[24] Like the railroad, however, the establishment of a bank was delayed until 1900.

The León administration took the first significant state actions in public health and the confinement of criminals. In 1897 the state government created the Office of Inspector General of Public Health. The inspector general, and his assistants stationed in the various towns, were authorized to inspect food industries, medicine sales, burial practices, outbreaks of contagious diseases (with the authority to impose quarantines), and all other matters affecting public health.[25] By the end of León's term, the state's first publicly supported hospital was nearing completion.[26] The state government was forced to begin building a penitentiary, according to León, due to "the scarcity of [financial] resources of the ayuntamientos of the *cabeceras* of the departments which has prevented the operation of jails due to weak security."[27]

THIS VICIOUS AND SPINELESS CUSTOM

For two decades, the practice of indebted servitude had given Chiapas a poor reputation. During the 1870s and 1880s, Chiapas came under attack by liberal and radical journalists as the "slave state" of Mexico.[28] Several Chiapanecos, in response, publicly defended indebted servitude as a humane, efficient, and legal contractual arrangement.[29] Flavio Antonio Paniagua, for example, editor of the Cristobalense *La Brújula*, reacted strongly in 1873 to an article published in the Mexico City periodical *Almavia* alleging that slavery flourished in Chiapas. Paniagua replied that "neither direct nor indirect, open or disguised slavery exists [in Chiapas]."[30] Fernando Zepeda, editor of the *Boletín de Noticias*, wrote in 1886 in the Mexico City newspaper *El Partido Liberal* that perpetual service did not exist in Chiapas. Zepeda said that "by speaking in favor of the servants, exaggerating their poor conditions, [the critics] are instilling in them imaginary rights such as the abolition of their debts, exciting in them the passion and disposition for rebellion, which would be without doubt unfortunate for society and, particularly, for the agricultural industry of the country."[31] Until the 1890s, landowners in Chiapas strongly supported indebted servitude.[32] Peonage appeared basic to the region's economy; "it constitutes," one hacendado noted, "the principal element of life of our fincas."[33]

Beginning in the 1890s, however, with the breakup of village communal lands and the increased availability of labor, many Chiapanecos began to believe that their economic interests were no longer bound to servitude; now they sought its demise. Liberal economic doctrine, many argued, supported the practice of free labor. In 1895, the conservative metropolitan review *El Economista Mexicana* recommended "the radical modification of the system of service in those states where there is the greatest scarcity of laborers; the increase of salaries, the decrease of the hours of work, in a word, the treatment of the peon as a man and not as a beast."[34]

The first public call for labor reform in Chiapas came in 1893. In that year the newly formed Sociedad Agrícola Mexicana de Chiapas, located in Tuxtla Gutiérrez and composed of the leading agriculturalists of the Central Valley, set forth its program. The Sociedad Agrícola recommended the promotion of scientific agricultural techniques, the establishment of banks, the construction of railroads, and the correction of labor abuses.[35] Later that year, Governor Emilio Rabasa criticized the system of service. He asserted in his annual *Informe* that this "problem," as he called it, paralyzed substantial amounts of capital that could be more efficiently employed, and therefore was prejudicial to both workers and capitalists.[36]

Governor León issued a call for an agricultural congress to resolve the question of indebted servitude as soon as he took office. The congress would meet in March 1896, with each municipality assigned one delegate.[37] There is no question that León wished to rid Chiapas of "this vicious and spineless custom."[38] One month before the meeting, however, a portentous warning appeared in *El Mundo,* one of the semi-official Mexico City newspapers. In a direct reference to the pending assembly in Chiapas, it censured those who would "attempt to change the economic face of the country."[39]

The congress that assembled in Tuxtla Gutiérrez in late March 1896 was certainly not a radical body; the eighty-eight delegates represented the wealthiest members of landed society. The geographical makeup of the congress was also weighted in favor of those departments where indebted servitude was most important. Apparently, areas where servitude had little importance did not send delegates.

The dominant concern of the sessions was not the humanitarian goal of improving the lives of rural workers but the economic one of increasing agricultural productivity, freeing the thousands of pesos tied up in debts, and finding a solution to the geographical maldistribution of the work force within the state. Clemente Robles, the representative of San Cristóbal and three other municipalities, summed up the feelings of most participants when he stated that "the present system of service is bad economics for the state."[40] Most delegates agreed that the system was antiquated and prejudicial to the worker and the hacendado. Economic self-interest, they believed, required the modification of indebted servitude.[41]

The congress divided into two committees to study and propose solutions to the labor problems facing the state. The agenda of the congress included six points; the First Committee was responsible for points one through three and the Second Committee for points four through six. The agenda was as follows:

First. The contract of domestic service as it is honored in the state: Does it merit the charge of slavery as has been alleged occasionally in the national press?

Second. The mentioned contract: Does it conflict with some of the established principles of the Federal Constitution?

Third. Does it conform to the accepted principles of political economy or can it be qualified as anti-economical?

Fourth. Has the occasion arrived to abolish the service known in the state as debt peonage?

Fifth. If affirmative: What are the most efficient means for the amortization of the debt and the substitution of this service, conciliating both the interests of the farmer and the servant?

Sixth. If negative: What means should be adopted for improving the actual system of service?[42]

Throughout the month-long congress, Governor León kept the president informed of the proceedings and, as a good Porfirian governor, constantly requested his advice and counsel. Díaz, for his part, did not hesitate to offer suggestions. Immediately before the congress Díaz, referring to the meeting's objective, wrote that "considering the great danger [of this effort], without losing any time I take this opportunity to inform you that for no reason should you permit it. You must believe that if [servitude] exists here it is because I cannot yet remove it; we are still not at the level of education where it is possible to bring such a benefit to the villages."[43] León responded that he would proceed with caution "without overly disturbing customs and with due respect for the consequences."[44] It is quite likely that from this point on, the question of meaningful reform became moot.

The course of the congress and of subsequent legislative action was one of progressive dilution of proposed reforms. Although no records reveal what took place behind the façade of the congress—the official record itself is edited and incomplete— the report of the work of the Second Committee is instructive. This committee, headed by Manuel Cano and José Lara, was responsible for proposing modifications of the labor system and clearly was the more important of the two. During the second week of the congress, Cano presented a fairly sweeping reform proposal that included the obligatory amortization of debts through wage deductions, a minimum wage of thirty centavos a day, the prohibition of all cash or credit advances, the final liquidation of all workers' debts within ten years, and careful supervision of the amortization process by the state government.[45] On April 19, the Second Committee, by a vote of thirty-two to eighteen, approved and presented its formal recommendation to the full congress. This proposal included Cano's amortization plan and the proposed prohibition of advances, but only to newly contracted servants. It made no mention of a minimum wage or the eventual liquidation of debts. Finally, at the end of the congress, the full assembly formally recommended to the governor that contracts for new servants prohibit the accumulation of any debt. Established debts were to remain unmodified and valid.[46] Indebted servitude, in short, was to die a natural death along with the servants themselves.

Although León had correctly sensed agreement among landowners regarding the economic problems presented by indebted servitude, he had miscalculated their willingness to do anything about it. The First Committee, for example, concluded that indebted servitude in Chiapas, although anti-economical, was not a form of slavery nor was it unconstitutional.[47] One minority delegate on the Second Committee argued that "there is no doubt that servitude is hostile to progress; but one cannot suppress it all at once, because this will bring worse wrongs."[48] The delegates were unwilling to undergo short-term injuries to their interests for the modernization of capitalist enterprise. Those who opposed any constructive reform, furthermore, had the full support of President Díaz.

On April 30 Governor León wrote Díaz, "I have the honorable satisfaction to inform you: that the Agrarian Congress has closed its sessions giving a solution to the Agenda that was previously formulated, but not without first adopting in the most part the dispatched plan which you appropriately indicated to me." León continued, "It is true that this leaves things as they were for now, but in the not remote future this vicious and spineless custom which no one loves will be reformed, without producing a disturbance and not in a radical manner."[49] Díaz, in response, indicated he wanted no more action:

The matter is over, and since it was decided only in part, it shows that it cannot be resolved and therefore you should not return to touch it; in so much as it is so important to landowners, it would damage your personal prestige and in this respect and if you agree, I invite you to leave it alone and I repeat, do not touch it further, even if a new opportunity indicates that you should do so.[50]

Although the Second Committee voted in the affirmative that the time had come to end indebted servitude, it nevertheless proceeded to include the sixth point on the agenda in its discussions: "What means should be adopted for improving the actual system of service?" The result was a legislative proposal redefining the rights and obligations of both workers and employers. This proposal required the witnessing by at least two persons of the signing of all labor contracts, written rather than oral contracts, and contracts that stated the amount of money promised and the exact nature and amount of work required. Employers were responsible for treating sick and injured workers and providing medicine for them. This legislative proposal was never acted upon by León.[51]

In 1897 Governor León decreed that all indebted servants had to be registered and their debts recorded by the jefes políticos. After November 12, 1897, the state government and its courts would not recognize any contract for new servants that recorded a debt exceeding two months' salary (or approximately 15 to 20 pesos).[52] The state's survey found 31,512 indebted servants in Chiapas who owed, collectively, more than 3 million pesos to their employers. (See table 2.) Later in the year, León observed that the law had been accepted by the "sensible part of the state" and would be "an important factor in the wellbeing of Chiapas, because it will expel innumerable abuses and a very bad system which has been one of the causes of the current backwardness of our agriculture."[53] This was putting the best face on what León clearly realized was a failure. He was absolutely correct when he told Díaz, "This leaves things as they were."

Governor León, Manuel Cano, José Lara, and others wanted to use the power of the state to remove what they perceived as an obstacle to full agricultural productivity. The modernizing entrepreneurs of Chiapas could convince neither the representatives of the landed class in Chiapas nor Porfirio Díaz of the need to regulate the labor market, to adapt it to the expanding regional economy. The experiment was vetoed, discouraging the evolution away from indebted servitude.

Francisco León nonetheless proposed in the summer of 1896 to reform "the custom of employing Indians as cargo carriers in place of beasts of burden." The governor informed the president that he wanted a "law prohibiting under the penalty of severe fines, the burdening of

TABLE 2

REGISTER OF INDEBTED SERVITUDE, CHIAPAS, 1897

Department or Partido	Number of Servants	Value of Debts (in pesos)
Mezcalapa	747	$72,570
Simojovel	2626	222,293
La Libertad	1142	105,701
Tonalá	832	76,033
Pichucalco	3242	506,675
Chiapa	1463	125,895
Chilón	3530	188,468
Las Casas	2238	117,733
Palenque	1131	n.d.
Comitán	4783	333,077
Soconusco	3997	467,840
Tuxtla	2339	214,904
Motozintla	714	50,971
Chamula	234	11,029
Frailesca	865	80,250
Cintalapa	1630	195,958
Total	31,512	$3,017,012

Note: The Soconusco figures are incomplete due to the absence of two account books. In 1898 the Secretaría de Hacienda registered a total of 6,500 indebted servants in Soconusco department. Motozintla, Chamula, Frailesca, and Cintalapa are partidos.

Source: *Periódico Oficial del Estado* (Tuxtla Gutiérrez), 30 July 1898.

Indians with a weight of more than one *arroba* [about thirty-five pounds]."[54] When this custom was forgotten, León believed, good roads would flourish. Díaz, however, commented that such a reform "could be counterproductive."[55] León dropped the idea—for two years. In 1898 he informed the president that there were more than 500 *tamanes*

(Indian cargo carriers) in Chiapas. They were paid a peso for each load and therefore many carried three or four loads at a time to earn more. Tamanes were held financially responsible for any loss or damage to the merchandise. This form of transport, according to León, monopolized commerce and impeded other forms of competition. "Regarding the merchants who traffic with these unfortunates," León wrote:

> they do not agree nor can they agree to the opening of highways or even less to the construction of railroads which would lead to the disappearance of this exploitation which leaves upon the bodies of many Indians the same lesions that beasts of burdens show on their backs. This explains why I have been offered thirty thousand pesos not to open a highway to San Cristóbal.

This time, however, perhaps anticipating Díaz's reaction, León advocated no reform. "It will be necessary to prohibit this traffic; but first we have to establish roads and railroads which will permit the passage of another kind of transport and then these improvements will render meaningless such prohibition."[56]

REBELLIOUS TO ALL ORDER AND PROGRESS

Francisco León pursued a political policy of centralization of authority in Chiapas and absolute loyalty to the national government. León, however, faced a far more volatile and dangerous political adversary in the Iron Circle in San Cristóbal than Emilio Rabasa had faced with Sebastián Escobar or Julián Grajales. This organization of Cristobalenses rested not upon the prestige or authority of one person but on a sacred cause. Rabasa, in fact, was the true target of Cristobalense wrath. His centralizing program, development and fiscal policies, and above all the transfer of the government to Tuxtla Gutiérrez had provoked certain Cristobalenses into organizing a sort of government-in-exile. Francisco León, a supporter of the Rabasa program but no puppet of the former governor, was their immediate target. His replacement by someone sympathetic to their cause was their goal.

León began his administration in a spirit of conciliation and unification. His secretary of government, Manuel Lacroix of Palenque, informed Díaz in January 1896 that "the governor has followed up to now a policy of unification, nominating for political posts men of all circles."[57] His most surprising nomination was that of Timoteo Flores Ruiz, one of the Iron Circle, as secretary of finance. Flores Ruiz served for fifteen days in Tuxtla Gutiérrez and then resigned and returned to San Cristóbal owing to a disagreement with the governor.[58]

León replaced a number of Rabasa appointees in the state government and the jefaturas with his own men, usually Tuxtlecos and Oaxaqueños.[59] The most important jefatura, that of Soconusco, was filled in 1896 by a Díaz appointee, a man unknown to León.[60] General Ignacio Bravo replaced General Topete in January as federal zone commander and moved the federal garrison from San Cristóbal to Tuxtla Gutiérrez, leaving detachments of thirty-five men each in San Cristóbal, Tapachula, Comitán, and Tonalá.[61]

As early as March 1896 León had lost all patience with San Cristóbal. His attitude from this point on toward the city and its residents certainly contributed to his later difficulties. A robbery of files from a state government office in San Cristóbal provoked this comment from León to Díaz: "You will see to what unlikely degree the perversion in that city has reached, obstinately rebellious to all order and progress. . . . It has reached such a degraded extreme that even the Cristobalense high magistracy is carelessly involved in illegal intrigues." San Cristóbal, concluded León, was "the most restless and hypocritical city in the Republic."[62] Díaz suggested in response that the governor "employ the least number possible of Sancristobalense lawyers."[63]

At the same time that the Agrarian Congress was in session, León created three new partidos: Chamula, Cintalapa, and Frailesca. The Partido of Chamula included the predominantly Indian municipalities of Chamula, Zinacantan, San Andrés, Santiago, Magdalena, Santa Marta, San Pedro Chenalhó, and San Miguel Mitontic.[64] Governor León justified this expansion of direct state supervision and protection as a legitimate response to the harsh exploitation of the Indians of these municipalities by the residents of San Cristóbal. "The Cristobalenses," wrote León, "are not content with squeezing the juice out of them, maintaining them in servitude for a peso a month, sucking their blood like voracious vampires in all kinds of little contracts; . . . I believe the opportunity has arrived to begin to give the Chamula a close protector who guarantees their rights and promotes their improvement."[65]

The establishment of the Department of Mariscal (formerly the Partido of Motozintla) and the partidos of Chamula, Cintalapa, and Frailesca was a way to place distant and difficult-to-reach subregions under closer supervision of the state government. The jefes políticos formerly responsible for these areas (with the notable exception of San Cristóbal) rarely visited them and exercised little control. The establishment of the Partido of Chamula was another attempt to reduce the control of San Cristóbal over the Indian population of the Central Highlands.[66]

Not unexpectedly, the formation of the Partido of Chamula, combined with the unhappiness in San Cristóbal over the Agrarian Congress and the location of the state government, produced the first political crisis of the León government. In July 1896, Cristobalenses cried that the Chamula were preparing another caste war. "Critical situation this capital," telegraphed former governor Miguel Utrilla, "rumors of barbarous Indian insurrection."[67] As far as León was concerned, "the Cristobalenses have created the pretext of a Chamula uprising in order to alarm the state and to have a plausible motive to buy arms."[68] In a long letter explaining the situation of Díaz, León commented:

> The Cristobalenses of today are the same as during the time of Ortega and Father Chanona: backward, troublemakers, hypocrites, and traitors. For this, Señor Rabasa transferred the government here and they are still calling him "the dead man" and since then have conspired to drag the capital back there.
>
> Since the abominable abuses of long ago are still being committed upon the Indian race in the neighboring pueblos, it made the creation of the jefatura in Chamula indispensable, and irritated those who exploit them; and in spite, they invented the story of the uprising, calculating to draw out of it all kinds of advantages; if they frightened the government to withdraw the jefatura they would remain masters of the flock.[69]

León, in a calculated move, declared a state of siege, "appearing to believe them," he noted, and to prevent the formation of a citizen's militia.[70] The crisis blew over, for the time being.

The gubernatorial election in the summer of 1899 rekindled regional and political discontent in Chiapas. In April seventeen of the leading hacendados, merchants, and professionals of the department of Pichucalco asked President Díaz not to re-elect Francisco León. This powerful group of Pichucaleños, originally Rabasa supporters, became disaffected for two reasons. They believed the state government had abandoned them by not promoting public improvements in their locality. They were also disconcerted by León's campaign to reform indebted servitude, an institution that was strongly rooted and pervasive in that department.[71]

> Here we have not one school well provided for the education of our children, this obliges us to send them to other states, or Europe, or the United States. . . . Even our attachment to work, our arduous dedication to agriculture has been considered a reviled enterprise, qualifying us as slavers, because of the system of domestic service that exists, as if its existence were not an institution of long persistence, outside of our social situation, and as if we were to be blamed for these historical antecedents. . . . In conclusion: the state government has not helped us; when it is not hostile to us, it scornfully abandons us, demanding higher taxes.[72]

Elite Comitecos, also part of Rabasa's original constituency, became disenchanted with the state's "progress" during the León administration. In 1897 León intervened to prevent the landowners of the City of Comitán from expropriating all of the city ejido, which had been in their possession before the reparto. They were simply transferring title to themselves without apportioning parcels to poor families or those who wished to buy plots. León set about to correct this abuse, making no friends in Comitán in the process.[73] Other Comitecos complained that "the jefes políticos and municipal presidents are frequently individuals that, even by their own account, abuse, extort, and are in open conflict with the best members of society."[74]

REELECTION AND RESIGNATION

The most intensive efforts to stop León's reelection were made in San Cristóbal. The Cristobalense camarilla tried to persuade Victor

Manuel Castillo to seek the post, which he refused. Francisco León, however, still possessed Díaz's confidence and in the spring the governor ordered all jefes políticos to establish reelection clubs. As a result no other candidates came forward.[75]

On May 25, 1899, less than two months before the election, one of the sentries at the government palace in Tuxtla Gutiérrez attempted to assassinate Governor León. The soldier fired once at the governor, who was walking to his office, but missed. He then tried to escape but was captured.[76] León reported to Díaz two days later that "two versions have come to my attention. The first presupposes responsibility to [Emilio] Rabasa, who would govern through Lacroix. The other, that the prisoner received 500 pesos from conspirators in San Cristóbal."[77] Two days after his first report, León was more certain. "Fron anonymous reports," he telegraphed to Díaz, "I know that a ring of conspirators exists in San Cristóbal with sympathizers in this city [Tuxtla Gutiérrez]; among those that are implicated is the Administrator of Stamp Taxes, Garmendía. In San Cristóbal, implicated as the leaders are Jesús Martínez Rojas, José H. Ruiz, Jesús Flores, Joaquín Peña; I am advised that they are preparing an uprising of Indians in Chamula and another here for the first of June."[78] In Mexico City, a press report indicated that "the clergy [of San Cristóbal] is the principal instigator, for not being pleased with the reelection."[79] In July, Francisco León was reelected governor of Chiapas for the term 1899–1903.

On June 12, Antonio Martínez, the soldier arrested in the assassination attempt, informed his captors that Major Romualdo Sánchez of the State Security Battalion had given him money to kill León.[80] Sánchez was then imprisoned and on July 9 confessed that he had received the commission to kill León from Cristobalenses Vicente Espinosa, Clemente Robles, and Ciro Farrera.[81] These three were imprisoned on July 14, two days after the election.[82] Others implicated in the plot—including José and Modesto Cano, Jesús Martínez Rojas, and J. Antonio Rivera G.—escaped to Guatemala.[83]

Governor León believed that the conspirators decided to kill him when it be came clear his reelection was a certainty. In this intrigue, as León noted, Judge Leonardo Pineda, Ciro Farrera's uncle, would be appointed interim governor and would then return the state government to San Cristóbal so that the conspirators would again have free access to the state treasury.[84] León's reconstruction of the crime and the motive is plausible. The documentary record, however, yields no definitive judgment. After so many years it is impossible to say whether Farrera and the others conpsired to have León killed or León used the assassination attempt to rid himself of political enemies.

In any case, León's decision to prosecute Farrera proved politically disastrous. Ciro Farrera was perhaps the richest man in Chiapas. Vicente Farrera, Ciro's father, had established the state's largest import-export house, Casa Farrera, in San Cristóbal in 1839. Since that time Casa Farrera had established branches in Tuxtla Gutiérrez, Tonalá, and Mexico City. The Farreras owned numerous haciendas and some coffee fincas throughout Chiapas and were related to the "best" and wealthiest families in the state. Farrera also had close political and familial ties to Victor Manuel Castillo, a national deputy from Chiapas and close friend and colleague of Emilio Rabasa.[85] Francisco León, the former army colonel from Oaxaca, had tackled too powerful a prey.

In preparation for a smooth and predictable trial, León asked for the resignation of Federal District Judge Abrahám López, who he believed was involved in the conspiracy. Perhaps under normal circumstances León would have succeeded and been able to call up First Alternate Judge Manuel Trinidad Corzo, who was close to the León administration. In the summer of 1899, however, in a case that was attracting national attention, López refused to be intimidated and step down.[86] León then sought the intervention of the federal Supreme Court and the president. After reviewing the preliminary proceedings of the Farrera case, the Supreme Court confirmed López's authority.[87] Díaz, for his part, wrote that "it is not possible to change judges if the elected judge [proprietario] does not resign."[88] Before the trial, León reported that "V. M. Castillo [defense counsel] in union with the district judge have made Major Sánchez retract his confession and in an amparo judgment freed Farrera."[89]

In August, Porfirio Díaz strongly advised Governor León to take a temporary leave of absence during the course of the trial and to appoint Rafael Pimentel interim governor. León agreed, although he had reservations about Pimentel, who according to the governor "was very friendly toward the defendants, especially Ciro, in whose house he stays each time he arrives and furthermore is not disinterested in work that has been carried out against me."[90] By September Porfirio Díaz believed that León's prestige was irrevocably damaged and that he had become a political liability to the regime. Díaz wanted to ease León out, promising that only a temporary absence would be necessary. Díaz also asked Castillo not to make derogatory statements aimed at his "good friend" León and suggested he return to Mexico City.[91]

Governor León delayed his departure. He wished to remain in Chiapas and in power until December 1, the first and inaugural day of his second term. "If it is your judgment that I resign," León informed Díaz, "your indication will be enough, but I would wish, in that case, that my leave not be the result of efforts by the conspirators or even appear to be the case."[92] Díaz was adamant that León leave as soon as possible, which he did on October 2, for "reasons of poor health." By then León realized he would not be returning and appropriated 10,000 pesos from the state treasury for "travel expenses." On November 30, León resigned as constitutional governor, giving up his second term, and the state legislature appointed Pimentel to be provisional governor.[93]

Less than a week after León took his "temporary" leave, Judge López resigned his seat, also citing poor health as the reason. Judge Raquel Ramírez then heard the Farrera case in January 1900. Ramírez ruled that the "declaration of [Major Romualdo] Sánchez, in which he accused Señor Ciro Farrera to be one of the authors of the attack, was extracted by means of threats and torture." Throwing out the only evidence against Farrera and the other defendants, Judge Ramírez ruled that the accused should be granted absolute liberty.[94]

The government of Francisco León continued the political and developmental modernization program begun by Emilio Rabasa in 1891 and proposed that state govenrment enter the virgin territory of social reform. León's bold venture into government regulation of labor practices failed for two reasons: divided elite opinion in Chiapas and opposition by the national government. The modernizing constituency in Chiapas, increasingly fragmented as the end of the Porfiriato neared, was not of sufficient strength to overcome both. Years later, during the Mexican Revolution, national governments made social reform national policy, thereby tipping the balance in Chiapas and throughout the nation against the element of society that was driven by short-run interests. By the 1920s the assumptions that had seemed so novel and dangerous in León's program in the 1890s became politically orthodox. Revolution was employed to serve the interests of commercial farmers by modernizing outdated social and economic institutions.

3

THE SPIRIT OF ENTERPRISE

FRANCISCO LEÓN'S FAILURE AS A REFORMER AND A POLITICIAN demonstrated the limitations of Porfirian-era modernization. It proved impossible in Chiapas to implement changes that directly and adversely affected even a minority of landowners. The state government was not sufficiently autonomous with regard to provincial landowners or the national government to make the painful but necessary reforms promoting the long-term development of modern commercial agriculture. By the first decade of the twentieth century the enlightened caciquismo had achieved about as much as it could (or wanted to) in transforming Chiapas. In the 1900s modernization was left primarily to the "spirit of enterprise": market forces, foreign investment, and the energy of entrepreneurs.

THE "UNENLIGHTENED" ADMINISTRATION

Rafael Pimentel was born in Oaxaca in 1855. His brother, Emilio, attended law school with Emilio Rabasa and the two became close friends, but Rafael never developed the same respect and affection for Rabasa. Due to the patronage of Porfirio Díaz, Rafael Pimentel held political posts in Oaxaca, Chihuahua, and Guerrero during the 1890s. When he became governor of Chiapas he was something of a political troubleshooter for the president.[1]

Pimentel accepted the governor's office in Chiapas, but he had little interest in the state and even less affection for it. In 1895 he had informed Díaz that "in all frankness, I feel no great sympathy [for Chiapas], because I see that its sons are more Guatemalan than Mexican."[2] His opinion had not changed by 1899. Early in his term he purchased a hacienda in the Central Highlands and spent most of his weekends there to enjoy the cooler climate. He developed a reputation for staying away from the government palace and spent as much time in Mexico City as he did in Chiapas.[3]

Several important modernizing projects were begun during the Pimentel administration, although the governor could take little credit for them. The most significant was the initiation of the construction of the Panamerican Railroad from Tehuantepec to Tapachula. Largely as a result of Emilio Rabasa's efforts, the Pan-American Railroad Company was incorporated in New Jersey in 1901 and obtained a joint federal-state subsidy totaling $10,000 (U.S., gold) for each mile completed. Payments were made at the termination of each fifty-mile segment. Construction began in 1901 and was finished in 1908.[4]

Early in 1902 the Bank of Chiapas was formed in Tuxtla Gutiérrez with 500,000 pesos capital from Mexico City investors. State Treasurer Ramón Rabasa was appointed manager and Ciro Farrera served on the board of directors. In 1908 the Bank of Chiapas merged with the Bank of Puebla and a branch office was opened in Tapachula. In both the railroad and the bank projects the Pimentel-Díaz correspondence suggests that the governor had only a small role.[5]

The Pimentel administration studied the cost, feasibility, and necessity of a highway from San Cristóbal to Salto de Agua (Palenque) and of an iron bridge across the Grijalva river between Tuxtla Gutiérrez and Chiapa de Corzo, but did not begin work on either project. Indeed, the roads constructed by Rabasa and León, according to one observer, "are almost lost, on account of not being cared for, despite the immense costs to the state in men and money."[6] From Soconusco came the complaint that "the governor promised [in July 1900] to take into consideration the improvement of roads, the reduction of the high taxes which burden the fincas, and other defects mentioned at that time, but so far nothing has really been done; on the contrary things have gone from bad to worse."[7]

The one area of government responsibility that interested Pimentel was education. In 1902 he proposed to erect a network of regional schools for Indians, a race he considered "the only significant obstacle to the development of commerce, agriculture, and industry."[8] The first and only school, The Escuela Regional Fray Bartolomé de Las Casas, opened its doors in Chamula in 1905. In 1904 Pimentel persuaded Sóstenes Ruiz, a well-known educator and Chiapaneco living in Guatemala, to open a private college for all grades that would be partly subsidized by the state. Ruiz's Liceo de Chiapas y Escuela de Comercio, located in San Cristóbal, educated many of the children of the regional elite from all departments prior to their professional training. Pimentel also founded the State Experimental Farm for the introduction and propagation of modern methods and new crops and established the private Sociedad Mercantil, which installed electric lights in Tuxtla Gutiérrez.[9]

Governor Pimentel gave his permission for the employment of highland Indians in the coffee plantations of Soconusco, a development that further tarnished the reputation of Chiapas. After enjoying very high prices from 1891 to 1897, coffee planters found thmemselves in a slump from 1898 to 1900. In March 1898 several of the largest Soconusense planters hired attorney Agustín Farrera to lobby the federal and state governments for tax relief. Farrera in his study of the coffee situation reported to Díaz and Pimentel that planters were selling their coffee for less than half the price they had received before 1898, yet "the cost of production is the same since the wages and transport find themselves at the earlier price."[10] Until 1900 coffee planters had received the bulk of their harvest workers from neighboring Guatemalan villages, although never in sufficient numbers. Instead of tax relief, Pimentel gave the planters permission to recruit highland Indians.[11]

At first only a few German planters used labor recruiters—called *enganchadores* (literally, hookers) or *habilitadores* (providers)—to contract Indians and bring them to the coffee plantations, although later the practice became widespread. The enganchadores would advance a small sum of money to establish a debt or large quantities of liquor to obtain signed contracts.[12] The *enganche* system clearly had an unsavory aspect. An editorial in the Cristobalense periodical *El Tiempo* in 1907 called enganche "the commerce in human flesh."[13] Yet most Indians signed on voluntarily and returned to the harvests year after year, since wages were nearly twice as high in Soconusco as in the Central Highlands. Population increase and the diminution of communal lands in the highlands created the economic necessity of yearly migration to the harvests.[14]

TRANSFER OF THE STATE CAPITAL?

In politics as well as in programs, Rafael Pimentel was a passive governor. *El Universal* reported that Ciro Farrera was the most influential advisor of the governor, which was likely since Pimentel had been close to Farrera before the assassination scandal. Furthermore, Ciro's brothers Romulo and Agustín were given important public posts during the Pimentel administration. It is not clear how close Pimentel was to the Cristobalense camarilla, although the administration did have a definite pro-Cristobalense slant. The one inhibiting element was State Treasurer Ramón Rabasa, whose appointment was owed to Porfirio Díaz (in fact, to Emilio Rabasa).[15]

Like his predecessors, Pimentel appointed a number of Oaxaqueños to public posts. He appointed a Oaxaqueño chief of staff—the third most important post in state government—in order, he said, to offset the influence of his Chiapaneco secretary of government.[16] Unlike his predecessors, however, Governor Pimentel made little effort to appoint honest jefes políticos or to moderate their behavior. According to Manuel Cruz, a hacendado and lawyer from Pichucalco, the jefes políticos under Pimentel "are commonly persons foreign to the departments, protected by the governor and at times, it is said, by some minister. With very few exceptions, these local officials are hungry bandits, men without conscience, who devastate the pueblos."[17] Under Pimentel, citizens complained about the low moral character of the jefes políticos and not, as in the 1890s, their execution of unpopular government policies. From the careful selection of jefes políticos by Rabasa and León, state government retreated to "business as usual," when government stood for thievery.[18]

In July 1903 Governor Pimentel was reelected, although apparently against the counsel of Emilio Rabasa and Victor Manuel Castillo.[19] Since he had done very little during his first term, Pimentel had stirred up little opposition within Chiapas and, most importantly, had maintained the confidence of the president. Having secured his political position, Pimentel embarked on the boldest move of his gubernatorial career—the return of the state government to San Cristóbal Las Casas.

Pimentel had various reasons for wanting to change the location of the capital. Perhaps the most important was his dislike of the people and climate of Tuxtla Gutiérrez and his sincere belief that dignified San Cristóbal was more suitable. His friendship with Ciro Farrera and Clemente Robles, men who strongly favored San Cristóbal, also probably contributed to his decision.[20]

With Porfirio Díaz's approval, Pimentel authorized the temporary transfer of the executive and legislative branches of the state government to San Cristóbal on September 20, 1905, ostensibly to attend to the construction of a road from San Cristóbal to Salto de Agua.[21] The real reason, Pimentel informed Díaz, was "to explore public opinion and study the obstacles to a definitive transfer."[22] Another, and more binding, reason for the temporary nature of the transfer and Pimentel's timing of the move was constitutional. Emilio Rabasa, during his tenure as governor, had amended the state constitution so that any definitive change in the location of the government required ratification during two legislative periods by the local congress. When Pimentel began the transfer, the 1903–5 legislature was ending and the 1905–7 legislature would begin its sessions in December. The governor could obtain the approval of two congresses in only months.

Pimentel foresaw some problems connected with the transfer, although not from Tuxtlecos who, he reported, were not "men of action." He did expect opposition from Emilio Rabasa, who would attempt to "sustain the blunder that he made," as Pimentel saw it.[23] A problem that weighed more on the governor's mind was "the preponderant and decisive influence which the clergy exercises [in San Cristóbal], particularly now that it is headed by Bishop [Francisco] Orozco y Jiménez, who is a soaring eagle who uses money to subjugate consciences, and to give you an idea of the fantasy state of this society, it is enough to say that there is not one lawyer who does not first consult the bishop even on the most insignificant matter." The power and influence of the bishop, furthermore, dominated not only Las Casas, but Comitán, La Libertad, Simojovel, and Ocosingo. Unless the bishop's influence was neutralized, wrote Pimentel to Díaz, "the action of the government will be of little importance."[24]

But before Pimentel had a chance to tackle the bishop, Emilio Rabasa intervened. In a report to the president, Rabasa outlined a powerful reason why the government should remain in Tuxtla Gutiérrez. "The decree authorizes the provisional transfer," wrote Rabasa, "and should remain in a provisional state."[25] Rabasa reported that the State of Chiapas owed 90,000 pesos. Nearly 30,000 of this sum was held by the Bank of Chiapas, managed by Ramón Rabasa, and by the Tuxtla commercial house of Cueto y Cía. These institutions, wrote Rabasa, "will close their doors to the government now that they have lost confidence in it by its transfer and negligence; but it will not obtain a centavo because in San Cristóbal there is no one to give it, because there is hardly anyone who has any." In short, Rabasa concluded, if the government was moved to San Cristóbal, the banks would call in their loans and the state would be bankrupted.[26] Rabasa played his strongest card and apparently it paid off.

If Governor Pimentel had the will to fight Rabasa, by the end of October he lost the strength to do so when he came down with malaria.[27] To take time to recover, Pimentel turned over the government temporarily to Miguel A. Castillo, one of the wealthiest hacendados in San Cristóbal. Pimentel returned to office in December at Díaz's urging, long enough to return the government to Tuxtla Gutiérrez and turn over power to Ramón Rabasa. He returned to Mexico City a sick man, but soon recovered. Perhaps in recompense, Díaz made him senator from Colima. Emilio Rabasa had won, and nearly everyone of importance in San Cristóbal was outraged.[28]

THE SECOND RABASA GOVERNMENT

Ramón Rabasa became provisional governor of Chiapas on December 25, 1905. A former state treasurer and municipal president of Tuxtla Gutiérrez, Rabasa was also manager of the Bank of Chiapas. In June 1906, to the unanimous dismay of San Cristóbal, he was elected constitutional governor for the period 1906–10.[29] In the interim, Porfirio Díaz had asked Bishop Orozco y Jiménez what he thought of Rabasa. "A good and honorable man," replied the prelate.[30]

Like his younger brother Emilio, Ramón Rabasa was a builder. He initiated work on the long-delayed San Cristóbal–Salto de Agua road, repaired the state highway, and expended 90,000 pesos in state funds to build the Grijalva bridge. He modernized Tuxtla Gutiérrez by building new streets, a water system, and public buildings appropriate to the state capital. Like Pimentel, Ramón Rabasa was attentive to the

Central Highlands, "above all San Cristóbal, which merits special attention since it is a city of true importance." He asked President Díaz for federal assistance (which was not forthcoming) to construct a road from the center of the state to Pichucalco and one from Comitán to Palenque.[31]

The governor's pet project and obsession was an interior railroad line, from the Panamerican Railroad station at Arriaga (Tonalá) to Tuxtla Gutiérrez, Comitán, and on through to Tabasco and Yucatán. In 1906 Rabasa's successor at the Bank of Chiapas, Romulo Farrera, proposed the idea to Díaz at the governor's urging. In 1908 Rabasa commissioned two studies on the best routes and projected expenses of the interior line and presented them to the president in person. Emilio Rabasa also discussed the project with Díaz, yet despite constant pressure the interior Chiapas railroad never captured Díaz's interest and was never constructed. No other single improvement would have had as much effect on Chiapas's economic development as the much-desired interior railroad, which would have made Chiapas the granary of Mexico.[32]

In 1907, in response to growing criticism of enganche, Governor Rabasa expedited a Servant's Law, which was essentially the same as the rights and obligations recommendation of the 1896 Agrarian Congress. This law sought to end the underhanded contracting methods employed by the enganchadores, but it was never adequately enforced.[33]

Rabasa was also active in education. The number of state-supported primary schools had actually decreased under the Pimentel administration, from 124 in 1898 to only 64 in 1904. Under Rabasa the number again climbed to 183 by 1907.[34]

Politically, the administration of Ramón Rabasa differed from those of his predecessors in that Tuxtlecos rather than Oaxaqueños dominated the upper reaches of state government and wealthy hacendados filled the jefaturas. In many ways Ramón Rabasa's administration was representative of the last decade of the Porfiriato, when a "modernizing oligarchy," the so-called Científicos, dominated the national government and made fortunes.

Appointees to top administrative posts were largely taken from the landowning elite of the departments of Tuxtla.[35] With the exception of Las Casas, most jefes políticos were wealthy hacendados from the departments they officially served. For Las Casas, Rabasa chose Tuxtleco José Joaquín Peña "because he is honest and energetic and will know how to handle those rogues that have caused so many problems in San Cristóbal, principally the group called 'la mano negra' [the black hand] whose chief is Jesús Martínez Rojas."[36] Martínez Rojas, on the other hand, considered Peña "the most hated person in this district and my worst enemy."[37] As a result of this appointment, Martínez Rojas left San Cristóbal and lived on his finca in La Libertad.[38] Other appointments were less controversial. The jefes políticos for Comitán, Chiapas, Tuxtla, Pichucalco, Soconusco, and Tonalá each owned haciendas valued at more than 10,000 pesos. The important municipal presidencies were held by close friends of the administration. Raul E. Rincón, for example, president of the Cámara Agrícola de Chiapas, presided over the ayuntamiento of Tuxtla Gutiérrez. Other important posts were filled by members of the Rabasa family. For example, the governor's nephew, Leopoldo Rabasa, was jefes político of Tuxtla (department), chief of police for Tuxtla Gutiérrez (city), and chief of the State Public Security Forces.[39]

A shadow clerical government in San Cristóbal took on an extraordinarily active role under Bishop Francisco Orozco y Jiménez in the early 1900s. The bishop arrived in Chiapas in 1902 and apparently saw himself as following in the footsteps of Chiapas's first bishop, Bartolomé de Las Casas. The comparison was not unwarranted. As a result of his efforts in Chiapas, Orozco y Jiménez did come to enjoy a reputation as one of Mexico's most progressive prelates. Like Las Casas, he worked for a Catholic utopia led by active priests like himself.[40] The bishop became the de facto leader of the anti-Rabasa camarilla of San Cristóbal and favored the return of the state government to San Cristóbal. He supported San Cristóbal's municipal president, José Manuel Velasco, for governor in 1910. In the fall of 1909 the bishop informed Porfirio Díaz that Ramón Rabasa

is entirely inept as governor. The consequences have been exceedingly sad in all the state in general and in particular in each locality, as it is understood he has given possession of the control and dispatch of all manner of business, above all in the area of justice, to a certain camarilla of perverse and poorly intentioned men. Everywhere, but beginning in this Capital [San Cristóbal], there is a general discontent, which is heightened even more by the terrible monetary crisis and the lack of business, and aggravated by the increase of taxes.[41]

Outside of San Cristóbal whatever discontent did exist in Chiapas was imperceptible until 1910, when Ramón Rabasa sought reelection and Francisco I. Madero began his anti-reelectionist campaign for president of Mexico. Until then, Chiapas appeared to be peaceful and progressing.

FOREIGN INVESTMENT AND NATIONAL RECESSION

The second great expansion of foreign capital in Chiapas occurred in the period 1900–1910, but particularly after 1905. The first expansion, that of German and other European capital, occurred in the late 1880s and 1890s and was concentrated in Soconusco. The second expansion primarily involved U.S. capital, employed in Soconusco and Palenque departments in the cultivation of coffee and rubber. The Zacualpa Plantation Company, organized in 1899 in San Francisco, California, went into operation in the early 1900s and placed 17,800 acres in cultivation of rubber in Soconusco, forming the largest rubber plantation in the world. By 1910 twenty rubber plantations were in operation in Chiapas, most of them owned by U.S. investors.[42] The German-American Coffee Company, incorporated in 1903, was the second most important North American capital investment in Chiapas. German-American owned the famous Triunfo plantation in Palenque, which covered some 43,000 acres and employed 3,000 Indians.[43] Even in Soconusco, U.S. interests owned six import-export houses.[44] During the decade 1900–1910, U.S. capital surpassed the value of German capital in all of Chiapas. By 1909 U.S. capital totaled 1.2 million pesos in Soconusco and 1.6 million pesos in Palenque, with a total for the entire state of nearly 3 million pesos. German capital totaled 1.8 million pesos—although it should be remembered that by 1910 a considerable quantity of German capital was invested in Mexican-owned properties and some Germans had become Mexican nationals.[45]

From 1907 to 1911 Chiapas, like most of Mexico, suffered an economic downturn. From 1907 to 1909 the industrialized countries sustained a business recession that contracted external demand and led to lower prices for raw materials on the international market. Reports from jefes políticos in Chiapas described the effects of the "crisis monetaria"—a decline in commerce, lack of credit, decline in production, and a lack of confidence in the future. Francisco Ruiz, a landowner from Chiapa de Corzo, complained in 1910 that the new Tuxtla Gutiérrez branch of the Bank of Mexico was limiting credit terms to only six months and had raised the rate to 3 percent a month, which was ruining the farmers. To compound problems, an epidemic from Guatemala had invaded the border departments in 1908 and 1909.[46]

At the end of the decade, perhaps in response to the economic crisis, two self-help and political pressure organizations of landowners were formed in the state. The Cámara Agrícola de Chiapas (Chiapas Chamber of Agriculture) was established in Tuxtla Gutiérrez in 1909 and pushed for easier credit, agricultural education, colonization, and the amortization of the debts of workers. It published a bulletin that reported on modern agricultural techniques and advocated the expansion of new crops in the lowland valleys. The organization was dominated by hacendados from Tuxtla, Ocozocoautla, Cintalapa, Jiquipilas, Chiapa, and Comitán—that is, the Central Valley—and its leadership was close to the Rabasa administration. The Cámara claimed only eleven members from Las Casas department.[47] In 1908 German and Mexican coffee planters created the Unión Cafetera de Soconusco (Coffee Planters' Union of Soconusco) to establish a uniform labor policy. The planters agreed to limit workers' debts to sixty pesos, not to give advances to laborers indebted to other planters, and to keep records explaining when and how the debts of their workers were incurred.[48]

THE TWO FACES OF MODERNIZATION

By 1910 Chiapas had undergone nearly twenty years of unprecedented economic development and modernization. The state government had begun to take an active role in the economic and social development of the region and had partially consolidated its own political power with regard to other power centers in the region. One indication of this shift was the increase of state revenue from 200,000 pesos in 1890 to 900,000 in 1906. In relation to subsequent progress, the efforts taken between 1891 and 1910 may appear slight. In the context of the time, the achievement was considerable.

By any standard, Chiapas was more "modern" in 1910 than in 1890. In just twenty years Chiapas had created an impressive transportation and communications infrastructure where previously none had existed. A good state highway traversed the state from the Panamerican Railroad at Arriaga through the Jiquipilas and Cintalapa valleys to Tuxtla Gutiérrez, across the Grijalva river to Chiapa de Corzo, and on to San Cristóbal and Comitán. (The Pan-American Highway follows much of this route today.) The Panamerican Railroad reached Arriaga in 1905 and Tapachula by 1908, extending the line to more than 250 miles. All the major towns and many haciendas were linked by a telephone and telegraph network by 1910.

The effect of these improvements on the economy of Chiapas cannot be overestimated. The railroad permitted shipment of Chiapas coffee to ports in the Gulf of Mexico, thereby reducing shipping costs by more than one half and leading to greater production, profits, and commerce in Chiapas. Production of coffee in Soconusco, for example, increased from 10 million to more than 20 million pounds from 1907–8 to 1908–10, while the total value of the crop more than tripled, reaching nearly 2.5 million dollars by 1910.[49] The railroad and the state highway opened up large parts of the interior of the state to wider markets by facilitating the movement of bulky commodities such as corn, cotton, sugar, and cattle to Mexico City. Lower shipping costs encouraged commercial agriculture in the interior valley so much that by 1910 the value of agricultural production in Chiapas was five times that of 1890.[50]

The valleys of Cintalapa and Jiquipilas in the department of Tuxtla were particularly favored by the changes between 1890 and 1910. In 1890 these valleys had no roads, no utilization of machinery in production, and only minimal trade, even with Tuxtla Gutiérrez, due to prohibitive freight costs. The value of all agricultural implements was only slightly more than 7,000 dollars and the total value of agricultural production was 45,000 dollars. Between 1890 and 1910, according to one observer, the valleys underwent "a rapid advance toward modern farming."[51] The digging stick began to be replaced by the steel plow—more than 300 such plows by 1910. To the seven animal-powered sugar mills of 1890 were added thirty-five additional animal- and thirteen steam-powered mills by 1910. The total value of agricultural implements reached 132,475 dollars by 1910, and the value of agricultural production in the valleys climbed to more than 200,000 dollars. Early in 1910 some 100 railroad cars of corn were shipped to Mexico City from Chiapas, to be sold for three to four times the local price.[52]

Commenting on the development of his area, *finquero* Raquel D. Cal y Mayor wrote in 1907 that "the vigor which has initiated the spirit of enterprise in the valley of Cintalapa is truly worthy of high praise." Cal y Mayor attributed this "violent development" to three causes. The first in importance was the "influence of Yankee energy" which built the Panamerican Railroad. Scarcity of laborers leading to the utilization of machinery was second. The third cause was the cooperation of the state government in its construction of roads and in its sensible tax policies.[53] It is not surprising that landowners and merchants in the Central Valley supported the program of the state government.

The indices of growth and development between 1890 and 1910 are impressive. The value of urban and rural property in Chiapas in 1885 was 0.5 million pesos and 3.3 million pesos respectively. By 1906 these reported values had increased to 3.6 million pesos and 30.7 million pesos. The number of fincas and ranchos had increased from about 1,000 in 1880, to 4,500 in 1896, and 6,800 by 1909. (See table 3.)[54] The United States consul in Chiapas noted in 1911 that "Chiapas is unique among the states of Mexico for the number of small holdings and peasant farmers."[55] Cattle, coffee, maize, *frijol,* wheat, and sugar production in the state increased over these two decades in both bulk and value.[56]

Although certain departments benefited more than others by the prosperity of the 1890s and 1900s—namely Soconusco, Palenque, Pichucalco, Tuxtla, Comitán, Chiapa, and Chilón—an increase in economic specialization benefited entrepreneurs in most localities. The increase of wheat production in the Central Highlands made it possible in 1895 to stop importing wheat and begin exporting it. Sugar grown and refined in the valleys of Jiquipilas, Cintalapa, and Tuxtla was utilized by the 200 distilleries in the highlands. Cotton grown in the departments of Chiapa and La Libertad was purchased by the textile factory La Providencia in Tuxtla Gutiérrez. Lowland cotton was also sold to highland Indians, who wove blankets sold throughout the state. Cattle stocks

TABLE 3

LANDHOLDINGS IN CHIAPAS, 1896–1909

	HACIENDAS			RANCHOS			OTHERS
Department	1896	1903	1909	1896	1903	1909	1909
Chiapa	48	—	130	527	115	232	528
Chilón	106	50	82	233	200	167	264
Comitán	88	132	143	396	317	905	72
La Libertad	48	—	77	138	—	98	133
Las Casas	59	—	0	105	80	348	3
Mariscal	—	—	32	—	—	73	116
Mezcalapa	100	—	19	50	—	310	349
Palenque	82	208	73	43	54	318	23
Pichucalco	93	270	208	529	767	572	461
Simojovel	136	67	53	34	110	170	195
Soconusco	123	520	240	530	725	1568	232
Tonalá	25	8	30	368	481	673	50
Tuxtla	60	99	33	240	276	308	1316
Partido							
Chamula	17	—	—	30	19	—	—
Cintalapa	37	46	—	115	132	—	—
La Frailesca	16	31	—	72	87	—	—
Motozintla	11	—	—	87	—	—	—
Total	1049	1431	1120	3497	3363	5742	3742

Note: The category "others" refers to economically insignificant, small property. There was no precise definition of *hacienda* and *rancho*. The best distinction that can be drawn is that *haciendas* (and *fincas*) were large estates while *ranchos* were middle-size farms or cattle ranches.

Sources: For 1896, *Datos estadísticas del Estado de Chiapas recopiliados en el año 1896* (Tuxtla Gutiérrez, 1898), p. 1; for 1903, *Anuario estadístico de la república mexicana* (Mexico: Sría. de Fomento, 1905), p. 418; for 1909, Wasserstrom, *Class and Society in Central Chiapas*, p. 111.

in Comitán, Chilón, Tonalá, Tuxtla, and Pichucalco increased as Chipanecos continued to send herds to Guatemala, Yucatán, and central Mexico.[57]

Modernization in Chiapas between 1890 and 1910 benefited landowners and merchants, not most people. It is difficult to chart the changes the rural population faced after 1890. Material standards and working conditions, which were certainly bad before, deteriorated, according to all available evidence.

Despite the substantial material and productive improvements during the two decades after 1890, daily wages remained static. The U.S. consul reported in 1910 that Soconusense planters "justify the low pay scale by the plea that the more money a Chamula is paid the more bad liquor he will drink."[58] Another justification was that "no one can get 100 cents worth of work out of them for each dollar spent."[59] In fact, low wages were one of the advantages of investing in Chiapas. Statements such as "the inhabitants are willing to work for low wages" were publicized to attract investors.[60] As reported in the state censuses, wages remained at the subsistence level of thirty-seven centavos a day for twenty years, and even declined in Mescalapa and Pichucalco.[61]

Descriptions of labor conditions in the plantation zones of Palenque, Soconusco, and Chilón confirm that modernization and misery advanced together. Karena Shields, who lived on a hacienda in Palenque in the early 1890s, reported that Mexican, German, and North American planters alike took merciless advantage of the workers. "As long as a man owed money to his patron," noted Shields, "his freedom was only a meaningless technicality."[62] Dr. C. L. G. Anderson, a stockholder in a rubber plantation company, was told on a visit to Palenque in 1905 that "eighty percent of the money paid out to labor came back through the Company Store."[63]

In Soconusco, the U.S. consul reported in 1911 that coffee planters secured their laborers under the peonage system, which he described:

> Their agents or labor contractors, called "habilitadores," go to the
> tableland and offer Indians loans of money, principally during the
> progress of a feast; this money is seldom paid, and cases exist where
> the debt and peonage conditions have been passed on from father to
> son. While this system is not legal under Mexican laws, it having been

copied from Guatemala, the Indians consider it binding, much more so since the authorities have connived to imprison peons for debt.[64]

Without doubt the worst working conditions in Chiapas (and perhaps in all of Mexico) were found in the *monterías* (mahogany lumber camps).[65] Hidden in the jungle where the borders of Chiapas, Tabasco, and Guatemala meet were approximately twenty large monterías. Unlike the largely voluntary labor in the Soconusco coffee or the Palenque rubber plantations, enganchadores for the monterías actually kidnapped highland Indians to form labor gangs and drove them into the jungle. Once there workers were chained at night and guarded during the day. One former montería foreman recalled in 1943 that "in those times there were no men who wanted to work in the monterías. For that reason Don Porfirio [Díaz] opened the jails and ordered the prisoners to work in the monterías."[66] The Díaz government also deported rebellious Yaqui and Maya Indians from Sonora and Yucatán to the camps.

The system of indebted servitude, temporary migrant labor, and slave labor did not exhaust the forms of labor expropriation in Porfirian Chiapas. In 1910, according to various accounts, there were from 75,000 to 150,000 agricultural workers in Chiapas out of a total population of 400,000. One third to one half were indebted servants. Workers not tied to a finca by debt worked as free *jornaleros* (day wage laborers), *baldíos* (sharecroppers), or *arrendatarios* (renters). Baldíos cultivated finca lands, usually two hectares, and in return gave the patron between 40 and 120 days per year of their labor. Arrendatarios turned over a portion of their harvest to the finquero or paid a cash rent, in return for using his land. These forms of labor were common outside the plantation zones. They provided the finquero with cheap labor and produce without the responsibility for crop failure or the expenditure of capital in workers' debts.[67]

The indigenous communities of the Central Highlands presented yet a different situation. In the department of Las Casas, some 40,00 Indians lived and made their living, yet the 1909 census reported only 3,000 jornaleros.[68] Many, sometimes entire villages, were tied to fincas. In addition, perhaps 10,000 Indians left the highlands each year for three or four months to work the coffee harvests. Most Indians, however, even those forced by economic necessity into migrant wage labor, still lived on communal lands. The Rabasa reparto had pressed least heavily on highland villages—which in any case had lost most of their lands earlier. Between 1892 and 1909, nearly 57,000 hectares of ejido land in the department of Las Casas had been parceled, leaving 50,000 hectares in communal possession.[69] The indigenous communities in the highlands, already pressed by population increases, were reduced even further into difficult, squalid, and impoverished lives. They still, however, had some land and a refuge.[70]

The reparto continued in Chiapas, although with less intensity after 1900, until 1909 when it was discontinued by the national legislature. Manuel Pineda, in his 1910 study of the reparto program, argued that it "constituted a true expropriation."[71] The citizens of Huistán agreed; they wrote President Díaz in 1909 that "Señores Flores and Morales, who try at all cost to extend their properties, are taking over our possessions on which we have small houses and fields where we produce what is necessary for our subsistence."[72] The people of Chapultenango asked Díaz to "permit us to leave as a whole the land by which the old law we occupy because we consider we will be injured once it is divided."[73] With the reparto, neighboring fincas purchased the portions put on the market. As Emilio Rabasa realized, "the Indians sell their lots as soon as they have them."[74] From 1892 until 1909 land was increasingly removed from village control, particularly in Soconusco—which became the center of the organized labor movement in the 1920s and 1930s.

REFLECTIONS

The "enlightened caciquismo" sought to work with the expansion of the national economy, using state government to remove the political and social obstacles to commercial agriculture and to build the infrastructure that would support it. In this respect the progressive governors of Chiapas in the 1890s and 1900s were not unlike the national científicos who possessed "a genuine vision of a dynamic, developing Mexico" and a "fervent commitment to social and economic change."[75] Events in Chiapas also reflected a broader, hemispheric development. "Much of Latin American history in the late nineteenth century and early twentieth century," contends Bryan R. Roberts, "is to be understood in terms of the struggles of various regional elites to expand their economies through a pervasive reshaping of local society."[76]

In Chiapas, as elsewhere in Mexico, the conditions favorable to a more commercial, efficient, and entrepreneurial agriculture began to take hold. To contemporaries, however, regional government in Chiapas appeared to be—and in fact was—an important catalyst and modernizing agent. Regional government did not play a similar important developmental role in those favored regions where capitalist expansion was more vigorous and geography more benign.[77] Yucatán became a booming enclave and monocrop (henequen) economy in the late 1890s and 1900s thanks to foreign demand, American fiber brokers, and productive hacendados. As Allen Wells notes, "Yucatan was at the right place at the right time."[78] The same was true for Soconusco; the difference being that Yucatán's henequen zone dominated the center of the state while Soconusco was isolated on Chiapas's periphery. The state government could claim little credit for Yucatán's "Gilded Age." Its efforts to promote the development of the state's southeastern hinterland, however, were inconsequential and unsuccessful. Similarly, in Morelos, which benefited from national and foreign demand for its sugar, the planters spearheaded the state's rush into "modernity." "*They* [emphasis added] astutely developed intersts in processing and selling to match their interest in production. *They* brought the railroad into the state, imported the new machinery, and planned how to get more land to grow more cane."[79] Foreign investment, easy transportation, and proximity to the United States favored Chihuahua after 1880. The powerful Terrazas family—even with its control of state government— did not create these conditions, but took full advantage of them.[80]

In those regions of Mexico where boom capitalism did not take hold, like Chiapas, local farmers and businessmen needed help and they looked to government.

Unlike many parts of Mexico, however, particularly the northern states, an entrepreneurial and progressive capitalist elite consolidated its power regionally and used it to promote its interests. In Chiapas there was little need for progressive capitalists—men like Coahuila's Venustiano Carranza, Chihuahua's Abrahám González, or Sonora's Álvaro Obregón—to rebel. In Chiapas they were making money and in power; their political careers and business opportunities were not closed by an aging oligarchy in league with foreign capitalists. The liberal Madero revolution, from the perspective of Chiapas capitalists, was irrelevant and bothersome.

The modernization of Mexico, wrote Frank Tannenbaum in 1929, "was coincident with lowering standards of life for the masses of the people."[81] Increasing alienation of village land and coercive labor practices, however, did not lead to popular mobilization and revolution in Chiapas, even when "the Revolution" was imported into Chiapas from outside in 1914. As elsewhere in southern Mexico, the *campesinato* of Porfirian Chiapas was weakened by ancient ethnic and cultural divisions, while the coercive labor system kept peace in the countryside and later prevented popular mobilization against landowners and their government. And, unlike some areas in central and northern Mexico, the Chiapas campesinato could not join forces with small landholders (*rancheros*) against the landed elite. Rancheros in Chiapas had benefited greatly from state government policies of the 1890s and 1900s and coexisted with the large finqueros and generally without complaint. The fuel of Mexico's agrarian revolution, the landless and exploited peasantry, in Chiapas and the southern regions generally was too divided, controlled, and isolated to burn down the old order.

Part 2

"Let's drink to the Revolution."
"First to peace."
"Viva Villa!"
"Viva Chiapas first!"

A toast overheard in a rebel camp somewhere
in the Central Valley.
La Patria Chica, February 29, 1920.

REVOLUTION
1910–20

(or the unfortunate convulsions—private and
extraneous—of the familia chiapaneca)

THE MEXICAN REVOLUTION THAT BEGAN IN 1910, WRITES HISTORIAN
William H. Beezley, "was no more than a series of regional struggles."
Each had distinct regional or local origins but evolved within the broader
context of other neighboring struggles, alliances and conflict among
insurgent groups, and contests for control of the national government.
The "revolutions" within the Mexican Revolution were popular struggles against privilege here, intra-elite struggles for power there, and
varied combinations of both in most regions. Long years of political
crisis and disintegration, civil war, economic disruption, and social
dislocation affected each state, each region, and each locality differently.
In time a revolutionary movement emerging from the frontier northeast
and northwest imposed itself on the nation, recreated central government, and for a time allowed regional caudillos to control provincial
Mexico.

Distant Chiapas was drawn into the storm by the vacuum of power
created by the overthrow of Porfirio Díaz in 1911. The first "revolution"
in Chiapas involved an attempt by Cristobalense elites to overthrow
Central Valley political power and return the state government to San
Cristóbal Las Casas. The modernizing farmers and merchants of Tuxtla
Gutiérrez and the lowlands successfully fought off this traditionalist
challenge. The second "revolution," an invasion by a northern Mexican
army in 1914, attempted to bring Chiapas under the control of the
Constitutionalist movement, later the national governnment, of Venustiano Carranza. The reformist vandalism of Carrancismo ignited the
third "revolution"—the rebellion of peripheral landowners in defense
of their properties, labor customs, and regional autonomy. Many fin-

queros and rancheros of Chiapas accommodated themselves to the national revolution and its modernizing reforms—some to Carrancismo, others later to Obregonismo—to preserve their power and defend their interests. The familia chiapaneca (the landowners of Chiapas) did not prosper during the revolutionary decade. And yet, at the conclusion of a national agrarian revolution, their lands were secure, their regional political power resecured. They had won.

Of course, none of these convulsions were truly social revolutions. As in other southeastern states, the exploited peasantry of Chiapas did not rebel. This defining feature of Mexico's agrarian revolution was missing here and in many other regions. As a result, the agrarian revolution did not thoroughly and irrevocably revolutionize the nation. Tight systems of social and economic control of laborers and villages; a campesinato divided ethnically, geographically, and linguistically; and the absence of progressive elite leadership for a peasant uprising precluded popular agrarian revolution in Chiapas and elsewhere in southeastern Mexico.

Chiapas was thrown into disorder because of a series of crises that rapidly led to the disintegration of the national state. Political crisis in Chiapas generated a slow-rising social crisis, however, by cracking the tight, paternalistic, repressive control of the landed elite over peasant villages and landless workers. Small acts of local defiance, popular violence, village independence, and individual rebellion—unplanned and informal—created a Chiapas that was far more difficult to govern, control, and farm. After 1910–20 the finqueros and políticos could no longer ignore villagers and campesinos in their political, private, and developmental affairs and schemes. "The people" accidentally had become politicized; thereafter they were organized in political parties, agrarian communities, and labor unions—in short, they were mobilized.

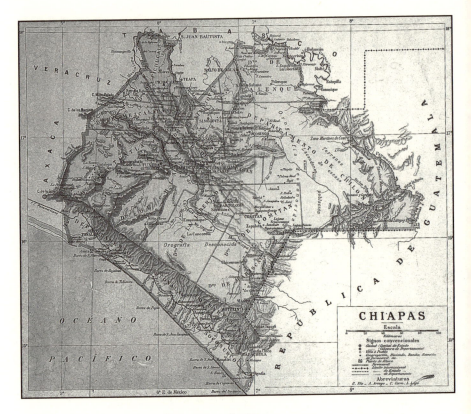

The State of Chiapas, 1911

La república mexicana: Chiapas, 1911
Latin American Library, Tulane University
Map Collection (LAL 349).

4

A PROFOUND POLITICAL DIVISION

"THE TRANSFER OF THE CAPITAL FROM SAN CRISTÓBAL TO TUXTLA," explained Romulo Farrera to the new interim president of Mexico in May 1911, "has created a profound political division between Tierra Fría and Tierra Caliente."[1] The Mexican Revolution that drove Porfirio Díaz from power did not engulf and transform Chiapas and the rest of southeastern Mexico. It was, in fact, transmogrified by regional politics for regional political ends—thus the need for Farrera's explanation. The sudden absence of the supreme caudillo and the triumph of a revolutionary movement out of northern Mexico created an opportunity for Cristobalense revanchists to acclaim the revolution and overthrow the "antiguo régimen" in Tuxtla Gutiérrez. With the national state in crisis, an old feud was rekindled.

The Cristobalense "revolutionaries," not unlike the Maderistas of the north, began to mobilize popular support for their political movement. Fear of a generalized "caste war" (the code phrase in Chiapas for social revolution) against ladinos, however, forced the rebel Cristobalenses to end their war against Tuxtla Gutiérrez once the national government had sided with the Tuxtleco government. Real revolution was avoided.

THE RIDICULOUS ANTI-REELECTIONIST MOVEMENTS

President Porfirio Díaz gave an interview to a North American journalist in March 1908. The president said he had prepared Mexico for democracy; therefore he could step down from office in 1910. Francisco I. Madero, scion of a wealthy landed family in the northern state of Coahuila, took Díaz seriously. He published a book that endorsed the

99

reelection of Díaz one last time in 1910 but called for a free and open election for the vice-presidency, meaning Díaz's presumed successor. Madero argued that the Porfirian dictatorship was a justified and necessary stage in Mexico's historical development. It had broken the seemingly endless cycle of revolution and civil war and prepared the nation for "the realization of the grandiose democratic ideal." To establish democratic constitutional government in Mexico, Madero proposed free voting with no reelections, later transformed into the revolutionary slogan, "sufragio efectivo, no reelección."[2]

Madero's *La sucesión presidencial en 1910*, published in December 1908, received an enthusiastic response and established its author as a popular figure in liberal circles. Madero was persuaded to become a candidate for president in the July 1910 election, and he toured Mexico setting up anti-reelectionist clubs and speaking for democratic government. Díaz had Madero arrested one month before the election, and released him thereafter. The arrest transformed the anti-reelectionist party into an insurrectionist movement. Under the Plan of San Luis Potosí (issued by Madero in Texas), essentially a program of political reforms, Madero revolted in November 1910.

After a disappointing beginning, this "Mexican revolution" picked up surprising popular support and military momentum in 1911 in the Mexican north. In Chihuahua, Coahuila, Durango, and Sonora the entrepreneurial well-to-do, as well as miners, day laborers, cowboys, and ranchers, joined together to fight local bosses, regional oligarchs, foreign capitalists, and the national dictator. A regional configuration gave rise to a rebellion of one group of elites (supported by lower-class rural rebels) against the elite establishment. On May 10, 1911, revolutionists captured Ciudad Juárez, a point of entry to the United States and a conduit for money and arms. The Científicos and the regime, although still in control of most of the country, had no desire for a long-drawn-out struggle and arranged for a conditional surrender and a transfer of power. Díaz and a few of his closest supporters resigned on May 25, leaving the government in the hands of the former ambassador to the United States, Francisco León De la Barra. The interim president prepared for the election of Madero in July and Madero's accession to the presidency in November 1911. The revolution had eliminated only the upper crust of the dictatorship; however, the Senate and the Chamber of Deputies, most governors and state legislatures, and the federal army and bureaucracy survived intact. This revolution seemed largely irrelevant to Chiapas.[3]

"Chiapas is indifferent to the ridiculous anti-reelectionist movements," wrote Raquel D. Cal y Mayor, a Central Valley finquero, in May 1910.[4] The Díaz regime and the Porfirista system might have lost their legitimacy elsewhere in Mexico, but not in Chiapas and the rest of the Mexican southeast.[5] Madero did not campaign in Chiapas, and no anti-reelectionist clubs were formed in the state during 1910. Two new publications, however, signaled an ever-so-slightly changing political climate in Chiapas. José Antonio Rivera G., a Comiteco and active anti-reelectionist since the 1890s, began publication of the review *Chiapas y México* in May 1910 in Mexico City. Rivera informed Díaz that his magazine was not hostile to the national administration; it was essentially anti-Rabacista and anti-Tuxtleco. He charged that Rabacista progress had relegated the Chiapas highlands to poverty and its Indian population to perpetual slavery. In order to rectify twenty years of misrule, the state government should be returned to San Cristóbal.[6] Juan Félix Zepeda, a sixty-year-old former judge and fervent Catholic, began publication of the periodical *Más Allá: Revista Católica Dominical Informativa* in October 1910 in San Cristóbal. Zepeda supported the return of the state government to San Cristóbal, the direct election of ayuntamientos, and the abolition of enganche. In December 1910 the paper was closed down and Zepeda arrested for revealing an abuse of privilege involving the governor's nephew.[7]

Criticism of the Rabasa government from San Cristóbal began to blossom in March and April 1911. As the national crisis deepened, Cristobalenses became bolder in their denunciations of the Rabasas, calling for "a political change as in some other states."[8] In April *La Voz del Pueblo* of San Cristóbal called for the end of caciquismo, meaning Rabacismo.[9] The first anti-reelectionist club in San Cristóbal was formed in April 1911 by Manuel Pineda, Jesús Martínez Rojas, Timoteo Flores Ruiz, and Juan Félix Zepeda—the "mano negra" camarilla. On April 20 this group called for the resignation of Governor Ramón Rabasa.[10]

Only in May, the last month of the Díaz regime, did armed groups appear in Chiapas. On May 8 about one hundred men on horseback proceeding from Tabasco captured Pichucalco, recruited the sixty men in the local jail, and robbed 30,000 pesos from the only bank in town. They returned to Tabasco the following day. Small groups of apolitical bandits began to appear in May as well, robbing trains, fincas, and even businesses in towns. Although they were branded as bandits, Lindoro and Isadoro Castellanos, finqueros from Ocosingo, rebelled in the name of Madero two days before Díaz resigned. Leading nearly 300 supporters, the Castellanos brothers charged that the people of the department of Chilón were oppressed by the jefe político and ignored by the state government. Don Lindoro, the self-proclaimed "Jefe Maderista" of Chiapas, captured and then abandoned Ocosingo on May 25, "liberating" 1,000 pesos from the jefe político. Three days later the same band briefly occupied Comitán, terrorizing local officials. Thus the revolution, such as it was, came to Chiapas.[11]

THE LIBERTY OF DESIGNATING A NEW GOVERNOR

Governor Ramón Rabasa resigned in favor of Manuel de Trejo on May 27, 1911 (two days after Díaz's resignation), and expressed his desire to give Chiapas "the liberty of designating a new governor."[12] Rabasa was followed a few days later by several members of his administration and six jefes políticos. The state legislature, however, remained intact, as did the municipal governments. Manuel de Trejo had been in and out of state government numerous times over the preceding twenty years and, although originally from San Cristóbal, was an unconditional supporter of the Rabasa brothers. The transfer of office from Rabasa to de Trejo, as Timoteo Flores Ruiz pointed out to the interim president, signified no real change. "The entrance of de Trejo," he informed De la Barra, "is the death of the revolution and the continuation of ferocious caciquismo."[13]

Chiapas experienced a political spring following Rabasa's resignation. Maderista clubs were organized in several cities and towns for the purpose of either maintaining power or winning it anew. The club "Chiapas" of Tuxtla Gutiérrez was formed by Ciro Farrera, Ponciano Burguete, and Cesar Cano—Rabacista hacendados—and promoted the candidacy of de Trejo for constitutional governor. The club "Chiapas" fairly represented the segment of society that had enjoyed political power since the 1890s.[14] Two hacendados from Pichucalco, Carlos A.

Vidal and César Córdova, proposed the separation of their department from Chiapas and its annexation to Tabasco. "We Pichucalqueños," charged Vidal, "have always been treated like Chiapanecan bastards."[15] In Tapachula the Maderista club "Soconusco" was composed of wealthy cattlemen who opposed the political pretensions of coffee planters.[16]

Early in June the anti-reelectionist club in San Cristóbal sent a five-man commission to Mexico City to see the interim president. The commission included Juan Félix Zepeda, Jesús Martínez Rojas, and José Antonio Rivera G. They tried to persuade De la Barra to name Eusebio Salazar y Madrid, a Cristobalense living in Mexico City, in place of Manuel de Trejo. They could not see the president but they did receive a sympathetic hearing from Secretary of Gobernación Emilio Vázquez Gómez, who was interested in placing revolutionaries in government.[17]

The naming of new governors was an important but difficult problem for the De la Barra administration. The Treaty of Ciudad Juárez permitted Madero to recommend to the state legislators his choices for interim governors. The old legislatures remained, however, and in several states they held the exclusive constitutional prerogative to name governors. Although Madero selected Venustiano Carranza interim governor of Coahuila, for example, the state legislature appointed a Porfirista instead. Madero called together the Chiapas colony of Mexico City for the purpose of advising him on the most acceptable candidate for Chiapas. Members of the colony met on June 19 and by sixty-seven votes designated Flavio Guillén, a close personal friend of Madero. Salazar y Madrid was second in the count with twenty-eight votes. With this indication, Madero recommended Guillén as his choice for interim governor to the Chiapas legislature, which was scheduled to meet on June 21.[18]

Flavio Guillén, although Madero's favorite, was unacceptable to many in Chiapas. The Club "Democrático Chiapaneco Independiente" of Chiapa de Corzo, among several others, telegraphed Madero saying they could not accept Guillén because he belonged to the "Científico element." They suggested, instead, Salazar y Madrid.[19] Guillén himself protested that many Chiapanecos "have made a crime of my friendship with Estrada Cabrera, Ramón Corral, and Emilio Rabasa."[20]

Vázquez Gómez intervened on June 20, one day before the state legislature met, by telegraphing Governor Manuel de Trejo and asking him to resign in favor of Salazar y Madrid. The gobernación secretary indicated that he was dissatisfied with the governor's progress in placing revolutionaries in office. With this indication Manuel de Trejo resigned. The following day the state legislature, refusing to be intimidated or pressured by Madero or Vázquez Gómez, selected Reinaldo Gordillo León, an engineer from Comitán, interim governor of Chiapas.[21] Gordillo León had served as municipal president of Comitán. One of his principal qualifications was his strong animosity for fellow Comiteco and intellectual leader of the Cristobalense revanchists, José Antonio Rivera G.[22]

In an attempt to force federal intervention and the assistance of Emilio Vázquez Gómez, the Cristobalense anti-reelectionists raised the banner of rebellion on July 3, 1911, and refused to recognize the legality of Gordillo León's appointment.[23] "The state legislature refused to accept the designation made by the Secretary of Gobernación," proclaimed the Cristobalenses, "for this and other reasons given: The nomination is not recognized and Manuel Pineda is named interim governor."[24] More than 100 prominent citizens of San Cristóbal signed the document of rebellion. In response the state legislature in Tuxtla Gutiérrez appropriated 60,000 pesos for the support of a volunteer battalion called the "Sons of Tuxtla."[25]

THE JULY PRONUNCIAMIENTO

By July each side had a clear perception of the other. *El Imparcial,* basing its report on a telegram for Tuxtla Gutiérrez, said the purpose of the Cristobalense rebellion was to sustain "the clerical predominance in the state."[26] Tuxtleco historian Luis Espinosa viewed the dispute as one between the "liberal element" in Tuxtla and the "clerical element" in San Cristóbal.[27] (A modern chronicler, Antonio García de León, believes Bishop Francisco Orozco y Jiménez organized the 1911 movement in San Cristóbal.[28]) The Cristobalenses saw themselves as true (gentlemen) revolutionaries fighting against an entrenched oligarchy in Tuxtla Gutiérrez. By July 1911 the issue of the location of the capital no longer appeared so prominently in Cristobalense propaganda. They had found a broader issue that attracted allies throughout the state:

"Death to caciquismo!"[29] Nevertheless, outside the two cities the contention was viewed—correctly—as a feud.[30]

The July *pronunciamiento* was designed to force the government in Tuxtla Gutiérrez to accept Vázquez Gómez's nominee for interim governor. The state elections were coming up in mid-July, and the composition of the new state legislature depended heavily upon the political inclination of the interim governor. The Cristobalense party feared that an unfriendly governor would subvert the election through the appointment of partisan jefes políticos. The election of an unfriendly legislature, in turn, would ensure the election of a full-term (1911–14) constitutional governor hostile to Cristobalense interests.

The July pronunciamiento did succeed in prompting Vázquez Gómez again to strongly recommend to the state legislature a compromise candidate, Dr. Policarpo Rueda.[31] This pressure from above was reinforced from below by a Cristobalense threat to march thousands of angry Indians into Tuxtla Gutiérrez.[32] Policarpo Rueda, president of the Club "Democrático Independiente" of Tonalá, was one of the earliest Maderistas in Chiapas. He was sympathetic, although not subservient, to the Cristobalense cause. Interim Governor Gordillo Léon resigned on July 5 and the legislature appointed Rueda to fill the office and keep the peace.[33]

Rueda tried to conciliate both sides by allowing each to control a geographical sphere of influence. He immediately replaced the jefes políticos named by Gordillo León and appointed Cristobalense leader Juan Félix Zepeda secretary of government to placate the opposition. On July 13 Rueda traveled to San Cristóbal and appointed jefes políticos for the departments of Las Casas, Comitán, Chilón, Palenque, and Pichucalco who were acceptable to the revanchist party. Manuel Pineda, for example, was given the jefatura of Las Casas. Rueda also tried, without success, to disarm both sides. In response to Rueda's "subversion" and to gain some time, the state legislature moved the elections back from July 11–13 to August 13–15, and still later to August 27–29.[34]

In early August Secretary of Gobernación Emilio Vázquez Gómez was replaced within the national cabinet by Alberto García Granados. The new secretary, in turn, appointed José Antonio Rivera G. secretary of government for the Federal District (Mexico City). Interim Governor

Rueda asked the state legislature for an indefinite leave of absence to visit Mexico City and seek reassurance and support for his government from the new gobernación secretary.[35] The state legislature then turned to another compromise candidate for governor, Manuel Rovelo Argüello. Before accepting, Rovelo Argüello first asked for the support of Rivera G. and pledged his complete neutrality. Rivera G. then threw his support to Rovelo Argüello and García Granados recommended him to the Chiapas legislature. That body made Rovelo Argüello Chiapas's fourth interim governor in as many months.[36]

Rovelo Argüello assumed office shortly before the August elections for the state legislature. On his first day he replaced the jefes políticos appointed by Rueda in five departments.[37] Only one of the appointments favorable to the Cristobalense party, that in Pichucalco, was overturned. As it turned out, however, the departmental electors did not always vote in line with the wishes of their jefes políticos. Comitán, for example, despite the presence of a pro-Cristobalense jefe, elected a pro-government legislator. The Cristobalense party, winning only in Las Casas, Simojovel, La Libertad, and Chilón, failed to obtain a majority in the new legislature.[38]

Two opposing explanations were forthcoming regarding the outcome of the election. Interim Governor Rovelo Argüello explained to De la Barra that "if San Cristóbal did not have a complete triumph in the elections, surely it was because it selected candidates absolutely unknown by the departmental electors."[39] Timoteo Flores Ruiz, on the other hand, charged that "the legislature gave a coup d'état; the current legislature, like the one before, continues to serve a camarilla."[40]

The four pro-Cristobalense state deputies arrived in Tuxtla Gutiérrez on September 13, on the eve of the convocation of the new legislature. The following day they were advised that San Cristóbal, under the leadership of finqueros Juan Espinosa Tórres and Manuel Pineda, had again withdrawn recognition of the state government, initiating rebellion. The four returned to San Cristóbal.[41]

BLOOD BETWEEN BROTHER TOWNS

The September 14 pronunciamiento had as its primary goal federal intervention, but this time the Cristobalenses were willing to install a friendly government by force of arms if necessary. On the same day "Comandante Militar y Jefe de las Fuerzas Libertadores del Estado" Juan Espinosa Tórres sent an ultimatum to Tuxtla Gutiérrez giving twenty-four hours to the state legislature to dissolve itself and demanding that the governor place the armed forces of the state at his disposal. "It being impossible, contemptible, and shameful to tolerate any longer the actual state of affairs, which pushes us to the edge of ruin and indefinite oppression," wrote the rebels in San Cristóbal, "we subscribers have resolved to sustain by arms the principles of the triumphant Revolution."[42] The first armed clash came the following day.

Gobernación Secretary García Granados, upon learning of the renewed rebellion, was quoted as saying that the problem in Chiapas was that "persons of the old regime are seeking to dominate the government, and this brings out discord on the part of the people of the new regime."[43] Francisco I. Madero was less understanding. He telegraphed Espinosa Tórres on September 17: "You have no motive which justifies such an assault and I am formally notifying you that if you continue to advance and attack Tuxtla, I will decidedly support the Government of Sr. De la Barra in order to punish you and others who are deserving in an exemplary manner and when I receive power I will also demand that you and your followers be held strictly accountable."[44] A conflict in policy clearly existed between the national government of De la Barra and the leader of the national revolution, Madero, regarding the situation in Chiapas. This lack of coordination encouraged the Cristobalense party to maintain their belligerent position all summer and, inadvertently, led to violence.

Upon hearing of the new Cristobalense pronunciamiento, Rueda left Mexico City and arrived in Chiapas on September 19 to resume his post of interim governor. To avoid this disagreeable prospect, the state legislature requested and obtained the resignation of Rovelo Argüello, repealed the appointment of Rueda, and named federal deputy Querido Moheno interim governor of Chiapas. The legislature refused to allow Rueda to return to Tuxtla Gutiérrez, but Moheno would not come to Chiapas, citing as his reason the illegal intervention of Secretary of Gobernación García Granados. Rovelo Argüello remained in office, if not completely in charge.[45]

The military conflict lasted not quite a month. The state government had at its disposal about one thousand well-armed men, while the Cristobalenses counted a few thousand Indians poorly armed and disciplined and an additional 800 ladinos.[46] The two forces clashed at points leading to Tuxtla Gutiérrez from the Central Highlands. The rebels remained on the offensive until the first week in October. By that time they had taken Ixtapa, Chicoasén, La Concordia, San Bartolomé, Copainalá, Simojovel, Chiapilla, San Gabriel, and Solistahuacán. Comitán, under the leadership of municipal president Belisario Domínguez, remained loyal to the state government. Chiapa de Corzo was occupied by Cristobalense forces and on September 24 withdrew recognition of the state government.[47]

Tuxtlecos charged at the time that the clergy in San Cristóbal and the bishop were responsible for the conflict and recruited Chamula villagers to take part. Indians did take part in most of the military actions under the command of a Chamula cacique, Jacinto Pérez, called "El Pajarito." The rebel leaders of San Cristóbal apparently offered land and the abolition of the head tax to recruit an Indian army. Their participation added to the bloody image of a caste war that horrified the people of the Central Valley and many in the highlands. Pérez's Indian army seized control of the indigenous highland villages, purged opposing Chamula factions, and took revenge on certain highland ladino landlords. Given the opportunity and leadership, highland Indians apparently were disposed toward rebellion and could have become a social revolutionary army.[48]

What was the role of the bishop, Francisco Orozco y Jiménez? There is no question that the leaders of the insurrection were fervent Catholics, particularly Manuel Pineda, and close friends of the bishop. Governor Rovelo Argüello firmly believed the bishop was involved.[49] We also know that the rebels, like the Zapatistas, carried the banner of the Virgin of Guadalupe as the symbol of their cause. After the conflict, however, several priests published their opinion that the leaders of the Cristobalense movement had used the bishop's name in support of their cause without his permission.[50] Luis Espinosa, the most thorough chronicler of the 1911 crisis, offers no hard evidence of the bishop's direct involvement other than letters, which show that the bishop was informed and concerned.[51]

On September 17, Orozco y Jiménez wrote Interim President De la

Barra requesting federal intervention: "Although I have never attempted nor do I now attempt to involve myself in politics, I believe it is my duty as Bishop, [responsible] for the well-being of my *diocesanos,* to manifest to you that this society is increasingly profoundly alarmed that at any time hostilities between this city and Tuxtla Gutiérrez will break out. Perhaps intervention by you, which for my part I seek and would give thanks for, can stop the flowing of blood between brother towns whose misfortune grieves me and upon which I cannot look with indifference."[52] One week later the bishop made another plea: "The situation now is extremely anarchic and distressing. My ecclesiastical authority is by today ineffectual, I have exhausted all means to help. Only you can remedy it and I urge that it be with quick and effective intervention."[53]

During the first three weeks of the conflict De la Barra declined to intervene on one side or the other.[54] He explained his inactivity this way: "If the federal forces operate, this will displease some. If they do not operate, this will displease others."[55] He looked for peaceful solutions instead. On the night of September 21, De la Barra and Rovelo Argüello held a telegraphic conference. The president twice suggested the desirability of asking the Senate to declare the *desaparición de los poderes* (federal intervention and removal) of the state government and the appointment of a military officer as interim governor. Rovelo Argüello replied that his government was in perfect accord with the constitution. De la Barra decided not to press the issue.[56] In communications with Espinosa Tórres, De la Barra emphasized that there were legal and peaceful means to protest election violations.[57] On october 4, De la Barra ordered General Eduardo Paz to go to Chiapas and seek a peaceful solution to the conflict. At the same time he ordered the Secretary of War to give arms and ammunition to the "Sons of Tuxtla," the volunteer forces of the state government.[58]

To the legal government of Chiapas and the people of Tuxtla, it appeared that the state had degenerated into a bloody caste war about which the federal government did nothing. After repeated requests for assistance to the executive branch, Rovelo Argüello turned for help to the Senate.[59] In response the Senate created a commission on Chiapas to investigate the crisis and propose a solution. The commission was led by none other than Emilio Rabasa and Víctor Manuel Castillo.[60]

Speaking before the commission on behalf of the federal government, Gobernación Secretary García Granados asked that the Senate declare the desaparición de los poderes and appoint a soldier interim governor until the November elections.[61] The commission, however, concluded that the established government in Tuxtla Gutiérrez was legitimate. On October 6, the full Senate voted to inform the president that it was the will of the Senate, and its constitutional prerogative under Article 116, that he order "federal forces to begin immediately active and energetic operations against the rebels that have risen in arms against the government of the state of Chiapas."[62] De la Barra complied and ordered General Paz to cooperate with the forces of the state government to bring about a military end to the rebellion.

The combined federal-state counteroffensive began on October 8 unexpectedly at Chiapa de Corzo. A misunderstanding between federal forces and the local militia led to a four-hour battle in which more than one hundred people were killed and many more wounded.[63] During the next four days federal and state troops retook most of the important towns under Cristobalense control. During one foray the "Sons of Tuxtla" captured ten Chamula soldiers and cut off their ears to make them examples of what would happen when Indians fought ladinos.[64]

The odds were too great. On October 12 the Cristobalense leadership agreed to enter into negotiations with General Paz.[65] A peace agreement was signed the following day by commissioners representing both sides. It is likely that the Cristobalense party agreed to a speedy peace settlement for fear that their Indian army was getting out of control.[66] The rebels agreed to recognize the state government of Rovelo Argüello in exchange for a general amnesty. This agreement also included the disarming of both sides, the establishment of federal detachments where necessary to ensure fair elections, and the appointment by the governor of a military officer as jefe político of Comitán. It was reported that Governor Rovelo Argüello was not happy with the agreement.[67]

THE GUBERNATORIAL ELECTION

The fighting over, Chiapas again turned its attention to electoral politics. The two candidates for constitutional governor in the November election were Reinaldo Gordillo León (former interim governor)

TABLE 4

THE GUBERNATORIAL ELECTION OF 1911

Department	ELECTORAL VOTES Rivera G.	ELECTORAL VOTES Gordillo León
Las Casas	110	0
Chilón	55	1
Chiapa	47	0
Pichucalco	30	0
Palenque	23	6
Tonalá	21	10
Simojovel	16	24
La Libertad	3	26
Motozintla	0	31
Soconusco	7	37
Tuxtla	0	71
Comitán	8	82
Total	320	292

Sources: *La Patria*, 23 November 1911; *La Voz del Pueblo*, 3 December 1911.

and José Antonio Rivera G. General Paz considered both unacceptable and proposed Dr. Policarpo Rueda, but there were no takers.[68] The election was close and representative of the political and regional division of the state. According to a variety of sources, including the secretary of gobernación, Rivera G. won the election with the 320 votes against Gordillo León's 292. (See table 4.)[69]

The state legislature, after waiting a month, finally declared that the voting in Palenque and Chilón had been fraudulent. Their votes were nullified and by a tally of 290 to 242, Gordillo León was elected and declared governor of Chiapas.[70] Gordillo León later admitted what everyone already knew, that the state legislature would never have confirmed Rivera G. He noted that Madero, who assumed the presidency in mid-November, did not want to give the victory to Gordillo

León but was advised to sacrifice Rivera G. for the sake of peace and stability.[71] Madero, however, did request that the new governor "bring into your administration some of the elements of the opposing párty."[72] At the beginning of 1912, to avoid yet another pronunciamiento in San Cristóbal, Madero named Gordillo León ambassador to Guatemala (after pressuring him to take a leave of absence) and finally obtained the office for Flavio Guillén.[73] A fragile truce ensued in Chiapas.

Landowning elites heaved a sigh of relief at the end of the conflict and the election of Gordillo León. "The great danger here," wrote the U.S. consul in August 1911, "is that a spread of agitation or revolutionary movement might reach the agricultural working classes and endanger the gathering of the coffee crop. . . . It is feared that should the masses awaken to the actual conditions of things danger might result to the coffee crop and even to the security of the plantations and planters."[74] Although there was some evidence of discontent, for the most part the countryside remained peaceful and orderly. In Tuxtla Chico workers protested the head tax, and there were scattered reports of labor trouble and the destruction of property.[75] The manager of the plantation "El Rosario" reported in August that "our laborers are still running away during the night in small bunches."[76] In July the anarchist "Juan Álvarez" club, which had formed in early 1911, took over the ayuntamiento of Tapachula in the elections and placed one of its members in the jefatura politica.[77] When Governor Gordillo León took office in December 1911 he ordered Víctor Constantino Herrera, the jefe político, to resign.[78] In February 1912, the U.S. consul reported that the new jefe político, Abelardo Domínguez, "has continued to make good his promises to assist the planters in every possible way and owners and managers report greater attempts to afford them assistance in managing their field hands than they have experienced for some time."[79]

CONCILIATION AND CONCORD

The dominant theme of the new Guillén administration was "conciliation and concord between brothers."[80] The governor, as befitting a true Maderista, encouraged a free political environment and competition between factions through political discourse. In Tuxtla Gutiérrez the Partido Liberal Chiapaneco, formed by Ciro Farrera in 1911, promoted lowland commercial and agricultural interests.[81] In San Cristóbal, Jesús Martínez Rojas formed the Partido Popular Chiapaneco to advance highland interests, including the return of the government to San Cristóbal.[82]

Governor Guillén's conciliatory policy was followed in the mid-1912 elections for senators and national deputies, and state legislators. The same legislature that had imposed Gordillo León chose two men loyal to the old regime, Leopold Gout and José Castellot, for the Senate. Belisario Domínguez was elected an alternate senator, presumably as a reward for his steadfast support of the government during the rebellion. There was a split in the election of national deputies. Romulo Farrera and Manuel Rovelo Argüello were elected as candidates of the Tuxtleco Partido Liberal, Adolfo E. Grajales represented Soconusco, and Jesús Martínez Rojas and César Castellanos were elected as candidates of the Cristobalense Partido Popular. The newly elected state legislature was, noted Martínez Rojas, "for the most part independent."[83] No better testimony of Guillén's political skill can be found than the change of opinion of the Cristobalense *La Voz del Pueblo*. In February 1912 Guillén's appointment was viewed as a "Científico triumph." By September the governor was referred to as "a man of good faith, of noble and honorable ideals."[84] Guillén also obtained the support of Bishop Orozco y Jiménez.[85] Surprisingly, Maderista democratic liberalism appeared to work in Chiapas.

Governor Guillén, cooperating with the new legislature, also decreed some meaningless reforms that did not touch the surviving Porfirian social and economic order. Although the division of ejidos had ended in 1909, the 1892 Ley de Ejidos decreeing the parceling of communal village lands was repealed in November 1912. In December a new labor law was promulgated. This law required employers not to carry workers' debts for more than a year, established a maximum ten-hour work day, prohibited debt inheritance, and required employers to provide a primitive form of insurance for disabled workers.[86] Guillén also established the Office of Servant Contractors to oversee the contracting of highland Indians, to prevent abuses. It quickly became, however, a corrupt and abusive agency. Finally, in response to the participation of Indians in the 1911 insurrection, the state government abolished the regressive head tax.[87]

Notwithstanding Guillén's program of conciliation and reform, banditry persisted throughout the state. Chiapas was plagued by a deep-rooted wave of violence. Landowners reported difficulties in keeping workers on their properties, and bandits roamed the state, burning some fincas, tearing up a few towns, and stealing cattle.[88] In Tonalá, for example, landowners and merchants felt compelled to form their own rural defense corps against bandits and rebellious workers.[89] Numerous petty political squabbles, often violent, erupted in the municipalities over the control of local government.[90] The end of the tight political control exercised during the Díaz dictatorship led to the venting of frustrations and the abuse of the freer political climate. Banditry, like violence by workers, was also partly economic in nature. While wages remained stable during the period after Madero began his revolution, prices of basic commodities soared. Between 1910 and 1912, for example, the price of five liters of corn in Tuxtla Gutiérrez increased from eight to thirty centavos and in Tapachula from twelve to twenty centavos.[91] Nevertheless, violence was never translated into a spontaneous jacquerie or an organized mass rebellion against the established order. Chiapas was revolution-resistant.

THE CONSTITUTIONALIST REVOLUTION

In February 1913 Governor Guillén took a leave of absence to travel to Mexico City. He wanted to lend his support to the Madero government in its struggle with Félix Díaz, the dictator's nephew, who had staged a revolt with Bernardo Reyes in the capital city. The state legislature then recalled Reinaldo Gordillo León from Guatemala to occupy the governor's office once again.[92] General Victoriano Huerta, the federal general in command of the defense of the Madero government, treacherously joined forces with Díaz and overthrew the Madero government. President Madero and Vice-President Pino Suárez were murdered on the night of February 21. The following day Governor Gordillo León professed his loyalty to the new administration of President-General Victoriano Huerta.[93] The governor also asked Senator Emilio Rabasa to work against the naming of a military governor for Chiapas, a change desired by certain Cristobalenses.[94] The governor of Coahuila, Venustiano Carranza, and Maderistas in Sonora took exception to

Huerta's coup d'état on the same day, February 22, and refused to recognize its legality. The Constitutionalist revolution began.

Most elite Chiapanecos—who had never converted to liberal democratic constitutionalism—were not really distressed at the fall of the Madero government. The state government, including the legislature, quickly and willingly accommodated itself to the new political order. In March, for example, Gordillo León asked all jefes políticos to help the political clubs supporting Félix Díaz and Francisco León De la Barra, candidates for president and vice-president.[95] The Cristobalense rebels of 1911 considered Madero a traitor to the principles of 1910 and their cause. Jesús Martínez Rojas supported the Huerta government (until October 1913), believing that the new president intended to comply with the promises of the revolution.[96] In Tuxtla Gutiérrez little had changed, as witnessed by the return of Ramón Rabasa to the municipal government.[97]

President Huerta replaced Gordillo León with General A.Z. Palafox in July 1913—a move made in conformity with the general militarization of the country and which, incidentally, pleased many Cristobalenses. During his one year in Chiapas, Palafox met his quota for enlisting soldiers in the federal army and kept Chiapas out of the hands of the anti-Huerta rebels. The military administration made an attempt to reform the office of labor contracting in San Cristóbal, set maximum prices for primary commodities sold in town markets, increased the number of school inspectors, and increased the budget for road construction and repair to a record 150,000 pesos.[98]

The Constitutionalist movement—that is, the anti-Huerta rebellion of Coahuilans, Sonorans, and Chihuahuans led by Venustiano Carranza—gathered military strength and political unity in the spring of 1913. Initially limited to the northern tier of states, the movement soon gained allies in Morelos, Zacatecas, San Luis Potosí, Campeche, and Tabasco.[99] By summer several Constitutionalist chiefs in Tabasco, such as Carlos Greene, Pedro Colorado, Juan Hernández, and Luis Felipe Domínguez, conducted military operations in both Tabasco and northern Chiapas.[100] Late in 1913 the Vidal brothers of Pichucalco, Carlos and Luis, offered their services to Greene and harassed Chiapas authorities in their home department.[101]

General Luis Felipe Domínguez, a hacendado from Tenosique, Tabasco, entered Chiapas in March 1913 in command of the "Usumacinta" Brigade. Over the next two years he marched from montería to montería liberating the mahogany workers.[102] Thirty years later one worker recalled: "I escaped from that hell because the Revolution liberated me. General Luis Felipe Domínguez came in 1913 and we all left with him."[103] One administrator of a montería reported in 1914 that the lumber camps "Santa Margarita" and "Santa Clara" had been reduced to ashes.[104] In each camp Domínguez decreed the absolute liberty of workers, the abolition of all workers' debts, and the execution of administrators and overseers. The "Usumacinta" Brigade put the monterías out of business for only two or three years but in doing so became a legend in Indian Chiapas.[105]

The other Domínguez who entered legend in 1913 was Senator Dr. Belisario Domínguez. He was elevated to the Senate in early 1913 on the death of Leopold Gout. Domínguez, a Comiteco and medical doctor trained in Paris, was a late Maderista who had been sickened by Huerta's climb to power over the bodies of Madero and Pino Suárez. In September 1913 the senator published in the congressional record a speech he was not allowed to read, which was a virulent indictment of the Huerta regime. Domínguez called on his colleagues to do their duty and depose the president, "a bloody and ferocious soldier who assassinates without hesitation anyone who is an obstacle to his wishes." He argued that "the country hopes that you will honor her before the world, saving her from the shame of having as chief executive a TRAITOR and an ASSASSIN."[106]

Two weeks later Domínguez was picked up by four policemen who drove him to a cemetery, shot him, and buried his body. When the senator failed to appear in the Senate chamber that day, October 8, the Chiapas delegation led by Jesús Martínez Rojas asked the secretary of gobernación about his disappearance and declared that the Chamber of Deputies would remain in permanent session until the matter was fully resolved. The following day rumors of Domínguez's assassination circulated in the capital city. Huerta dissolved both chambers of the national legislature on October 10 to prevent the congress from withdrawing its recognition of the government. The Huerta regime no longer had even a shadow of legitimacy.[107]

Violence became more widespread in Chiapas in 1913 and 1914. In the confused political climate it was often impossible to distinguish between bandits and revolutionaries. In June 1913 the jefe político of Soconusco captured a large quantity of Constitutionalist revolutionary propaganda being smuggled into the state.[108] By September 1913 Governor Palafox was asking the federal government for arms to use against the rebels of Pichucalco, Palenque, and Mariscal.[109] In February 1914 an uprising occurred in Tapachula and was immediately suppressed. In the process the jefe político and coffee planter Fernando Braun detained the leaders of the anarchist "Juan Álvarez" club, had them shot, and burned the bodies.[110] Ricardo Caracosa led a small band of revolutionaries near Comitán in 1914, supported by Guatemalan President Estrada Cabrera.[111] Other similar small rebel grops appeared: in Cintalapa led by Luis Espinosa, in Villa Flores led by Santana Córdova, in Ocosingo led by Aarón Castellanos. These bands neither individually nor collectively threatened the Palafox government in 1914 given their failure to incite a popular insurrection.[112]

The Huerta regime, defeated militarily by the Constitutionalists, collapsed in the summer of 1914. The president-general resigned on July 15, and the first chief of the Constitutionalist movement, Venustiano Carranza, entered Mexico City on August 20. Governor Palafox resigned on August 13, and the state legislature named José Cano, a Tuxtleco and Rabasa intimate, interim governor. Faced with incipient rebellion within his own movement in the north, Carranza set about to secure his control over the southeast. In late August Carranza appointed three military governors, revolutionary proconsuls, for the south: Salvador Alvarado for Yucatán, Francisco J. Mújica for Tabasco, and Jesús Agustín Castro for Chiapas. Castro, and the northern revolution, arrived in Tuxtla Gutiérrez on September 14, 1914.

"The revolutionary movement of the State of Chiapas," reported the secretary of gobernación in 1911, "has an exclusively local character."[113] The Maderista revolution provided an opportunity for Cristobalense elites to attempt to break the political power of the Central Valley landowners. The political establishment in Tuxtla Gutiérrez, however, successfully defended itself from enemies within Chiapas and without. There was much at stake. It is no coincidence that the three most prosperous districts in the state, Tuxtla, Comitán, and Soconusco, cast their votes for the government candidate in the November 1911 gubernatorial election. The modernizing elites defended their progress against a retrograde alliance of clerical landlords and separatist, communalist Indians. The 1911 conflict was the last major political expression of a long regional struggle, the last conflict of the nineteenth century.

The Mexico Revolution that began in 1910–11 constituted the most serious crisis of the national state since the Reform. The Mexican state was so intimately bound up with the personality and political machine of Porfirio Díaz that his disappearance led to a period of political fragmentation. Chiapas was drawn into "the Revolution" but not into social revolution. The civil wars of the second decade of the twentieth century were elite struggles for power and in defense of interests. All the same, they had important social consequences.

To Feel the Effects of the Revolution

"CHIAPANECO COWARDS, WHILE THE NORTH IS STRUGGLING, YOU ARE enjoying peace," General Jesús Agustín Castro informed a crowd of Tuxtlecos, "but I will teach you to feel the effects of the Revolution."[1] Chiapas was invaded by a Mexican revolutionary army in the fall of 1914. Never before had regional autonomy been so violated; never before had the national state extended its power so directly and forcefully in Chiapas; and not since the Reform had the power and the interests of the liberal Central Valley elites been so threatened. The result was a profound political crisis—another regional convulsion—manifested as a civil war. It was three conflicts in one: the region against the national center; some finqueros against other finqueros; and, to some extent, workers and campesinos against landowners. Chiapas experienced the "effects of the Revolution," but was not itself revolutionized. To avoid a bloody "caste war," Mexican revolutionaries and their Chiapanecan allies, remembering Pajarito and 1911, did not dare mobilize peasants to overthrow the old social order and advance the goals of the Revolution. Paternalistic reform, not popular mobilization, characterized the official Mexican Revolution in Chiapas.

INVASION OF THE NORTEÑOS

General Jesús Agustín Castro and the Brigada Veintiuno, comprising 1,200 officers and men from north central Mexico, reached Tuxtla Gutiérrez on September 14, 1914. Their primary task was to incorporate "the benighted, provincial south into Constitutionalism."[2] As military governor, Castro assumed all executive, legislative, and judicial power. All important positions in state, district, and municipal government were staffed by military officers or loyal Carrancistas. As federal garrisons were demobilized, military detachments were stationed in each department cabecera. In less than two weeks Constitutionalist (that is to say, Carrancista) rule was imposed in Chiapas.[3]

General Castro was twenty-six years old when he undertook the task of revolutionizing Chiapas. A native of Durango, he had joined the Maderista movement in 1910 and by 1914 had ascended to the rank of general in the Second Division of the Center under the command of Jesús Carranza, brother of Venustiano Carranza. As a middle-class Norteño and a member of the "radical wing" of the Constitutionalist movement, Castro was "a natural Carrancista."[4] He was appalled by the social conditions of the Mexican southeast and sought to effect revolutionary changes in Chiapas.[5] "While endorsing order, property, and centralized government," writes Knight, the Carrancista proconsuls were "hostile to tradition and privilege, both secular and clerical."[6] Castro outlined his revolutionary vision on arrival in the state:

> If yesterday the despotic government degenerated men and converted them into slaves, the Revolution will raise them up and make them dignified citizens; if the tyranny sustained ignorance, the Revolution will destroy it and bring enlightenment; if the privileged robbed the poor, the Revolution will return to them their rights; if there was one justice for the rich and another for the poor, the Revolution will impose equality before the law; if the ambitious misused their power through fraud and crime, the Revolution will see to it that officials will be chosen by the popular vote. All the conquests of the Revolution speak eloquently and proclaim a great future for the country.[7]

Castro's first official act was to declare October 7—the anniversary of Belisario Domínguez's assassination by, or on behalf of, Huerta—a day of mourning. Thereafter he pronounced official reform decrees in rapid succession. In mid-October priests were prohibited from wearing ecclesiastical dress in public and from saying mass more than once a week, convents were closed, and the property of Bishop Orozco y Jiménez was confiscated. The "Ley de Obreros o de Liberación de Mozos" abolishing indebted servitude came on October 21, the confiscation of all church property on December 5, and the nullification of mortgages of less than 3,000 pesos on December 8. On January 16, 1915, the post of jefe político was abolished in conformity with Carranza's conviction that no political intermediaries should exist between the municipalities and the state government. In April ayuntamientos were authorized to expropriate lands and a Local Agrarian Commission was organized to supervise the return of land to despoiled villages. A law permitting divorce and remarriage was decreed on May 22.[8] These laws and decrees, in harmony with the principles of the Constitutionalist movement, sought to liberate workers, small property owners, Indians, women, and municipal governments from the control of economic, spiritual, political, and domestic bosses. They were designed to force Chiapas to become part of the modern "civilized world."

The Ley de Obreros was by far the most significant and potentially the most economically and socially disruptive decree of the early Constitutionalist period in Chiapas. In one action Castro had abolished in law the system of indebted servitude, the most important labor practice in Chiapas. The debts of all workers were forgiven; company stores and child labor were prohibited; days and hours of labor were regulated; decent housing, schools, and medical care for laborers and their families were to be provided by employers; and a regionally varied minimum wage scale was mandated. Military commanders of the departments, and later state government work inspectors, were responsible for enforcing compliance by landowners.[9] Throughout the state military commanders liberated servants, permitting and sometimes forcing workers to abandon haciendas.[10] "I have not only lost 30,000 pesos in debts, but all of my workers as well. Of more than 300, only three stayed with me," complained the owner of the finca "Prusia."[11] A North American landowner in Pichucalco complained that the soldiers drove all her servants away. The officer in command asked the workers, "Don't you want to mount your patron's horse and put on his spurs, and be a Señor?"[12]

Castro, as promised, set about to teach Chiapanecos "to feel the effects of the Revolution." General Castro's secretary general of government, Lieutenant Colonel José C. Rangel, permitted the Carrancista soldiers to commit "every kind of abuse, robbery, and murder of good and honorable people."[13] Executions of "enemies of the people" com-

menced immediately. State *rurales,* municipal policemen, and hated local political bosses made up many of the victims. The most notable
victim was Arturo Paramiro, chief of the state secret police under Governor Palafox, who was executed in October. Jacinto "Pajarito" Pérez,
the Chamula leader of the 1911 rebellion, was captured and shot in
October after military authorities in San Cristóbal were advised that
he constituted a potential danger to public order.[14] Carrancista military
expeditions took the form of punitive raids against fincas, churches,
and towns. The soldiers burned estates, murdered landowners, stole
cattle and crops, and encouraged workers to disobey their masters. They
broke into churches, destroyed altars, and took anything of value.[15]
The term *Carrancear,* in Chiapas, was synonymous with "to rob."[16]
The U.S. consular agent in Ocos, Guatemala reported, "It appears these
Constitutionalists are determined to commit all the possible damage
before they are defeated. They have committed no end of depredations
in the state of Chiapas."[17]

The new authorities sanctioned disorder. In a trip to the Central
Highlands in early 1915, General Castro visited several Indian villages
and explained the principles of the Revolution through an interpreter
to the thousands who had gathered to hear him. His government, Castro
explained, was their friend and the enemy of their ladino exploiters.
He told villagers they could retake the land that had been stolen from
them. In Oxchuc Castro supervised the division of an abandoned finca.[18]
Campesinos took revenge on neighboring landowners, repossessed land
once believed to be theirs, and offered assistance to the soldiers from
the north. "As the revolution developed in intensity," declared a resident
of Tonalá, "the peons and laborers working on the claimants' haciendas
became more and more restless. Many became insolent and refused to
work, some joined various bands of revolutionary forces, and still
others became bandits and thieves."[19] Complaints like this one were
common in late 1914 and early 1915, yet no popular mobilization
occurred or was permitted.

The Carrancista revolution in Chiapas in the fall of 1914 was like
an invasion of barbarians to the landowning and commercial elites of
the region. This was true in many areas throughout Mexico. Many of
the best and wealthiest families in the Central Valley and the Central
Highlands fled to Guatemala or Mexico City. The German coffee plant-

ers of Soconusco successfully pressured German diplomats in Mexico City to obtain guarantees from the Carranza government that their properties and businesses would not be molested.[20] Many landowners throughout the state, but particularly in the department of Tuxtla, collaborated with the Carrancistas. They had no choice, since opposition meant expropriation or worse. Collaboration with, and even participation in, the Carrancista revolution by Chiapaneco finqueros and merchants was a way to buy time, maintain local power, and protect interests. Many finqueros and rancheros, however—those of the more isolated and distant localities of Chiapas—chose a different course of action. They rebelled.

LA MAPACHADA: IN DEFENSE OF CHIAPAS

The rebellion against Carrancista rule in Chiapas began when Don Venustiano's movement seemed nearly defeated. The Constitutionalist victory over the government of Victoriano Huerta in the summer of 1914 was accompanied by serious friction between First Chief Venustiano Carranza and his most powerful and popular general, Francisco "Pancho" Villa. The growing split in the Constitutionalist movement was largely a struggle for personal and factional power. Carranza governed dictatorially and tolerated little dissent or independence on the part of his military commanders. Villa, chief of the División del Norte, chafed under Carranza's tight control. The first chief considered Villa too insubordinate. Each came to distrust and loathe the other.[21]

Mexico verged on civil war once again in the fall of 1914. In September Carranza called for a national convention to determine a date for national elections and, many hoped, to resolve the factional dispute and prevent war. Supporters of both Carranza and Villa wanted a peaceful resolution but expected the convention to champion their leader. The convention that met in Aguascalientes on October 10, however, at first assumed a neutral position and made itself a sovereign government, much to Carranza's disgust. In early November Villa recognized the authority of the convention government and placed himself and the División del Norte under its command. Carranza refused to do likewise since Villa now controlled the convention. The convention government then declared Carranza an insurgent. The loyal Constitutionalist generals, the most important being Álvaro Obregón, remained with Carranza. By the end of November the Carrancistas were forced to abandon Mexico City to Villa's army and flee to Veracruz. At the end of 1914 the future of Carranza and his movement appeared bleak.[22]

During this desperate time, the first uprising occurred in Chiapas. In response to General Castro's heavy-handed treatment of the regional elites and the apparent imminent collapse of the Carranza government, which had sent Castro to Chiapas, forty finqueros met on December 2, 1914, on an estate in the department of Chiapa. They signed the Acta de Canquí, which proclaimed the sovereignty of Chiapas; pledged the signatories to drive the "Carrancista filibusters" from the state; and made a young finquero, Tiburcio Fernández Ruiz, chief of "la revolución chiapaneca." They insisted they had risen in arms:

> in view of the vandalistic acts which have victimized the Familia Chiapaneca by the odious armed group that has invaded Chiapaneco soil, sent by the Carrancista government without any other objective than to destroy our political institutions, end our sovereignty, and make themselves masters of our lives and haciendas, sowing everywhere pain and misery and attacking the most sacred possession of man, the home.[23]

The military government in Tuxtla Gutiérrez attributed the rebellion simply to finquero opposition to the Ley de Obreros.[24] Salvador Alvarado, chief of the Army of the Southeast (headquartered in Mérida, Yucatán), blamed the uprising on the abuse of power by Castro or his subordinates.[25] A U.S. resident of the state noted that the insurgents "are men of good reputation who call themselves Villistas."[26] Fernández Ruiz, who was a law student of Emilio Rabasa when the Maderista revolution began and an officer in the "Sons of Tuxtla" during the 1911 rebellion, served in the División del Norte of Pancho Villa until his return to Chiapas in 1914.[27] The Chiapas insurgents adopted the Villista label because, like Villa, they opposed Carranza. In time, however, the Chiapas rebels acquired the popular name *mapaches* (raccoons) because they moved at night and ate uncooked maize in the fields.[28]

"La revolución mapachada" did not represent the reaction of "the landed class" of the Central Valley to reformist government. Lowland landowners formed the leadership of the Mapaches, but other land-owners gave their support to the Carranza government in Tuxtla Gutiérrez and Mexico. Finqueros and merchants of Tuxtla Gutiérrez and the surrounding area, particularly the owners of the largest estates—and therefore those with the most to lose—cooperated with and often joined the Carrancista government and in time made it their own.[29] In the words of Alan Knight, they "colonized the Revolution." The Mapache leaders were frontier finqueros and ranchers—owners, it was said, of "fincas pobres." Their soldiers were foremen, cowboys, ex-soldiers, rurales, and loyal servants and day workers. Their home territory was the southern foothills of the Sierra Madre around Villa Flores, Villa Corzo, and La Concordia. They rebelled to defend their valleys against abusive outsiders. The modernization program of the Rabasa era had barely penetrated into this periphery of the department of Chiapa. Only one of the Mapaches, Fernández Ruiz himself, owned property valued at more than 10,000 pesos, although he was one of nearly 900 such finqueros in Chiapas. The Mapache leaders were finqueros who valued their autonomy more than any assistance they might gain from regional or national government. They saw themselves as revolutionaries who struggled under terrible conditions for Chiapas, for their way of life, and in defense of their fincas.[30]

At first the Mapache insurgency comprised a loose coalition of *guerrillas,* later organized as regiments, which recognized the leadership of Tiburcio Fernández Ruiz. The Ruiz and Fernández clans operated in the Chiapa de Corzo and Tuxtla Gutiérrez area; Salvador Méndez in the Custepedes valley; Federico and Enrique Macías in La Frailesca; Ernesto Castellanos, Abelardo Cristiani, and Manuel Rovelo Argüello in Comitán; and Virgilio Culebro and Tirso Castañón in Tonalá. Two former federal army officers, Rosendo Marquez and Teofilo Castillo Corzo, resided in Guatemala and aided the rebellion by recruiting men and rounding up arms and ammunition. The guerrillas attacked Carrancista garrisons in towns, ambushed government columns, raided trains on the Panamerican Railroad, and harassed supporters of the government.[31]

In December 1914 Ángel María Pérez, José Domingo Pérez, and other Mexican cattlemen of Soconusco rebelled against the Carrancistas in Tapachula. This group fielded a force of about 400 armed men, took possession of Tapachula and Huixtla, and professed loyalty to the convention government in Aguascalientes. In January a large Carrancista force from the Isthmus counterattacked, dispersed the rebels into the mountains, and killed the two leaders. A second attempt was made in March, when Francisco Pino led 80 men to capture Union Juárez. They were quickly routed and driven into Guatemala. Soconusco thereafter remained relatively peaceful, productive, and solidly in the Carrancista camp.[32]

LA MISERIA

The opposing "revolutions" became a bitter civil war in 1915. Mapache raids brought government counterattacks, arrests, and executions. Both sides plundered and killed in the name of military necessity, while numerous bandit gangs took advantage of the disorder to help themselves. As life in the countryside became more and more dangerous, families moved to towns and agricultural production declined. Food became scarce and expensive, and hunger took its toll.[33]

Ladino and Indian campesinos suffered as much at the hands of the Carrancistas as from the Mapaches. Mateo Méndez Tzotzek of Chamula recounted that the Carrancistas "were awful to Indians and Ladinos alike. They made women stay and be raped while they sent the men to look for food for their horses. They stole food, livestock, everything from the Chamulas."[34] Xun Vaskis, of Zinacantan, remembered that the Mapaches "stole coils of woven palm. They stole pants. They stole shirts, money, everything."[35] For most Chiapanecos the civil war was a powerful force beyond their control and comprehension. They did understand its effects: hunger, rape, murder, theft, abduction, and fear. As late as the 1960s, residents of San Cristóbal Las Casas referred to the war years as "la miseria."[36]

On June 3, 1915, the state legislature of Oaxaca withdrew its recognition of the Carranza government, and General Castro was ordered to contain this defection. Castro withdrew from Chiapas with two brigades of the newly named División Veintiuno, leaving General Blas Corral as military governor. Corral, with only one brigade, had sufficient forces to control most towns but not to pacify the countryside.[37] In central Mexico, meanwhile, Carrancista forces took the offensive in the spring of 1915. By the summer, Pancho Villa was, according to General Obregón, "defeated as a general and . . . a nullity as a politician." By October the convention government in Aguascalientes came to an ignominious end at about the same time the U.S. government extended de facto recognition to Carranza.[38]

In 1916 the Mapaches were forced to abandon their disorganized and uncoordinated ways and establish greater cohesion. Early in the year former Chiapas governor Flavio Guillén, Pancho Villa's agent in Guatemala, attempted to gain control of the insurgency in Chiapas. With the assistance of Guatemalan dictator Manuel Estrada Cabrera, who provided arms and ammunition, Guillén named Comiteco Virgilio Culebro chief of the Villistas in Chiapas. This move forced Tirso Castañón, leader of a rival band in Comitán, to establish a closer alliance with Fernández Ruiz. In April the two leaders met in Villa Flores and formed a government. Castañón was designated provisional governor of Chiapas while Fernández Ruiz assumed the more important post of general-in-chief of the "Brigada Libre de Chiapas," which was divided into four regiments. Together they forced Culebro into Guatemalan exile. Castañón retained Estrada Cabrera's patronage, without Guillén as middleman, and the Mapache chief claimed the allegiance of most rebel factions in the region.[39]

To seal the bargain, Fernández Ruiz and Castañón, joined by the Macías brothers and Castillo Corzo, combined forces to attack the Carrancista garrison in Comitán. The assault by 1,000 men—the largest military action in Chiapas to that time—began at three in the morning on April 15, 1916. The government troops, vastly outnumbered, held out for four hours and then abandoned the city. Following their victory, drunken rebel soldiers sacked most of the commercial houses in the city and broke into private homes looking for money, liquor, and women. A disapproving Fernández Ruiz protected a few of the homes in the center of town but left the rest to the mercy of Castañón's troops. The following day government reinforcements from San Cristóbal forced the Mapaches to evacuate Comitán, to the relief of the townspeople.[40]

In July 1916 the rebellion received a further boost when Alberto Pineda Ogarrio, the son of 1911 Cristobalense leader Manuel Pineda, took up arms. Early in 1915 the government had arrested four highland finqueros including Pineda as rebel sympathizers. They were detained in Tuxtla Gutiérrez and released when family and friends paid a "fine" of 20,000 pesos. Again in early 1916 Pineda and twenty other gentlemen were rounded up and jailed. Although soon released, Pineda had endured humiliation enough and went to see the Mapache chief. Fernández Ruiz gave Pineda the rank of colonel. Along with some other highland landowners he formed the "Las Casas" brigade. Pineda operated primarily in the department of Chilón, and also in Las Casas, Palenque, and Simojovel.[41]

SIDESHOWS: GUATEMALANS, FELICISTAS, ZAPATISTAS

In 1916 General Blas Corral received orders from Carranza to end both the rebellion in Chiapas and the abuses of the military government.[42] Corral believed that the rebellion could be sustained practically forever so long as the government of Guatemala actively supported the insurgents and gave them sanctuary. The Estrada Cabrera government treated the Mexican government as a natural enemy.[43] In 1916 alone, Guatemala supplied certain factions of the Mapaches with 250 rifles and 100,000 shells. In retaliation, Corral supported (with little success) Guatemalan revolutionaries operating near Huehuetenango with arms and money.[44] Despite secret negotiations between the Mexican and Guatemalan governments in 1916 and 1917, no agreement was reached and each side continued to interfere in the internal affairs of the other.[45] In 1918 General Salvador Alvarado, then operating in Chiapas, captured the archive of Fernández Ruiz and Hector Macías. Much to his surprise he learned that the Mapache leader refused to take munitions from the Guatemalan government. Nearly all the ammunition used by most Mapache groups had been purchased or stolen from the government's own troops.[46]

Félix Díaz, Don Porfirio's ne'er-do-well nephew, initiated a rebellion in the state of Veracruz to overthrow Carranza in February 1916. The Felicista movement, however, was no match for the armies of the government, and Díaz's forces were forced from Veracruz into Oaxaca and finally into Chiapas by November. Of the 3,000 men Díaz had raised in Veracruz, fewer than 100 managed to flee into Chiapas, most unarmed and on foot. General Díaz believed Chiapas would be fertile ground for his movement, but before he could join forces with the Chiapas rebels he suffered a devastating attack at Pueblo Nuevo. This engagement reduced the Felicistas to a pitifully small band of refugees. Díaz did confer with both Fernández Ruiz and Pineda, inviting both to enlist in his revolution. Fernández Ruiz cordially received and aided Díaz and his entourage but rejected any alliance. The Mapache chief asserted that he was fighting only in defense of his native state. Alberto Pineda publicly rejected Díaz's offer but apparently adopted the failed counterrevolutionary until he returned to Oaxaca and Veracruz.[47]

Díaz's second-in-command, Juan Andreu Almazán, years later gave a candid assessment of the Mapaches. Although their leaders were landowners of high quality, he commented, "unfortunately, perhaps due to the incredible amorality of the principal chiefs, the revolutionary movement had degenerated into the most criminal conduct in the history of all the civil wars of Mexico. . . . The Mapaches did not attack the enemy who carried carbines, no sir, like sickly hellbound bastard goats they attacked women, without deference to age, social position, or health."[48]

Another rebellious element injected itself into Chiapas in 1916. In April, Emiliano Zapata, caudillo of the agrarian revolutionaries in the state of Morelos, appointed Rafael Cal y Mayor chief of military operations in Chiapas, Tabasco, Campeche, and Yucatán. Cal y Mayor was from one of the most distinguished landholding families in the department of Tuxtla; he had been a law student along with Fernández Ruiz in Mexico City before he joined Zapata. The Chiapaneca Zapatista staked out the Chiapas-Veracruz-Oaxaca border in the department of Mezcalapa as his base of operations and in the next three years established several small military-agrarian communities based on small private landholdings. Due to the size of his group and his failure to mobilize a peasant army, Cal y Mayor was not much more than an irritant to the government in Tuxtla Gutiérrez.[49]

REVOLUTION AS GUIDED SOCIAL REFORM

Government in Chiapas remained in the hands of Mexicans—non-Chiapaneco military officers—from September 1914 to 1920. Throughout this period the "revolutionary government" enacted significant reforms, but it never attempted to mobilize Chiapas's peasant masses to defeat the Mapaches and revolutionize the established social and economic order. Ladino Chiapanecos' ancient fear of "caste war," a fear Tuxtlecos had known as recently as 1911, governed the counsel that Carrancista Chiapanecos gave Castro and Corral. The price for local collaboration was guided reform—social progress, not social revolution. Thus the new purpose of government was, as General Blas Corral maintained, to regulate "the relationship between the capitalist and the workers, toward the end of obtaining equilibrium."[50]

The agents of executive will in the countryside throughout the war were Carrancista military officers with various titles. When the jefaturas políticas were abolished in 1915, General Castro created the post of executive delegate to perform the same duties. This post was abolished in June 1915 and revived in 1917. Areas under government control were essentially ruled by "foreign" military officers with considerable power and opportunity to abuse that power.[51]

The military government beginning in 1915 distributed circulars and sent translators throughout Chiapas advising villagers how to legally claim lands that had been stolen from them during the Porfiriato.[52] Some villages did proceed through administrative channels to request the return of communal lands, although some other communities simply took over lands they considered rightfully theirs.[53] Despite the government's early emphasis on agrarian reform, however, between 1915 and 1920 only six grants of land to villages were approved, providing a total of 17,300 hectares.[54]

Work inspectors charged with the enforcement of the Ley de Obreros were located in each department.[55] Finqueros and planters attempted to preserve their labor practices as though nothing had changed. Some maintained two debt registers, one for the Carrancista authorities showing the cancellation of all debts and another, true list to be used when the Carrancistas would be driven from the state.[56] The executive delegate for Palenque, for example, fined several finqueros a total of 1,250 pesos for infractions of the Ley de Obreros. He also found that finqueros had close ties with local government officials and Indian caciques in procuring laborers and maintaining obedience. To enforce the law, executive delegates were forced to depose more than a few municipal presidents and secretaries. The military government also set about to end the practices of baldiaje and arrendamiento. Executive delegates were instructed to publicize the prohibition of these practices and to announce fines of between 500 and 1,000 pesos for finqueros who continued demanding labor or commodities in rent.[57]

In 1918 a state labor relations board was established to resolve fairly conflicts between workers and employers. Local boards were set up in each department.[58] One month after the labor board's creation a strike of coffee workers began on some plantations in Soconusco. The strikers, led by Michoacán socialist Ismael Mendoza, demanded the reduction of the *cuerda* (coffee workers were paid by volume rather than by hour), provision of medical attention, the elimination of company stores, and payment in cash. The government in Tuxtla Gutiérrez refused to support the strike, which was broken by the planters.[59]

Nowhere did the Carrancistas rule with such a light hand as in Soconusco. As a result the department was quiet and peaceful throughout the revolutionary period. This anomalous condition was the product of different forces all working to maintain the production of coffee. In contrast to Alvarado's control of henequen marketing in Yucatán, the Carrancista authorities in Chiapas did not attempt to regulate the production or marketing of coffee because of the region's small market share. The national government, noted the U.S. consul in Guatemala City, "in that part of Chiapas, is friendly in the extreme." As a result, he continued, "business is active and there is a great deal of seeming prosperity."[60] Higher wages, land reform, and private police forces discouraged worker discontent. Competition for workers, noted one observer, "is going to eat up a large share of the profits."[61] Most of the government-approved land reform petitions during this period, furthermore, came from Soconusco.[62] Planters with private guards cooperated with municipal authorities to prevent labor violence, vandalism, and land seizures. Coffee was too valuable to both the planters and the government to let a revolution disrupt production.[63]

Carrancista military control of Soconusco had a subversive effect indirectly upon the agricultural workers of the region. The soldiers from the north did enforce the Ley de Obreros and also spread their "revolutionary" ideas about unions, fair wages, education, and so on. According to Daniela Spenser, "it was during these years [1914–20] that a class consciousness developed among the peons of the fincas which at the beginning of the 1920s was translated into the foundation of the Chiapaneco Socialist Party."[64] A group of labor contractors for the coffee plantations complained in 1918, for example, that workers would take their cash advances, sign work contracts, and then not show up or work for someone else.[65] In the rest of Chiapas as well, Carrancista reformist administration combined with the dislocation and disruption of war led to the beginning of a popular revolutionary climate. (In central and northern Mexico, meanwhile, "the popular insurgence of 1910–11 and 1913–14 gave way to the popular quiescence of 1916–20."[66]) Under the cover of war, and sometimes with military protection, the rural people of Chiapas began to take greater control of their lives. They stopped paying rent, seized land and livestock, and ran away from their former employers.[67] Villagers began to complain to the authorities of conditions they had passively accepted during the Porfiriato.[68] Significantly, what they still did not do was organize to defend their interests and struggle for control of local government.

The military governments maintained and even gave greater emphasis to the Porfirian priorities of road construction and public education. In 1915 an unprecedented 50 percent of the state budget was devoted to roads and schools. To pay for these improvements and to finance the war, the Corral government increased taxes by 40 percent on rural properties valued at more than 1,000 pesos, on commerce, and on coffee production.[69]

In 1916 Carranza reduced the financial independence of the federal states. The first chief cut from 50 to 20 percent the scope of the state governments in the kinds of taxation earmarked for the states.[70] While federal per-capita expenditure increased from thirty-four pesos in 1910 to fifty-three pesos in 1921, Chiapas state per-capita expenditure declined from eight to only five pesos in the same time span. Carranza made state governments even more dependent than before on the federal government for the financing of capital-intensive development projects. The federal government increased its political control over state governments through the provision and denial of subsidies and grants. Furthermore, given the limited size of the national budget and the responsibility to direct funds where they were most economically or politically beneficial, the federal government favored some regions and states over others. Unfortunately for Chiapas, the state had never been very important to politicians in Mexico City, and the revolution did not alter this status.[71]

Finally, the most progressive Carrancistas wrote a new constitution for Mexico in 1916 and 1917 which, while not immediately relevant or important to Chiapas, provided the political framework for a stronger, more centralized, and more active national state. The Constitution of 1917 sanctified land and labor reforms, gave the state control of natural resources, further limited the civil rights of the clergy, and established a preeminently presidential form of government. The new charter ratified the social reforms that had emerged pell-mell from the popular revolution and legitimized the planned Carrancista reconstruction of a Porfirian-like national state. Following the election of a national congress and his own election as constitutional president, Carranza authorized provisional governors (except those in rebellious regions like Chiapas) to hold elections for regular state governments. The Mexican Revolution was officially over. "On 1 May 1917 the new Mexican state formally appeared. The First Chief was sworn into office in Mexico City as the new president, to serve until 30 November 1920. And the new constitution went into effect."[72]

HOME RULE IN OCCUPIED CHIAPAS

As it became clear that the military government could not crush the rebellion in Chiapas by force, Mexico City ordered the implementation of a new strategy. In September 1916 First Chief Carranza appointed Colonel Pablo Villanueva interim governor, while General Blas Corral was shifted to chief of military operations of the region. Villanueva planned to end the war through conciliation and negotiation. To facilitate his peace offensive the new governor brought a number of Mapache sympathizers into his government, including Humberto Consuelo Ruiz, brother of the Mapache leaders Francisco and Fausto Ruiz. Consuelo Ruiz was appointed secretary general of government, the second most important civil post in state government. Villanueva's other significant appointment was that of Rafael Macal, an old friend of the Rabasas, as treasurer general.[73] Home rule—or so it appeared to some— was instituted in occupied Chiapas.

Civil administration generally was returned to local hands in late 1916, while an army of occupation still ruled Chiapas. Landowners and merchants, however, had served earlier military administrations. Luis Espinosa, César Córdova, the Vidal brothers, Victórico Grajales, Moisés E. Villers, Eduardo Castellanos, and José Farrera, to name only a few, joined the División Veintiuno when it arrived in Chiapas in 1914.[74] Finquero Raquel D. Cal y Mayor served in several capacities in the govenrments of Castro and Corral.[75] Still, the appointment of Villanueva "transformed the public spirit" in Tuxtla Gutiérrez and cemented greater elite support for the Carrancista regime.[76] In late 1916 the Villanueva government sent eight delegates, all substantial landowners, to the constitutional convention in Queretaro.[77] Finqueros Diego Coeto Lara, Prudencio Pastrana, and Ezequiel Burguete sat on the state supreme court.[78] The Carrancista regime in Chiapas, particularly after 1916, had the support and active participation of many of the most respected names in Chiapas society.[79] The senators from Chiapas during the Carrancista period were wealthy finqueros, while the deputation to the national congress was composed largely of professionals. "The Carrancista administration," writes García de León, "was almost entirely taken over by lawyers and doctors whose family names were the same as those of the resistance."[80] No simple class war ensued in 1914. Rather, the Revolution in Chiapas was—among other things—a conflict within the elite, between one segment that cooperated with and integrated itself into the Carrancista movement and another segment that rejected any outside intrusion. The Revolution turned into a civil war between those who compromised with the national state and used it to gain power, and those who would not, at least not yet.

Villanueva's first moves were steps to end the abuses committed by the military in Chiapas and to open negotiations with the Mapaches.[81] Fernández Ruiz, however, held a secure military position in the field and demanded nothing less than the immediate withdrawal of all Carrancista troops and the election of a civil government composed entirely of Chiapanecos. Villanueva could not accept these conditions, but before the end of the armistice Tirso Castañón attacked San Cristóbal, ending discussion. The governor then ordered General Corral to resume active military operations. Consuelo Ruiz resigned from the government, and the policy of accommodation was in ruins.[82]

WAR AND MORE WAR

The most successful and active year of the Mapaches during the revolution was 1917. The total number of rebels under Fernández Ruiz may have reached 2,000, rivaling and perhaps surpassing the number of government troops in Chiapas.[83] All travel between the major towns was organized in convoys with military escorts. One such convoy between Tonalá anad Tuxtla Gutiérrez early in 1917 contained eighty-three ox carts and a guard of thirty mounted soldiers.[84] Train service between Tehuantepec and Tapachula occupied only the daylight hours, and even the trains with heavy guard were derailed and held up.[85]

By June Fernández Ruiz felt strong enough to strike a crippling blow. He ordered diversions along the Panamerican Railroad as well as in the Central Highlands. Early in the morning of June 5, he sent a force of 500 men under the joint command of Colonels Fausto Ruiz and Wulfrano Aguilar into Tuxtla Gutiérrez. The attack had been well planned, for the capital city was defended by fewer than 60 soldiers, while General Corral and more than 1,000 men were in the Frailesca valley looking for Mapaches. The insurgents quickly took control of the city, although not of the military garrison, began to loot businesses and homes, and burned the government palace. (Colonel Aguilar was dismissed by Fernández Ruiz for the destruction of the palace.) The Mapaches were more interested in plunder than defense, it seems, for Carrancista reinforcements from nearby towns soon retook the city. Fernández Ruiz ordered a second assault on Tuxtla on July 29, this time under the command of Tirso Castañón. They again quickly took the town and held it for twenty-two hours, but failed to block the road from Ocozocoautla and the reinforcements it carried. The Mapaches, secure in the countryside, could not hold the cities of Chiapas.[86]

Nineteen seventeen also saw a division in Mapache ranks between Alberto Pineda and Tirso Castañón. Pineda had become disgusted by Castañón's "vandalistic behavior," as he termed it, particularly Castañón's treatment of Comitecos.[87] Pineda bleieved that Castañón damaged the common cause and that Castañón was jealous of his prestige and authority in the highlands. This feud led to frequent minor clashes between the two rebel bands. In March 1918 Fernández Ruiz sided with Pineda and expelled Castañón from the movement.[88]

Frustrated in the lowlands, Fernández Ruiz ordered an offensive in the highlands in January 1918. He sent his four brigades to serve under Pineda and elevated the Cristobalense to brigadier general. With about one thousand soldiers, Pineda left his base in Ocosingo and over the next two months took Simojovel, Palenque, Salto de Agua, Sivaca, Copainalá, and Pichucalco. This successful campaign was abruptly halted by Salvador Alvarado in March.[89]

The failure to successfully prosecute the war in Chiapas by 1918 led President Carranza to call in one of his most respected generals, Salvador Alvarado. Alvarado arrived in Chiapas from Yucatán in late March with more than four thousand soldiers. In Tuxtla Gutiérrez, Alvarado formed a citizen's committee to negotiate a political settlement with the Mapaches. Negotiations did begin and took place on an isolated hacienda in the department of Chiapa, but during one of the sessions a column of government troops under the command of Carlos Vidal closed in on the negotiators. A skirmish killed some on both sides, although the principal rebel leaders escaped. This was the same kind of treacherous tactic that led to Emiliano Zapata's assassination in April 1919, also at the hands of Carrancistas. Alvarado then turned to total war.[90]

On March 20, following the example of the Spanish army in Cuba, the U.S. army in the Philippines, and the Carrancista army in Morelos, General Alvarado ordered a program of population reconcentration in strategic hamlets ("aldeas estratégicas"). The departments of Tonalá, Tuxtla, Chiapas, and La Libertad south of the Grijalva were declared rebel zones. All inhabitants in those areas were required to resettle in government-controlled towns or they would be considered and treated as rebels after May 31, 1918.[91]

The reconcentration program, more than any single action during the revolution in Chiapas, devastated the regional economy and brought hunger and hardship to the state's population. The U.S. consul at Salina Cruz among others charged that the main result of reconcentration was "to fill the pockets of the government generals and their lieutenants, who are thus enabled to buy up the livestock and other belongings of the reconcentrated population at nominal figures, and to embitter the people against the government."[92] More people than ever, particularly small property owners, abandoned the state or joined the rebellion in 1918 rather than be shot at in the country or go hungry in the towns.[93] Governor Villanueva was not willing to pursue victory at any price and worked at cross purposes with Alvarado.[94] When villagers, rancheros, and finqueros requested permission not to reconcentrate, the governor nearly always assented.[95]

Faced with an aggressive campaign by nearly five thousand Carrancistas, Fernández Ruiz avoided battle with Alvarado. Alvarado's two lieutenants, Generals Blas Corral and Carlos Vidal, divided the state between them, the former going after Pineda and the latter after Fernández Ruiz. In April Corral attacked Pineda's base, Ocosingo, with 1,500 regulars. Pineda, with only 300 men, held out for fourteen days. On the fourteenth day Alvarado personally led an additional 500 regulars and 500 Indian troops, forcing Pineda and his men to escape during the night.[96] Corral continued to harass the Pinedistas, forcing them to break up into small groups and move into Tabasco and Guatemala. He recaptured Simojovel and Pichucalco, although in October Pineda resurfaced and briefly occupied San Cristóbal.[97]

Alvarado returned to Mexico City in the fall of 1918 to report to Carranza. He told the president with considerable exaggeration that the rebellion had been crushed and in a newspaper interview stated that three fourths of Chiapas had been pacified.[98] Alvarado returned to the state near the end of the year to mop up, although by that time much of his expeditionary force had been transferred to other parts of Mexico. Fernández Ruiz demonstrated the deficiency of Alvarado's pacification when he ambushed the famous general near La Concordia. Alvarado barely escaped to Tuxtla Gutiérrez and returned from there to Mexico City. He covered his withdrawal with declarations of victory.[99] The stalemate continued, however; the government could not pacify the countryside, the rebels could not hold the cities.

Although Alvarado left Chiapas unsuccessful, he had in fact nearly accomplished his mission. Due to the hardships imposed by this aggressive campaign the Mapaches had been reduced to fewer than 600 men by late 1918 and were runing low on arms and ammunition.

Furthermore, in late 1918 and throughout 1919 the entire state was hit hard by the Spanish influenza epidemic and a bout of malaria. Both devastated the Mapaches. In October one of the Macías brothers showed up at the Mexican legation in Guatemala asking the ambassador to arrange suitable peace terms between the warring parties. Fernández Ruiz, it seemed, was ready to talk. The legation communicated this desire to General Alvarado, who refused to discuss any terms except unconditional surrender. The legation then reported to Mexico City that due to the demoralization of the Mapaches and their lack of arms and men, 1,500 men commanded by any "respected general" (Alvarado's star was obviously in decline) could end the rebellion. The Carranza government did not heed this advice.[100]

The year 1919, from a military point of view, was relatively quiet. The only significant military action occurred near the end of the year. In November and December Fernández Ruiz routed two different Carrancista columns near Villa Flores.[101] The most heated conflict during 1919, however, took place on the political battlefield within Carrancista ranks.

POLITICS AS USUAL, POLITICS IN TRANSITION

In 1918 President Carranza ordered gubernatorial elections to be held in May 1920 in the remaining states still ruled by preconstitutional regimes. Chiapas then turned its attention to political rather than military campaigns. Two rival political camps immediately formed in Tuxtla Gutiérrez, one supporting Pablo Villanueva and the other supporting the Pichucaleño general, Carlos Vidal. State government employees, personal friends, and important Tuxtlecos formed the pro-Villanueva Partido Liberal Chiapaneco while Vidal's supporters, many of them military officers, formed the Club "Liberal Joaquín Miguel Gutiérrez." The opposing political parties were not completely unfamiliar to Chiapas. Behind Villanueva was Ramón Rabasa, Raquel D. Cal y Mayor, Raul E. Rincón, and Lisandro López—Rabacistas all.[102] Vidal had the support of the anti-reelectionist club in San Cristóbal; its leader Jesús Martínez Rojas, was Vidal's campaign manager.[103]

Vidal, more than anything else, was the all-round opposition candidate, and his program reflected his diverse constituencies. The Vidal platform was an interesting combination of Constitutionalism (support for Carrancista reforms), 1911 revanchism (economic development of the Central Highlands), and Mapachismo (a free and autonomous Chiapas).[104]

Both candidates campaigned as outsiders: Villanueva resigned his commission and ran as a civilian against a government (his own) of soldiers; Vidal ran as the military officer unstained by sordid political compromises.[105] In the towns and villages factions competing for local offices endorsed either Villanueva or Vidal. Preparations for the first round, the municipal elections of November 1919, occupied most of that year. The real issues of the local political contests had little or nothing to do with broader revolutionary, national, or even Chiapaneco questions and issues but pitted the "outs" against the "ins," one clan against another, one part of town against another.[106] Yet beginning in 1919–20 politics began to take on a new character in some areas in response to the politicization of the countryside during the long years of conflict. Political polarization appeared: Indios against ladinos, landless against landed, poor against rich, and workers against capitalists. The politics of class was beginning in Chiapas.[107]

The evolution of politics from traditional family rivalry to class polarization in Motozintla, the cabecera of the department of Mariscal, in 1919 and 1920 was pivotal in the transformation of regional politics in the 1920s. Motozintla is located in a small valley in the Sierra Madre just north of the coffee-producing region of Soconusco. For decades the Indian villages in Mariscal had provided a large part of the labor force on the coffee plantations. Thanks to the difficult terrain and their distance from Tapachula the villages had remained free, although they had been adversely affected by the reparto program before the Revolution. This unique environment provided the birthplace for the first socialist party in Chiapas.

In 1919 two political clubs were formed in Motozintla around two alliances of political clans to participate in the upcoming elections. The Club "Liberal Mariscalense," run by the Avendano, García, and Ruiz families, was organized to maintain control of the ayuntamiento and support Villanueva. Since this was the party in power it was also the party of the enganchadores, the ever-present labor contractors. The Club "Liberal Belisario Domínguez," dominated by the Velázquez, Pérez, and Zunúm families, was the opposition party. It supported Vidal, the opposition candidate.[108]

Villanueva won the first bout with Vidal when he put his supporters in most of the municipal presidencies in the 1919 elections.[109] Not surprisingly, the Club "Liberal Mariscalense" won in Motozintla.[110] Following the election the Club "Liberal Belisario Domínguez" underwent something of a transformation. Under the influence of Raymundo Enríquez, an agronomist working for the Carranza government in Soconusco, and Ricardo Alfonso Paniagua, originally from Motozintla and in 1919 a representative of the Socialist Party of Michoacán, the party broadened its base to include Indian workers and women. In the last days of December 1919 the district judge in Motozintla reported that "for several nights Mendoza [leader of the Club "Liberal Belisario Domínguez"] and others have held secret meetings, with the indigenous class armed with clubs, machetes, and firearms; it is rumored that the leaders will effect an uprising tomorrow."[111] Several meetings were held during the first two weeks of January 1920, leading to the formation of the Partido Socialista Chiapaneco (PSC) on January 13.[112]

The PSC, reported Motozintla municipal president Avendano, was a "true workers' mob" of more than 200 members, which he characterized as "very advanced bolshevik socialism."[113] The PSC, according to Paniagua, "was founded with the principal object to procure the improvement of our proletarian classes."[114] The party's general program called for the socialization of land and all instruments of production, social equality, and the institution of communism in Mexico.[115] The municipal government in Motozintla used every means at its disposal to destroy the PSC: The party was denied permission to organize, meetings were disrupted by the police, and party members were arrested for agitation. Paniagua was busy organizing PSC branches elsewhere in Mariscal when the Carranza government in Mexico City and Chiapas was overthrown.[116]

VICTORY BY PERSEVERANCE

Venustiano Carranza's term of office expired in December 1920 and under the Constitution of 1917 he was ineligible for reelection. On June 1, 1919, General Álvaro Obregón announced his candidacy for the presidency of Mexico. No individual in the country had as much prestige and popularity as Obregón, who was widely believed to be Carranza's choice as his successor. Early in 1920, however, the "official" government newspaper *El Demócrata* formally launched the candidacy of Ignacio Bonillas, the Mexican ambassador to the United States and a man generally unknown in Mexico. It was a poor political move by Carranza, since as president he had alienated many generals and organized groups, and it led to his downfall.[117] Like Díaz in 1910, Carranza was "out of touch with a changing political reality, [and] sought to perpetuate his own rule in defiance of public opinion and jealous competitors for power."[118]

In April 1920 a revolutionary movement formed in the state of Sonora—Obregón's home state—under the leadership of Governor Adolfo de la Huerta. The rebellion originated in response to Carranza's efforts to impose central control, but quickly evolved into a drive to prevent Carranza from imposing and dominating his successor. Obregón, who feared government imprisonment when he was ordered to appear before a Mexico City court, joined the movement. By late April Carranza was faced with a serious revolt. Most of the revolutionary military chieftains, along with anti-Carrancistas of all colors from Zapatistas to Felicistas, followed Obregón and joined the Agua Prieta movement, named for the Sonoran town where the rebellion was proclaimed. As in late 1914, Carranza abandoned Mexico City for Veracruz. His train was attacked before it reached the port city, and the president was obliged to escape into the Puebla countryside on horseback. On the night of May 20 his pursuers found the camp of the presidential party, and the first chief of the Constitutionalist revolution was killed.

The political repercussion of these events in Chiapas, as in most states, was considerable. In March Provisional Governor Alejo González (Villanueva resigned in 1919 to run for governor) met with Fernández Ruiz, and the two agreed to suspend hostilities until mid-April. In the subsequent peace negotiations, the Mapache caudillo agreed to drop his demand for the immediate withdrawal of federal troops from Chiapas if the new government incorporated the Mapaches into the federal military. Fernández Ruiz also sought forgiveness of rural property taxes during the period of the revolution and the suspension of future taxes for three years for the purpose of reconstruction. He demanded agreement by the federal government to build a railroad into the interior of Chiapas, the division of national lands for the benefit of the "proletarian class," and the free election of an entirely Chiapaneco government.[119]

In April the question of negotiation became irrelevant as the Carrancista government of Alejo González began to collapse. Early in the month Albino Lacunza, the commander of the government garrison in Villa Flores, joined the Mapaches in seconding the Agua Prieta Movement. Fernández Ruiz declared himself first chief of the Obregonista movement in Chiapas. On May 1, the 150-man garrison in Chiapa de Corzo pledged its loyalty to Obregón and Fernández Ruiz. Five days later gubernatorial candidate Carlos Vidal went over to the Agua Prieta movement, and most of the federal army in Chiapas followed his lead.[120] General González abandoned Tuxtla Gutiérrez on May 18 with nearly 1,000 men and tried unsuccessfully to join Carranza in Veracruz. Fernández Ruiz occupied the state capital four days later. Perseverance had won the war; "la revolución mapachada" had triumphed.[121]

Throughout the country, as in Chiapas, Agua Prieta "afforded an opportunity for wholesale deals, surrenders and submissions, which achieved, within months, a degree of pacification the country had not known for years."[122] By declaring his adherence to the Agua Prieta movement in its early stages Fernández Ruiz won the goodwill of the new authorities in Mexico City. Early in June, Interim President Adolfo de la Huerta chose Francisco Ruiz, a Mapache commander, interim governor of Chiapas. Fernández Ruiz was designated chief of military operations in the state of Chiapas and his rank of general of division was confirmed by the president. The Mapache army was incorporated into the federal army. In July Carlos Vidal, Francisco Ruiz, Héctor Macías, and Alberto Pineda endorsed Tiburcio Fernández Ruiz for constitutional governor of the state. Running unopposed, Fernández Ruiz won the November election and took office on December 1, 1920.[123]

Another, very different group also won political power late in 1920. The collapse of Carrancista rule had local as well as statewide consequences. In some localities Vidalista parties joined the Agua Prieta movement and, with military support, overturned local governments. Such was the case in Motozintla. Ricardo Alfonso Paniagua placed Partido Socialista Chiapaneco members in the Mariscal electoral college and elected in November a "socialist" municipal government.[124] The stage was set for the politics of the 1920s and 1930s.

REFLECTIONS

The Mexican Revolution in Chiapas was a strange affair. As in previous national upheavals, political-military struggles for power among different elite groups convulsed the region. The landowners of the Central Valley successfully defended their power against an opposing regional elite in 1911. The unity of the Central Valley was shattered in 1914 by an invading army of a distant revolution. Some finqueros and rancheros of tierra caliente, primarily those near Tuxtla Gutiérrez, accepted the new order and made it their own, benefiting from modernizing capitalist reforms. Others, landowners from the more isolated reaches of the Central Valley and the highlands, resisted the invaders and their reforms and eventually came to power.

The specter of class conflict, along with the earlier defeat of Cristobalense revanchists in 1911, redirected the attention and energy of the familia chiapaneca from the rivalry between tierra fría and tierra caliente. Hard feelings survived in San Cristóbal, but the city's champion, Alberto Pineda, was incorporated into the national army and transferred to Tabasco in 1923. His participation and defeat in the 1923–24 de la Huerta rebellion put a stop to his political career until the mid-1930s. Elected mayor of San Cristóbal in 1936, Pineda saw his municipal government dissolved by the state government in Tuxtla one year later, allegedly for financial irregularities.[125] Regionalism no longer propelled provincial politics in postrevolutionary Chiapas.

And what about the rural population of village farmers and landless campesinos? They were drawn into a storm of destruction and suffering. They fought on both sides. Many left their patrons and repudiated their debts, refused to pay rent, took land, and overturned local bosses. This was not their fight, however; they had not risen up in insurrection. Certainly the rural Chiapanecos were more politicized by 1920, but they were not mobilized for political action as in many regions of Mexico. The campesinos of Chiapas emerged from the civil wars freer but directionless and therefore open to mobilization and control from above by soldiers, politicians, bureaucrats, and . . . landowners.

PART 3

"Unfortunately, nothing has yet been done to
free the peasant from the politician."

Marjorie Ruth Clark, *Organized Labor in Mexico* (Chapel Hill: The
University of North Carolina Press, 1934), pp. 161–62.

Copy of a card that reads in part: "The servant
Tomás Morales is from today under the protection of
the Chiapanecan Socialist Party. July 20, 1922." This
document shows the birth of modern politics.

MOBILIZATION
1920-50

(or the revolutionary organization of the "popular masses" in their own political and economic marginalization)

THE RETURN TO PEACE AND ORDER WAS THE IMMEDIATE AND MOST important task facing Mexican government in 1920. The process of returning to an orderly national political system, supervised by the government in Mexico City, would not be quick or easy after a decade of civil war, political fragmentation, peasant rebellion, and labor organization. The reality of regional warlords was an additional obstacle. The mechanisms used by Porfirio Díaz and Venustiano Carranza for political consolidation were no longer applicable. Mexico was entering the age of broad and popular participation in politics, and therefore the support of organized workers and organized campesinos, as well as generals, bankers, and the United States, was necessary. Postrevolutionary governments were forced to mobilize popular support for political survival. Workers and campesinos mobilized in the expectation of pressuring reluctant governments to fulfill the promises of the Revolution. Nothing was done, however, as Marjorie Ruth Clark put it in 1934, "to free the peasant from the politician." And the politician in Chiapas, after as well as before the Revolution, was increasingly indistinguishable from the merchant and the landowner.

Campesinos in Chiapas had not rebelled against the Porfirian order either before or during the Revolution, whether under the leadership of one of their own or that of a champion from the "progressive bourgeoisie." Mass mobilization in Chiapas, as in Yucatán, Veracruz, Michoacán, and other states, came in the 1920s and 1930s in the context of local and regional political struggle. The development of labor unions and agrarian leagues was not spontaneous; the Partido Socialista Chiapaneco began in 1920 as a small but genuinely popular movement—

"from below"—of social and economic struggle. Before the PSC had a chance to become a politically powerful and autonomous threat to landowners, it was patronized and coopted by regional politicians who represented the progressive, flexible branch of the familia chiapaneca and who granted reforms, asked for votes, and required submission. This "secondary mobilization," as Hans Werner Tobler terms it, which took place not only in Chiapas but throughout Mexico, was insufficient to protect the interests of rural workers and campesinos against landowners and the state. Moreover, like the Trojan Horse, it appeared at the moment of victory surreptitiously carrying the forces of conquest.

During the early 1930s, when the state and federal regimes were in the hands of conservative modernizers, the mobilized sector in Chiapas split into "official" and "dissident" wings. Opposition *agrarista* and worker organizations attached themselves to the populist presidential campaign of Lázaro Cárdenas, and subsequently were integrated into the new national and state regime. Campesinos and workers and their organizations became dependent upon the state for land, credit, work, and security. They became pawns in regional and national politics. By the 1940s the mobilized masses were immobilized by a powerful state and their own internal divisions, new-found conservatism, and—perhaps—enervation from past struggles.

Through it all the landowners of Chiapas emerged with their modernizing program and economic interests largely intact. This result was not owed to class solidarity or any Machiavellian strategy of reformism. The familia chiapaneca, always a most fractious clan, both resisted and adapted to changing circumstances. Rivalry between tierra caliente and tierra fría was supplanted by rivalry between progressive reformers and conservative modernizers. In retrospect, it is clear that the division and conflict among landowners was most fortuitous for them, since it allowed some to champion and lead a popular yet measured struggle against others who were depicted as "reactionary capitalists" and "latifundistas." Social reform served the cause of modernization in ways rarely expected or understood, but it was the impressive results that counted most. Modern commercial agriculture expanded and prospered. On the other hand, ejido and smallholder subsistence agriculture, the economic base for most of the population, stagnated—thereby providing surplus laborers to the commercial farmers. Chiapas, as a result, remained a rich land with poor people.

6

IN DEFENSE OF CLASS INTERESTS

THE MAPACHE GOVERNMENT OF TIBURCIO FERNÁNDEZ RUIZ FROM 1920 to 1924 concerned itself primarily and almost exclusively with the welfare of the landed class. Ironically, the Mapaches demonstrated how not to protect the interests of finqueros in an age of mass politicization and nationalized politics. An alliance of former Carrancistas, organized workers, and agraristas arose in opposition. It politically defeated the Mapache regime with central government help and established a reform government in 1925. Political struggle in Chiapas during the 1920s was, in the words of Socialist Party leader Ricardo Alfonso Paniagua, "in defense of class interests."[1] Regional history of the 1920s, in fact, provided two quite different examples of government defense of the interests of landowners: one narrow and obsolete, the other inclusive, modern, and ultimately successful. Mobilization of the masses in Chiapas from above, manifestly for their economic liberation and advancement, ultimately served to further modernize the regional economy and preserve the great inequalities of wealth and power.

MAPACHE RECONSTRUCTION

The priorities of the government of Tiburcio Fernández Ruiz (1920–24), for the most part, matched those of President Álvaro Obregón who was similarly elected to a four-year term in 1920. Both began the task of political consolidation and economic reconstruction. The crucial difference was Obregón's recognition of the political importance of the organized working class and agraristas.

Much needed to be done. Evidence of the destructive nature of the civil war existed in nearly every district and municipality in Chiapas. Ángel Primo, a finca manager from Mapastepec, wrote in 1920 that "all the neighboring ranches and plantations have almost disappeared owing to the past revolution."[2] Governor Fernández Ruiz informed the president in 1921 that all telegraph and telephone lines as well as roads had been "totally destroyed and neglected during the period of struggle."[3] The Panamerican Railroad was in serious disrepair, numerous fincas and businesses had been abandoned, and towns like Ocosingo, Villa Flores, La Concordia, and others that had been militarily contested stood nearly abandoned and destroyed.[4]

The reconstruction program proposed by Fernández Ruiz was Rabacista as well as Obregonista in its emphasis on roads and schools. The governor informed Obregón early in 1921 that he wished to "introduce modern systems" to regional agriculture. He asked the president to help him establish several agricultural schools and research stations; to rebuild the Industrial-Military School, a technical preparatory destroyed during the Revolution; and to grant Chiapas 250,000 pesos for road construction.[5] Despite stringent national budgets throughout his term of office, Obregón managed to meet at least in part the governor's major requests. The national government provided funding for one agricultural school, 20,000 pesos for the new Industrial-Military School, and (in 1923) a 15,000-peso monthly subsidy for road construction.[6]

Mapache reconstruction in the area of labor and agrarian reform was exactly that—the reconstruction or restoration of the Porfirian social order as much as possible. The Fernández Ruiz regime ended enforcement of the 1914 Ley de Obreros, which had abolished indebted servitude, by budgeting no funds for inspection and enforcement. Servitude, montería slavery, enganche, and tiendas de raya—abuses that had never completely disappeared—again became normal in the countryside of Chiapas.[7]

The landed class of Chiapas included 13,000 families in all, of which 300 to 500 could be classified as the elite. This group had a friend and defender in Tuxtla Gutiérrez.[8] The Mapache administration forgave unpaid property taxes during the war years and extending into 1920 and 1921. Scores of landowners were given liberal postponements and dispensations.[9] The Carrancista land reform had not really affected regional finqueros, since 72 landowners still owned 20 percent of all private property. The Mapache regime was certainly not inclined to alter land tenure in any meaningful way. In 1921 the state government promulgated a state agrarian law that affected only properties of more than 8,000 hectares, or about 70 fincas. In accordance with this law landowners were required to designate the 8,000 hectares they wished to keep. Then, working with the State Commission of Fractional Division, finqueros were required to sell the excess property to willing buyers in twenty annual payments.[10] A few villages, frustrated by the interminable delay of the federal agrarian reform program, purchased land under the terms of this law. Unlike the federal program, which was centered on the restitution of land to villages, state legislation favored individuals with sufficient capital to establish small to medium-size farms. Chiapas's ceiling limit of 8,000 hectares was one of the highest in the nation.[11]

In Chiapas the federal agrarian program was administered with little enthusiasm or energy. According to the enabling legislation, only villages with political status (thus excluding residents of fincas) could petition for the restitution of lands illegally alienated or for outright grants of land. Petitions were first presented to the state Agrarian Commission (CLA) and investigated by agricultural engineers as to the validity of the claim and the need for land. Petitions approved by the CLA and the governor were then passed on for inspection to the National Agrarian Commission (CNA) while at the same time the land was provisionally granted to the village. When petitions were approved by the CNA, the president would sign the title, making definitive the grant or restitution.[12] "The powers granted to the state governors by the agrarian laws," notes Dudley Ankerson, "gave them control over the pace of land reform."[13] The Chiapas CLA was staffed by landowners who held little sympathy for even the idea of land reform.[14] The Mapache CLA employed only two agricultural engineers, a reduction from six during the Carrancista period. Judicial interference—restraining orders from district judges—also contributed to the near nullity of land reform in Chiapas.[15] According to the *Memorias* of the National Agrarian Department, the Fernández Ruiz regime approved only nine provisional restitutions benefiting just over 1,000 families. (The governor, on the other hand, claimed fourteen restitutions.)[16] In comparison, Governor

Adalberto Tejeda of Veracruz during the same time span pushed forward 154 grants or restitutions benefiting 24,000 campesinos.

The political composition of the state government was almost entirely Mapachista. This annoyed the important political families of Tuxtla, including the newly returned Rabasa group.[17] The composition of Fernández Ruiz's government also alienated some Mapaches who expected but did not receive important positions. The Ruiz clan led by Fausto and his brothers Sóstenes, Amado, and Francisco opposed the Mapache chief (whom Fausto called "a vulgar cacique") in 1922 and 1924.[18] Fausto Ruiz, according to Luis Espinosa in 1922, "publicly swore that he would avenge the mockery of the liberty of suffrage in Chiapas with weapons in hand."[19] This split in time allowed some Mapaches to join "revolutionary" governments. The government was also oblivious to the economic needs of the Central Highlands and the Gulf Plain. Fernández Ruiz emphasized the reconstruction of the state highway from Arriago to Tuxtla Gutiérrez (by now called the National Highway) but abandoned work on the still-unfinished San Cristóbal–Salto de Agua road. Tax concessions, furthermore, were generally granted to landowners in the Mapachista departments of Chiapa and La Libertad.[20] The discriminatory nature of the Mapache regime alienated the former Carrancistas of Chiapas and their nominal chief, General Carlos Vidal, as well as highland finqueros led by Alberto Pineda, villagers petitioning for land, farm workers, and individuals who had suffered under the sometimes brutal treatment of the Mapaches during the Revolution.

PARTIDO SOCIALISTA CHIAPANECO

Despite the state government's efforts to restore Porfirian Chiapas, that era had passed. Carrancista governance and the years of disorder had disrupted the absolute power of the finqueros over villagers and workers. The number of independent villages in Chiapas had doubled between 1910 and 1921, from 300 to 600.[21] Mobilization of the rural population for land, for unions, and for power had begun throughout Mexico, and Chiapas was no exception. Popular grassroots resistance to the old social order—late in relation to many regions in Mexico—finally had begun.[22]

In the fall of 1920 PSC President Ricardo Alfonso Paniagua proposed to Carlos Vidal that they join forces. Paniagua, a genuine socialist revolutionary, was much like the Yucatecan socialist Felipe Carrillo Puerto, whom Gilbert Joseph characterizes as an "astutely pragmatic revolutionary leader."[23] Vidal, a Pichucaleño finquero and former Carrancista general, who was soon to be chief of the General Staff Division in the War Ministry under Obregón, enthusiastically agreed. He directed his friends in Tuxtla Gutiérrez to work with Paniagua to create a "Great Socialist Party." Vidal also informed Paniagua that "at all costs we need the unionization of all workers' organizations of the state in order that, as a socialist base, we can introduce in that region the dictatorship of the proletariat and end once and for all the caciques and kings who attempt to dominate that unfortunate entity."[24]

In many ways this was an ideal political alliance. Paniagua needed a powerful patron with contacts in the national capital and in Tuxtla Gutiérrez if the PSC was to have more than a local influence or even to survive. Vidal also provided the PSC federal military protection in Chiapas. Vidal, on the other hand, needed a broad base of support in his native state to further his political ambitions. Vidal, like Obregón, recognized the political usefulness of a mass base. Having secured a patron, the PSC took the offensive.[25]

During 1920 the PSC remained in the mountains of Mariscal, affecting Soconusco only to the extent of hampering the work of the enganchadores in Motozintla.[26] Beginning in 1921, however, the party began to extend its influence into the coffee zone. PSC agents visited coffee plantations—often with a guard of fifty mounted and armed men—organized unions, and tried unsuccessfully to negotiate collective contracts with the coffee planters.[27] Assisting the PSC in this region was agrarian engineer Raymundo Enríquez who was well known in the villages as a sympathetic agrarian.[28] In April 1921 a special commissioner, appointed by Fernández Ruiz to look into the planters' complaints, reported that the PSC had caused "demoralization, disorder, and the abandonment of work, leaving the coffee enterprises in a difficult situation."[29]

Agitation by the socialists led to the formation in the spring of 1922 of the Sindicato de Obreros y Campesinos de Soconusco (the Workers' and Peasants' Union of Soconusco), headed by Pompeyo Cárdenas of Tuxtla Chico and affiliated with the powerful national labor sindicate, the Confederación Regional Obrera Mexicana (CROM). The Sindicato, according to a manifesto by local planters, "is pursuing an effort sufficiently pernicious to society and to the hacendados of this region."[30] In particular, the planters complained of the issuance of cards by the PSC to members of the Sindicato informing contractors, foremen, and local officials that the holder of the card was not to be molested. These cards, according to the planters, made campesinos believe that "they should respect no authority."[31]

By the fall of 1922 the first workers' organization in Chiapas confronted the coffee planters. With only one or two weeks before the beginning of the harvest, the PSC called a strike in the coffee zone by members of the Sindicato de Obreros y Campesinos.[32] The strike, which began on September 22, 1922, with the participation of between 5,000 and 7,000 workers, lasted only two days. State government troops killed one of the strike leaders and jailed twenty more, while planters provided a large payment to the federal army zone commander to restore order.[33] Fearful of losing the harvest, however, the planters agreed to an eight-hour work day, schools on the major plantations, and the liquidation of workers' debts at the end of each year. This first confrontation, although not entirely successful for the workers, did foment "true alarm among the finqueros of the coffee zones."[34] The PSC also began to mobilize workers and villagers to act on behalf of their political as well as economic interests.

THE 1922 ELECTIONS

Politics in Chiapas in the 1920s was significantly more complicated than it had been before the Revolution. The political channels of control, administration, and communication had expanded from 12 powerful jefes políticos to 110 weak municipal presidents. The diffusion of political power was enhanced by powerful finqueros, whose extralegal power and authority exceeded that of many municipal presidents. This political environment was further complicated by federal military commanders, labor unions, and village agrarian committees. The potential for conflict among these different and often rival power centers was substantial and multiplied the difficulties of any state government in establishing and maintaining political control. The one significant exception to this was the indigenous municipality. The state government was able to reestablish in Indian villages the high degree of political control that existed before 1910.[35]

The government of Fernández Ruiz certainly spared no effort to establish political dominance in Chiapas in preparation for the 1922 elections. The regime elevated villages to municipal status or diminished them to *agencias municipales* depending on their degree of support for the regime. Communities pushing for land reform were frequently converted into agencias municipales governed by officials appointed by the governor.[36] Another method of political control was the cooptation of village agrarian committees. In the village of Copoya (Cintalapa), for example, the agrarian executive committee was appointed by the CLA, an illegal action. Besides politically supporting the state government this agrarian committee relegated landless campesinos to poor-quality national lands and even charged rent for the parcels.[37] In Soconusco the state government was closely identified with the political party "Orden, Unión, y Trabajo," which had been formed by the Tapachula Cámara de Agricultura, an organization of coffee planters.[38]

The political opposition that developed in 1922 previewed the "new politics" of postrevolutionary Chiapas. The opposition leadership at the state and local levels was not significantly different, in terms of social class, from that of the Mapache government. Landowners, large and small, predominated. Prominent Central Valley finqueros, such as Juan Cano, Reynaldo Yañez, Ezequiel Burguete, Carlos Castañón, Pomposo Castellanos, and others, were Vidalistas.[39] The opposition incorporated those who had been frozen out of the Mapache regime—namely, former Carrancistas—and notable political figures of Tuxtla Gutiérrez, San Cristóbal, Tonalá, and Pichucalco.[40] (Only in Soconusco was political conflict essentially organized as class conflict.) The significant difference between the two political groups was in their base of support in the countryside. The Mapaches relied on the traditional hierarchical relationship between the principal landowner, neighboring rancheros, and their dependent foremen, workers, and villagers.[41] The socialist opposition, in contrast, depended upon a small but expanding base of labor unions and agrarian committees. These groups were mobilized to struggle on behalf of their own local interests in wages and land and of local power that advanced the regional power of the leadership.

General Carlos Vidal became the titular head and political director of the opposition. Manuel de J. León directed the ex-Carrancista wing in Tuxtla Gutiérrez as president of the Comité Chiapaneco de la Confederación Revolucionaria (Chiapaneco Committee of the Revolutionary Confederation, or CCCR). The CCCR proposed "revolutionary socialism" as its program, nominated Carlos Vidal for senator, and presented a slate of candidates for the national legislature, state legislature, and municipal governments.[42] The PSC in Mariscal and Soconusco, although part of the CCCR, had its own regional slate of candidates, which included Raymundo Enríquez for national deputy. Vidalistas throughout the state used village agrarian committees as ready-made political action groups and shadow municipal governments. In Soconusco and Mariscal the Vidalistas had a well-organized base in the Sindicato de Obreros y Campesinos and were protected by a federal regiment commanded by Colonel Luis Vidal, brother of Carlos.[43]

The Mapaches were determined to win the fall elections despite the apparent growing unpopularity of the government in the towns and the countryside. They employed various forms of political imposition. In Huehuetán (Soconusco), for example, the pro-regime ayuntamiento held no elections at all and simply named its own replacement.[44] "The municipal president," noted Luis Espinosa in an interview, "was the soul of the official imposition."[45] Opposition leaders throughout the state were arrested before the election, voting booths were set up on pro-Mapache fincas, and ballots were selectively given to voters in several localities to ensure favorable outcomes.[46] Nevertheless, Vidalistas won elections in about forty-two of fifty-seven towns in the state. Governor Fernández Ruiz, however, with control of the state legislature, "did not hesitate to declare such elections null and void and name members of his own political party to substitute for those who were imposed."[47] This blatant political imposition met with resistance.

THE PEOPLE ROSE UP IN ARMS

Immediately following the state legislature's nullification of the pro-Vidalista election victories and the installation of the new ayuntamientos, violence broke out in the departments of Mariscal and Soconusco. The U.S. vice-consul reported that "the people rose up in arms against the governor of the state."[48] Imposition in Motozintla sparked a demonstration march to the municipal palace and demands for a change of power. The city police fired into a crowd, and the mob then attacked the building, killing the new municipal president and some policemen.[49] The district judge subsequently ordered the army to arrest and imprison more than eighty campesinos, all members of the PSC.[50]

In January 1923 an "ejército reorganizador" was formed in Soconusco by Colonel Luis Vidal. This people's army included as many as 1,000 coffee workers, most of whom were members of the Sindicato de Obreros y Campesinos. It threatened ayuntamientos in Huehuetán, Tapachula, Huixtla, Tuxtla Chico, Escuintla, and Metapa, sparking federal intervention.[51] President Obregón sent Gobernación Secretary Plutarco Elías Calles, Secretary of War Francisco Serrano, and a confidential agent to investigate the Chiapas uprising.[52] Calles failed to reach an understanding with Fernández Ruiz, so Obregón called the governor to Mexico City, told him to appoint a provisional governor to enact the necessary conciliatory measures, and threatened to remove all federal army units from the state if he did not cooperate.[53] As a result, Fernández Ruiz appointed Manuel E. Cruz, a member of the state administration's inner circle, as provisional governor. Cruz placed the blame for the impositions on Fernández Ruiz's right-hand man, Secretary General of Government Amadeo Ruiz, who was dismissed. He also ordered two new municipal elections and the reinstatement of duly elected officials who had been deposed after the elections. Cruz asked the state legislature to pass an amnesty law clearing the Vidalistas of criminal liability, but the deputies refused. When Fernández Ruiz returned to office he decreed the amnesty desired by Obregón.[54]

The final results of the 1922 elections were mixed. The state legislature returned with a Mapache majority, and there was a fairly even split in the political composition of the municipal governments. In the Chiapas deputation to the national legislature, however, only two Mapaches were elected.[55]

The Fernández Ruiz regime, despite the rebellion and Obregón's disapproval, repeated the same "electoral tactics" in the 1923 municipal elections. In November Miguel Pino y Farrera, an officer of the PSC and editor of the Arriaga newspaper *Hombre Libre,* was arrested for sedition, apparently for promoting several socialist candidates.[56] Notwithstanding numerous abuses and illegalities, the state government again lost political elections in the most important towns in the state. And again, the state legislature voted to give the governor the power to name "provisional" ayuntamientos if citizens' groups in the municipalities requested the nullification of the election. This technique permitted the governor legally to impose politically acceptable municipal governments throughout Chiapas.[57] Again, Vidalistas took up arms to resist imposition—this time during a national insurrection.

THE DE LA HUERTA REBELLION

The dominant political theme of the government of Álvaro Obregón was accommodation and conciliation. Only by such a policy could his regime hope to survive in the dangerous political climate of postrevolutionary Mexico. Nevertheless, this government alienated several powerful groups in the country, a situation which perhaps was unavoidable. In his campaign to reform and tame the new revolutionary military, Obregón discharged nearly one half of the army and numerous generals. His diplomatic agreements with the U.S. government on claims, petroleum, and agrarian expropriations won the disapproval of ultranationalists, and his designation of the then-perceived radical Plutarco Elías Calles as his successor frightened conservatives. The succession question also antagonized former interim president Adolfo de la Huerta, the finance secretary under Obregón and a presidential hopeful.[58]

In December 1923, thirty-six generals leading fully one half of the army joined Adolfo de la Huerta in rebellion against Obregón and his "impositional tendencies." Originating in Veracruz, the movement was rapidly seconded by political and military leaders in several states, including Chiapas's neighbors Oaxaca and Tabasco. Fernández Ruiz remained loyal to Obregón, but his state government faced serious threats from without and within.[59]

Inside Chiapas a popular rebellion broke out against the Mapache regime of greater magnitude than the one that had begun the year. On December 28, Colonel Victórico Grajales, municipal president of Chiapa de Corzo, initiated the uprising. "Chiapas is one of the states," he proclaimed, "perhaps the only one in the republic, that is ruled by an antirevolutionary government."[60] Grajales, a former Carrancista and political ally of Vidal, was careful to affirm that his movement, although locally seditious, was loyal to the government of Obregón. The rebellion in Chiapa de Corzo was soon joined by independent groups in Comitán, Jiquipilas, Cintalapa, and Pichucalco.[61] The Partido Socialista in Mariscal and Soconusco formed the Voluntary Socialist Corps of the Southeast to defend the Obregón regime against Delahuertistas but was prepared to watch the Fernández Ruiz regime be overthrown.[62] While agrarians in many parts of the country came to the defense of the Obregón government, in Chiapas the emerging agrarian movement not only supported Obregón but also rebelled against a loyal state government.

The most serious defection originated outside Chiapas. Alberto Pineda and his 2,500-man sixty-seventh Mounted Regiment joined rebel general Carlos Greene in a successful siege of Villahermosa, state capital of Tabasco. Early in 1924 Pineda invaded Chiapas and took San Cristóbal Las Casas. Fernández Ruiz, as a precaution, moved his government to Tapachula, the headquarters of federal zone commander Donato Bravo Izquierdo. Of all the insurrections in Chiapas, only Pineda's was genuinely Delahuertista (anti-Obregón) and considered a serious threat by General Bravo.[63]

General Bravo, now the real power in Chiapas, negotiated a temporary truce with Colonel Grajales for the duration of the national rebellion and permitted no state government military action against the anti-Mapache rebels. This decision was motivated by Bravo's assessment that the real enemy was Pineda and by Bravo's reluctance to declare war against the political allies of his military superior, General Carlos Vidal.[64] General Bravo reactivated Colonel Grajales's commission and transferred him and his volunteer regiment to fight in Tabasco. The general also armed the PSC, which sent its workers' battalion to fight Pineda. Bravo Izquierdo understood local politics and prevented the state from becoming a redoubt for the Delahuertistas, which would have prolonged the rebellion.[65]

Having successfully postponed the political struggle in Chiapas until after the suppression of the national rebellion, General Bravo began his campaign against Pineda in April 1924. Pineda, in league with generals César A. Lara and Candido Aguilar, held several defensive positions in the Central Highlands. Throughout April and May, state and federal forces pushed Pineda back in several bloody encounters. Although Pineda was finally forced into Guatemala in July, he had fought one of the most aggressive campaigns in the state's history.[66] The Delahuertista rebellion signaled the first phase of the 1924 electoral struggle for power in Chiapas. Fernández Ruiz's poor handling of the agrarian question in Chiapas, which produced the incipient rebellion, undermined his usefulness to Mexico City. Vidal's socialist allies emerged in a stronger position since they had been armed by federal forces. They were mobilized and prepared to wage an aggressive political campaign.[67]

THE TRIUMPH OF LABORISM

"The man that will augur the triumph of laborism in Chiapas,"[68] Carlos Vidal, met with President Obregón in mid-1924. Vidal came away from the interview believing he had the president's tacit support for his bid to become governor of Chiapas. Vidal and his campaign manager, PSC chief Ricardo Alfonso Paniagua, then launched an all-out political struggle, secure in the knowledge that the federal government would support the effort.[69]

Governor Fernández Ruiz, as before, spared no effort to control and win the July election. In June, the governor took a three-month leave of absence to direct the campaign for his hand-picked successor, Luis Ramírez Corzo, and to promote his own candidacy for the federal Senate.[70] He appointed his nephew, Félix García, provisional governor and placed nearly one thousand state militiamen in the municipalities to ensure an orderly and predictable election.[71] According to a confidential agent of the gobernación secretary, the governor removed all municipal presidents not in sympathy with the Mapache regime. "Systematic opposition was practiced toward Vidal and the candidates for the legislature on his ticket. . . . The municipal governments refused to register their candidacies, stamp their ballots or allow their representatives to be part of the electoral colleges."[72] The state Agrarian Commission (CLA) installed several village agrarian committees that worked to elect the government's slate of candidates rather than, according to one complaint, "attending to our petitions for land."[73]

The Vidalistas were better organized in 1924. The PSC had become the parent political organization encompassing a federation of opposition clubs and parties, nearly sixty in all, located throughout the state.[74] Vidal had formidable grassroots support in Chiapas and a critical asset in the friendship of the next president of Mexico, Plutarco Elías Calles.[75]

Vidalistas and Mapaches exercised little restraint in collecting votes in 1924. In one extreme case a group of Vidalistas, led by a federal army captain, captured Tuxtla Chico and stuffed the ballot box.[76] The more "normal" electoral procedure, however, involved the installation of rival polling booths, the collection and invention of votes, and the declaration of victory by each side.[77] The retiring Mapache legislature in the summer of 1924 discarded the returns of fifty-eight districts, out of a total of sixty-two, which favored Vidal for governor. In response, Colonel Julio Gutiérrez, garrison commander of Tuxtla Gutiérrez, angrily arrested the entire state legislature on October 23.[78]

At the end of October 1924 Chiapas had two state legislatures. On the day that Colonel Gutiérrez arrested the Mapache legislature, the Vidalista legislature, led by its presiding officer Ricardo Alfonso Paniagua, invaded and took possession of the legislative chamber of the government palace. Obregón ordered the federal garrison to provide security for the governor's offices but not to expel the Vidalista body.[79] On November 30, one day before the beginning of the new legislative session and the new state government, both governors-elect, Luis Ramírez Corzo and Carlos Vidal, gave President Obregón notice of their impending accession to office and both professed their loyalty.[80] Obregón let his successor, Calles, resolve the Chiapas problem.[81]

On December 1, President Calles turned the problem over to the Senate. Calles recommended that state autonomy be revoked owing to the "state of anarchy" existing in the state, and the Senate complied four days later. On December 6 Calles sent three names to the Senate, César Córdova, Eduardo Román, and Virgilio Figueroa, asking that the senators choose one as the interim governor who would preside impartially over new elections. After learning that Calles favored Córdova—an ex-Carrancista, ally of Vidal, and a director of the CNA—the Senate named him interim governor of Chiapas.[82]

Córdova arrived in Chiapas in early January 1925 and scheduled the municipal elections for April and the gubernatorial election for May. Although Córdova protested his complete neutrality, his selection as interim governor indicated Calles's support for Vidal. His first official action in Chiapas was to suspend the authority of all ayuntamientos and to name new municipal councils which, claimed the supporters of Fernández Ruiz, were completely Vidalista.[83] Ramírez Corzo, the Mapache candidate, dropped out of the race for governor.[84] The elections, although marked by violence here and there, overwhelmingly favored Vidal and his party. The Chiapas deputation to the national legislature, however, which had been accepted by the legislature, remained Mapache. Córdova turned over power to Vidal on May 20, 1925.[85]

The Vidalista political triumph in 1925 was dependent upon two interrelated advantages. First, the Chiapas opposition had organized a political base of grassroots popular support. Labor unions, socialist clubs, and agrarian committees provided Vidal with votes, fighters, and "revolutionary" legitimacy. Because these proletarian organizations were linked to national labor syndicates and agrarian and socialist parties, Vidal had allies in Mexico City. Second, Vidal had the political backing of the incoming Calles regime, which was not eager to keep in power in Chiapas a loyal Obregonista. Carrancista, and now Callista, Vidal, not Mapachista and Obregonista Fernández Ruiz, was a member of the faction—the "revolutionary family"—which had fought for the Revolution.

VIDALISMO: SOCIALISM CHIAPAS-STYLE

When Carlos Vidal became governor of Chiapas his key political ally, socialist party leader Paniagua, became director of the state Agrarian Commission and president of the state legislature.[86] The close political relationship between Vidal and Paniagua formed the true axis of Vidalismo. As soon as the new regime assumed power, the PSC established the Confederación Socialista de Trabajadores de Chiapas (the Socialist Confederation of Workers of Chiapas), Chiapas's first official labor syndicate, to unionize all workers in the state. The Confederation, of which Governor Vidal was titular head, became associated with the national labor confederation, CROM.[87]

The Partido Socialista Chiapaneco became, in effect, the official party of the state. The radical wing of Vidalismo now was the new Partido Socialista de Soconusco, headed by Ernesto C. Herrera. Calles's attorney general, Octavio Paz, on a trip to Chiapas in April 1925 described

Soconusco as "the only place in the state where the division is perfectly demarcated between the Capitalist Bourgeois Reaction and the revolutionary element which is composed almost entirely by workers and campesinos of the region, who are now perfectly organized."[88] Paniagua, it is safe to say, wanted to "Soconuscize" all of Chiapas.

Once in office Vidal cleared out all employees remaining from the previous government, reaffirmed all decrees of the pre-Constitutionalist period (1914–16), and reassured small landowners that their properties would not be subject to expropriation. Despite the administration's radical socialist guise, Vidalismo was—as G. M. Joseph characterizes Salvador Alvarado's program in Yucatán—a "blueprint for state capitalism via a populist brand of bourgeois revolution."[89] The Carrancista objective of using the state to create an equilibrium between workers and capitalists was the essence of Vidalismo. The government sought to regulate labor relations, accelerate the return of land to villages, increase the tax share of finqueros, and build schools and roads. Vidal, perhaps best described as a "revolutionary developmentalist,"[90] mobilized and befriended the impoverished and dispossessed without threatening a wholesale transformation of the social and economic order. Vidalismo represented an effort to modernize the social system as well as the economy by means of a more powerful and active state.[91]

The Vidal regime decreed three labor laws to protect the interests of both workers and employers. The first decree in 1926 established Investigative Offices of Contracts in San Cristóbal, Comitán, and Motozintla. These offfices were responsible for regulating the contract agreements and employment of Indians on the coffee plantations. All contracts had to be signed before government officials and conform to the Ley de Obreros of 1914. Inspectors from these offices were required to visit Indian villages and coffee plantations to enforce the labor reform law.[92] Also in 1926 the Vidal regime revived the Central Board of Conciliation and Arbitration, which had disappeared in 1920. The Central Board, located in the state capital, was charged with forming municipal labor relations boards composed of three representatives of workers' organizations, three representatives of employers, and a government representative. These boards were responsible for resolving all conflicts between workers and employers regarding contracts, wages, work conditions, and unionization. All labor-employer disputes first were heard before one of the municipal boards. If the dispute was not resolved at the local level and the workers were judged to have a legitimate complaint, the Central Board could then authorize a strike. The Central Board was also assigned the task of forming several regional minimum wage commissions to study and establish appropriate minimum wage scales for the different regions and agricultural tasks.[93]

The Labor Law of 1927 attempted to replace individual contracts with collective work contracts. This law required that all contracts be made with labor unions whenever possible and prohibited employers from replacing striking workers. The law also introduced the principle of profit sharing, although regulations governing this feature were never enacted. Finally, the law increased the minimum wage for unskilled labor to 1.20 pesos a day and established, for the first time, a minimum wage for piece work of 1.20 pesos for each 220 pounds of coffee beans harvested.[94] Vidalista labor legislation had three main goals: to build political support for the state government among agricultural workers; to bring the incipient regional labor movement under state government regulation and control; and to rationalize the relationship between workers and employers so as to ensure justice and productivity.

In the area of land tenure the Vidal government initiated the first serious and populist redistribution program in Chiapas, more than ten years after First Chief Venustiano Carranza had decreed national agrarian reform. The state agrarian law of 1927 permitted villages to expropriate adjoining lands and pay for them in ten annual payments at the value set forth in the notoriously undervalued tax declarations.[95] To encourage village petitions the government distributed volumes of the agrarian handbook, *Catecismo agrario,* to each municipality.[96] As a result the number of agrarian petitions increased from an average of ten per year in 1920–24 to sixty-eight in 1925 and thirty-four in 1926.[97] During the Vidal period, thirty-nine petitions were provisionally approved, distributing 80,000 hectares to 6,634 heads of families. Vidal's agrarian record compared favorably with any other state program in Mexico at the time. Realizing that campesinos needed not only land but money to work the land, Vidal sought to establish a state lending agency to provide low interest loans to poor farmers, small businessmen, and incipient industrialists. The governor proposed this plan to President Calles and asked for a three-year loan of 2 million pesos, but the president, pleading budgetary difficulties, did not back the project.[98]

Vidalista land reform, like that of the Mapache government, was not an onslaught on productive private property. The state Agrarian Commission, for the most part, provisionally granted national lands and idle lands to new ejidos.[99] Land reform was also a method of striking at political enemies and defusing agrarian radicalism, while at the same time building political support in the countryside for the state government and its semi-official party.[100]

When Carlos Vidal became governor of Chiapas the state government was bankrupt and owed back wages to its own employees. To remedy this deficit and reverse the very mild and inequitable Mapache tax policies, Vidal raised property valuations and taxes across the board. The U.S. Consul in Salina Cruz (Oaxaca) reported that "on real estate particularly, in the states of Chiapas and Oaxaca, there had been a heavy increase, not only in the rate but in the assessed valuations on both urban and rural properties."[101] One businessman reported that he had to pay 50 percent more than during the preceding year.[102] A coffee planter from Soconusco complained that on a crop of 800 tons that grossed 580,000 U.S. dollars, he had to pay 94,901 dollars in taxes, of which fully two thirds went to the state.[103] Vidal, of course, was not antagonistic to all landowners. The 1925 tax decree permitted the governor to reduce by 10 percent the fiscal value of cultivated lands if the property had suffered damages during the Revolution or the de la Huerta rebellion. This clause permitted Vidal to favor finqueros supportive of his government.[104]

Governor Vidal considered school and road construction two of the most revolutionary activities the state government could pursue. Although Vidal increased the number of state-supported primary schools in Chiapas from 60 to 90, the most significant development during the 1920s was the increase of federal intervention in education in the state. In July 1924, Professor Ricardo Sánchez, inspector of rural schools for the federal Department of Education, arrived in Chiapas to begin an intensive federal effort to increase rural schooling.[105] By 1927 the federal government financially sustained 182 schools in Chiapas, of which 159 were primaries. The federal government allocated more spending for education in Chiapas than the state government.[106] The Vidal regime did pursue a vigorous policy of requiring finqueros to build schools and employ teachers for the education of the children of workers.[107] Vidal considered road construction to be the key to future prosperity and increased spending from 5 percent of the budget under Fernández Ruiz to nearly 25 percent. The state government established a new department of roads, the Dirección General de Caminos, which employed highway engineers to survey and plan new routes. As in education, however, the federal government began to assume greater responsibility for road construction through subsidies to the state and by assigning projects to the army.[108]

The Vidalista program of reform and development was certainly not radical. In the day-to-day implementation of state programs, however, the government often squarely sided with agricultural workers and landless villagers. Governor Vidal appointed socialist party members as tax collectors, work inspectors, municipal secretaries, and municipal agents. These officials in turn established socialist party branches, labor unions, and agrarian committees across the state. In one village, for example, Vidal replaced as municipal agent an employee of the largest finca in the district with Ricardo Ruiz, a PSC member. Ruiz, according to the legal representative of the finca, "has told us that his special mission for the government is to improve conditions for workers."[109] On the finca of San Juan Chicharras in Soconusco, another municipal agent organized a union and began a strike of 200 workers to increase daily wages to one peso.[110] When Lotario Schamme, administrator of the finca "Germania," dismissed 200 workers for joining the Confederación Socialista de Trabajadores de Chiapas, the governor ordered their immediate reinstatement and mandatory arbitration.[111]

The state government often looked the other way when landless villagers invaded and seized private property. Finqueros complained frequently that "bad elements" were exploiting the workers and forcing them to take land they did not need or know how to use. One finquero complained, for example, that an agricultural engineer employed by the state, aided by the municipal president and fourteen armed men, forced himself onto his land to survey a division. "Unfortunately, many authorities in towns, like this municipal president," he correctly surmised, "believe they can win the sympathy of the governor with such savage orders."[112]

The existence of an agrarista state regime encouraged the appearance of "agrarian caciques," local bosses who used the agrarian reform system for selfish benefit. The president of the agrarian executive committee of the ejido "El Caucho," for example, used his position to sell parcels of land to residents of other villages while leaving twenty-nine of his own people landless.[113] The Indians of Cancuc (Chilón) complained in 1926 that their municipal agent forced them to carry loads for less than they earned before 1910, forced them into indebted servitude, and made most of his money by selling liquor to Indians. All the reforms of the Revolution, they wrote, "have only served to worsen our situation."[114] Marcos and Agustín Bravo, posing as agraristas, ruled the ejido "El Naranjo" in Soconusco as finqueros. The brothers alternated as president of the ejidal administrative committee and as municipal agent. They did not work the land but paid themselves from the ejido treasury, and expelled or brought in new members as it suited them. When CLA president Paniagua heard of this situation he expelled the pair from the state. Unfortunately there were many more unscrupulous agraristas who were not disciplined.[115] The other problem was collusion between landowners and local governments in opposing land reform. "Some municipal authorities with sufficient frequency," the governor declared, "not only obstruct the [agrarian] labor of Executive and Administrative Village Committees but even harass these Committees, even to the point of committing abuses against them, notoriously violating the law."[116]

The Vidal government in Chiapas in the mid-1920s may have represented, as Marx and Engels wrote in the *Communist Manifesto*, "a part of the bourgeoisie . . . desirous of redressing social grievances, in order to secure the continued existence of bourgeois society."[117] It is safe to say, however, that Vidal and Vidalistas did not possess such a farsighted understanding of Vidal's place in (regional) history. He was a "revolutionary caudillo," and as such he believed not only in the importance of his reforms in creating a more just and equitable social system but also—and more importantly—in the political utility of reform in mobilizing worker and peasant support for his regime.

HELL HAS BROKEN LOOSE IN CHIAPAS

Postrevolutionary federal-state relations during the 1920s constituted a mosaic of alliances between governors and regional caudillos,
and national leaders. Governors were Obregonistas or Callistas of vary-
ing loyalty and sincerity. An analyst for the U.S. War Department wrote
in 1926 that "a governor who wishes to retain his Governorship must
be in accord, or pretend to be in accord, with the leaders who control
the Federal Administration. If he is not, means are generally found to
put him out and to replace him, eventually, by a person who will support
the plans of those who rule."[118] Vidal learned this lesson in 1927.

In 1926 former president Álvaro Obergón violated the most sacred
tenet of the 1910 Revolution when he decided to seek reelection and
succeed Calles in the presidency in 1928. At the end of the year the
Obregonista bloc in the federal legislature led a successful effort to
amend the constitution to permit one nonconsecutive presidential reelection. Two presidential hopefuls, however, generals Arnulfo R. Gómez
and Francisco R. Serrano, continued their candidacies. In June 1927,
Gómez was nominated for president by the Anti-Reelectionist Party and
Serrano was nominated by the National Revolutionary Party. Obregón
officially announced his candidacy the same month.[119] As in 1910–11,
1920, and 1923, the problem of presidential succession led to a national
crisis.

The presidential campaign put the "socialist government" of Chiapas
at risk. Governor Vidal, an old friend and colleague of Serrano, became
the general's national campaign manager. According to one close observer, Vidal was "the principal axis of Serranismo."[120] Under Vidal's
instructions the Chiapas legislature refused to approve the amendment
reforming Articles 82 and 83 of the federal constitution to permit presidential reelection. (Only Veracruz took a similar defiant position.)
Senator Fernández Ruiz, not surprisingly, viewed Obregón's return to
power as the means of a Mapache restoration in Chiapas. The senator
unsuccessfully petitioned the full Senate in August 1927 to rescind the
state's autonomy and appoint a provisional governor. Fernández Ruiz
revived the Mapache (now called Obregonista) party in preparation for
the electoral struggle in 1928.[121]

In the fall of 1927 Governor Vidal took a temporary leave of absence from the state government in order to devote his full time to the presidential campaign. He appointed his brother, Luis, provisional governor. By now, however, the Serranistas correctly realized they could not peacefully compete with Obregón and Calles, and plans were made for a rebellion in conjunction with the party of General Gómez. "With these elements [against us]," argued Vidal, "it is impossible to triumph democratically, but it is possible to carry out a bloody ridicule of the vote."[122] The revolt planned for October 2, 1927, was discovered and almost immediately repressed by Calles and Obregón. The leading members of the Serranista party were captured in Cuernavaca the following day. Calles ordered the execution of the fourteen prisoners, and on the Cuernavaca–Mexico City road, near the village of Huitzilac, Vidal and the others were shot and killed.

At midday on October 3 General Manuel Álvarez, commander of the federal garrison in Tuxtla Gutiérrez, received orders from President Calles to seize control of the state government.[123] General Álvarez ordered his troops to occupy all public buildings, disarm the state and municipal police, and capture Provisional Governor Luis Vidal, PSC chief Paniagua, police chief Julio Sabines, and other high officials of the regime. As soon as Luis Vidal turned over the state treasury to General Álvarez, they were all executed.[124]

On October 4, the chief of military operations in Chiapas, General Jaime Carrillo, arrived in Tuxtla Gutiérrez from Tapachula and assumed the post of provisional governor. Carrillo replaced the ayuntamientos of every municipality in the state with appointed *juntas de administración civil* (committees of civil administration). Federal troops and Mapache vigilantes also executed tens (perhaps as many as a hundred) of Vidalistas and jailed hundreds of local and state officials throughout Chiapas. Municipal and state officials of Arriaga and Mapastepec, for example, were arrested and placed on a train for Tapachula; they were executed in transit. The municipal president of San Cristóbal Las Casas, Juan Manuel Gutiérrez, was rounded up and shot. Reports of similar executions, particularly of socialist party members, indicate a general bloodletting.[125] A North American resident of Chiapas summed up the situation fairly well in a letter to the consul: "I suppose you know that hell has broken loose in Chiapas. They have jailed or shot all the authorities and the new ones are simply playing thunder with us."[126]

Vidalismo was smashed. *Excelsiór* reported in early November that Senator Fernández Ruiz and his "Committee of Pro-Obregón Propaganda" controlled all political parties in the state.[127] This was an exaggeration. The Vidalista-socialist movement in Chiapas had been decapitated but its heart was still beating. The local socialist parties, labor unions, and agrarian committees survived. Here was the base for future state governments.

Tiburcio Fernández Ruiz would have made a good Porfirian governor of Chiapas. A law student of Emilio Rabasa and a member of the Central Valley landowning elite, he was a "modernizer" in the Rabacista mold. The times of Don Porfirio and Don Emilio were past, however. In postrevolutionary Mexico the Mapache leader practiced a "rude and anachronistic nineteenth-century political style" featuring loyalty to the national caudillo and government of, by, and for Central Valley finqueros.[128] Fernández Ruiz's obsolete politics in an age of politicized and mobilized workers and campesinos was not only unworkable but, from the perspective of the landowning elite, counterproductive. His policies served to radicalize and thus better organize the dispossessed of Chiapas against landowners. There was a better way to defend "family"—that is, landowner—interests: lead the masses through reform and politically incorporate them into the system of government. This way, they could be brought, "albeit shackled, weaponless and vulnerable,"[129] into "a situation of negotiated dependence."[130]

Carlos Vidal, one of the new breed of postrevolutionary politicians, did precisely that. A "revolutionary finquero," Vidal certainly did not seek to destroy his own class. Perhaps he understood that landowners would have to bend to survive, protecting their long-term interests by means of (in the eyes of many landowners) odious concessions. There is no doubt, however, that Vidal understood the politics of postrevolutionary Mexico. Government-controlled reform and mass mobilization bought political support and regional power. As Vidal informed labor leader Luis Morones in 1927, "The complete organization of our [labor] Confederation, gives us absolute and firm control of local politics."[131]

Vidal's mistake was to gamble on the downfall of Obregón. Vidal, not Vidalismo, failed.

7

FOR THE PURPOSE OF POLITICAL ORDER

AFTER THE FALL OF CARLOS VIDAL THE "REVOLUTIONARY ALLIANCE" HE
had fashioned with the labor and agrarian movement was institutionalized as an integral part of the state government apparatus. Labor and
agrarian support became necessary, as one dissident labor leader complained, "for the purpose of political order." Political opponents also
sought popular support in their struggles for power and influence. Because of politics as well as opposing ideologies and interests, the labor
and agrarian movement in Chiapas split into official and dissident organizations. These became part of national labor and agrarian organizations, thus integrating regional and national political struggles and
ultimately serving the cause of national political centralization. Politics
in Chiapas was also institutionalized by means of an official party that
was part of a new national revolutionary party. Centralization at the
state and national levels advanced using these new institutions—the
"official" party, the "official" labor confederation, and the "official"
agrarian league. Mobilization was becoming a straitjacket.

THE MACABRE SHADOW OF VIDAL AND PANIAGUA

At the end of 1927 the Gran Partido Obregonista de Chiapas, led by
Tiburcio Fernández Ruiz, appeared to own Chiapas.[1] As in 1920, the
elevation of Álvaro Obregón to the presidency was to be the Mapache
ticket to power. But two obstacles stood in the way. First, Plutarco Elías
Calles was president of Mexico. In 1923 Calles, as gobernación secretary, had conferred with Fernández Ruiz and come away with a distinct dislike of the governor. In 1925 Calles had helped Carlos Vidal

become governor over the opposition of Fernández Ruiz, and it was unlikely that Calles would help the staunchly Obregonista Mapaches in 1928. Second, Raymundo Enríquez inherited the political leadership of the socialist movement in Chiapas and announced his candidacy for governor in January 1928. In February, Enríquez, with the assistance of the new president of the Partido Socialista Chiapaneco, Ernesto Herrera, formed the Unión de Partidos Revolucionarios, which included twenty-two socialist, labor, and agrarista parties and organizations in the state.[2] As the Mapachista *La Voz de Chiapas* editorialized: "The macabre shadow of Vidal and Paniagua still blooms on the horizon of the Chiapaneca landscape, announcing to the people a new era of pain and misery."[3]

One week after the federal purge of the Vidalista government, the military governor appointed Federico Martínez Rojas interim governor. Martínez Rojas, municipal president of San Cristóbal Las Casas, was the son of 1911 rebel leader Jesús Martínez Rojas. He appointed Manuel Rabasa, son of former governor Ramón Rabasa, secretary general of government.[4] This political team, made up of the sons of two political enemies, demonstrated how the politics of local conflict had diminished in the face of what appeared to be a class threat. Martínez Rojas was also a partisan of Fernández Ruiz. Those Vidalistas remaining in power in the municipalities after the October purge were deposed by this new government.[5]

From the moment of the appointment of Martínez Rojas, the socialist parties, labor unions, and agrarian committees of Chiapas sent a stream of protests to Mexico City complaining how "our state has fallen into the hands of the reactionary element."[6] The governor was accused of pursuing anti-worker and anti-agrarian policies and of conniving with the clerical element.[7] Calles sent confidential agents to Chiapas who confirmed the allegations. In March, at the request of the president, the Senate removed Martínez Rojas and appointed former Carrancista Amador Coutiño interim governor. Coutiño placed Enriquistas in the municipal presidencies in preparation for the gubernatorial election.[8]

Three candidates entered the campaign in 1928: Luis C. García, Raymundo Enríquez, and Rafael Cal y Mayor. The relatively unknown Colonel García was the Mapache candidate. The Garciístas claimed the support of fifty-seven parties in the state and the moral support of the former governor of Tabasco (and anti-Vidalista) Tomás Garrido Canabal. The best the Garciístas could say about their candidate was that his opponent, Enríquez, was a Vidalista.[9] Raymundo Enríquez, originally from Chiapa de Corzo, was thirty-five years old in 1928. He was a graduate of the National Agricultural College and had served two terms (1920–22 and 1926–28) in the national legislature. In 1920 Enríquez was instrumental in creating the PSC, and in 1922 he helped establish the first labor federation in Chiapas. He had been a close friend and political ally of Ricardo Alfonso Paniagua (and therefore Carlos Vidal) and possessed impeccable agrarian and labor credentials; he was Vidal's logical successor.[10] Almost at the last moment, former Zapatista Rafael Cal y Mayor joined the race. Cal y Mayor, president of the Partido Nacional Agrarista, had little organized support in Chiapas. He believed, however, that he was the most acceptable candidate to the national government.[11]

The campaign and election in 1928 were fairly typical for Mexico during the 1920s. Enríquez was firmly supported by Governor Coutiño who suspended payment of government salaries to fund the campaign.[12] The Garciísta party attacked socialist party offices and ran a slanderous campaign against Enríquez complete with forged documents implicating him in the assassination of Obregón.[13] In September all three candidates claimed victory, and in November all three parties installed separate state legislatures in Tuxtla Gutiérrez. Calles, however, recognized only Enríquez, which prompted Cal y Mayor to withdraw immediately. On November 24 the state police arrested the entire Garciísta legislature as well as the staff of La Voz de Chiapas. Raymundo Enríquez became governor of Chiapas on December 1, 1928.[14]

A REGIME OF INSTITUTIONS

The assassination of President-elect Álvaro Obregón in July 1928 exposed the fragility of Mexico's postrevolutionary political consolidation. The partisans of Obregón had suspicions that Callista labor leader Luis Morones was the intellectual author of the crime. They were also adamantly opposed to Calles remaining in the presidency beyond the end of his term. In deference to these powerful sentiments, President Calles reassured Obregonistas that he would leave office and proposed that Mexico conclude the age of caudillos and establish "a regime of institutions." The president worked with moderate Obregonistas in the national legislature and chose one of them, Emilio Portes Gil, interim president until an election was held to choose someone to finish Obregón's term. Portes Gil, a politician who "represented the frontier between Obregonistas and Callistas," assumed office on December 1, 1928.[15]

The "regime of institutions" proposed by Calles began to take shape in late 1928 and early 1929. Before leaving the presidency, Calles formed the organizing committee of the Partido Nacional Revolucionario (PNR). A party convention was planned for March 1929 in Queretaro to inaugurate the party and select a presidential candidate. The party was organized as a coalition of existing "revolutionary" (Obregonista, Callista, and so forth) national and regional parties. Portes Gil described the PNR as

a party of the State. The Partido Nacional Revolucionario is frankly a government party. We are not going to deceive public opinion, as it has been deceived in the past, by presuming that the [PNR] will be an independent party. The revolution makes it necessary that the government have an organ of promotion and defense.[16]

Aarón Sáenz, governor of Nuevo León and director of Obregón's reelection campaign, appeared to be the popular choice as the PNR's presidential candidate. Calles, however, saw Sáenz as a potential threat to his authority and chose Pascual Ortiz Rubio, a little-known and even less distinguished regional politician turned diplomat. The PNR convention nominated Ortiz Rubio on March 2, 1929. The following day diehard Obregonistas rebelled, led by General Gonzalo Escobar. The government put down the rebellion in May, and Ortiz Rubio was elected president in July and took office in December.[17]

The political posturing between Obregonistas and Callistas was replicated in Chiapas. Interim Governor Coutiño, an Obregonista with agrarian credentials, had no intention of giving Raymundo Enríquez a free hand in governing Chiapas. The Unión de Partidos and the state legislature were led by partisans of the former interim governor. In November 1928 the Unión de Partidos endorsed Aarón Sáenz and in

December it loyally adhered‧to the PNR. At the PNR convention in Querétaro the Chiapas delegation was instructed to vote for Sáenz even though it was clear that Calles supported Ortiz Rubio.[18] The Enríquez government, however, quickly maneuvered to take political control of Chiapas. In February 1929 the governor traveled to Mexico City to consult with Calles. After his return, Enríquez visited Mariscal and Soconusco dispensing favors and conferring with the leaders of the local labor movement seeking political support. In March the state government established a 2,000-man "social defense force," which was placed under the authority of a trusted Enriquista.[19]

Enríquez made his first overt move in May when he deposed the pro-Coutiño municipal government of Tuxtla Gutiérrez. In August he forced the resignation of César Ruiz, the Coutinista director of the Unión de Partidos. By September the Unión de Partidos was solidly Enriquista with the exception of Propaganda Secretary Ernesto Herrera, president of the Partido Socialista de Soconusco (PSS) and municipal president of Tapachula.[20] The Coutiño group then struck back. On September 18 six state legislators met in a Tuxtla Gutiérrez hotel, accused the governor of misappropriation of public funds, withdrew their recognition of the government, and called on the Senate to intervene and depose Enríquez. The governor promptly arrested the dissident deputies, expelled them from the legislature, and called up six loyal alternates. Calles, the Senate, and the national leadership of the PNR backed the governor. In early October Ernesto Herrera resigned his post as municipal president and socialist party president, and left Chiapas in forced exile.[21] By the end of 1929 Governor Enríquez had consolidated his power in Chiapas by allying with Calles and becoming part of the new institutionalized political order. Powerful enemies still threatened from without.

PEASANT AND WORKER CONFEDERATION OF CHIAPAS

Others besides Amador Coutiño sought political influence in Chiapas: Tomás Garrido Canabal, caudillo of the state of Tabasco; former Zapatista Rafael Cal y Mayor; and the small but growing communist-led labor movement in Soconusco. These threats forced Enríquez to seek not simply an alliance with the labor movement in Chiapas as had

Vidal, but total government domination through institutionalization. The defection of Ernesto Herrera had shaken Enríquez's confidence in the political fidelity of the Soconusense socialists. The labor movement, furthermore, was much larger and more heterogeneous than in 1925. Enríquez was forced to create, in political self-defense, a new mechanism for the political control of organized rural farm labor.

Thomás Garrido Canabal, governor of Tabasco (1922–26) and a staunch Obregonista, had been strongly opposed to the government of Carlos Vidal because of its lenient anti-clericalism and its attachment to the national labor federation, CROM. In 1926 Garrido had even demanded Vidal's resignation. An additional source of conflict was the desire by both governors (like Felipe Carrillo Puerto before them who tried and failed[22]) to unify in one labor organization all rural workers in Chiapas, Tabasco, and Yucatán. Vidal envisioned this unification taking place under the direction of CROM and his own Confederación Socialista de Trabajadores. Garrido, on the other hand, wanted it carried out by his Liga Central de Resistencia.[23]

Garrido made his move into Chiapas one month after Vidal's execution in Huitzilac. Two Ligas de Resistencia were formed in the departments of Pichucalco and Palenque.[24] At the same time several small unions of banana workers were established in Chiapas under the control of the Garridista Liga de Productores de Rotán (League of Banana Producers). This move into Chiapas was facilitated by the fact that Pichucalco and Palenque were under the military authority of the chief of military operations of the state of Tabasco.[25] Garrido also had a close relationship with Fernández Ruiz, and in 1928 the Mapachista Gran Partido Obregonista named the Tabasqueño honorary vice-president.[26] Garrido became governor of Tabasco a second time in 1930 and continued efforts to extend his influence in Chiapas.

Enríquez also faced competition from Rafael Cal y Mayor, another Obregonista, who was ambitious to become governor of his native state. Beginning in 1929 the Portes Gil government in Mexico City showered favor on a national agrarian organization led by Cal y Mayor, the Liga de Comunidades Agrarias (League of Agrarian Communities, LCA). The national government thus attempted to check the growth of the more radical Liga Nacional Campesina (National Peasant League, LNC), which had affiliates in sixteen states and a membership of at least

300,000.[27] Cal y Mayor's LCA never came close to surpassing the influence of the LNC; it did, however, work to undermine Enríquez's control of campesino organizations within Chiapas. The LCA established leagues in Cintalapa in 1929 and in Huixtla and Pijijiapám the following year.[28] Cal y Mayor also encouraged these organizations to follow his instructions exclusively. In 1930, for example, the LCA ordered its league in Cintalapa to disregard a state government order to vacate a certain piece of property.[29] Cal y Mayor, like Garrido Canabal, was working to erode the authority of the government of Chiapas within the working-class movement.

In 1930 the communist labor movement in Chiapas offered an even greater political threat to Enríquez than Coutiño, Garrido Canabal, or Cal y Mayor. In 1928 a Bulgarian, S. Mineff, using the name "Juan Groham Bukovich," assisted by propagandists from Veracruz and local labor radicals, organized the Bloque Obrero y Campesino (Peasant and Worker Bloc) in Tapachula. (The Communist Party of Soconusco was formed at the same time.) Although avowedly communist, the Bloque remained independent of the Mexican Communist Party (PCM) from 1928 until 1931. By 1930 the organization, now called the Oposición Sindical Revolucionaria (Revolutionary Syndical Opposition), included nearly eighty local unions and agrarian committees that called themselves either communist or socialist, but not Enriquista. The communists of Soconusco furnished the most consistent opposition to expanding state government control over the worker and campesino organizations during the 1930s and 1940s.[30]

Partisans of Cal y Mayor and Amador Coutiño participated in the state elections of 1930. The PNR state committee—which was also the directorate of the Unión de Partidos—however, firmly controlled the electoral process and elected its entire slate.[31] "Before the invincible political force of the state executive committee of the P.N.R.," wrote the Enriquista *La Vanguardia,* "there is no resistance." The Coutinista *El Baluarto Chiapaneco* in Mexico City agreed but put it somewhat differently: "A government that centralizes all power solely in the person of the governor, deserves no other name than that of dictatorship."[32]

In response to the political threats of Obregonistas and communists, the Enríquez government began in mid-1930 to unify and control the labor movement of Chiapas. Following lengthy and difficult negotiations between the government and unions, the state executive committee of the PNR assembled in Ocozocoautla "the first great campesino and worker convention" and created the Confederación Campesino y Obrera de Chiapas (Peasant and Worker Confederation of Chiapas, CCOC) in March 1931. The CCOC superseded the agrarian and worker committee of the Unión de Partidos. The Sindicato de Obreros y Campesinos de Soconusco, led by Gonzalo Méndez, brought 200 representatives and formed the majority of the assembly. The communist Bloque de Obreros was not recognized by the government and was not invited. The convention disagreed only over the inclusion of migrant Indian laborers into the Soconusense federation, a modification desired by the government but resisted by Méndez, who feared a "dilution of the revolutionary fervor." The CCOC did, however, begin the unionization of highland Indians, separate from the independent socialist unions and directed and led by state politicians. The first executive committee of the CCOC was made up of genuine labor leaders, not politicians, and most were Soconusenses.[33]

One year before the state PNR selection of the next official candidate for governor, Raymundo Enríquez had begun to institutionalize within the state government the regional labor movement. In exchange for labor support of Enríquez and the state PNR, the government of Chiapas favored labor arbitrations (and sometimes agrarian petitions) of member organizations of the CCOC. Those "semi-proletarian peasants," as contemporary communists called them, were not part of the federation and had no protection from landowners. The official labor union, "one component in the government machine,"[34] had become a reality in Chiapas.

Near the end of 1929 former president Calles, the "Jefe Máximo de la Revolución," having just returned from Europe, indicated that he believed the agrarian reform program was doing more harm than good. In June 1930 he remarked that "each one of the state governments should fix a relatively short period within which the communities still having a right to petition for lands can do so; and once this period has passed, not another word on the subject."[35] The Ortiz Rubio regime then invited state governors to Mexico City and asked them to enact "stop laws" terminating the agrarian commissions in their states. Some governors, due to conviction or political pressure, did not cooperate. Raymundo Enríquez was one, for both reasons.[36]

In 1930 land tenure in Chiapas remained highly concentrated. There were 29 fincas that possessed more than 10,000 hectares; together they held more land (roughly 900,000 hectares) than the 15,000 properties of 500 hectares or less (roughly 760,000 hectares). The 1,500 fincas of 500 or more hectares possessed 79 percent of all land; the 15,000 properties smaller than 500 hectares possessed 18 percent; and the 67 ejidos listed in the 1930 census possessed only 3 percent. Agrarian reform, it seems, had barely touched Chiapas.[37]

In June 1931 the Chiapas PNR responded to a call from the national legislature for the termination of land reform in twenty days. The State PNR announced that "it would be prejudicial for Chiapas to terminate the agrarian effort."[38] Indeed, Chiapas was one of the few states to increase rather than slow the pace of its agrarian reform in 1929–32.[39] In the period 1928–32 the Enríquez government provisionally awarded 126 ejidal grants totaling some 200,000 hectares and benefiting 14,000 families. This record compares favorably to that of Governor Lázaro Cárdenas of Michoacán who during the same period granted 140,000 hectares to 180 communities.[40] In August Enríquez informed President Ortiz Rubio that "the Government of the State has resolved the agrarian question so as to abolish the law. Up to now more than one hundred thousand hectares of land have been divided."[41]

Despite Enríquez's agrarian reform effort, no wholesale transformation of the countryside took place. Finqueros organized private armies—the Mapachista valleys were especially well "defended"—to fight agraristas and intimidate villagers. The agrarista leadership of San Bartolomé was assassinated in the late 1920s; not until 1945 was another effort made to utilize the machinery of agrarian reform.[42] Landowners also divided their property among family members in order to qualify as "pequeña propiedad" (small farms) and avoid expropriation. Land granted to ejidos was often of the worst quality, poorly suited for farming and supporting families.[43] The reform bypassed the indigenous highlands altogether, as finqueros of the area prohibited the formation of any agrarista movement. And, without political pressure, the state

Agrarian Commission did not act on petitions.[44] Reform also bypassed the coffee plantations of Soconusco and elsewhere in the state. By the early 1930s there were ninety-one principal coffee plantations in Soconusco; seventy-five were the property of sixteen families.[45] Coffee groves remained secure against agrarian expropriation in both state and federal legislation until 1936. This fact helps explain the high degree of social and economic control exercised by the planters during the 1920s and 1930s. Despite a depressed world market, coffee production in Chiapas was simply too profitable and fiscally important to permit disruptions by agraristas. State taxes on coffee plantations, production, and export brought to the state treasury 60 to 80 percent of all revenue from agriculture and constituted about one third of all state income.[46] As coffee prices declined, and in response to demands by the Coffee Growers' Association of Soconusco, Governor Enríquez reduced state taxes on coffee production to help the industry.[47]

The Enríquez government also pushed labor reform, and certainly this was needed. Maya explorer Frans Blom observed in 1925 that in the Central Highlands "Indians living at large on the distant lands of the haciendas are held liable for a certain amount of labor each year, in lieu of rent. While so working they are paid, largely in credit at the local store and fed."[48] Historian Frank Tannenbaum noticed in San Cristóbal in 1927 that "the people here live largely by supplying labor to the coffee plantations in the southern part of the state.... After many months and years of labor an Indian may succeed in working off his debt, but not always."[49] To rectify abuses such as these, the state government established the Department of Labor, Proletarian Defense, and Social Welfare. This agency provided free legal counsel to workers and villagers regarding land and labor procedures or disputes, supervised labor contracting and enforcement, and supervised the municipal labor relations boards. The eight work inspectors employed by the department had the impossible task of making periodic visits to every finca within their jurisdiction to observe working conditions, negotiate collective contracts, and enforce the minimum wage law.[50] By the end of 1931 the department had supervised the negotiation of collective contracts covering 14,000 workers. There were numerous reports, furthermore, of improved conditions, payment of minimum wages, indemnification of injured workers, and fines levied on finqueros.[51] Still, the task was too enormous for the small state bureaucracy to make more than superficial improvements in the lives of rural workers.

Although Enríquez gave emphasis to rural education, the state of Chiapas continued to fall behind the pace of the national government in advancing primary education. Increased assistance from Mexico City, however, also brought meddling federal bureaucrats who sometimes came into conflict with state authorities.[52] No project interested Enríquez more than road construction. "The only three great problems of the present government," wrote the semi-official *La Vanguardia* in 1929, "without doubt are roads, roads, and roads."[53] Despite the empty treasury that he found upon taking office, Governor Enríquez devoted 20 percent of the budget to road construction, the single largest item of state expenditure. Enríquez began paving the state highway and initiated construction of three major roads. The federal government also began a yearly subsidy of 300,000 pesos for these works. "Roads," noted Enríquez (echoing Rabasa), "will be the best legacy I can leave my children."[54]

VICTÓRICO GRAJALES: GOBERNADOR FINQUERO

The struggle over succession that took place in late 1931 and early 1932 revealed the diminished political influence of the state labor-socialist movement following the creation of the Confederación Campesino y Obrera de Chiapas. In December different constituencies began to put forward possible gubernatorial candidates. Factions within the "official" labor federation proposed state deputy Antonio León as well as CCOC founder Martín Cruz. Conservative Enriquistas, headed by dissident Mapache Fausto Ruiz along with former Carrancistas César Lara and Benigno Cal y Mayor, proposed state deputy Victórico Grajales. Grajales was a well-to-do finquero and former Carrancista colonel from Chiapa de Corzo who had no formal ties with the labor-agrarian movement. In 1923 he had revolted against Fernández Ruiz and later supported the candidacy of Carlos Vidal. For these reasons, then, Grajales was a politician who was well known and respected by "the revolutionary element"—the políticos—throughout Chiapas. Most important, he was the choice of Governor Enríquez, who was also a native of Chiapa de Corzo. In April 1932 Grajales became the official nominee for governor of the Chiapas PNR–Unión de Partidos.[55]

Grajales was the only candidate for governor in 1932, and he won the election in July without one opposing vote. There was little violence, and all state PNR candidates triumphed. Antonio León and Martín Cruz were sent to Mexico City as federal deputies, out of Grajales's way. The political complexion of Chiapas changed immediately after Grajales assumed office in December 1932. Fausto Ruiz became the president of the state legislature; his brother, Sóstenes Ruiz, was elected municipal president of Tapachula. As the post in Tapachula had previously been assigned to socialist party members, ex-Mapache Ruiz's imposition was particularly insulting to organized labor and indicative of its declining political influence. The final blow, however, came during the third worker and campesino congress in March 1933. At this meeting Fausto Ruiz was elected president of the CCOC. The other seats on the executive committee were filled by politicians rather than labor leaders. The official labor organization of Chiapas was further reduced to a submissive organ of state government.[56]

The Grajales government was entirely a regime of cattlemen from the Central Lowlands. Two cattle-raising families from the department of Chiapa, the León and Ruiz families, almost monopolized official positions as local deputies, municipal presidents, district judges, tax collectors, and administrative department heads.[57] By 1935 six of the nine deputies in the state legislature were natives of the governor's *patria chica*. Perhaps most surprising was Grajales's close rapport with Tabasco's Governor Tomás Garrido Canabal.[58] Raymundo Enríquez quickly had second thoughts about his successor.

Even before six months had passed in Grajales's term, a break occurred between the present and former governors. Captain Gustavo López Gutiérrez reported that Grajales in mid-1933 "began to hound to death all those who still felt sympathy for those who had power in the previous administration."[59] Enríquez, along with national deputy Antonio León, charged in the national press that Grajales was smothering proletarian elements and was opposed to the candidacy of Lázaro Cárdenas for president, which was true. Grajales replied that it had been necessary to purify his administration of those elements which had been introduced by the preceding government.[60] Grajales was forced on the defensive from the beginning of his term. He won the battle for domination within Chiapas, but he ultimately lost the war in Mexico City.

THE GRAJALES MODERNIZATION PROGRAM

Reform took a back seat to modernization during the Grajales period. The Enríquez era had been tranquil and his government politically successful because the governor supported the federal authorities and accelerated the pace of agrarian and labor reform. Grajales, on the other hand, deemphasized both kinds of reform.

In 1935 Grajales promised to complete the division of lands in the state and terminate the program entirely by 1936. Like Obregón and Calles the governor wanted "to contain agrarian reform within a political framework and . . . complete it quickly, in order to pass on to modernization and productivity."[61] Grajales also reformed the 1921 state agrarian code to conform with the 1933 federal agrarian law. The new state law fixed a sliding scale for maximum land ownership, from 150 hectares of well-watered land to 5,000 hectares of mountainous land. The state government assumed financial responsibility for the land surveys, which previously had been paid for by the villages, and established an agrarian debt to grant land to petitioners without charge. Plantations of sugar cane, coffee, and cacao were granted the maximum extension of 5,000 hectares.[62]

Grajales remarked in his first Informe that "nothing is more important for Chiapas [than roads]; they will resolve the problem of agricultural production."[63] During his tenure state expenditures for road construction increased from 300,000 pesos in 1933 to 500,000 a year by 1936. In 1935 the state completed its first all-weather road, from Arriaga to Chiapa de Corzo. That old panacea, an interior railroad line, was realistically set aside for a less costly network of roads and highways traversed by cars, buses, and trucks. This began to open the region to wider markets at lower cost. In 1925, for example, there were only 7 trucks in Chiapas and most produce was carried in animal-driven carts, but by 1939 there were more than 400 trucks in operation. Transport costs of one ton per kilometer were 1.50 to 3.50 pesos by cart but only

12 to 20 centavos by truck on a paved road.[64] Commerce was motorized in Chiapas in the 1930s.

The Partido Nacional Revolucionario's first six-year plan, written in 1933, urged all states to implement Article 191 of the 1931 federal labor code, which regulated sharecropping and land rental. Grajales complied in 1935 with the Agricultural Partnership Law. This piece of legislation prohibited landowners at the risk of expropriation from leaving their properties uncultivated. It also regulated the nature of contracts between landowners and "partners" (sharecroppers and renters). Partners were allowed to cut all the wood they needed and to use water for domestic (non-farming) purposes without charge. Rent was regulated at between 5 and 30 percent of the harvest, either in produce or cash, depending upon the amount and quality of land cultivated and whether the landlord provided animals, tools, seeds, machinery, and so on.[65] The Agricultural Partnership Law signified that the age-old practice of baldiaje, although reformed and regulated by the state, would continue in Chiapas.

The Grajales government was the most overtly favorable to landowners since the days of Mapache rule. Early in 1933 the governor cut rural property taxes across the board. To promote industrial development, the government suspended taxes for ten years for new as well as existing industries. All state taxes on the lumber industry were repealed. In 1934 the government established the Central Economic Council and 15 local councils to give official support for "diverse economic activities." The Central Council, for example, encouraged cattlemen to organize self-help and self-defense organizations. The first such association, the Cattlemen's Cooperative of La Frailesca and Custepeques, was formed in Mapache country in 1934. In 1935 other cooperatives were established in Tonalá, Villa Flores, Ocosingo, and Comitán. They became effective as political pressure groups and in warding off agraristas.[66]

The Grajales government initiated a systematic effort to integrate and "civilize" the indigenous population of Chiapas. In 1934 the governor remarked that the Indians were the greatest obstacle to modernization and progress in the state. Grajales, like all governors since Rabasa, wanted to turn Indians into "civilized" Mexicans and "productive citizens." In 1934 the new Department of Social Action, Culture, and Indigenous Protection created 14 cooperatives and 71 official unions, and arbitrated 162 conflicts between workers and employers in the Central Highlands. An Indian Credit Bank and 10 centers of Spanish language teaching were also established. The department began an unsuccessful "pants campaign" to persuade Indians to wear trousers instead of their traditional costume. The substitution of collective contracts in place of individual contracts (or more commonly no contract at all), was the most significant development in the highlands. Officials of the department formed Indian labor unions, negotiated collective contracts with coffee planters, and obtained the minimum wage for migrant laborers. More than 8,000 coffee workers were involved in this system by the end of 1934, and more than 20,000 by 1936.[67] Grajales's indigenous policy was paternalistic and also politically useful since the unionized Indians automatically became "supporters" of the state PNR.

Chiapas was quiet during the church-state conflict in Mexico from 1926 to 1929, the Cristero rebellion against the revolutionary state. Carlos Vidal refused to initiate an anti-clerical campaign, and Raymundo Enríquez limited the number of priests allowed in Chiapas to eleven. This restriction, however, was not enforced. During the Grajales period, anti-clericalism reached such an intensity that this era became widely known as the "time of closed churches" and the "burning of saints."[68]

In August 1933, Governor Grajales—influenced no doubt by Tomás Garrido Canabal—ordered the closing of all churches in the state, an order that was enforced and continued until the end of 1936. He sent a detachment of troops to San Bartolomé de los Llanos, for example, to close the church and destroy all parish records as well as religious relics and images of saints. In Tuxtla Gutiérrez the government ordered public bonfires to destroy religious objects. In February 1935 Grajales expelled all priests, including the bishop, from Chiapas.[69] Under the banner of anti-clericalism, state forces attacked and killed troublesome agraristas.[70] In conformity with the PNR's six-year plan the governor also began to institute socialist, or "rational," education—a program intended to fight fanaticism and give children a better conception of their "social obligations."[71] The most ethereal anti-clerical measure prohibited the inclusion of the names of saints in place names. As a result, San Cristóbal Las Casas became Ciudad Las Casas, San Bartolomé de los Llanos became Venustiano Carranza, San Lorenzo Zinacantan became simply Zinacantan, and so on.[72] Grajales's anti-clerical campaign did not have its intended effect, as one municipal president suggested in 1936: "Today, fanaticism has resurged with even more force."[73] In 1937 Grajales's successor opened the churches and invited the bishop to return to Chiapas.

The centralization of the national state in Chiapas in the early 1930s is perhaps best demonstrated in the movement of municipal, state, and federal bureaucrats. From 1930 to 1935 the number of municipal officials and employees in Chiapas declined from roughly 1,700 to 1,300. Over the same time span the number of state bureaucrats increased from 900 to 1,100 and the number of federal bureaucrats more than doubled, from 600 to 1,300.[74] The penetration of the national government into the states and the localities of Mexico, the expansion of direct and continuous institutional authority from the center into the periphery, constituted an important avenue of national political consolidation.

CARDENISMO: LABOR-AGRARIAN ALLIANCE

General Lázaro Cárdenas became a candidate for president of Mexico in the spring of 1933. He had the backing of President Abelardo Rodríguez (1932–34),[75] most of the army, and two powerful regional caudillos, Juan Andreu Almazán and Saturnino Cedillo. Also, according to labor leader Vicente Lombardo Toledano, "the left wing of the PNR nominated Cárdenas and with our help, that of the labor movement, General Calles ... had to accept Cárdenas."[76] In May 1933 several governors visited Calles at his ranch in Baja California to discuss the succession. Upon learning that the "Jefe Máximo" supported Cárdenas, one of the visitors noted that General Cárdenas was uncultured, excitable, and had extreme ideas. Calles replied that Cárdenas "is a young and honest revolutionary ... [and] with a good rein, he can establish a good government."[77] As before, Calles intended to remain Mexico's political boss while the president administered the government.

Cardenismo, as Lombardo noted, was formed by an alliance between the labor and agrarian movements. The agraristas opposed Calles's deceleration of land reform. Agrarian moderates, such as Emilio Portes Gil, Graciano Sánchez, Enrique Flores Magón, and Marte Gómez, formed the Confederación Campesina Mexicana (Mexican Peasant Confederation, CCM) in early 1934 to push for the nomination of Cárdenas by the PNR. By July 1934 the CCM had affiliations in twenty-four states and was rapidly becoming one of the strongest campesino organizations in Mexico. It found little "official agrarista" support in Tabasco, Yucatán, and Chiapas.[78]

The other element of Cardenismo was organized labor, the traditional political foe of the agraristas. Both had come on hard times politically and—due to the Great Depression—economically between 1928 and 1934. Both envisioned their return to political influence and power with the candidacy and election of Cárdenas. Just as the agraristas opposed the Callista land reform policy, the labor movement opposed the Federal Labor Law of 1931. This law, designed to federalize state labor statutes, denied labor unions the right of independent struggle against capitalists. Labor organizations were required to register with the government. Those which did not register or could not obtain registration did not exist officially and could not appeal to government protection or intervention in labor-management disputes. Unions not registered with the government, furthermore, did not possess the right to strike. In short, according to Lombardo, the 1931 law gave the government the power to impose tranquility at the expense of workers.[79]

In reaction to the Federal Labor Law, Lombardo organized the Alliance of Worker and Peasant Groups, a temporary congress that formulated a detailed criticism of the legislation. In 1933, with CROM nearly in ruins after five years of official neglect, Lombardo converted to Marxism and formed a new "pure CROM" (without Callista labor boss Luis Morones), dedicated to the absolute independence of union organization with respect to the state. The "pure CROM," renamed the Confederación General de Obreros y Campesinos de México (the General Federation of Workers and Peasants of Mexico, CGOCM), was supposedly apolitical. The close personal relationship between Lombardo and Cárdenas, however, was an important source of support for the Cárdenas candidacy.[80]

In the summer of 1933 the PNR began work on a party platform, a six-year plan originally designed to follow Callista principles, which would guide and moderate Cárdenas once he was in office. At the PNR national convention in Querétaro in December, Cárdenas was officially nominated, and the agrarian wing of the party modified the six-year plan. The convention approved recommendations by Graciano Sánchez permitting hacienda residents (*peones acasillados*) to petition for land and the creation of ejidos, and sanctioning the establishment ·of an Agrarian Department to replace the Comisión Nacional Agraria. The continuation and expansion of land reform became party policy. The convention also modified the organizational structure of the PNR. Regional parties, the base of the PNR since 1929, lost their autonomy and became direct dependencies of the party's national executive committee. In Chiapas the Unión de Partidos was replaced by the PNR State Committee, which placed local committees in every district and municipality. The PNR was becoming a genuine national party at the expense of local and regional political organizations.[81]

The modifications of the six-year plan did not affect the articles of concern to organized labor. Still, labor had an ally in Cárdenas. In the 1934 presidential campaign the influence of Lombardo on Cárdenas was clear. On one occasion, candidate Cárdenas declared that "the union is the best weapon of the workers and is worth much more than the protection of the laws and the authorities."[82]

The election of Lazaro Cárdenas in the summer of 1934 and his assumption of office in December led to important changes in the Mexican state. Under Cárdenas the postrevolutionary state began to take on the corporate form we are familiar with today. Cardenismo also infiltrated politics in Chiapas.

THE HARD LINE

The Grajales government got under way in 1933, at the same time as national Cardenismo. As Grajales began to politically subdue labor and agrarian organizations in Chiapas, Cárdenas emerged on the national scene giving encouragement to the independent agrarian and labor movements. The opposition to Grajales, both inside and out of Chiapas, rallied around the Cardenista banner. A fierce struggle between the two went on for four long years. Grajales considered independent labor organizations a threat to social and economic stability and to his political power and applied the policy of "la línea dura"—the hard line.[83]

The leadership of the Confederación Campesina y Obrera de Chiapas became more conservative and led by finqueros; genuine labor leaders came to have little influence on state government policy, on agrarian reform, and on labor-management disputes. As a result, defections occurred from the official labor organization. The Longshoremen's Union of Tapachula left the CCOC in April 1934, for example, "having observed that we are vilely exploited."[84] Independent labor and agrarian organizations had two places to go: the communist Cámara del Trabajo de Chiapas, which was organized in 1934 and was a member of the Mexican Communist Party; or the national Confederación Campesina Mexicana, which was Cardenista.

At the end of 1934 the newly organized Liga Central de Comunidades Agrarias of Chiapas, a constituent organization of the CCM, sent a detailed report to President Cárdenas. Governor Grajales, according to the League, "saw in the unions a threat to the stability of his government and from the beginning has placed obstacles in the path of their development."[85] One tactic, continued the authors of the report, was the formation of *sindicatos blancos*, official unions. In Tapachula the Sindicato de Lecheros was formed by the municipal president, Sóstenes Ruiz, and Fernando Braun, a leading coffee planter. The state government also encouraged the formation of *guardias blancas*, ranchers' private guards, which menaced unions and agraristas. Cattlemen in the municipality of Villa Flores, for example, formed twenty-one separate guardias blancas; there were eight in Cintalapa, five in Chiapa, and too many to count in Tonalá and Soconusco.[86]

The laws and institutions of the state government, which were originally designed to protect workers, came to benefit employers at the expense of workers. The Grajales government refused to register numerous unions, usually communist and Cardenista. The labor relations boards almost without exception favored employers, labor inspectors reportedly made more money from the bribes of employers than from their salaries, and several high officials in the state government were also legal advisors to finqueros appealing land reform decisions.[87] Municipal officials also served as labor contractors for coffee plantations, various fees and deductions made a mockery of the minimum wage, and company stores and indebted servitude were common.[88] "The few workers' organizations that exist [in Chiapas]," complained the Social Revolutionary Bloc of Soconusco, "are only political groups that have no worker control and have been formed with the only object of serving as instruments of political opportunists. These pseudo-proletarian groups, such as the so-called Confederación Campesina y Obrera de Chiapas and the district federations, are composed only of the members of their board of directors, who are public officials, capitalists, or unconditional servants of either."[89] Membership in an organization not associated with the CCOC, many believed, was sufficient reason for imprisonment or assassination.[90] The authorities, wrote the Liga Central Socialista de Resistencia in Tapachula, "will not let up on those workers and campesinos who do not belong to the CCOC, the official organization of the state."[91] According to the candid state public defender, "organizations belonging to the [Cardenista] CCM in Chiapas enjoy no guarantees [of their legal rights] since they are enemies of the government of the state."[92] The entire 41-member Masons' Union of Tapachula, affiliated with the communist Cámara de Trabajo, was jailed and fined simply for holding a meeting.[93] Slayings of agrarian and labor leaders were common and occasionally had a gangland flavor, as in the machine-gunning from a speeding car of a Cardenista party office in Tapachula. The denunciations were many.[94]

The Cárdenas regime did not intervene in Chiapas except to send arms to agrarian communities and ejidos that wanted to establish "social defense guards."[95] The national administration in 1935 did express its concern over the "systematic repression" of workers in Chiapas by local officials.[96] Grajales, however, in a letter to the president in response, noted that his government had raised the standard of living for workers and campesinos. The complaints, wrote the governor, "are simply intrigues of political enemies."[97]

INTRIGUES OF POLITICAL ENEMIES

An odd assortment of mutual enemies—Raymundo Enríquez, Amador Coutiño, Ernesto Herrera, and Rafael Cal y Mayor—came together in 1934 to oppose and oust Victórico Grajales under the banner of Cardenismo. The crusade against Grajales in many ways resembled that against Tiburcio Fernández Ruiz in the early 1920s: it was populist and it succeeded. The tone of the crusade was established quite early by former governor Enríquez. In the summer of 1933 Cárdenas designated

Enríquez director of the Cardenista presidential campaign in Chiapas, and Enríquez immediately charged that Grajales was hampering the operation.[98] Grajales supported the candidacy of Manuel Pérez Treviño until he dropped out of the race in July. The governor then took over the Cardenista campaign in Chiapas using his authority as president of the Chiapas PNR.[99]

Grajales's adversaries faced a powerful political machine in Chiapas. The governor controlled the state PNR, the state labor federation, the state legislature, and most municipal governments. Even in the region where unionization was the most developed, Soconusco, the state regime managed to impose a coffee planter as municipal president of Cacahoatán and another in Motozintla.[100] In 1934 the Partido Socialista de Soconusco (PSS) reappeared, after several years of political hibernation. Calling itself Cardenista, the PSS had close ties to the CCM and was headed by Ernesto Herrera, Alberto Domínguez, and Génaro Marín. In mid-1935 Marín was arrested by the local authorities in Tapachula and shot in his cell; he remained paralyzed.[101] The PSS and other opposition parties entered the state and local elections in 1934 and 1935 but won only jail terms.[102]

The Cárdenas regime finally intervened in Chiapas in 1936. In March the newly established federal Department of Indigenous Affairs, in an obvious attack on the state government, declared that "conditions of virtual slavery exist in Chiapas."[103] The report, authored by former CCM chief Graciano Sánchez, charged that the practice of enganche persisted in the Central Highlands. Despite the minimum wage of 1.30 pesos a day, the report stated, "Chamula workers labor for thirty centavos a day, and have to pay a twenty peso tax which the state labor inspectors demand for authorizing the hiring, as well as various excises charged by municipalities for passage through the area."[104] The department then sent a commission to Chiapas to study Indian labor conditions.[105] In April 1936, in the middle of the gubernatorial campaign, the commission issued its report, alleging that state officials tolerated inhuman working conditions. In their role as middlemen between the Indian unions and coffee planters, it was charged, labor inspectors profited from bribes, graft, and theft of wages.[106] Although politically inspired for the purpose of discrediting the Grajales government, the report was accurate.[107]

President Cárdenas forced Governor Grajales to dismiss several state officials as a result of the report. The Department of Indigenous Affairs also forced some planters to cancel around 24,000 pesos in illegal salary advances.[108] At the end of 1936 the department also formed the Sindicato de Trabajadores Indígenas (Syndicate of Indian Workers, STI) to represent 25,000 migrant Indian workers. The Sindicato, at first supervised by the federal government, was responsible for supervising contracts, transportation, and payment of salaries. It distributed obligatory "work tickets" to local Indian authorities, who in turn distributed them in the villages.[109] One student of ethnic relations in Chiapas contends that "the state restored forced salaried work, controlled it, and guaranteed it."[110] The benefit to the planters—a large and dependable work force—was considerable despite the increase in labor costs. The formation of the STI marked the beginning of the federalization of the Chiapas "Indian problem." As with rural education, Indians increasingly became the responsibility of the national government.

Intervention in Chiapas by the Department of Indigenous Affairs in March 1936 was essentially a political measure, the first part of a larger campaign to remove Grajales and his group from power. It turned into a power struggle between the state and federal governments.

THOSE WHO GO AGAINST THE PNR

The initial phase of the gubernatorial campaign in Chiapas coincided with a national political crisis. In mid-1935 Jefe Máximo Calles implicitly criticized President Cárdenas for tolerating an increase in strikes. Cárdenas, many believed, would be forced to heed the advice of Calles or resign. Instead, Cárdenas reorganized the cabinet and the leadership of the PNR, dismissing Callistas from both. General Calles then retired temporarily from Mexico and from public life. He returned from the United States in December 1935 and published a defense of his government and his political views. For this provocation, Cárdenas expelled Calles from the PNR and on April 10, 1936, forced him into exile along with Luis León and Luis Morones.[111] The defeat of Callismo made Chiapas more vulnerable to direct federal intervention. During the crisis Governor Grajales frequently was labeled a Callista in the national press and his opponents even planted rumors that he was planning a revolt against Cárdenas.[112]

Two gubernatorial candidates appeared at the end of 1935. Cárdenas and the anti-Grajalista coalition found a suitable candidate in Efraín Gutiérrez. In 1914 Gutiérrez had interrupted his studies at the National Agricultural College to join the Zapatistas in Morelos. He returned to school in 1916, took a degree, and joined the Comisión Nacional Agraria. From 1928 to 1932 he served in the state government of Michoacán under Governor Cárdenas. During the first two years of the Cárdenas presidency Gutiérrez served as the first director of the National Bank of Ejidal Credit and later as secretary general of the Agrarian Department.[113] The official Grajalista candidate was Dr. Samuel León Brindis, secretary general of government in 1933–34 and vice-president of the state legislature in 1935. Dr. León, naturally, was a close personal friend and political ally of Victórico Grajales.[114]

The state PNR plebiscite to choose party candidates was scheduled for April 1936. Early in March the national executive committee of the party designated a new state chairman for Chiapas. This chairman proceeded to purge Grajalistas from the state, district, and municipal party commissions.[115] Although the PNR had carried out an efficient and quiet coup d'état in Chiapas, Grajales did not submit. In preparation for the April vote, the state government used harassment and assassination against the Gutiérrez camp and attempted to purchase the necessary votes.[116] The PNR, however, was unbeatable. Ejidos, agrarian communities, and municipal governments were more dependent upon the national party and federal largess than upon the state government. On April 5, Efraín Gutiérrez and his delegates won 97 of the 110 PNR municipal committees. The state PNR convention three weeks later officially nominted Gutiérrez as its candidate for governor of Chiapas. Grajalistas cried "official imposition."[117]

The general election was held on July 6. Although Dr. León dropped out of the race, Governor Grajales still refused to back down and advanced another candidate, Águiles Cruz. The governor also pulled the state's official labor organization out of the PNR. "Since the PNR recognized the triumph of Ing. Gutiérrez," wrote Excelsiór, "assassinations and political persecutions are committed almost every day."[118] During the general campaign the state PNR informed a municipal party official in Huixtla that "those who go against the Partido Nacional Revolucionario, go against President Cárdenas."[119] In May the national PNR executive committee expelled the federal deputies from Chiapas who still opposed Gutiérrez.[120] On election day loyal Grajalista state and municipal officials:

> made use of all means within their reach to commit outrages against
> the persons of workers who went to the booth to vote for the PNR
> ticket. . . . In most of the municipalities the police, led by official
> elements of the state, resorted to the most arbitrary procedures,
> assaulting polling booths and injuring some voters.[121]

Efraín Gutiérrez won the election, and Grajales still fought on. An assassination squad of about twenty-five *pistoleros* (gunmen) assaulted the governor-elect's house one night following the election, but Gutiérrez escaped unharmed. Grajales swore he would never turn over power to Gutiérrez and President Cárdenas took the threat seriously.[122] On September 22, acting on a request from the president, the Senate intervened and deposed Grajales. Former governor Amador Coutiño was appointed provisional governor, and the army closed all state government offices and occupied the government palace.[123] Efraín Gutiérrez became governor of Chiapas on December 1, 1936, without incident.

Raymundo Enríquez and Victórico Grajales were quite different in their philosophies of government. Enríquez was a reformer, like his predecessors Francisco León, Jesús Agustín Castro, and Carlos Vidal. Grajales, like Emilio and Ramón Rabasa, and Tiburcio Fernández Ruiz, was a modernizer. Modernization and reform, however, in the 1890s as in the 1920s and 1930s, were never viewed as contradictory processes. Rather, they were seen as complementary means—but employed in different compositions—to make Chiapas modern and agriculturally prosperous. Both Enríquez and Grajales, out of political necessity, began the institutionalization within the state apparatus of the labor and agrarian movement in Chiapas. This development, which was completed and nationalized in 1937 and 1938, provided one of the key mechanisms of national political consolidation and of regional political control of worker and agrarian power. "The age of the machine politician and the agrarian [and labor] bureaucrat was dawning. . . ."[124]

8

ONLY FOR POLITICS HAVE THE POSTULATES OF THE REVOLUTION BEEN PROSTITUTED

IN 1939 PAULA CAL Y MAYOR COMPLAINED TO THE AGRARIAN DEPARTMENT that the agrarian petition against her finca was economically unfounded. More than 80 percent of the land of neighboring ejidos was uncultivated. The purpose of the petition, she wrote, was to increase the power of local agrarista caciques. "Only for politics," she concluded, in a comment more truthful and transcendent than she probably knew, "have the postulates of the Revolution been prostituted."[1]

From the late 1930s through the 1940s the government of Chiapas completed the political mobilization of workers and campesinos, fully integrated the regional "revolutionary" party into the national party of the state, and carried agrarian reform to the indigenous Central Highlands and the coffee plantations of Soconusco. In the process the power and authority of the national government greatly expanded at the expense of local and regional power and autonomy. But the regional landed elite—the familia chiapaneca, which comprised nearly the same families who had owned Chiapas in the 1890s—understood that it could only defend and advance its interests as part of the national state. This truth was personified by Isidro Rabasa: A great-nephew of Governor Emilio Rabasa, he was a Mapache during the late 1910s and became a Cardenista in the 1930s. The same truth was demonstrated during the "radical phase" of the Revolution in the late 1930s. Labor federations and agrarian leagues were incorporated into the political apparatus of the state, their leaders were transformed into interchangeable politicians, and their constituent unions and ejidos sank into fratricidal struggles for short-term gain. Reforms were transformed, by means of the corrupting influence of "politics," into instruments of pacification, manipulation, and control. The "new Chiapas" of the 1940s came to look remarkably like what Emilio Rabasa probably had in mind in the 1890s.

THE NEW STATE OF THE MOBILIZED MASSES

The Constitution of 1917, far from repudiating the authoritarian centralism of the Mexican state as it developed under Porfirio Díaz, expanded the responsibilities and extended the reach of government. Aside from the provision for a strong chief executive, the constitution did not and could not outline precisely how the state's power would be consolidated and its legitimacy established. One thing was certain in the immediate postrevolutionary era: the politicization and mobilization of part of the urban and rural working class made the methods of Díaz insufficient. "No future regime dared disregard popular feelings as blatantly as Díaz had."[2]

The first governments following the revolution developed ties with organized workers and campesinos, trading mild reforms and limited political participation for political support. This informal policy came temporarily to an end at the national level with the assassination of Álvaro Obregón. Part of the price of peace between Obregonistas and Callistas was severance of all ties between the regime and organized labor. The revolutionary family, headed by Plutarco Elías Calles and embodied in the Partido Nacional Revolucionario, was to be the sole arbitrator of national politics. Organized workers and campesinos, however, were disturbed by the increasing conservative drift of the national government. They helped bring to power a friend of unionization and agrarian reform, a "populist Callista," Lázaro Cárdenas.[3]

Cárdenas confronted the task of consolidating the power and giving legitimacy to the authority of the state by aligning the organized masses. Cárdenas created an institutional alliance, "conceived as a union and a commitment," between the state and the masses.[4] He reorganized the party of the state as a party of social corporations, divided among labor, campesino, military, and middle-class sectors. Along with the party reorganization, indeed as part of the bargain, came an intensification of reform. The very success of the long-delayed reforms of the Revolution led to a partial demobilization of the working class. The acceleration of agrarian reform created many communities that were grateful to the state for land, depended on it for credit and markets, and were less concerned about class solidarity and struggle. Ejidos and unions became embroiled in conflicts with one another. Ejidatarios often found that working with the Bank of Ejidal Credit was as oppressive as working for a hacendado. Cárdenas's successor, General Manuel Ávila Camacho, undertook to "consolidate the conquests of the Revolution" between 1940 and 1946. The electoral reform of 1945 and the last major reorganization of the official party in 1946 caused the labor sector as well as state governments to lose a significant degree of political influence and local or regional autonomy. "The resignation of the popular masses, expressed through silence," writes Luis Javier Garrido, "once again became the fundamental dominant note of Mexican political life."[5]

UNIFICATION IN MEXICO AND CHIAPAS

From the start of the Cárdenas regime the government patronized the Confederación General Obrera y Campesina de Mexico (General Confederation of Workers and Peasants of Mexico, CGOCM) led by Vicente Lombardo Toledano. The CGOCM had evolved from Lombardo's "pure CROM" and had supported Cárdenas for president in 1934. Both Cárdenas and Lombardo sought an increase in unionization and the integration of workers' organizations into a unified front that would end inter-syndical conflicts and give workers a more effective political voice and a mechanism of defense and struggle. This united front was established during the second CGOCM congress in February 1936. More than 3,000 workers' organizations with 600,000 members combined to form the Confederación de Trabajadores de Mexico (Confederation of Mexican Workers, CTM). Lombardo remained at the head of the labor movement and a dedicated Marxist. The CTM, according to one scholar of the labor movement, "was, without doubt, the organization that Cárdenas considered indispensable . . . and was the intervening instrument by which the working class would be mobilized in support of the decisions of the state and in defense of the established regime."[6]

In July 1935 Cárdenas called for the unification of all campesino organizations as well. Lombardo wanted to unify both rural and urban workers within the CTM, but Cárdenas was adamant that they remain separate. He ordered the PNR to "call conventions in every state of the union to meet for the purpose of having but one League of Agrarian Communities. . . . Once the Leagues of Agrarian Communities have been organized in the states, the National Executive Committee of the Party shall call a Great Convention to organize the Peasant Confederation."[7] Cárdenas preferred a single industrial workers' union, the CTM, and a separate and less independent campesino organization, the Confederación Nacional Campesino (National Peasant Confederation, CNC), which was formed in 1938.[8]

The unification of workers and campesinos in separate "umbrella" institutions constituted only the first phase in Cárdenas's drive to establish a corporate state. Beginning in 1936, the CTM with the president's support put forward labor candidates for elective office. These candidates became PNR nominees, thus strengthening the alliance between the PNR and the CTM. In December 1937 Cárdenas proposed to formalize sector participation in the PNR. At the party's national assembly in March 1938, the Cardenistas created the Partido de la Revolución Mexicana (PRM) to replace the PNR. The PRM was divided into three sectors or interest groups: workers, campesinos, and soldiers. The workers' sector was dominated by the CTM and the campesino sector by the CNC. Membership in the PRM was automatically bestowed by membership in an affiliated labor union, cooperative, ejido, or by inclusion in the armed forces.[9]

The most notable difference between the PRN and the PRM was the manner of selecting candidates for public offices. Names were advanced by sectors and, through high-level negotiation, official candidates emerged. The PRM transformed labor and campesino representatives into politicians. Sector leaders came to identify more with the interests of the state or a particular government than the interests of class. In this way, notes historian Paul Nathan, "a federation of interest groups within a party cannot 'facilitate' the class struggle, but mollify it."[10] The PRM, however, did help legitimize the state within the ranks of the organized masses. The PRM represented the reinstallation and institutionalization of the policy of alliance and collaboration, with the state holding the strongest position.[11]

Efraín Gutiérrez took office in late 1936 with the nearly unanimous support of organized labor. The labor groups that the Grajales regime had refused to register, including the communist unions, had joined the CTM and supported Gutiérrez in the campaign. After the election, Provisional Governor Amador Coutiño reorganized the state Confederación Campesino y Obrera de Chiapas by placing Gutierristas in charge.[12]

In July 1937, after less than seven months in office, Gutiérrez convoked the First Workers' Congress of Chiapas. This assembly established the Confederación Obrera y Campesina del Estado (Worker and Campesino Confederation of the State) in place of the CCOC. The new state labor federation was composed of two subordinate affiliations: the Confederación Obrera and the Confederación Campesina.[13]

The Confederación Obrera was made up of 145 local labor unions in 1937, and 271 by 1939 with a rank and file of around 33,000 members.[14] In August 1937 the Sindicato de Trabajadores Indígenas, claiming 18,000 members, joined the confederation.[15] The Confederación Obrera, subsidized by the state government, assisted nearly 5,000 sharecroppers and renters to obtain legally registered contracts and helped unorganized rural workers obtain individual parcels of land through the Law of Idle Lands.[16] The Confederación Obrera's main task was to unionize workers. One result of the acceleration of unionization was a fourfold increase in strikes from the Grajales period.[17]

At the end of 1938 Vicente Lombardo Toledano, secretary general of the CTM, flew to Chiapas to formally integrate the Confederación Obrera into the CTM. The most important task of the confederation, proclaimed Lombardo at the second State Workers' Congress, was the organization of hacienda residents, or peones acasillados. These campesinos composed the majority of rural workers in Chiapas but were excluded from the Confederación Campesina because they were not residents of legally constituted agrarian communities.[18] The CTM became the primary channel through which local unions voiced their complaints and requests to the state and national governments.[19]

The other wing of the new state labor confederation, the Confederación Campesina, represented all ejidal governments (*comisariados ejidales*) and the agrarian executive committees of communities petitioning for land. In 1938, in conformity with President Cárdenas's campaign for campesino unification, the Confederación Campesina officially became the Liga de Comunidades Agrarias y Sindicatos del Estado (League of Agrarian Communities and Syndicates of the State), and joined the CNC.[20] The CNC, like the CTM, replaced the state government as the primary channel of communication between campesino organizations and the state and national governments.[21]

Businessmen and industrialists were also unified in the late 1930s. Cárdenas wanted class conflict to take place peacefully and legally among powerful corporations and he considered the organization of capitalists necessary for state regulation. In 1936 the Law of Chambers of Commerce and Industry was enacted, replacing an obsolete 1908 law. The new legislation maintained that businesses were institutions with public responsibilities; it defined chambers of commerce as organs of collaboration with the state. Businesses and industries valued at more than $500 were obliged to join the National Chamber of Commerce and Industry. They were also required to register with the government, since only registered enterprises could participate in arbitrations conducted by the labor relations board.[22] The Tuxtla Gutiérrez Chamber of Commerce joined the National Chamber in 1938 and continued its policy of close consultation and collaboration with the state government.[23] By the late 1930s and early 1940s the organization of the regional bourgeoisie in political pressure groups of cattlemen; coffee, cacao, and platano growers; and merchants and industrialists was well advanced. Certain of these associations, according to César Corzo Velasco, "demonstrated great political force."[24]

As in other states, the Chiapas PRN was converted into the PRM in mid-1938. The leadership of the party, the Regional Committee for Chiapas, was composed of the president of the state party, local deputy (and former Mapache) Isidro Rabasa; one representative of the Confederación Obrera; one from the Liga de Comunidades Agrarias; and, later, one from the popular sector.[25] The Regional Committee of the PRM, in close consultation with the governor, appointed and discharged municipal and district party committee members. Candidates for public posts were named by party conventions. Final authority in the Chiapas PRM resided in the National Executive Committee in Mexico City.[26]

Mario J. Culebro, secretary general of the Confederación Obrera, in 1939 ordered all labor unions in Chiapas to abstain from supporting any potential candidates for local, state, or national office. The Confederación, Culebro stated, would present its slate of candidates to the PRM Regional Committee behind closed doors. The affiliated organizations and members would then support as a bloc the labor slate during the state PRM convention.[27] The high degree of integration among state PRM, CTM, and CNC affiliations was demonstrated in 1939 when the Regional Committee reported that 1,361 separate constituent organizations in Chiapas supported General Manuel Ávila Camacho, a presidential hopeful, for the PRM nomination.[28] In early 1940 the Regional Committee of the PRM persuaded gubernatorial condidate General César Lara to drop out of the race and support Dr. Rafael P. Gamboa, the official candidate and PRM nominee. President Cárdenas picked Gamboa through careful consultation with state party sectors and the National Executive Committee to avoid a repetition of the 1936 campaign. Gamboa was unanimously and peacefully elected in 1940.[29]

Political unification of worker and campesino organizations within the national ruling party diminished the political importance of state government. It was bypassed as the key mediating institution between the localities and the national government by national interest groups that were part of the state and organized at the local, regional, and national levels. In addition, as the federal government acquired more and more functions that had once been exclusively state functions, the state government became a regional branch of the national government better adapted to administer national policies than to defend and promote regional priorities. Politics, not unexpectedly, also became less important and contentious. Political competition and discontent became a matter for bargaining among state officials, national bureaucrats, and sector representatives, all usually indistinguishable bureaucrat-politicians. The state government as a political institution in Mexico was becoming increasingly marginal.

THE RISE AND CORRUPTION OF INDIGENISM

The state government of Chiapas assumed the task of converting Indians into Mexicans in the 1890s and erratically continued its labors until the 1950s. Before 1890 few public officials considered it worthwhile or even possible to truly "civilize" the indigenous population.

After 1950 the federal government, through the Instituto Nacional Indigenista (National Indigenous Institute, INI), assumed primary responsibility for the "Indian problem." The period 1936–44 was, in terms of state government policy, the high point of indigenous reform.

Indigenismo became a tenet of the ideology of the Mexican Revolution, replacing the racist notion that native ethnicity was uncivilized and therefore prevented Mexico from becoming a great nation. In the 1920s artists, writers, and intellectuals viewed Indian society, past and present, as a positive presence and heritage of the nation. The national agrarian reform program, for example, revived the communal tenure of land, the village ejido. At the level of government policy, indigenismo encompassed two intertwined goals by the 1930s: the incorporation of the Indian into national society without total cultural obliteration; and the improvement of Indian life through education, political and economic organization, and the reform of the larger surrounding society. The revolutionary aspect of indigenismo was the idea that Indian poverty was largely the result of inequalities in Mexican society and not simply a consequence of ethnic or racial inferiority.[30]

In 1937 Governor Gutiérrez established the Department of Rural Education and Indigenous Incorporation, later renamed the Department of Indigenous Protection. This new department replaced the Grajalista Department of Social Action, Culture, and Indigenous Protection created in 1934.[31] The new department's first director, Erasto Urbina, had assisted in the formation of the Sindicato de Trabajadores Indígenas in late 1936 and would later serve as a Gutierrista state deputy and municipal president of San Cristóbal. Under Urbina the state indigenous department initiated a massive effort to increase Spanish literacy, sending 250 teachers to Indian villages. The department also established collection agencies in San Cristóbal, Comitán, and Motozintla to supervise the contracting and transport of Indian workers to the coffee plantations of Soconusco.[32] Urbina also had some success in getting planters to provide radios and install film theaters, to construct better housing for migrant laborers, and to stop selling liquor to Indians.[33]

Urbina was the prime mover in the formation of new and energetic agrarian committees in the native highlands. According to anthropologist Robert Wasserstrom, "Urbina was able to transform the basis of landed wealth in the region." Between 1936 and 1944, fifty-three ejidos were formed in the Central Highlands, affecting almost all of the approximately nine hundred fincas of the area. More than 500,000 hectares were granted to approximately 60,000 families.[34] Even with a sympathetic state and federal government, the petitioning for land and creation of ejidos involved a violent struggle against landowners who attacked agrarian communities, burned settlements, and murdered agraristas. Highland finqueros led by Alberto Pineda also were not passive in the face of official agrarian reform procedures. They were able to salvage their best lands as well as their buildings. Landowners frequenty sold or gave away tracts of uncultivated land to tenants and agrarian committees to protect productive land. The ejidos of Indian municipalities, unable to provide land to all families, without sufficient capital and irrigated or arable land, did not significantly improve the standard of living of highland Indians. The ejidos, however, were important politically—they were incorporated into the state Liga de Comunidades Agrarias y Sindicatos Campesinos, and thus into the official party.[35]

One result of the formation of agrarian committees in Indian villages and Urbina's policy of turning over local political authority to Indians was the rise of the modern Indian cacique after Urbina's departure in 1944. These new caciques, skilled middlemen who were bilingual and able to work with and even manipulate ladino officials, came to control tightly municipal and ejidal governments. They became prosperous businessmen, money lenders, landowners, and employers.[36] Mariano Zarate and Salvador Oso, for example, were caciques of Zinacantan and Chamula respectively from the 1940s to the 1960s.[37] With political support at the state and federal levels, Indian caciques often became a pernicious power in Chiapas. The caciques of the ejido of La Libertad, for example, made a very unfair and unequal division of lands in 1939.[38] The cacique of Tenejapa in 1944 used the police to break up a market in Yochib and thus maintain his monopoly over the Sunday market in Tenejapa, which he taxed.[39]

Indigenous mobilization was to be the cornerstone of indigenismo in Chiapas. The only way the Indian population might escape ladino exploitation and a capricious, patronizing government was through the organization of a labor union. That organization was the Sindicato de Trabajadores Indígenas. From 1936 to 1939 the STI functioned more or less as Urbina had planned. It negotiated collective contracts with coffee planters and obtained the minimum wage, free meals, transportation, and free medical treatment.[40] The STI briefly succeeded in mitigating the worst abuses of migrant labor in Chiapas.[41] By 1939, however, the Sindicato began to lose its reforming mission. In September 1939, for example, the STI refused to support a strike by the Sindicato Único de Trabajadores de la Industria de Café de Soconusco (SUTICS), which derailed the strike movement.[42] After Urbina's transfer out of Chiapas in 1944, his successor as chief of the Departamento de Asuntos Indígenas from 1946 to 1948, Alberto Rojas, was a prominent landowner who served powerful interests.[43] Rojas did not renew the charter of the STI and it came to an end. The STI was reestablished in 1953, not as an instrument of self-defense and reform but—in effect—as a center of robbery and a compliant contracting agency for the coffee planters' cartel, the Asociación Agrícola Local de Caficultores de Soconusco.[44]

AGRARIAN REFORM: SOCONUSCO

Governor Efraín Gutiérrez, after twenty years of agrarian reform in Mexico, finally brought that program to the indigenous Central Highlands and the coffee plantations of Soconusco. In September 1937 Gutiérrez reported to the state legislature that within a few days he was sending a team of thirty agrarian engineers to Soconusco to study the problem of land concentration and begin to act on petitions for land.[45] The governor's initiative was in response to a new wave of agrarismo— and planter repression—in Soconusco. Beginning in 1937 SUTICS, the principal Cardenista labor union in the coffee zone, began to organize agrarian committees on the coffee plantations that petitioned for land.[46] The governor gave notice to the planters that their lands would no longer be exempt from expropriation. Long before, however, they had planned for such an eventuality. In the 1920s German nationals obtained permission from their government to become Mexican citizens only for the purpose of preventing the expropriation of their properties, which were within fifty kilometers of the international border and thus, under the constitution, not permitted to be held by foreign nationals.[47] After Cárdenas modified the federal agrarian code to permit the expropriation of coffee lands, the planters began to divide their properties among family members, sell parcels to friends and neighbors, and give less valuable land to villagers to defuse agrarian sentiment.[48] Planters directed ferocious attacks against radical agraristas, tried to bribe agrarian committees, and launched a propaganda campaign to convince the federal government that expropriation of the coffee groves of Soconusco would mean the economic ruin of Chiapas.[49] Planters had a useful ally in the federal army zone commander, General Ríos Zertuche, a coffee planter himself, who cooperated with the guardias blancas in repression of agraristas. Coffee planters also permitted or encouraged the less "troublesome" Guatemalan migrant laborers to form agrarian committees, believing that the Guatemalans would be easy to control and also would be denied land due to their nationality.[50]

The preliminary surveys were completed by the end of March 1939, at which time the governor traveled to Tapachula to give provisional grants to three new ejidos.[51] In April Gutiérrez established seven collective ejidos in the coffee zone. This first wave granted 8,000 hectares of first-class coffee land to benefit 1,600 peones acasillados. More than 3,000 hectares were expropriated from the seven properties belonging to coffee magnate Fernando Braun.[52]

Agrarian reform in Soconusco in 1939 left the coffee-processing machinery, not to mention the marketing companies, still in the hands of a few powerful German planters. During the 1939–40 harvest they tried to bankrupt the new ejidos. The planters refused to process (dry and shell) or purchase ejido coffee for export. Gutiérrez stepped in to force the planters to process the crop, and a few processing plants were seized by ejidatarios. The Bank of Ejidal Credit (a federal agency) gave emergency credit to eight ejidal credit societies, and the state government contracted with the firm of A. C. Muller of Houston, Texas, to purchase the ejidos' coffee. These difficulties prompted the federal government to step in and initiate the second phase of land reform in Soconusco.[53]

In the spring of 1940 President Cárdenas visited Soconusco and supervised expropriations affecting nearly every large plantation in the departments of Soconusco and Mariscal. Cárdenas added another 20,000 hectares to the ejidal coffee zone and expropriated several processing plants.[54] The plantations affected, however, were then declared "small property" and their owners were granted "certificates of inaffectability," exempting those properties from additional agrarian litigation.[55] Planter Ad Giesman's conversion into a small property owner prompted some peones acasillados in 1941 sarcastically to remark, "With six fincas in operation, it is a curious small property."[56]

President Manuel Ávila Camacho in 1941 ordered the termination of agrarian activity in Soconusco during his term, thus initiating the final phase of land reform in the coffee zone. This phase included the upgrading of provisional grants to definitive grants, the processing of petitions still under consideration, and the provision of certificates of inaffectability, which up to 1941 had benefited only about half of the planters and landowners of Soconusco.[57] Part of the resolution of remaining agrarian problems during the early 1940s involved the breakup of the two largest communal ejidos, Unión Juárez and Cacahoatán. Both had been formed by combining several independent agrarian communities and rival agrarian committees. The union of nine communities in the Cacahoatán ejido led to the formation of nine political factions that could agree on hardly anything. This in turn led to factional violence and agricultural inactivity. The federal Agrarian Department was forced to divide these two ejidos into smaller ones which, however, were still worked communally.[58]

By 1946 the present agrarian contour of Soconusco was largely in place. About 50 percent of all coffee plantations had been affected by agrarian expropriations that created more than 100 ejidos. Most of the ejidos were organized into 31 credit societies—essentially business corporations with ejidatarios as shareholders and workers. These credit societies assigned tasks to the workers, processed and marketed the coffee, and paid the ejidatarios. More than half of these credit societies, sixteen out of thirty-one, accepted credit from the federal Bank of Ejidal Credit. The bank determined salaries and the number of days per week ejidatarios could work, and oversaw the harvest, processing, and marketing of the coffee. The bank became a bureaucratic "planter"; the ejidatario, the "peon" of the bank.[59]

The agrarian reform program of the 1930s and 1940s included not only the formation of ejidos but also the creation of a complex bureaucratic structure to assist, supervise, and control ejidatarios. In 1937 the federal Agrarian Department established the Division of Ejidal Promotion, a dependency of the state Agrarian Mixed Commissions. This office divided Chiapas into eighty ejidal zones, each supervised by a jefe de la zona who was responsible for channeling government assistance to ejidos. These jefes provided tools, livestock, schools and teachers, roads and trucks, and improved seed to ejidos. They assisted ejidal governments to expand their original grants, a duty that occasionally made them targets of assassination.[60] Jefes also arbitrated conflicts within and between ejidos. The jefes were trained agronomists and career bureaucrats who carried out the directives of the federal Agrarian Department, further diminishing the role of the state government in ejidal affairs.[61]

Land without the resources to fully and profitably work it could not raise the standard of living of ejidatarios, thus the absolute necessity of credit. Most credit in Chiapas before 1939 was dispensed by the National Bank of Agricultural Credit to private producers of coffee and cacao.[62] The Bank of Ejidal Credit, established by President Cárdenas in 1935 to provide credit to ejidal credit societies, opened an office in Tuxtla Gutiérrez in 1936. The following year a central office was established in Tapachula and branch offices were set up in San Cristóbal, Tonalá, and Huixtla. Loans to credit societies increased from 100,000 pesos in 1936 to 3 million in 1940, and to 31 million by 1948.[63] The number of ejidal credit societies in Chiapas multiplied proportionally, from 36 in 1936 to 160 by 1950.[64] Despite this apparently impressive increase in ejidal credit, it was woefully inadequate. Ejidos were, and remain today, monuments of poverty and underdevelopment; ejidatarios, poor people in a rich land.

The private coffee plantations of Soconusco remained productive and, following World War II and the rise of coffee prices, still highly profitable enterprises. "Agrarian reform in the region," Wasserstrom correctly notes, "served to surround large landholdings with a protective buffer of underproductive and undercapitalized ejidos which contributed [by means of cheap labor] to the prosperity of private growers."[65]

President Lázaro Cárdenas and Governor Efraín Gutiérrez came to power in the mid-1930s at the head of a politically powerful labor-agrarian coalition. In Chiapas this coalition was based in Soconusco, the most unionized region in the state and the home of the state's principal productive enterprises—coffee plantations, which still were in private hands. The coalition pledged its political support to Gutiérrez; the governor in turn was committed to extending land reform to Soconusco. Whether it was planned or not, the agrarian program ul-

TABLE 5

AGRARIAN REFORM IN CHIAPAS 1917–48

Administration	Petitions	Settlements	Provisional Grants (in hectares)
Villanueva: 1917–19	41	10	17,295
Fernández Ruiz: 1920–24	47	19	20,754
Vidal: 1925–27	102	43	87,061
Enríquez: 1928–32	n.d.	126	192,517
Grajales: 1932–36	n.d.	104	105,602
Gutiérrez: 1936–40	n.d.	424	449,150
Gamboa: 1940–44	n.d.	27	62,225
Esponda/Lara: 1944–48	n.d.	74	98,627

Source: *Anuario de 1930;* Gutiérrez, *Informe 1939;* Gutiérrez, *Trayectoria de un Gobierno,* pp. 40–41; and De la Peña, *Chiapas Económico,* II, pp. 375–376.

timately benefited private agriculture, pacified the agrarian movement, and weakened organized labor. Agrarian reform reinforced and preserved the bifurcated agricultural economy in the state: a small but prosperous commercial agricultural sector and a large but impoverished subsistence and semi-subsistence agricultural sector. (For the course of agrarian reform in Chiapas, see table 5.)

SEQUESTRATION OF GERMAN PLANTATIONS

Mexico declared war on Germany, Italy, and Japan on June 2, 1942, after two Mexican oil tankers were torpedoed by German U-boats. Nationals of the Axis nations were reconcentrated to interior cities and their properties impounded and administered by the federal government.[66] The Board of Administration and Supervision of Foreign Property seized sixty-six German coffee plantations in Chiapas (most located in Soconusco), which were collectively valued at more than 12 million pesos. The sequestration lasted until 1946.[67]

Administration of the impounded German plantations in Chiapas was turned over to the Fideicomiso Cafeteros de Tapachula (Coffee Fiduciary), which was a dependency of the Bank of Foreign Commerce. Officials of the Fiduciary were neither good businessmen nor social reformers, and it seems quite likely that corruption was rampant. Despite the increase in coffee prices during the war, production in the impounded plantations dropped by more than half during the sequestration. When the properties were finally returned to their owners in 1946, machinery, houses, roads, and the coffee groves were in bad condition since no funds had been used for repair and upkeep.[68] The Fiduciary tolerated no strikes and even lowered salaries but did allow the organization of peones acasillados in labor unions.[69] The Fiduciary also hired Guatemalan workers in preference to Mexican workers since they accepted less than the minimum wage; undoubtedly the difference was diverted into the pockets of the administrators.[70] The sequestration of 1942–46 marked the end of agrarian reform in Soconusco. Although the Sindicato Único de Trabajadores de la Industria de Café de Soconusco repeatedly demanded the total nationalization of all impounded properties, the agrarian reform department left each plantation with a minimum of 300 hectares, as required by law.[71] Since the planters had previously divided their properties among family members, they managed to retain a good portion of their properties. In 1946 more than 10,000 hectares of the richest and most productive land in Mexico were returned along with certificates of inaffectability to the German planters of Soconusco. With the doubling of coffee prices between 1945 and 1950, the establishment of a system of export quotas among producing nations, and security against further expropriation, coffee planters enjoyed considerable profits in the postwar period.[72]

DEVOURED BY THE STATE

The unification of campesinos and workers into what appeared to be powerful confederations integrated into the party of the state, and the flawed but extensive advance of agrarian reform in Chiapas, led to the political debilitation and even immobilization of the organized masses. It was a decline of political influence, class solidarity, and independent struggle, rather than a disbanding of formal organizations. Once-aggressive labor unions and agrarian leagues turned away from the broader struggle for class power and interests to focus on internal rivalries, disputes with the state apparatus, and self-preservation and aggrandizement. The always fragile yet potentially powerful mobilization of workers and campesinos in Chiapas peaked and then subsided between 1936 and 1945.[73] The movement, as Arnaldo Córdova vividly describes it, was "devoured by the state."[74]

Land reform in the Central Highlands restored and strengthened the separate indigenous *municipios* at the expense of broader Indian or campesino solidarity. Because land was distributed within municipios to landowning and landless Indians, agrarian reform aggravated internal community stratification and discouraged class-based organization spanning Indian municipios. Agrarian reform, by restoring the territorial integrity of Indian municipios, also reinforced "municipios as parochial domains." Furthermore, writes George A. Collier, "the administration within a municipio of an ejido was turned over to a governing body, the Comisariado ejidal, through whose officials the State party generally controlled municipal politics."[75]

The formation of ejidos created communities that were, and remain in the 1980s, closely tied to the state; "a gift always compromises the recipient," writes Jean Meyer.[76] They had received their land from the state and were dependent on the state for credit, material assistance, and amplification of their original land grants. Ejidatarios became loyal, conservative, and self-interested citizens. "We the organized campesinos of this colony," wrote the leadership of one new ejido in 1938, "are disposed to join the new National Party of Workers and Soldiers [the

PRM] and we will be with [President Cárdenas] at all times."[77] In 1940 ejidatarios in Chiapas numbered 40,000, composing around 12 percent of the male population but possessing 20 percent of all cultivated land. By 1970 ejidatarios numbered nearly 150,000, composing 20 percent of the male population but possessing 50 percent of all land in cultivation.[78] Most ejidatarios were and remain poor, but within the regional campesinato they are the privileged poor.

Ejidatarios had something to defend. Their solidarity with members of neighboring ejidos, with unionized agricultural workers, and with unorganized sharecroppers, renters, and day laborers disappeared. The ejidatarios of Independencia (Mariscal department) in 1936, for example, encroached upon 100 hectares of the best land of the neighboring ejido of San Isidro Siltepec. In 1943, assisted by an agrarian engineer who was probably bribed, the same ejidatarios helped themselves to an additional 120 hectares, provoking a violent feud.[79] Forty-two baldíos of Tierra Colorado in the municipality of Zinacantan opposed the formation of an ejido comprising lands they had cultivated for thirty years. When the Chamula ejidos were formed in 1940 the ejidatarios ordered the baldíos to move off the land. In 1956 the baldíos of Tierra Colorado petitioned the government for their own ejido. The Chamula ejido then gave them membership rather than risk losing some of its land to a new ejido.[80]

Internal ejidal conflicts were, and still are, serious and commonplace. Governance of ejidos almost always fell into the hands of a few powerful caciques whose authority derived from the support of government officials and from their skillful employment of favors and punishments. Bartolomé Vásquez Chahal was the cacique of Venustiano Carranza from 1939 until his death in 1947. He rented ejidal land to cattlemen, which not only made him a wealthy man but won him the backing of the ladino municipal government and party officials.[81] Parcels were usually unfairly distributed to ejidatarios, according to one faction in Carranza, and were occasionally sold to outsiders.[82] Internal conflicts in ejidos also permitted the expansion of landowner influence. In Socoltenango the municipal president, supported by local landowners, intervened in an ejidal feud to bring to power a "friendly and cooperative" comisariado ejidal.[83] Conflicts within ejidos often arose between factions linked to the Bank of Ejidal Credit and those opposed to the bank. One group in 1942, voicing a common complaint, did not like working "to promote a group of favorites of the Bank of Ejidal Credit."[84]

The Bank of Ejidal Credit, in fact, became the most heated issue of conflict within ejidos in the 1940s. Referring to the situation in Chiapas, the secretary general of the national League of Agrarian Communities commented that "the property owner has not changed, now he is called 'the bank' and the exploitation could not be more iniquitous."[85] The Ejidal Bank's control of ejidos that accepted government credit was substantial. The bank placed its employees in charge of ejidal credit societies and paid a low price for ejidal coffee but sold it to exporters for a much better price. In an especially corrupt action in 1942, the bank used 800,000 pesos belonging to the collective ejidos of Unión Juárez and Cacahoatán to purchase 300 hectares and the processing machinery of planter Enrique Braun. The price was quite high, leading some to conclude that the bank and Braun were in collusion. The bank, furthermore, kept control of the land and the machinery instead of turning both over to the credit society. In response, some mutinous ejidatarios created the Unión Central de Credito Ejidal Colectivo to get out from under the control of the bank. The bank, however, "killed this new organization."[86] In 1943 the leadership of the coffee workers' union of Soconusco demanded "that the employees of the Bank of Ejidal Credit be replaced by others who do not steal from ejidatarios."[87]

To avoid the capricious domination of caciques and bankers, factions appeared in the collective ejidos of Soconusco demanding parcelization—the working of the coffee groves not as a whole but in small individual plots. "In view of the scandalous misuse of money that can be observed in the ejidos," wrote one ejidal faction, "we demand that the ejidal parcels be emancipated and that in these ejidos new comisariados ejidales be organized."[88] The president of the dissident Liga de Acción Política y Social of Chiapas informed President Manuel Ávila Camacho that "the ejidatarios are longing, truly longing to obtain: parcelization; title to authentic property that will protect a portion of land which is their property; and individual credit. These are the true desires of ejidatarios."[89] The bank, and officials linked to the bank, responded that those who wanted parcelization were either Guatemalans, who had no legal right to land anyway, or communists.[90] In fact, communists did support the parcelization effort, an interesting ideological shift from their earlier collectivization demands.[91] Parcelization of the collective ejidos, however, from an economic and fiscal perspective was out of the question. It would lower productivity and thus lower the Ejidal Bank's rate of return and the state's tax revenue.[92]

Agrarian reform combined with the aggrandizement of the ejidal bank led to antagonism between ejidos and labor unions. In 1945, when the finca "Numancia" of Cacahoatán was converted into an ejido, the local SUTICS section (whose members were not included in the ejidal census) found itself in a difficult situation. The leaders of the ejido, wrote section chief Alberto Guzmán, "not only took away our jobs before dissolving the Section but until now have not recognized their obligation to indemnify us." Guzmán continued, arguing that "the ejidal bank, Señor Presidente, manages these señores ejidatarios. . . . Ours is not the first case; many union sections have been dissolved, and the ejidatarios possess the coffee region to the detriment of union members."[93]

According to a SUTICS memorandum, "once the Credit Societies were constituted, the agency of the [Ejidal] Bank in Tapachula began to apply a policy of separation between ejidatarios and unionized workers."[94] The Ejidal Bank jailed union leaders who voiced opposition to its activities, and it even organized an armed defense force, allegedly to help ejidatarios defend themselves against planters but in fact "to control all the workers of Cacahoatán."[95] In 1945 the Agrarian Department granted land not to the SUTICS members who lived and worked on the land but to a neighboring agrarian colony linked to the bank.[96]

By 1945 the Ejidal Bank not only controlled the operations and finances of fifteen credit societies (representing between fifty and seventy ejidos) but also owned and operated several coffee plantations and processing plants. "At the moment the bank acquired these properties," wrote SUTICS, "it demanded the cancellation of collective work contracts affecting 147 workers." The bank informed these workers that "it could recognize no union rights, in view of the fact that [the bank] is not an enterprise but an official apparatus." According to the union, "one finds in this same situation the workers of the fincas 'Santa Rose' in Tuxtla Chico; 'El Palmar' and 'California' in Tapachula."[97] The bank, an agent of the state, had become in less than six years one of the most powerful institutions in Soconusco and Chiapas generally.

The debilitation of organized labor came not only at the hands of the Ejidal Bank but also as a result of hiring practices of private land-owners in the 1940s. In 1941 the migration authorities in Motozintla called attention to the "ruinous competition" of Guatemalan workers who came to Mexico to escape a deteriorating economy in their own country and to look for land and higher wages to the north.[98] Coffee planters and the Fideicomiso Cafetero preferred non-unionized Guatemalan *braceros* who would work for less than the minimum wage.[99] By 1950 the migration of Guatemalan workers into Chiapas had become a flood of 30,000 a year.[100] The flow of Guatemalan braceros into the coffee zone had two important consequences. First, Mexican labor unions lost what leverage they once had with the planters, since threats of a strike carried little weight. (The number of strikes declined significantly after 1940.) As a result, "the standard of salaries has remained stagnant for over four years [1939–43]; the same salary that a worker earned when a kilo of maize cost 6 centavos, is the same he earns now, when this same kilo of maize is valued at 18 centavos."[101] The second consequence was the decline in the number of Central Highland Indians who were contracted to work in Soconusco, from around 30,000 in 1940 to fewer than 10,000 by 1950.[102]

Debilitation and immobilization took place on many fronts and for different reasons, but the result was the same: the shifting of responsibility for the welfare of workers and campesinos from independent class-based organizations to the state, which was informally allied with landowners. It was a poor bargain for campesinos and agricultural workers. But as Arturo Warman soberly notes, "Those who did not resign themselves to participating in the apparatus or to following its rules did not have many alternatives."[103]

ECONOMIC RECOVERY

During the interwar period, the 1920s and 1930s, the regional economy of Chiapas was impaired and altered by agrarian reform (or the threat of agrarian reform) and the world depression. Due to lower prices and a general hesitancy to invest in commercial crops, Central Valley finqueros shifted from cotton and sugar cane to cattle. Cattle ranching had long been a mainstay of the economy of the Central Valley, but in the 1920s and 1930s landowners understood that investment in cattle herds could not be expropriated by agraristas. The finqueros also rented their vacant land to Indians from the Central Highlands who needed more land to support their families. Indian renters and sharecroppers cleared small fields for maize plots, which were converted to pasture land after three to four years—thus doubly benefiting the landowners, who earned rent and obtained free Indian labor that expanded their pastures. The Indian renters, furthermore, could not take advantage of the agrarian reform since they did not live on or near the rented fields. The new economy of the Central Valley was not yet very profitable for the finqueros, but it was an excellent entrepreneurial response to impinging political and economic conditions.[104]

The coffee economy of Soconusco also suffered from the twin plagues of agrarianism and depression, but not at first. During the 1920s coffee prices rose and naturally so did production. German economic dominance in the region increased, since the North American colony had left during the Carrancista years and their properties had been purchased by old and new German planters. During the 1930s and the first half of the 1940s, prices declined by more than one half and the threat of agrarian reform became reality. Many small coffee plantations were bankrupted, but the real danger for the large plantations was agrarianism and, later, sequestration. Although the state and federal governments expropriated around 30,000 hectares in the coffee zone and impounded 66 plantations owned by German-Mexicans, the coffee industry was far from destroyed. State regimes during the 1930s and 1940s responded to depression prices by lowering taxes on property and coffee exports. More importantly, coffee planters received certificates of inaffectability protecting their truncated but more intensively cultivated plantations from further expropriation. The German plantations were returned to their owners in 1946, which coincided with the increase of coffee prices on the world market. The coffee zone once again became the bonanza region of Chiapas.[105]

The economic recovery of the Central Valley began in the late 1930s but accelerated during the 1940s. The deceleration of agrarian reform, the widespread distribution of certificates of inaffectability, the decline of government support for organized labor, and the increase of commodity prices all encouraged landowners to reinvest in agriculture, particularly wheat, sugar, and cotton. The expansion and paving of a regional network of roads and highways in the 1940s and the construction of a Gulf Plain railroad from Veracruz through Pichucalco and Palenque to Yucatán in 1940 decreased transportation costs and facilitated greater labor mobility. The combined effect of these diverse developments can be seen in the expansion of land in cultivation (see figure 3). The greatest production increases for most commodities came in the period from 1945 to 1950. Cattle ranching, however, remained the predominant economic activity in the Central Valley.[106]

It should also be emphasized that economic recovery in Chiapas was also in part the result of thirty years of social and economic reform. Labor and agrarian reform, although temporarily harmful to regional landowners, essentially served to provide the state with a large pool of agricultural workers tied to their communities but forced by economic necessity into poorly compensated migrant labor. The "revolutionary" reforms also politically pacified workers and campesinos by providing them with weak organizations of protection and integrating them into the political system. After World War II, organized workers and campesinos were passive supporters of a political system led by wealthy landowners. "By 1948, when the Pan-American Highway was completed in central Chiapas," writes Wasserstrom, "state officials and local landowners had worked out the mechanisms whereby social peace was restored and the appearance of reform might be maintained. . . . In the Grijalva basin, at least, land remained highly concentrated in the hands of men who had entitled and monopolized it since the 1840s."[107]

Despite the remarkable perseverance of the familia chiapaneca in preserving its lands, it was never closed to new talent. The agrarian reform not only divided some large landholdings but also indirectly contributed to the formation of new latifundia. A smalltime ladino ranchero in Teopisca, for example, became a leader of local agraristas in the 1930s. As administrator of the neighboring ejido, he successfully expanded its lands while at the same time protecting the best lands—the irrigable valley portins—of private landowners. In 1935 he became municipal president and used his political influence to increase his own wealth and landholdings. "He managed to buy up remnants of three

Figure 3

Land In Cultivation
Chiapas, 1926 - 1950

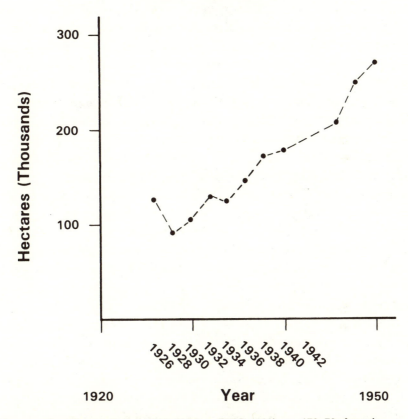

Sources: Anuario estadístico. 1938 (México: DAPP, 1939), pp. 178–79; Anuario estadístico de los Estados Unidos Mexicanos. 1940 (México: Sria. de la Economía Nacional, 1942), p. 503; Anuario estadístico de los Estados Unidos Mexicanos. 1951–1952 (México: Sria. de la Economía Nacional, 1954), pp. 529–589.

fincas in the Río Blanco basin from owners whose fortunes had waned. . . .
With the help of his growing and able sons, he consolidated these three
fincas into a single enterprise and managed them profitably by introducing coffee, expanding and improving the pasture area for the production of beef, and increasing the maize yields by irrigation works on
suitable portions of these holdings." In the 1940s he marketed local
grain, transported produce and manufactured goods, and rented lands.
"In short, he built an economic empire that had no rival in Teopisca."[108]
This was not an uncommon process.

Finally, there is little evidence that regional economic recovery benefited peasant farmers to any significant degree. Although many received
land, the price of the most important crop to campesinos and ejidatarios, corn, failed to keep pace with the general level of inflation of
the 1930s. This meant, as Warman explains, "the peasants, somewhat
perplexed, found themselves obliged to work twice as hard to obtain
barely the same things as ten years earlier: to keep on living, just barely,
with debts, commitments, harvests that faded away in bills."[109] In Chiapas, primarily in the Central Valley during the 1940s, renters and ejidatarios put more land in cultivation and produced more corn while
real income remained stagnant. The peasant economy, cheaply feeding
Mexico's cities, was being robbed by inflation.

Over the course of half a century, from the 1890s to the 1940s, the
national and provincial Mexican state intervened in the regional economy, modernizing both its material infrastructure (primarily roads and
railroads) and the social relations of production (land tenure and labor
utilization). State intervention, in the final analysis, strengthened and
modernized the commercial agricultural economy of Chiapas at very
little cost to the familia chiapaneca. From the 1940s to the 1980s the
expansion of the commercial agricultural economy of Chiapas was
considerable. Yet, as any casual observer realized, most Chiapanecos—
the country people—were very poor.

THE POLITICS OF CONSOLIDATION

The accelerated pace of agrarian reform, policies favorable to labor
and toleration of strikes, the expropriation of the foreign-owned oil
companies (in 1938), and the radical rhetoric of the Cárdenas regime

produced a serious division in Mexican society and politics. President Cárdenas realized the potential danger to political stability that continuation of his program signified and in 1938 began to moderate the reform agenda. It was widely assumed, even by the Marxist labor leader Vicente Lombardo Toledano, that the continuation of Cardenismo would lead to irreparable internal division and possibly civil war, which in turn could provoke intervention by the United States. The times seemed to call for a period of consolidation.[110]

Cárdenas and the revolutionary family of the PRM chose General Manuel Ávila Camacho as the next president—someone who represented the middle ground in national politics. The large segment of Mexican society that opposed any continuation of Cardenismo supported the independent candidacy of General Juan Andreu Almazán. It is believed that Almazán, in fact, had more popular support than Ávila Camacho. Nevertheless, PRM candidate Ávila Camacho was declared winner in the general election in July 1940, although not without considerable violence and electoral fraud. The general impression in the country was that the official candidate had not really triumphed. These circumstances further induced Ávila Camacho to follow a course of conciliation, moderation, and, as he stated in his inaugural address, "consolidation of the conquests of the Revolution."[111]

In Chiapas the official gubernatorial candidate, Dr. Rafael P. Gamboa, was as much a choice of the officials of the national executive committee of the PRM as of the state committee. He was a close friend of Veracruz Governor Miguel Alemán, who was an important Avilacamachista and became gobernación secretary in the new regime. Gamboa had served as secretary general of government in the Gutiérrez regime and had moved on to the Senate where he made valuable contacts with the right politicians. His government in Chiapas (1940–44) represented no sharp break with that of his predecessor in terms of personnel. It was also reported that he was well regarded by coffee planters and businessmen.[112] Juan M. Esponda, secretary general of government from 1940 to 1942, succeeded Gamboa in 1944. Although unpopular in Chiapas, particularly with the official agrarian sector, Esponda was Gutiérrez's and Gamboa's man, and he was elected.[113]

The government of Ávila Camacho gave special emphasis and encouragement to private commercial agriculture, industrial expansion, and foreign investment. It also expanded public investment through the Banco de Mexico and the Nacional Financiera (the National Investment Bank). These new policies were pursued during the favorable economic climate engendered by the national mobilization during World War II. It was at this time that Mexico seriously embarked on the road to industrial development.[114]

The national government also undertook, at the end of the war, political reforms that strengthened the power of the federal government at the expense of local and regional government and the labor sector of the PRM. In December 1945 the Ávila Camacho regime revised the 1918 Electoral Law. The new statute removed from municipal and state authorities the power of establishing and redrawing electoral districts, forming census lists for voting purposes, overseeing the electoral process and computing vote tallies, and declaring a winner. The system of local control of elections had led to innumerable cases of fraud, violence, and general political disorder, most recently in the presidential election of 1940. The president wanted to avoid a repetition of that embarrassing episode and centralized the electoral process at all levels of government in the Federal Commission of Electoral Supervision.[115]

The Partido de la Revolución Mexicana was also reformed during the Ávila Camacho government. In 1940 the military sector was dropped from the party structure and two years later a "popular sector" was added to represent government employees, small businessmen, and the middle class generally. In 1943 the party's campesino sector welcomed "small property owners" as members. In the national party convention of January 1946 the PRM was dissolved and the Partido Revolucionario Institucional (Institutional Revolutionary Party, PRI) was born. The convention also nominted Miguel Alemán Valdés for the presidency. In the PRI, sector independence and influence was diminished, while the power of the party president, a presidential appointee, was strengthened. In the internal selection of candidates, individual voting replaced sector votes. The transformation of the PRM into the PRI reduced the power of the party's single most powerful organization, the Confederación de Trabajadores de Mexico. The Electoral Law and the formation of the PRI also increased the power of the national regime and the presidency. "The regional executive parties and the municipal committees," writes historian Luis Javier Garrido, "did not have after 1943 more than a purely formal existence."[116]

The reformed political system immediately affected Chiapas. In the municipal elections of 1946, Chiapas Governor Juan M. Esponda (who was notorious for selling local offices to the highest bidder) imposed Michoacano Guizar Ocequera as municipal president of Tapachula. On the day Guizar assumed office, December 31, the opposition faction, the Partido Cívico Tapachulteco, staged a protest rally. The fifty police agents sent from Tuxtla Gutiérrez panicked and fired into the crowd, killing twelve and wounding forty-three unarmed citizens.[117] The provisions of the 1945 Electoral Law, although derelict in preventing the scandal, were applied to restore order. The Federal Electoral Commission and the Permanent Commission of the national legislature began an investigation of the incident and concluded that the governor and several state deputies had illegally intervened in the municipal election. Governor Esponda took an unlimited leave of absence rather than face federal intervention.[118]

The state legislature, guided by the new government of President Miguel Alemán in Mexico City, appointed General César Lara provisional governor. Lara's appointment ended the Cardenista-Gutierrista era in Chiapas. Lara, an old Delahuertista (he fought with Alberto Pineda in 1923–24) and a Grajalista in the 1930s, brought the Mapache-Grajalista faction back to power in Chiapas. The Liga de Comunidades Agrarias viewed the shakeup as simply a case where "landowners took over the [state] government."[119]

Francisco Grajales, a Mapachista captain during the Revolution, was elected for the period 1948–52.[120] His regime, and all subsequent state regimes, administered the regional apparatus of government with the passive or calculated political support of the official labor and agrarian organizations of Chiapas and with the active support and close collaboration of the associations of cattlemen, "small property" farmers, cacao and coffee planters, and merchants.[121] The most important and active division of the state government was the Department of Agriculture and Animal Husbandry, which promoted modern farming and husbandry methods, vaccinated cattle, established an institute for artificial insemination, protected cattlemen and farmers from cattle rustlers and squatters, and so on. In his 1949 Informe, Governor Grajales concluded that Chiapas had "two cardinal necessities: communications and education."[122]

Roads and schools were priorities that evoked the modernization program of Emilio Rabasa in the 1890s. How much had really changed since then? A gubernatorial candidate in 1951 offered one answer: "All of the previous governors have come from the Interior of the State, that is Tuxtla Gutiérrez and Chiapas de Corzo and from the same dynasty."[123]

REFLECTIONS

By 1920 the revolutionary process in most regions of Mexico, the important northern and central regions, had come to an ambiguous close. In Chiapas, however, the revolutionary process began at the same time that state government was handed over to the rebellious Mapache finqueros. With the formation of the Partido Socialista Chiapaneco, a genuinely popular mobilization from below challenged the social and political status quo. By forming a politically necessary alliance with Carlos Vidal, the PSC came to power with Vidal in 1925 and began the process of social and economic reform, but in the process abdicated its popular and autonomous character. Vidal began the institutionalization of the popular movement, which began in Motozintla in 1919 and 1920. And Vidal's immediate successors, Raymundo Enríquez, Victórico Grajales, and Efraín Gutiérrez, completed the transformation to controlled mobilization in Chiapas, which in turn facilitated centralization from Mexico City. Controlled mobilization to further reform could be, and was, eventually turned against the reformers and the mobilized.

"I think that extreme centralization of political power," wrote Alexis de Tocqueville, "ultimately enervates society . . . so much that in the end each nation is no more than a flock of timid and hardworking animals with the government as its shepherd."[124] In Chiapas the flock of the impoverished masses, following a brief flirtation with freedom and power, were herded into new corrals by the good shepherds of the government of the familia chiapaneca. By the mid-1970s this flock, no longer timid, was beating against the gates.

EPILOGUE

The government and the finqueros are the same thing (1950s–90s)

CHIAPAS REMAINS AS BEFORE: A RICH LAND AND A POOR PEOPLE. THIS is neither an accident of geography nor a consequence of poor economic planning. The prosperity beside mass poverty in Chiapas as elsewhere in Mexico, writes Gustavo Esteva, "has been brought about by men, by power."[1] The distribution of power and wealth within Chiapas has changed very little since the 1950s. While politically subservient to Mexico City, government in Chiapas continues to serve particular local interests. As one agrarian leader complained in 1980, "The government and the finqueros are the same thing. They are together and they want to screw the Indian."[2] In Chiapas, a journalist explained in 1983, "the finquero and the cacique, the rancher and the lumberman govern, in other words, force."[3] Three years later an opposition congressman declared that "the governor does not rule. It is the caciques, the latifundistas who exercise power."[4] In 1990 the Mexican Commission for the Defense and Promotion of Human Rights denounced the "sordid association" in Chiapas among caciques, finqueros, and the police.[5] An intimate nexus of power and interests still keeps people poor in a rich land.

ECONOMIC EXPANSION AND SAFETY VALVES

Chiapas experienced remarkable economic expansion during the 1950s and 1960s. Cattle raising led the way. Ranchers increased their herds by 65 percent between 1950 and 1960, from 480,000 to more than 790,000 head. By 1970 the cattle stock had reached 1.25 million head (or more than 2 million, according to one estimate.) Production of the export crops of coffee, cacao, sugar cane, and cotton also increased significantly. Coffee remained the single most important agricultural product of Chiapas, representing 40 percent of the total value of agricultural production in the state while taxes on the crop constituted one third of state revenue. During this time Chiapas became the largest coffee producer in Mexico. Sugar cane and cotton, crops that had nearly disappeared during the 1920s and 1930s, once again became economically important. Cultivated land increased from 270,000 hectares in 1950 to over 850,000 in 1975 (See Figure 4). The total value of agricultural, livestock, and lumber production increased more than thirty times from 1950 to 1975.[6]

This economic expansion was due to several favorable external and internal developments. The increase in the world market prices of the most important export crops and the opening of central Mexico as a market for Chiapas cattle, while outside regional control, played an important role. In Chiapas, the frenetic pace of road building, an increase in private and public credit, and the mechanization of agriculture were no less important. To Chiapas's paltry 1,400 kilometers of roads in 1940 more than 6 million kilometers had been added by 1970, opening long-forgotten valleys and villages to commerce. The number of trucks and pickups that used these new roads to transport crops, merchandise, and workers increased substantially, to approximately 2,300 by 1970 (compared to about 500 in 1940). The number of tractors in use increased from about 500 in 1960 to 1,500 by 1970.[7] Although it cannot be quantified, state government support for private agriculture has been no less important. One independent agrarian confederation charged in 1955 that in Chiapas

> the landowners daily take advantage of their friendship with Municipal Presidents and Local and Federal Deputies who have them use the law so that they can persecute and jail those campesinos who request the amplification of an ejido, or simply seek for the first time to petition land from some hacienda that still has not been touched by the Agrarian Reform, like those which have been protected by the so-called Titles of Inaffectability for Cattle Concession although in reality everyone knows that they are purchased by landowners so that their great latifundia will not be affected.[8]

The official labor confederation, the institutional defender of the worker, became a shadow of its former self. In 1948 Salvador Durán Pérez, head of the coffee workers in Soconusco, was "elected" (from Mexico City)

Figure 4

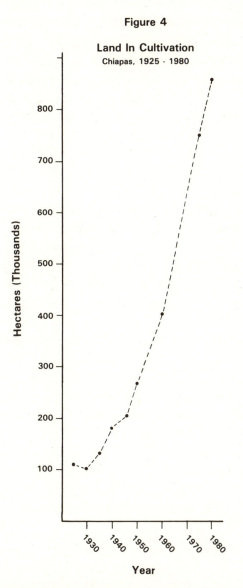

Land In Cultivation
Chiapas, 1925 - 1980

Sources: Anuario estadístico. 1938 (México: 1939), pp. 178–179; Anuario estadístico. 1939 (México, 1941), pp. 392–393; Anuario estadístico. 1940 (México, 1942), p. 503; Tercer censo agrícola, ganadero y ejidal. 1950 (México, 1956), p. 65; VI censos agrícola, ganadero y ejidal. 1960. Resumen General (México, 1965), p. 161; Anuario estadístico de Chiapas, 1985, Tomo II (México, 1986), pp. 1779–1780.

secretary general of the Chiapas Confederación de Trabajadores Mexicanos (CTM). Under the leadership of the "maximum leader," the Chiapas CTM gradually lost the core of its former strength and support, the coffee workers' union, which by the 1980s was "practically nonexistent." The Chiapas CTM since the 1960s has been composed of taxi drivers and construction workers. It has lost its ability to influence or control in any meaningful way the working class of the state.[9]

The economic expansion of the 1950s and 1960s in Chiapas was far more beneficial to private landowners than to ejidatarios.[10] All indices point to the underdevelopment of the ejidal sector. In 1960, for example, while some 900 ejidos supported 92,000 families, as compared to about 30,000 landowning families, the ejidal sector earned one third as much, owned one tenth as many tractors, and possessed land valued at one third of the amount of the private sector.[11] Although the ejidal sector increased its landholdings substantially, most ejidos were overpopulated by the 1960s. Many if not most ejidal parcels were too small to support a family, which forced members to work on neighboring estates or as migrant laborers.[12] The high density of population in ejidos led to soil degradation, severe deforestation, and the near-disappearance of wild game (see figure 5).[13]

Within the private agricultural sector, two classes coexisted, one very poor, the other very wealthy.[14] By 1960 the *minifundistas*—the very small landowners who possessed properties of less than 10 hectares and constituted nearly one half of all landowners—occupied less than 1 percent of all land. The *latifundistas*—the large landowners who owned properties of more than 1,000 hectares and constituted only 2.4 percent of all landowners—owned nearly 60 percent of all land. Just 44 fincas monopolized 25 percent of the land.[15]

Cattle ranching was and remains the dominant activity of the large estates across the state. Although the first certificates of ranching inaffectability (certificados de inafectabilidad ganadera), protecting the property of cattlemen from the agrarian reform, were granted in the late 1930s, the counter reform process was spurred by federal regulation in 1948. "The rise of certificates of immunity thereafter undid many of the reforms undertaken by Cárdenas in the 1930s."[16] Large landowners, not surprisingly, own most cattle and machinery, employ most day laborers and migrant workers, and dominate local and state politics.[17] In the cof-

Figure 5

Population Growth
Chiapas, 1910 - 1985

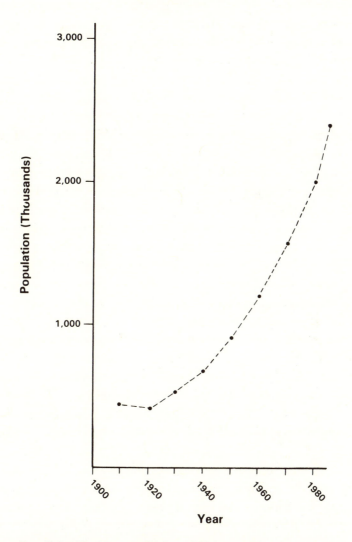

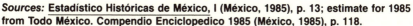

Sources: Estadístico Históricas de México, I (México, 1985), p. 13; estimate for 1985 from Todo México. Compendio Enciclopedico 1985 (México, 1985), p. 118.

fee zone of Soconusco, the private sector is dominated by the "largest coffee fincas in the country" and owned by seven families descended from the Germans who began cultivation during the Porfiriato.[18] In Chiapas, as elsewhere in rural Mexico, government and private agricultural investment, credit, and technical assistance during the 1950s and 1960s were channeled almost entirely into commercial and export agriculture.[19]

For the most part, social peace was preserved in the Chiapas countryside during the 1950s and 1960s less through economic growth than as a result of socioeconomic safety valves. The most important of these was the continuation and expansion of agrarian reform. It was during these two decades that the ejidal sector came to possess roughly one half of all land worked in Chiapas. The quality of these new ejidal lands, by all accounts, was very poor.[20] The number of ejidatarios doubled from approximately 71,000 in 1950 to more than 148,000 by 1970. Seasonal labor on the coffee plantations of Soconusco, rental of land in the Central Valley, and immigration into the eastern frontier also provided income (or land) to the landless as well as additional and very necessary income for ejidatarios.[21] For the most part this movement constituted an "avalanche of the indigenous population" from the Central Highlands.[22] "In a sense it can be argued that without the [coffee] plantations," notes a student of migrant labor, "Chamula would have probably undergone near total economic disintegration."[23] The fragile Lacandón forest served as an agricultural frontier absorbing in recent decades 150,000 Tzeltal, Chol, and Tzoltzil Maya from the Chiapas highlands and Ocosingo valley, postponing an agrarian crisis.[24]

The federal government intervened with programs to promote stability in the underdeveloped countryside through modernization. In the central highlands in the 1950s, the federal Instituto Nacional Indigenista (INI) began a program of social and economic improvement by constructing roads, building schools and health clinics, organizing cooperative stores, and introducing more modern agricultural methods.[25] In 1949 the federal government established the Comisión Nacional de Café, which sought to increase production, improve cultivation, and provide a better system of credit for small holders and ejidatarios in Chiapas and the other coffee-producing states of Mexico. Beginning in 1958 the Comisión was replaced by the Instituto Mexicano del Café (INMECAFE), which sought in addition to regulate the national coffee market by providing guaranteed prices.[26]

This is not to say that these developments provided anything resembling prosperity or even a decent living for most rural Chiapanecos—they certainly did not. Studies based on census data have quantified what most already assumed: postwar Chiapas is one of the most impoverished regions in Mexico. Paul Lamartine Yates, using the 1950 census, created an "index of well-being" (based on levels of literacy, mortality, houses with running water, and so forth) and concluded that, after Oaxaca, Chiapas possessed the lowest level of well-being in Mexico.[27] Historian James W. Wilkie developed a similar but more realistic "poverty index," which placed Chiapas after Oaxaca and Guerrero with one of the highest levels of poverty based on the 1960 census.[28] Finally, an agency of the federal government created in 1977, Coplamar,[29] created an "index of marginality" based on nineteen indicators taken from the 1970 census. To no one's surprise, the states of Oaxaca, Chiapas, and Guerrero had the highest levels of marginality because of their large rural and indigenous population.[30]

Clearly most Chiapanecos from 1940 to 1970 remained very poor; but was poverty in the state declining (if ever so slowly) or increasing? The evidence is contradictory. Wilkie, looking at the 1940-60 period, sees some improvement: a decline in the level of poverty from 61 percent to 49 percent of the population.[31] Regional specialists contend, however, that these were years of growing pauperization and marginalization in the Chiapas countryside. As Wasserstrom has found for the Central Highlands, "the entire program of modernization and transculturation which the state and federal agencies had since 1952 put into effect there had, in reality, caused living standards to decline."[32] And Gustavo Esteva, writing in 1980, states: "Socio-economically, Chiapas is the most backward of the states, a situation which has worsened over the last 25 years."[33]

Still, by means of barely adequate safety valves and occasional repression, Chiapas was politically quiescent and socially "stable" in the decades before 1970.

THE 1970S: BLOODY POPULISM

Beginning in the 1970s, a grassroots, widespread, and increasingly organized agrarian struggle unfolded in Chiapas. It was caused by a complex conjunction of conditions that compelled campesinos to take over plots of (generally) unused but private property to feed their families. They also, however, began to protest and demonstrate to publicize their increasingly desperate plight and the corrupt alliance between wealthy landowners and the government, which rendered ineffective the official organizations long ago established to advance campesino interests and influence. As campesino activism and organization increased, the level of repression and violence directed by private interests and government (often in tandem) against campesino leaders and followers escalated. A low-level, locally-focused agrarian war, bitter and bloody, matured in Chiapas.

At first consideration, the 1970s seem to be an unlikely time for the outbreak of rural discontent. Never before had the national government poured so much money into the development of Chiapas. The construction of the Grijalva-Usumacinta hydroelectric complex in the central valley during the 1970s provided lots of jobs and, in time, half of the electricity for the entire country.[34] By the mid-to-late 1970s the exploration and development of the Reforma oil fields of northern Chiapas and Tabasco had brought considerable investment and employment to the region.[35] The federal administration of President Luis Echeverría (1970-76) redirected attention and resources, after decades of neglect, to the underdeveloped Mexican countryside. The extension of greater credits, agricultural price supports for small private and ejidal producers, and the provision of subsidies for popular consumption items and more public services benefited Chiapas as well as other states.[36] Beginning in 1971 the government of Chiapas, assisted by the United Nations in coordination with the federal government, initiated the Socioeconomic Development Program of the Chiapas Highlands. PRODESH, as it was called, took over the programs of the INI Coordinating Centers and substantially increased expenditures in the indigenous regions of Chiapas.[37]

The state government of Manuel Velasco Suárez (1970-76) was especially active in building roads, providing irrigation works, and purchasing industries of special importance to the state. In the Central Highlands the state encouraged the formation of artisan and consumer cooperatives. The governor's son boasted that by 1976 thirteen federal dependencies, six state agencies, and five international organizations were working to raise the standard of living of Chiapas's Indians.[38]

These developments, however, contributed more to economic stress than to prosperity and stability. The large construction and developmental projects of the 1970s increased the cost of living, on top of an accelerating national inflation, more than offsetting any benefit from increased employment. This was particularly true in northern Chiapas, where most jobs in the petroleum industry were filled by unionized migrants while prices climbed for local residents.[39] The hydroelectric complex—including the dams of Malpaso, La Angostura, and Chicoasén—created lakes that submerged more than 200,000 hectares of productive land in the Central Valley, thus crowding ejidatarios even more. The federal government, according to a report from *Excelsior*, "intervened with such an impact that it upset the balance of regional life."[40]

The diversion of resources into Chiapas in the 1970s was a case of too little, too late. By this time several factors had combined to create an explosive situation: soil erosion and depletion, the pernicious corruption of government agencies that had dealt with campesinos, rising prices and stagnant wages, increasing concentration of private farmlands, the expansion of cattle pastures at the expense of farmland, and—worst of all—fraud, delay, and languor in the agrarian reform process.[41] Despite the impressive economic expansion of the previous three decades, in 1970 more than 90 percent of economically active Chiapanecos earned less than 1,000 pesos a month, or slightly more than eighty dollars. Nearly 40 percent of the population was illiterate; about 50 percent of all the houses were without running water and electricity; and 80,000 day laborers worked on fincas and plantations, often living in miserable huts and receiving less than the minimum wage. Chronic alcoholism, malnutrition, and diseases such as tuberculosis, typhus, and intestinal parasites plagued Indian communities. Perhaps 90 percent of Indian children were undernourished.[42]

By the 1970s the process of *ganaderización*—the expansion of pastures for cattle at the expense of cropland—had gone too far in Chiapas. Cattlemen converted lands formerly rented or sharecropped by corn farmers into pastures; they took over abandoned lands and "rented" ejido lands; and they expanded into forested areas, causing destructive deforestation and soil erosion.[43] Following peasant farmers into the Lancandon forest on new government-built roads, cattlemen purchased or simply appropriated the cleared plots to form large ranchos.[44] "Supported by generous bank loans, these colonist-cattlemen joined the state's politicians in envisioning the rainforest as one vast cattle ranch."[45] As cattle herds expanded and pastures increased in Chiapas, land erosion and exhaustion accelerated, pastures displaced milpas, the production of corn and other basic grains stagnated, and an agrarian crisis developed (see figure 6).[46]

However, the key to campesino activism was the problem of land and the unresponsiveness of the Secretaria de la Reforma Agraria to campesino land petitions, as well as the inability of the Confederación Nacional Campesina (CNC) to help its clients. By the 1970s there were nearly 4,000 agrarian petitions pending; many were decades old and apparently forgotten. Hundreds of government resolutions favorable to communities and ejidos had been suspended due to injunctions requested by landowners while they appealed the decisions.[47] The CNC, however, writes Neil Harvey, "had become increasingly ineffective in achieving land redistribution" while its leaders were denounced "for their collaboration with landowners and government officials in assuring that land was *not* redistributed."[48] The local CNC, in turn, blamed the agrarian reform bureaucracy. When land *was* granted, the different agencies and departments were known to award two different campesino groups the same ejidos, which then became the so-called "two-story ejidos" and sources of conflict.[49] The campesinos, said the president of the Liga de Comunidades Agrarias de Chiapas, "are witnesses of the indifference and apathy of the Secretaria de la Reforma Agraria to resolve their old and grave problems."[50]

The recent history of one community tells much about the renewal of agrarian struggle in Chiapas. In 1945 the residents of Venustiano Carranza (formerly San Bartolomé de los Llanos) petitioned for the restitution of lands they claimed had been stolen from them during the Porfiriato. In 1965 President Gustavo Díaz Ordaz awarded the petitioners provisional title to 50,000 hectares, of which 20,000 were in possession of local cattlemen who refused to give up the land. (Nineteen families controlled 40 percent of private property in the municipality in 1970.[51]) In 1974 the Department of Agrarian Affairs and Colonization ordered these ranchers to relinquish control of this land, but nothing happened. In the meantime, the construction of La Angostura dam considerably reduced the size of Venustiano Carranza's ejido, which put

Figure 6

Cattle Raising
Chiapas, 1880 - 1983

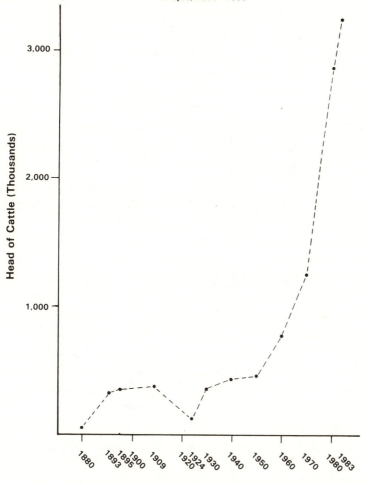

Sources: Emiliano Busto, <u>Estadístico de la república mexicana</u>, I, Cuadro de Agricultura Num. 6 (México, 1880); Rámon Rabasa, <u>El estado de Chiapas</u> (México, 1895), p. 118; <u>Chiapas su estado actual</u> (México, 1895); Moises T. De la Peña, <u>Chiapas económico</u>, II (México, 1951), p. 470; <u>Anuario estadístico</u>. 1940 (México, 1942), p. 496; <u>Compendio estadístico</u> (México, 1950), p. 181; <u>Tercer censo agrícola, ganadero y ejidal</u>. 1950 (México, 1956), p. 162; <u>VI Censos agrícola-ganadero y ejidal</u>. 1960 (México, 1965), p. 462; <u>Anuario estadístico de Chiapas, 1985,</u> III (México, 1986), p. 1831.

severe pressure on the community. Finally, early in 1976 several hundred campesinos "invaded" the disputed land, built houses, and started farming. Mexican army units moved in during the spring and forced the campesinos off the land, burned down their houses, and jailed their leaders. Several of the "invaders," including women and children, were killed or wounded.[52] In 1978 the ejidatarios seized the municipal palace for five days to force the release of their leaders and, in 1979, attempted another "invasion" and again were expelled. The army has remained in Carranza since 1976.[53]

Similar takeovers, violent explusions, and confrontations with landowner's *pistoleros* and public security forces multiplied during the 1970s throughout the Chiapas countryside.[54] What was going on? According to the Mexican government, due to "the atomization that land distribution is producing in the state, invasions of peasants against cattle ranchers and vice versa are very frequent."[55] One analysis of 115 serious agrarian disputes in Chiapas during the 1970s concluded that 87 had been caused by the takeover of ejidal lands by cattle ranchers.[56]

By the end of the decade, local jails and the state prison were being filled with community agrarian leaders, who were essentially political prisoners.[57] They were the lucky ones. From 1966 to 1975, for example, the first four leaders (comisariados de bienes comunales) of the Venustiano Carranza ejido were assassinated, presumably by pistoleros acting on behalf of the local caciques. Reports of assassinations and deadly assaults, generally in relation to forcible explusions from private property, were all too common. Amnesty International observed "a pattern of apparently deliberate political killings."[58] The Indian villagers of San Francisco reported that in 1975 soldiers from the 46th Battalion "assaulted them, burned their homes, and drove them from their land—which was then handed over to non-Indians with political connections."[59] In May 1976 soldiers shot and killed five agraristas in Venustiano Carranza. In 1978 four ejidatarios were killed when the state police, accompanied by guardias blancas, expelled 300 campesinos from a parcel of land in Suchiate. In 1980 fifteen persons were killed and twenty-two wounded when soldiers attacked the community of Colonchán in Chilón. "Governor Juan Sabines Gutierrez was the one who ordered us killed," said one resident of Colonchán, "because he's in with and defends the interests of the landowners."[60]

This was the infamous "bloody populism" of governors Jorge de la Vega Domínguez (1976-78), Salomón González Blanco (1978-80), and especially Sabines Gutiérrez (1980-82): increased government spending for rural development coupled with greater violent repression of rural "troublemakers."[61] This formula, in fact, would reappear in the 1980s and again in the 1990s. Money was channeled into Chiapas in the hope that it would smother conflict and purchase peace. Infusions of money, however, with no change in the intimate nexus of power and interests in the state, bought only time, an occasional temporary truce. And in time, as most of the money found its way into the pockets of politicians and the rich, desperation and outrage forced campesinos to take direct action, and landowners and caciques brutally defended their interests.

AN EXPLOSION OF PEOPLES' ORGANIZATIONS

Learning through long and bitter experience that the CNC and its regional member organization, the Liga de Comunidades Agrarias de Chiapas, not only would not help them but often participated in attacks against them, Indian and ladino workers, campesinos, and ejidatarios organized independent community, labor, and agrarian organizations in the 1970s and 1980s. "The events of this period gave rise to an explosion of peoples' organizations."[62] The rebellion that erupted in 1994, writes Carlos Tello Díaz, "is the natural continuation of the movements of the 1970s."[63]

Indian politicization and organization were assisted by the First Indian Congress in Chiapas, sponsored by Bishop Samuel Ruiz in San Cristóbal de Las Casas in 1974. The Congress brought together Tzotzil, Tzeltal, Chol, and Tojolabal leaders representing more than 300 communities. Many of the leaders of the new agrarian organizations which later emerged had been delegates in 1974. "The Congress produced," Ana Bella Pérez Castro writes, "a massive, well-organized movement."[64] Local organization was also assisted by activist priests, members of regular orders, and catequistas as well as radical political activists (refugees from the Student Movement of 1968).

Three broad and fractious, popular and independent movements developed in the most contentious and conflictive regions in Chiapas: the eastern frontier (Las Cañadas and the Selva Lacandona), the Simojovel area of the north, and at Venustiano Carranza in the center. Mobilization in Soconusco, still the region of "the most highly developed agrarian capitalism in Chiapas,"[65] was stifled as a result of the large number of temporary Guatemalan migrant laborers who worked the coffee harvests. One finca administrator explained why he hired Guatemalans: "field hands are cheaper, they don't ask for loans and they don't think they can invade the property just because it is large."[66]

The migrant Tzeltal communities and ejidos of the Las Cañadas region of eastern Chiapas, encouraged by the Echeverría government (for reasons of efficiency and productivity), formed three separate Uniones de Ejidos (UE) in 1975-76: UE "Quiptic Ta Lecubtecel" (United by our Strength, in Tzeltal) located in the valley of San Quintin in the municipality of Ocosingo, UE "Tierra y Libertad" (Land and Liberty) and UE "Lucha Campesina" (Peasant Struggle) both in the municipality of Las Margaritas. The new UEs, writes Neil Harvey, "were not controlled by interests loyal to the PRI but by the delegates who had participated in the Indian Congress." They were also influenced and advised by several Church catequistas as well as Maoist political activists from northern Mexico, a group known as Línea Proletaria (See Figure 7).[67]

The Uniones de Ejidos were also born of agrarian insecurity. In 1972 the Echeverría government granted 600,000 hectares to a small number of Lancandón families (in conjunction with a lumber company). The communities of migrants began to organize to modify the 1972 concession and obtain definitive title to the lands they worked. During the 1970s certain communities were declared by the state government to be "invaders" of the lands they had long possessed and worked, and were attacked and burned by soldiers. The UEs, organized and determined to hold onto their lands, embarked upon a long struggle of negotiation with government agencies.[68]

In 1980, led by Quiptic, the three UEs joined other, smaller producer groups in the Selva, along the Guatemalan frontier, and in the highlands, to form the Unión de Uniones Ejidales y Grupos Campesinos Solidarios de Chiapas (UU). This organization of approximately 150 indigenous communities scattered throughout 11 municipalities comprising about twelve thousand families "was the first and largest independent campesino organization in Chiapas."[69]

While the communities of the UU did not obtain secure and guaran-

Selva Lacandona

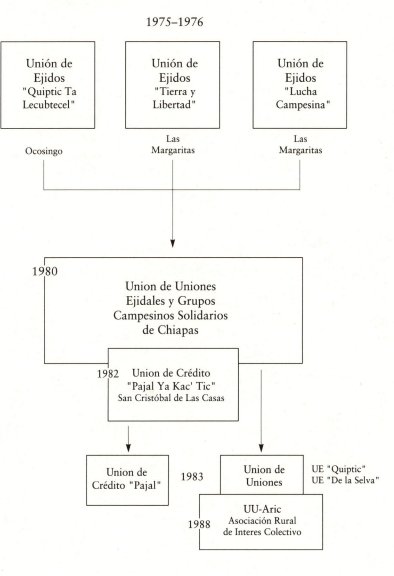

Catazaja

La Libertad

Palenque

Tumbala

Yajalón   Chilón

• Ocosingo   • Monte Libano

Oxchuc

← To   Las Cañadas
San Cristóbal   Altamirano

Guatemala

                                              San Quintin •

Comitán •   Las Margaritas   • Guadalupe Tepeyac

             La Indepencia

0   50   100

kilometers

La Selva Lacandona

teed titles to their ejidos until the late 1980s, the land problem was increasingly overshadowed by more immediate economic necessities. Their concerns in the 1980s focused on credit, production, and marketing and how government agencies might assist them. As a result, the advisors and leaders of the UU embraced a strategy of negotiation and cooperation with the state. This approach led to the formation of the Unión de Crédito "Pajal Ya Kac' Tic" ("We Work Together," in Tzotzil) in 1982, an effort to end financial dependency on government bureaucrats.

The manner in which the Unión de Credito was formed, however, led to a schism in the organization. The leaders of the "Quiptic" and "Tierra y Libertad" Uniones de Ejidos opposed the rising influence and power of an agrarista leader, Adolfo Orive, of Línea Proletaria, and left the Credit Union. The two successor organizations, however, continued to pursue similar policies. Both collaborated with government agencies in order to increase the autonomy and efficiency of their economic apparatuses. The Orive faction, the Unión de Crédito, for example, purchased a coffee processing plant in 1983 while the anti-Orive faction, which kept the UU name and joined the Asociación Rural de Interes Colectivo (ARIC) in 1988, developed organic coffee production for export to Europe. Both organizations, indeed, all of the communities and ejidos of the Selva (and elsewhere in Chiapas) have struggled to survive since 1989, when the international price of coffee declined by half.[70]

In the north of Chiapas, in the coffee producing municipios of Simojovel, Huitiupán, Sabanilla, and El Bosque, independent campesino mobilization has been focused on land. There agrarian reform established 25 ejidos between 1934 and 1959, but "the lands which were granted were surplus finca lands: lands of poor quality."[71] By the 1970s the ejidos were greatly overpopulated and the region had a large population of peones acasillados working in coffee fincas and petitioning for land. Frustrated with the CNC, agrarian "invasions" of fincas began in 1975 and 1976, only to be followed by repression by army and landowner-organized "counter-insurgency militias."[72]

A central committee (comité central) of seven ejidos in Huitiuapán, a tangible consequence of the Indian Congress, followed legal avenues to free imprisoned campesinos and to further agrarian reform. Getting nowhere, the organization adopted in 1976 a strategy of direct action—

land invasions. By 1977 the Central Committee represented 37 ejidos in Huitiuapán, Simojovel, Sabanilla, and El Bosque and over the next three years invaded and held onto parts of 19 fincas. Late in the decade, the Central Committee invited the assistance of the Central Independiente de Obreros Agrícolas y Campesinos (CIOAC) in the establishment of a union of agricultural wage laborers. The Sindicato de Obreros Agrícolas was established in 1980, uniting groups of acasillados from 20 fincas. A wave of strikes broke out in the coffee fincas of the north. CIOAC was established in Chiapas (See Figure 8).[73]

At the same time the CNC countered CIOAC and established its own union of agricultural workers, "Solidaridad," which promptly obtained legal registration by the Commission of Conciliation and Arbitration. "Solidaridad" petitioned Reforma Agraria for land, organized strike breakers against the CIOAC actions, and even "invaded" properties previously "invaded" by CIOAC groups. The state government not only assisted the official union but attempted to repress the independent union. Legal registration was denied at first, and even after it was approved in 1983, the campaign of arrests and murders of CIOAC leaders in Chiapas continued.[74]

With legal registration the CIOAC sindicato organized locals in other parts of Chiapas, established a credit union, supported leftist political parties in the state, organized highly publicized protest marches (one from Chiapas to Mexico City in 1983), and fought for better wages and benefits for wage laborers. CIOAC also conceived of the class struggle in Chiapas as one uniting labor and land rights. As a result, it pushed and negotiated with Reforma Agraria for land and took direct action, occupying numerous fincas. Finally, in 1987, the government authorized entitlement of CIOAC members to 16 ejidos.[75]

The struggle for land in Venustiano Carranza gave rise to the third independent campesino movement in Chiapas. "The movement of the People's House" (Casa del Pueblo) took its name from the building, constructed in 1972-73, that served as the offices and center of the comuneros (the members of the Carranza agrarian community entitled to land). The failure of the DAAC to implement fully the 1965 agrarian decree led the comuneros to adopt a more direct course of action. In 1974 the comuneros, led by their fourth comisariado, Bartolomé Martínez Villatoro, seized and occupied the DAAC offices in Tuxtla

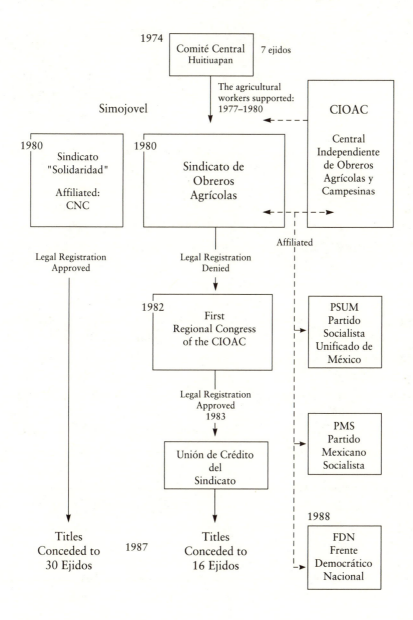

Gutiérrez and, as a result, obtained an agreement to begin work on implementing the decree (See Figure 9).[76]

The struggle, however, was just beginning. Martínez Villatoro, like all of his predecessors, was murdered in 1975. The following year the army seized the Casa del Pueblo building and ignited a shootout that led to the deaths of seven soldiers, two comuneros, and the arrest of the leaders of the movement. The repression led some members of the movement to call off the land struggle and accept government assistance, credit, and patronage. (The comuneros viewed this as a "spurious group" composed of outsiders and policemen and formed by the authorities.)[77] These *coras*, as they came to be called, joined the CNC and were officially recognized by SRA as the legitimate agrarian community of Carranza. The comuneros, denied official recognition and government help, countered the 'divide and conquer' strategy of the government with their own approach of bridging campesino isolation by making alliances.[78]

In 1979 representatives from the Casa del Pueblo attended the founding congress of the Coordinadora Nacional Plan de Ayala (CNPA) at Milpa Alta. The comuneros began to build bridges nationally and, with the help of catequistas, within Chiapas. The following year the Casa del Pueblo joined with communities from various municipalities, from Simojovel in the north to Las Margaritas in the southeast, to form the Coordinadora Provisional de Chiapas. In July 1982 this emerging organization of communities and ejidos adopted a new name: the Organización Campesina Emiliano Zapata (OCEZ). With member groups in four large zones of Chiapas, the OCEZ became the broadest of the popular organizations formed in Chiapas at this time. It also became, writes Neil Harvey, "the most combative of the independent organizations in Chiapas."[79]

The OCEZ during the 1980s pursued a strategy of uncompromised independence, economic autonomy, mobilization and negotiation. The OCEZ, unlike the CIOAC, has stayed out of party politics and unlike the UU-ARIC and the coras, has avoided entangling relationships with government agencies. (It is for this reason, perhaps, that some former CIOAC communities have joined OCEZ as well as one Unión de Ejidos.) It has established food and transport cooperatives, organized protests and marches, and negotiated with government dependencies regarding

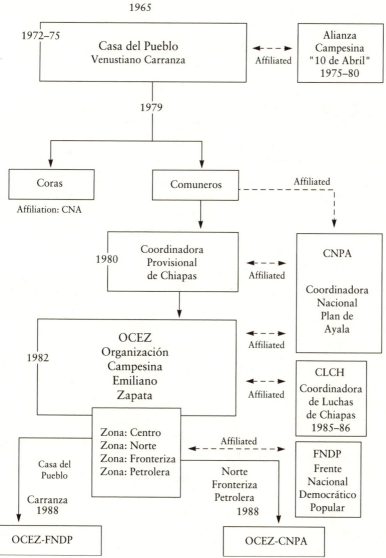

the provision of services, justice, and land. The OCEZ continued its bridge building tradition in the 1980s by joining the broad-based but short-lived and repressed Coordinadora de Luchas de Chiapas (CLCH) and the Frente Nacional Democrática Popular (FNDP).[80]

Unfortunately, the OCEZ, like the UU, could not avoid a schism. In 1988 the organization split into two groups over the issues of alliances and internal democracy. A faction led by Arturo Albores, a former student activist who arrived in Chiapas in the mid-1970s, opposed the Casa del Pueblo's alliance with the FNDP, which Albores believed was infiltrated by government agents. The Casa del Pueblo, on the other hand, denounced Albores for his "caudillismo."[81]

These popular and independent organizations were not the only ones to emerge in Chiapas in the 1970s and 1980s. The teacher's movement, for instance, a struggle for a democratic and independent union, won control of the local and was influential in the national struggle. In the Frailesca there was also an early attempt at ending the isolation of the various agrarian groups in the Central Valley in 1975. The Alianza Campesina "10 de April" (named after the date of Emiliano Zapata's assassination) coordinated "land takeovers by various soliciting groups from the municipalities of Villa Flores, Angel Albino Corzo, Chiapa de Corzo, Venustiano Carranza, Socoltenango, Tzimil y Comalapa."[82] Along the Pacific coast the Alianza Campesina Revolucionaria appeared, which, beginning in 1982, led invasions of fincas.[83] The Solidaridad Campesino-Magisterial organization of the mid-1980s was a coalition of campesinos and teachers that was repressed by the state government not long after its formation. The Comité de Defensa de la Libertad Indígena was established in the late 1980s and early 1990s to publicize government abuses and neglect.

All of this activity represents profound and widespread discontent with the status quo, a new-found politicization, and enormous distrust and repudiation of established, official "popular" organizations. In a manner reminiscent of the grassroots activism of the 1920s, campesinos and workers in Chiapas were, and are, reconstituting themselves as determined, independent, and democratic movements of popular struggle. As before, this most recent and current mobilization is weakened by factionalism sponsored by government but also generated by the inevitable disagreements which arise over leadership, strategy, and ideology.

As before, "outsiders," that is, political activists originally from other parts of Mexico who became "naturalized Chiapanecos" through long residence and sacrifice, have played an important role in this mobilization. Ultimately, however, it has been the campesinos of Chiapas themselves who have built these organizations through their participation and by building bridges with similar groups within Chiapas and in the rest of Mexico.

THE 1980S: AN ESCALATING REPRESSION

The crisis in rural Chiapas during the 1970s did not abate in the 1980s. On top of the worsening agrarian struggle three additional calamities befell the state: an invasion of Guatemalan refugees; the eruption of the volcano Chichonal; and the imposition of a new governor, General Absalón Castellanos Domínguez. With war and revolution in neighboring countries and a low-intensity agrarian war in Chiapas, the federal and state governments began to militarize Chiapas. By 1987 approximately 4,000 soldiers were stationed in the state. The two state police forces, the Public Security Police and the Judicial Police, were placed under the command of military officers. "Chiapas has been turned into another one of the principal operations of the armed forces," commented one reporter.[84] Two Soconusense observers declared that "Chiapas lives under a state of siege. General Absalón Castellanos Domínguez tries to solve the region's problems by the least adequate means: repression."[85] Jesús Heriberto Noriega, an opposition politician, explained that it was all part of a strategy "to establish security zones in order to weaken, in particular, the left."[86]

Beginning in mid-1981, more Guatemalans than ever before fled into Chiapas to escape the murderous counterinsurgency campaign of the new military government of General Efraín Ríos Montt. These unwanted refugees, Indian campesinos for the most part, filled more than ninety camps along the Chiapas-Guatemala border during the next two years. Mid-decade estimates of the number of refugees ranged from the low official count of 50,000 to the Catholic Church's figure of 100,000. "One politically dangerous aspect of the refugee problem," one scholar wrote, "is the attention it focuses on the suffering of Mexico's own citizens. This is particularly true in Chiapas."[87]

There was also concern in Mexico City, among business leaders and conservative politicians, that Central American guerrillas could take advantage of the mass exodus to establish themselves in Chiapas and spread the virus of social revolution, which could threaten the Reforma oil fields.[88] "The Chiapas area is considered especially vulnerable to insurrection," reported an American journalist, reflecting the unofficial but real concern of Mexican officials.[89] The actual threat was different. The Guatemalan army began to make frequent incursions—sixty-four raids between 1981 and 1984—across the border to attack the camps and torture and murder supposed guerrillas and guerrilla sympathizers.[90] Genuinely concerned about the insecurity of its southern border, the Mexican government increased the number of army units in the state. Military roadblocks were set up to search vehicles for weapons. The federal government began construction of the Southern Frontier Highway along the border parallel to the Rio Usumacinta to better secure the region. And in 1984 the federal government began to relocate about 18,000 refugees to Campeche. The war in Guatemala aggravated the crisis in Chiapas.[91]

In March 1982 in the area of Ixtacomitán, "the sky blazed and the earth burned."[92] The eruption of the Chichonal volcano killed 1,500 people, devastated a large area that included an ejido and 67 private fincas, and uprooted about 14,000 Zoque Indians. Governor Sabines Gutiérrez responded by announcing that the state would purchase the affected lands and relocate the people. The landowners were well compensated, but the Zoques were placed in areas with insufficient and poor quality lands. Many emigrated to Zoque regions in Veracruz and Tabasco, others have been forced into migrant labor, and many Zoque women have become prostitutes at the Las Penitas dam construction site. Most of the 2.5 million pesos allocated to assist the Zoques disappeared when Governor Sabines Gutiérrez left office.[93]

In 1982 General Absalón Castellanos Domínguez, the commander of the 31th military zone at the time of the army massacre of Indians at Golonchán in 1980, was "elected" governor of Chiapas. The PRI's selection of a career military man, many speculated, was a response to increasing disorder within Chiapas as well as in neighboring Central America. The new governor, a member of an old and wealthy landowning family, was identified in Chiapas as a modern Mapache.[94] Six months after taking office, General Castellanos granted an interview to *Excel-*

sior. "Chiapas," the governor noted, "is a paradox. It is one of the country's three main food producers but also one of the three states with the most malnutrition and hunger." It is the first-ranking state in coffee production and corn but also first in illiteracy. It is second in importance in cacao and banana production and also second in the nation in fatalities caused by infectious and parasitic diseases. And how did the governor explain the causes of these problems? "During the [campaign] tour," Castellanos said, "I encountered the age-old problems besetting us: caciquismo, alienation, lack of education and public health, meager productivity, the poverty of the Indians and campesinos, and irrational use of our resources; all stemming from a single cause—lack of communications." His first priority as governor, he continued, would be road building.[95]

The governor, perhaps accidentally, identified one of the keys to the "paradox" of Chiapas. "We have no middle class," he asserted, "there are the rich, who are very rich, and the poor, who are extremely poor.[96] The governor—who owns an ostentatious mansion constructed by the state Department of Public Works and two fincas which, allegedly, include lands that in part had been legally granted to two ejidos as a result of agrarian reform—has ensured that his family remains one of the "very rich."[97]

The new decade and administration in Chiapas did witness two more programs of social development. During the 1982 campaign, PRI candidate Miguel de la Madrid promised to initiate a major development program in Chiapas. The federal government, in conjunction with the World Bank, unveiled the six-year, 300 million dollar Plan Chiapas in January 1983—although the funding arrangement was not agreed upon until the spring of 1985. The president, in explaining the necessity of the program, said that "the Mexican Revolution has not yet fulfilled its mission in Chiapas and there are places where the Revolution is unknown." The immediate objective of Plan Chiapas was to increase the production of foodstuffs by "small farmers" through the construction of irrigation works and roads.[98] Beginning in 1984, the state and federal governments also attempted to resolve land disputes with the Programa de Rehabilitación Agraria (PRA). The approach was to compensate finqueros for lands "invaded" and occupied by campesinos. The PRA was focused in those areas with the greatest conflict (Simojovel, the Selva, and Venustiano Carranza) and provided title to land to campesinos affiliated with the CNC, primarily, but also independent organizations. "The principle beneficiaries of the PRA," writes Neil Harvey, "were the landowners and some agrarian reform officials." Between 1984 and 1987 these fortunate constituencies devoured the 100 million dollar budget.[99]

These new programs, existing ones, and larger market forces benefited commercial agriculture in Chiapas: cash crops and cattle. Campesinos were encouraged to produce coffee (which was hardly a new policy) by high prices and government credit. By the early 1990s there were more than 70,000 coffee producers in Chiapas—70 percent were minifundistas, 60 percent were Indians. Campesinos were moving into the commercial agricultural sector but there were still many, many campesino corn farmers and their economy was in a precarious position. During the 1980s the government steadily reduced the provision of subsidized credit, lowered guaranteed prices paid to farmers, and generally reduced investment in the Mexican countryside. Not surprisingly, productivity and production in basic grains, like maize, declined and imports of the same increased.[100] "The growth of private sector commercial agriculture," on the other hand, "boomed in Chiapas."[101]

The agrarian crisis in Chiapas, meanwhile, worsened. As pressure for land distribution increased due to campesino mobilization, the administration of President Miguel de la Madrid (and of Governor Castellanos) during the sexenio of 1982-88 accelerated the "protection for private owners against expropriation." During the sexenio of President José López Portillo (1976–82), for example, 61 certificates of agricultural inaffectability (certificados de inafectabilidad agrícola) and 45 certificates of ranching inaffectability (certificados de inafectabilidad ganadera) were issued to Chiapas landowners. During De la Madrid's (and Castellanos's) sexenio, 2,932 (agricuture) and 4,714 (ranching) certificates were issued. More than a million hectares were legally protected against land reform during the 1980s, more land than in the preceeding forty-five years combined.[102] In 1984 Reforma Agraria declared in Tuxtla Gutiérrez that "the national government cannot provide land to all campesinos who ask for it."[103]

Campesinos, however, were not deterred. The agrarian and labor organizations established in the 1970s continued their struggle during the 1980s. "Invasions" continued. At times the struggle involved poor landless campesinos encroaching upon the tiny holdings of poor farmers and ranchers. Generally, however, the class lines were well drawn. In 1983 it was reported that campesinos invaded 128 fincas in Chiapas.[104] Luis López Vázquez, secretary general of CIOAC in Chiapas, announced in 1985 that "his people" had occupied 109 large fincas in various municipalities around the state.[105] The tenacious people of Monte Líbano in the municipality of Ocosingo settled on "their land" in 1976 only to have their houses burned down. They returned in 1979 and 1982 and suffered the same outrage. In 1983 they wrote the president saying: "the blood bath is not over and the God of War in the state of Chiapas has not stopped harrasing all of the Indians. . . . Our struggle has been difficult and unequal, the rich with their money have bought authorities of all sizes and we just shout that we are right. Our town has suffered the violence of landowners and caciques." They concluded their plea by promising: "the experience has been hard and bitter but this we have learned: if we don't do it, no one will, and we are prepared to struggle for the recovery of our lands."[106]

Invasions were followed by explusions, usually by violent means with tragic ends. In 1982 Chiapas had the dubious honor of being the second most violent state in the country (Veracruz was first).[107] In spite of this, Governor Castellanos claimed in 1983 that in Chiapas, "there are no serious problems."[108] The Castellanos administration sought to avoid the necessity of expelling campesinos from private property by preventing invasions from occurring at all. The police or the army, at the first sign of an invasion or in response to requests by landowners, would move into a community rapidly and jail the leaders.[109] PSUM's *Así Es* during the early-to-mid 1980s constantly reported "persecution, imprisonment, and harrasment of all the native and campesino movements of Simojovel, Villa de las Rosas, Villa de las Flores, Venustiano Carranza and the border with Guatemala."[110]

International and Mexican human rights organizations monitored and documented repression in Chiapas.[111] In 1986, for example, Amnesty International observed in Chiapas "a pattern of apparently deliberate political killings." The report continued: "The majority of the reported victims were supporters of independent peasant organizations or rural trade unions. The killings appear to have occurred in nearly all cases in the context of long-standing land disputes."[112] In 1987 the Academia

Mexicana de Derechos Humanos characterized the Castellanos government as one of the most repressive in the country.[113] John E. Mendez, director of Human Rights Watch/Americas, in testimony before the United States Congress, noted that in Chiapas "disputes over land are resolved by force, and social and political organizations that are formed to represent peasants are ruthlessly persecuted. . . . In our view, a pervasive culture of human rights violations has marked PRI rule in Chiapas."[114]

The 1980s witnessed, thus, "an escalating repression."[115] Chiapas experienced more than an agrarian crisis, more than an economic crisis. Perhaps more fundamental, the responses of poor people to hunger and hardship and the responses of finqueros and politicians to the actions of the poor, created a severe crisis of justice. The new administration of President Carlos Salinas de Gortari compounded both problems, leaving many campesinos in Chiapas believing they had few options.

THE 1990S: ONE STEP FROM GUERRILLA WAR

At first, the new decade brought only more of the same to Chiapas: more "new" government programs, more independent grassroots organizations, more hardship, more protest, more repression. But with the start of 1994 came rumors of groups of armed revolutionaries, *guerrilleros*, in the state. Ten years earlier, in the time of Central American revolutions, Guatemalan refugees, and a severe national economic crisis, the Episcopado Mexicano had feared that Chiapas was "one step from guerrilla war due not to the presence of Guatemalan refugees but because of worsening injustice."[116] The immediate crises passed and the fears diminished. Ten years later, in the midst of a new crisis, and now rumors, sightings, and isolated confrontations with armed uniformed men, Chiapas was once again considered "one step from guerrilla war." The possibility of guerrilleros in Chiapas, however, was inconceivable (or at least inadmissible) to those in government, given the apparent triumph of 'Salinastroika,' which was modernizing Mexico and bringing it into the First World as an economic partner of Canada and the United States. "There are no guerrillas in Chiapas," proclaimed Joaquín Armendáriz Cea, the state attorney general. "This is definitely a false alarm and it comes from those who seek to discredit the government and frighten the Chiapanecan people."[117] Of course, in 1993 there *were* guerrillas in Chiapas and their dramatic appearance in early 1994 exposed the authoritarian and impoverished reality of Mexico, which had been hidden from the rest of the world under the bright and shiny economic transformation that Salinas was engineering.

In typical fashion the new federal and state administrations of President Salinas and Governor Patrocinio González Garrido, beginning in 1988, gave new benefits in Chiapas with one hand and took away existing benefits with the other. It was not, many campesinos believed, a good bargain. They protested, and the repression continued.

Soon after taking office, President Salinas established the National Solidarity Program, an anti-poverty program that has provided funding to local groups (Comités Locales de Solidaridad) for small projects of community development and improvement. The central element of Solidarity was local participation in the design and execution of projects. In Chiapas specifically, Solidarity provided credit to subsistence farmers and campesino coffee producers. No state received more money from Solidarity during the Salinas sexenio than Chiapas. Solidarity provided funding for schools, health clinics, hundreds of basketball courts, repairs of public buildings, roads and bridges, and more. The results seem impressive. "Yet this massive investment," writes Jessica Kreimerman about the town of Villa Corzo, "has not improved the day-to-day lives of its inhabitants."[118]

Despite increasing budgets and the multiplication of projects, Solidarity can hardly hope even to dent the massive poverty and vast income disparity in Chiapas. "The problems of poverty cannot be solved through money," Jorge G. Castañeda writes, "because the problems are related to structures, not spending."[119] Anthropologist Andrés Medina has calculated that spending by Solidarity nationally is about one dollar per Indian per year.[120] Like many other past development programs, Solidarity appears to have more of a political than a developmental function. The governor of Chiapas prior to 1994 controlled Solidarity disbursements and rewarded local political allies while bypassing politically independent communities and organizations.[121]

The benefits of the one-and-a-half million new peso investment by Solidarity in Chiapas from 1989 to 1993 were offset by a number of more harmful developments. The federal government began to eliminate agricultural price supports, credits, and subsidies prior to 1988 but the Salinas administration accelerated the transition to a free market. This policy was ratified by the North American Free Trade Agreement (NAFTA) in 1993. Although the agreement provides a fifteen-year phase-out of trade protection for maize and beans farmers, and the administration established a new agricultural support program in the fall of 1993, campesino farmers fear their extinction as cheaper North American corn eventually floods into Mexico.[122]

Although previous presidents (José López Portillo, for instance) declared the termination of agrarian reform, President Salinas has done more than any other president to ensure its death. He also radically reformed the ejidal system of land tenure in 1991-92. The central problem of Mexican agriculture, both private and ejidal, Salinas believed, is the lack of investment. Investment is discouraged by the insecurity of private land ownership (due to the constant threat of land invasions and agrarian reform) and the prohibition of corporations from owning lands or other kinds of holdings within ejidos. To encourage investment in agriculture, therefore, the Salinas government reformed Article 27 of the Constitution and wrote a new Agrarian Law. These reforms removed the right of campesinos to petition for land redistribution and permitted the privatization of ejido land. Ejidatarios could rent or sell their land, use land as collateral, and form joint ventures with capitalists.[123]

While Mexico's technocrats and intellectuals debated these reforms, campesinos and ejidatarios, always cautious and distrustful of decrees from on high, feared the end of a system (ejidos and agrarian reform) which was familiar and secure, even if it was impoverished and bureaucratized. And they dreaded the beginning of a system (free trade and NAFTA) which threatened to flood Mexico with inexpensive grain and thus extinguish corn farming as their way of life. Alberto Huerta, during the summer of 1993, spoke with Indian campesinos in San Cristóbal de Las Casas. One asked Huerta if he knew that the president of Mexico had changed the constitution and Huerta recalled the conversation: "Did I not know that Article 27 had changed their lives? Before, their paraje (hamlet) could not be sold. The dismantling of Article 27 had privatized all lands. Now they could sell, and would probably be forced to sell by local landowners or the Mexican army. Miguel added: 'Already we hear that the Japanese want a part of the Chiapas Highlands for timber.'"[124]

This proposed and legislated transformation of Mexican agriculture occurred at the same time that the world price of coffee collapsed. In 1989, after the International Coffee Organization failed to set any production quotas, coffee prices fell by 50 percent. In Chiapas, where tens of thousands of campesinos grow coffee on small plots, the "crop of dreams" turned into another source of disillusionment. Sr. Pérez de León, a coffee grower with just a few hectares and 3,000 coffee plants, for example, earned $320(US) in 1993, or less than one dollar a day.[125]

Disconcerting reform and economic deterioration were accompanied by more repression in Chiapas. Although President Salinas upon taking office gave amnesty to those "jailed while involved in social and political battles," his governor in Chiapas presided over a new wave of assassinations and imprisonment. Conditions were such that Bishop Samuel Ruiz established a diocesan human rights center to expose the abuses. The governor, in turn, began to agitate for the removal of the bishop, and after January 1993, when González Garrido was promoted and put in control of Gobernación, he continued the campaign at a higher level, negotiating with the papal nuncio Geronimo Prigione.[126] The governor's public relations offensive against the bishop unleashed the pent up ire of regional landowners and cattle ranchers against the bishop and his "radical" priests, friars, and catechists in the countryside. They blamed the "political clergy" for organizing invasions, blockading roads, and other kinds of protests: "we have proof that they have used the pulpit to incite campesinos and Indians."[127] In the summer of 1992 vague death threats aimed at the bishop surfaced in Chiapas (and denied, of course, by leaders of the landowners and cattlemen's organizations).[128]

In these harsh yet propitious seasons, a new grassroots independent organization was formed in the highlands, the eastern frontier, and the north: the Alianza Campesina Independiente Emiliano Zapata. In early 1992 it became the Alianza Nacional or ANCIEZ. Little is known definitively about this organization. Some observers, like the Jesuit priest Mardonio Morales who has lived in the state for 30 years, believe ANCIEZ is related in some way to the OCEZ: "It appears that the OCEZ and the ANCIEZ are the same but with different names and fronts."[129] In October 1992 ANCIEZ participated in the Columbus day protest march in San Cristóbal de Las Casas which toppled the statue to the conquistador of Chiapas, Diego de Mazariegos. Later came accusations regarding "subversive groups that struggle in the ANCIEZ."[130] Neil Harvey claims that in early 1993 "ANCIEZ went underground, presumably to begin training for the armed rebellion."[131]

The story of Francisco Gómez reveals something of the continuity of struggle in Chiapas in recent decades. A Tzeltal of Las Cañadas, Gómez served as president of Quiptic Ta Lecubtesel in the late 1970s and as secretary of the Unión de Uniones—ARIC—during the late 1980s. In the 1990s he was one of the leaders of ANCIEZ. He surfaced in early January 1994 as captain Hugo of the EZLN and revealed in an interview that he had been a Zapatista for almost nine years. He was killed during the battle of Ocosingo in early January 1994.[132]

Following the outbreak of the rebellion, interviews with rebels have revealed that the rebel organization, the Ejercito Zapatista de Liberación Nacional (EZLN), began as a self-defense force. "When we came here," explained the rebel Marcos, "the people said, 'Yes, we have to take up arms to defend ourselves . . . to protect the villagers, not to attack.' And that's how we grew."[133]

While the origins of the EZLN are as yet still obscure, its turning point, all agree, was 1992. That was the year of the "reform" of Article 27. "The end of Article 27," said Vicente, an inhabitant of a Zapatista village, "was what made us decide we'd had enough."[134] Marcos also emphasized that they "were driven to even greater desperation" by the constitutional "reform."[135] 1992 was also the quincentennial of the "Discovery of America," a year of demonstrations throughout Indian Chiapas. In San Cristóbal the statue of the conquistador was brought down by protesters: "According to some of the participants, that moment marked a turning point."[136] In 1992, Marcos recalled, "the compañeros said, 'We have been struggling for 500 years. Now is a good year to say enough is enough.' So they told me that they wanted to start the war." In 1992 "the communities voted to make war."[137]

The following year the North American Free Trade Agreement was debated and ratified. NAFTA did not inspire the rebellion; the trade pact is unimaginably complicated and not a little abstract, and its supposed consequences cannot be known with any certainty. The Mexican left, however, opposed NAFTA and so did the Zapatistas. Their manifesto characterized NAFTA—which took effect on the day they rebelled—as a "death sentence" for Mexico's Indians.[138]

There were warning signs of the impending rebellion. Tensions increased palpably in Chiapas in 1993. Groups of landowners and cattlemen in eastern Chiapas were reported to be forming "citizens defense organizations" (despite the existence of guardias blancas in the area for decades).[139] In March of 1993 two government soldiers disappeared and presumably were murdered; the army unofficially blamed and punished a Tzotzil community and criticized the "provocations" of Bishop Ruiz and his priests.[140] In May a minor confrontation between the army and (in the words of Defensa Nacional), "a group of individuals who presumably are involved in some illegal activity," left one soldier and one unidentified civilian dead. A rebel uniform, propaganda, and various kinds of arms and ammunition were also discovered and displayed.[141] In fact, Marcos has stated that the army came upon Zapatista camps several times in 1993 and found an arms cache in October.[142] During the year both landowners and campesinos reported "paramilitary groups," and ranchers forced the municipal president of Altamirano to resign because he protected, they claimed, "subversive groups that belong to the ANCIEZ."[143] In September the Jesuit Mardonio Morales told Proceso—and Proceso told the nation on its cover—"There are guerrillas in Chiapas."[144] Throughout the year, however, the federal and state governments blindly repeated, as one official of the attorney general's office put it, "there is no reason to think that Chiapas has a guerrilla problem."[145] But as Alberto Huerta realized later, "all one needed to do was listen."[146]

JANUARY 1, 1994: THE AWAKENING

The Ejército Zapatista de Liberación Nacional, whose members numbered perhaps 2,000 fighters, many of them Tzeltal Indians, seized San Cristóbal de Las Casas, Ocosingo, Altamirano, and Las Margaritas on New Year's Day. The rebels also took over a radio station, attacked an army garrison, and kidnapped former governor Absalón Castellanos Domínguez. (The Zapatistas later subjected the former governor to judicial tribunal, found him guilty of the massacre at Colonchán in 1980 and other crimes, and then magnanimously released him.) Within days the Mexican army in Chiapas was reinforced, mounting a total force of 12,000 to 15,000 soldiers, and quickly recaptured the towns. During the two weeks of fighting approximately 400 people were killed, mostly rebels and civilians.[147]

The guerrillas retreated into the eastern frontier of Chiapas, toward the Selva Lacandona, and prepared to fight a prolonged war against the Mexican government. The rebellion greatly embarrassed President Salinas but he and his advisors realized that continued conflict, bringing with it inevitable reports of human rights abuses against poor Indians, would further damage the reputation (and investment climate) of Mexico and its government. Ten days after the outbreak of the uprising, the Salinas government announced it would negotiate with the rebels and seek a political rather than a military solution. Two days later the president declared a cease-fire. On February 21 formal negotiations between the government and the EZLN, mediated by Bishop Samuel Ruiz, began. Preliminary accords were signed on March 2 but they solved nothing and were not ratified by the rebel communities.[148]

The "propaganda war" began on the second day of January.[149] The Salinas government, of course, immediately blamed the rebellion on "outside agitators." President Salinas told a gathering in Europe that "serious problems, disputes, exist [in Chiapas], but this is not an indigenous revolt."[150] Much of the public discussion regarding the rebellion has centered on this issue. Iconoclast Enrique Krauze agrees: "Mexico is witnessing today a typical Latin American guerrilla movement in which the Indians are the cannon fodder and their leaders, the comandantes, supply the quasi-religious ideology and strategy to achieve their objectives: separate Chiapas from Mexico and create a 'liberated zone'—in short, a scenario of succession and civil war."[151] Krauze's mentor, Octavio Paz, similarly argues that outsiders, extremists, "have penetrated Indian communities for a long time now and, due to miserable conditions of life, they have found it relatively easy to form 'military and revolutionary bases.'"[152]

Academics and the political left viewed the rebellion as the rebels wished it to be viewed: a popular uprising of exploited people fighting for a just cause. Jorge G. Castañeda, for example, rejected the government's racist view of "poor Indians being manipulated by people from outside, white college graduates."[153] Lorenzo Meyer noted that "injustice provoked violence"[154] and that the United States, European, and Latin American press tended to view the rebellion sympathetically and, for the first time in five years, penetrated the gloss of Salinismo to see "the reality of 'deep Mexico'."[155]

In interviews, Marcos and other Zapatistas proclaim, naturally, the popular, indigenous, and Chiapanecan character of the rebellion. "The government says that this is not an indigenous uprising," Marcos commented ironically, "but we think that if thousands of indigenous people rise up in protest, then it is indeed an indigenous revolt."[156] Cristóbal, a rebel captain, similarly noted that "we have people everywhere, we are more than ten thousand men and women in struggle."[157] Both Marcos and Indian campesinos freely admit that some of the military leaders of the revolt are neither Indian nor Chiapaneco. Marcos has told journalists that he and a small group of political activists went to Chiapas in 1983; Cristóbal revealed that his military instruction "was imparted by people who had been in the Selva for more than ten years."[158] The rebellion may be led by some ladinos, like Marcos himself, but he and others declare that the revolutionary movement is led by representatives of self-governing Indian communities who form the Comité Clandestino Revolucionario Indígena (CCRI). Marcos stated that his role was "subordinate to the leaderships of various 'clandestine committees' made up almost entirely of Mayan Indian peasants."[159] When the reform of Article 27 was announced, according to Marcos, the CCRI held a referendum as to whether to take up arms. When the preliminary accords were signed with the government, the CCRI took the agreement back to the communities.

The fighting lasted only two weeks. Its effect (in sociological terms, its "demonstration effect") in Chiapas and throughout Mexico, however, has been significant.[160] The metaphor most commonly used to describe the change is "awakening." One week after the start of the rebellion, a 20-page pamphlet, "El despertador mexicano" (the Mexican Awakener), described as the official organ of the EZLN, was delivered to the press in Mexico City.[161] The Zapatista Cristóbal told a journalist: "We fight because we know the poverty of our country, of our communities. . . . We campesinos therefore have awakened and realize that, in such poverty, we cannot advance."[162] Outside of Chiapas in various rural areas of Mexico angry campesinos protested injustice and demanded the removal of corrupt officials, demanded land redistribution. In some localities campesinos organized land invasions. And throughout Mexico on April 10 (the anniversary of Emiliano Zapata's assassination) campesinos expressed solidarity with the Zaptistas of Chiapas. In Teopisca, in the state of Mexico, campesinos poured into town in the first week of February and took over the palacio municipal. One local corn farmer, Miguel Hernández, told a journalist that "the Zapatistas have opened our eyes." That journalist, Tim Golden of the *New York Times,* described hundreds of farmers, their wives and children, gathered in the central square. "The word they used again and again," Golden writes, "was 'awakened' [despertado]. That was what the Zapatistas, they said, had done to them."[163]

In Chiapas, meanwhile, 'the awakening' has taken on a more recognizable, Chiapaneco character. Campesinos, first in the east, have invaded tends of thousands of hectares of land they have petitioned or claimed for years. The OCEZ, reversing its earlier opposition to Zapatista methods, began to organize land invasions. This wave of invasions in April and May extended to regions of Chiapas outside the control of the EZLN: Soconusco and the Pacific coast, Los Altos, Simojovel, and Pichucalco. More than 80,000 hectares by the spring had been occupied by campesinos outside the Zapatista zone of control (and approximately 100,000 hectares inside the zone). The president of the Business Center of Chiapas declared on April 16, "there are people from the Frente Cardenista, from the CIOAC, and distinct groups alligned with the EZLN; all of them are invading lands."[164]

Violence between campesinos and landowners, and between campesino organizations and landowners' organizations, has increased in the Chiapanecan countryside since the formal ceasefire between the Zapatistas and the army in mid-January. These longtime enemies have accused each other of assassinations, kidnappings, and rapes. Cattlemen claim campesinos are not only stealing their land, but their cattle as well; and, as a result, they have lost more than $100 million (US) in revenues and destroyed property. Cattlemen threatened to rebel themselves if their lands were not soon returned and security in the countryside restored. In mid-April José Luis Aguilar, president of the Cattleman's Association of Altamirano, stated: "The situation is deteriorating. We have no support from the authorities. We're desperate."[165] Negotiations with the state government a month later obtained for landowners a generous monthly compensation to offset loses, which was retroactive to January.

The rebellion itself has shown itself over time to be more theatrical performance than military campaign.[166] "What made the Zapatista insurrection different from any other recent Latin American guerrilla movement," Guillermo Gómez Peña writes, "was its self-conscious and sophisticated use of the media."[167] Starting on the first of January, Subcomandante Marcos quickly produced a large and sophisticated epistolary revolutionary testament (his letters with their characteristic postscripts overshadowed the official EZLN communiques). His extended conversation with the nation has been part history lesson, part critique of Mexico's political system, and part report on indigenous Chiapas. It represents, perhaps, a new kind of revolutionary discourse: utopian but non-dogmatic, nationalist without being chauvinist, intellectually sophisticated but also grounded in peasant reality. Few insurrections in history have had such an articulate and charismatic spokesman.[168]

Negotiations with the government in the cathedral of San Cristóbal in February and March 1994 gave national and international attention to Zapatista demands (see Appendix). The rebel communities rejected the peace accords after an extensive consultation process as being too narrowly regional. The Zapatistas then called for a National Democratic Convention ("their culminating theatrical event"[169]) to meet in Chiapas in August. This "Mexican Woodstock" as some called it, brought together progressive elements from every corner of Mexico to support a national democratic transition (and, not incidentally, the Zapatista cause).[170] Talk, however, did not prevent the PRI from electing a new president and governor of Chiapas. Thereafter the Zapatista propaganda juggernaut began to drift.

During the fall the EZLN threatened war if the PRI candidate was inaugurated governor on December 8. The Zapatistas rejected new peace talks in October and unilaterally ended the truce on December 8. Ten days later Zapatista forces seized six new towns and popped up in thirty-eight municipalities outside of their zone of control in Chiapas. Despite this grandstanding, the Zapatistas remained militarily surrounded and contained in the eastern frontier and regionally isolated. Furthermore, the government blamed the Zapatista offensive for the collapse of investor confidence in Mexico and thus, at least in part, for the new economic crisis. While the charge was ludicrous, the crisis diverted attention from Chiapas. Time was not on their side, yet the Zapatistas refused to negotiate with the new national regime of Ernesto Zedillo.[171]

The president used Zapatista intransigence as the pretext for his offensive in early February 1995. Zedillo ordered the arrest of rebel leaders, figuratively stripped off their ski masks by revealing their civilian identities, and directed the attorney general to restore the "state of law" in eastern Chiapas. The national army aggressively moved into Las Cañadas and the Selva Lacandona unopposed by the Zapatista army. Rebel communities were occupied, food supplies were confiscated, and thousands of campesinos fled into even more remote corners of the Selva. Although Marcos and most other leaders escaped arrest, any remaining mystique of the EZLN as a military force was now thoroughly shattered. Zedillo called off the offensive after a month, suspended the arrest warrants, and called for new peace negotiations. This time the Zapatistas agreed. Face-to-face talks began in April but by mid-summer no agreement had been reached.[172] As this epilogue is written—in June 1995—the stalemate continues.

REFLECTIONS

The final chapter on the Zapatista rebellion, indeed, on the modern history of Chiapas, has yet to be observed and analyzed, let alone written. No matter how the rebellion itself is resolved, the fundamental polarization in Chiapas that provoked it will surely persist. Increasingly well-organized but desperate campesinos will continue to face powerful and politically connected private landowners. While the national government has dramatically increased spending in the state in an attempt to smother discontent, it has proven unwilling or unable to reform the basic socioeconomic structure of Chiapas, which gave rise to the conflict in the first place.

What at first appears to be an historical turning point can be deceptive depending on the context from which it is viewed. "Intellectuals are saying," the *Wall Street Journal* wrote in February 1994, "Chiapas could turn out to be a defining moment in Mexican history."[173] Ironically, the rebellion may contribute to greater change in Mexico generally than in Chiapas specifically. Chiapas is fairly resistant to genuine progress, and the future there seems to be a hostage to the past. This temporal pessimism, it would seem, is a particularly 'southern' characteristic in both

Mexico and the United States. William Faulkner was certainly thinking about his own rich land and poor people when he wrote: "The past isn't dead. It's not even past." His words apply nevertheless to Chiapas, "the Mississippi" of Mexico. Chiapas's contemporary chronicler, an historian with a Faulknerian sense of tragedy intermingled with the bizarre, Antonio García de León, echoes the maestro of Oxford: "Elements of the past linger here."

APPENDIX

THE ZAPATISTA DEMANDS
FEBRUARY 1994

THE GOVERNMENT RESPONSE
MARCH 1994

1. We demand free and democratic elections with equal rights and obligations for all political organizations contending for power, true liberty to choose one or another proposal, and respect for the will of the majority. Democracy is a fundamental right of all indigenous and nonindigenous people. Without democracy there can be no liberty, justice, or dignity and without dignity there is nothing.

1. Attending to the problem is a means to make a political solution possible.

2. To ensure free and truly democratic elections, it is necessary for the Federal Executive and occupants of state offices who reached their positions of power through electoral fraud to resign. Their titles do not come from majority consensus but rather are the result of usurpation. Consequently, it will be necessary for a transitional government to be formed.

2. This month an extra congressional session will be called to discuss a reform that guarantees a fair electoral process with no advantages for any politcal forces.

3. The recognition of the EZLN as a belligerent force.

3. Full guarantees to the EZLN and a dignified treaty that is respectful of all involved parties. The Zapatista Army will decide on the nature of their social and political participation in the future.

4. A new pact between federation members to do away with centralism and allow regions, indigenous communities, and municipalities to govern themselves with political, economic, and cultural autonomy.

5. General elections in the state of Chiapas and the legal recognition of all the state's political forces.

6. It is of the utmost importance that all Chiapan communities receive electricity and that a certain percentage of the taxes earned from the commercialization of Chiapan petroleum be applied to industrial, agricultural, commercial, and social infrastructure projects for the benefit of all Chiapanecos.

7. The revision of the North American Free Trade Agreement signed with the United States and Canada. In its present form it does not take into account the indigenous population. Furthermore, it represents a death sentence because it does not include any labor qualifications whatsoever.

8. Article 27 of the Magna Carta should respect the original spirit of Emiliano Zapata: land is for the indigenous people and peasants who work it, not for latifundistas.

9. We demand that the government build hospitals in the capitals of all municipalities, to be equipped with specialized doctors and sufficient medicine to attend to all patients, and rural clinics in smaller communities

4. The promotion of a General Law for the Rights of Indigenous Communities (which takes into account the communities' demands to govern themselves with political, economic, and cultural autonomy).

5. The carrying out of general elections in Chiapas and the legal recognition of all the region's political forces. This implies drawing up a new electoral law which guarantees the impartiality of the electoral process.

6. To elaborate programs to bring electricity to rural communities that will double their annual rate.

7. A careful evaluation by the Ministry of Trade and Industrial Development of the impact of NAFTA on indigenous communities and on the various productive activities in the state of Chiapas.

8. To generate a solution to the numerous agrarian conflicts. The process to attain this solution will be connected to the discussion, approval, and elaboration of the General Law for the Rights of Indigenous Communities.

9. Health. To rehabilitate hospitals and promote investment in the area of health in order to strengthen the network of primary and secondary-level medical attention.

with training and fair salaries for health representatives.

10. That indigenous people be guaranteed the right to information on local, regional, state, national, and international levels through an independent radio station that is directed and operated by indigenous people.

11. We demand that housing be built in all rural communities in Mexico to be provided with necessary services such as light, running water, roads, sewage systems, telephones, public transportation, etc. Also that we be granted the benefits of the city such as televisions, stoves, refrigerators, washing machines, etc.

12. We demand an end to illiteracy in indigenous communities. For this we need better elementary and secondary schools in our communities which provide free materials and have teachers with university degrees who are at the service of the people and are not just defending the wealthy.

13. That the languages of the various ethnicities be made official and that they be taught in primary, secondary, and high schools and at the university level.

14. That our rights and dignity as indigenous people be respected and that our culture and tradition be recognized.

15. We do not want to be subject to discrimination and scorn which we, the indigenous, have suffered for a long time now.

16. As indigenous people we de-

10. The Ministry for Communication and Transport (SCT) will apply for the necessary permit to found an independent indigenous radio station, headed and operated by indigenous people.

11. Housing. To support the construction and improvement of housing in indigenous and rural communities, including the introduction of basic services such as electricity, running water, paths and roads, and projects to improve the environment.

12. Education. To establish programs to evaluate the quality of public education in the region.

13. To implement bilingual education in indigenous communities.

14. To respect the culture, traditions, and the rights and dignity of indigenous communities which includes the concrete expression of these in government, judicial, and cultural spheres.

15. To modify the values of children and the youth in an effort to prevent discrimination against indigenous people.

16. The creation of new municipali-

mand that we be allowed to govern ourselves autonomously, because we no longer want to be subject to the will of national and foreign powers.

17. That justice be administered by the indigenous communities themselves according to their customs and traditions, without intervention from illegitimate and corrupt governments.

18. We demand dignified jobs with fair salaries for all workers both in the cities and in rural areas so that our brothers are not forced to resort to bad things such as narco-trafficking, delinquency, and prostitution in order to survive.

19. We demand fair prices for our products. For this we need to have free access to a market to buy and sell without being subject to the coyotes who exploit us.

20. That the extraction of wealth from Mexico and especially Chiapas, one of the Republic's richest states but one in which hunger and misery grow every day, cease.

21. We demand that all debts whether they be credits or loans for taxes with high interest rates be canceled as these cannot be paid back due to the poverty of the Mexican population.

22. We want an end to hunger and malnutrition because they have caused the death of thousands of our brothers both in the city and the countryside. In

ties in the present territories of Ocosingo and Las Margaritas.

17. Reforms to the Political Constitution of Chiapas, the Law of Judicial Power of the State of Chiapas, the Police Law of the region and other orders.

18. Dignified jobs and fair salaries for workers which require increased training and education. Efforts will be made to increase productivity and stengthen legislation in defense of workers' rights.

19. To make decisions regarding the prices of rural products which partially compensate for the effects of abrupt international price fluctuations in indigenous communities.

20. The protection of the region's natural resources. A compromise on the part of the federal government, international institutions, foundations, environmental groups, and indigenous communities to respond collectively by supporting technology transfer and soliciting financing for the conservation of natural resources.

21. The establishment of a Commission of the Ministry for Finance and Public Credit to evaluate the magnitude of the region's financial problems, examine the effects of the conflict, and present a proposal.

22. The realization of a medical attention program for children between the ages of zero and six who are afflicted with severe malnutrition.

every rural community there should be cooperative stores supported economically by the federal, state, and municipal governments and the prices in these stores should be fair.

23. We demand the immediate and unconditional release of all political prisoners and poor people who are being held unjustly in Mexican and Chiapan jails.

24. We demand that the federal army and judicial and public-safety police be prohibited from entering rural zones as they only go to intimidate, clear out, rob, repress, and bombard peasants who are organizing to defend their rights.

25. We demand that the federal government compensate families that have suffered material losses due to air raids and actions by federal troops during the conflict. We also demand indemnity for widows and orphans of the war, both civilians and Zapatistas.

26. We, indigenous peasants, want to live peacefully and tranquilly and demand that we be allowed to live according to our rights to liberty and a life of dignity.

27. That the Penal Code of the state of Chiapas be eliminated as it does not allow us to organize except by taking up arms, because legal and peaceful struggles are repressed and punished.

28. We ask and demand an end to the expulsion of indigenous communities by the local tyrants who are supported by the state. We demand that all

23. On the day following the signing of the peace agreement, the Law of Amnesty, both federal and state, will be applied in favor of the people against whom penal action has been taken as a result of their participation in the conflict.

24. To reconcile the objective of attaining legal order with that of respecting the rights of indigenous communities.

25. Monetary support for victims, widows, and orphans of the conflict.

26. Combining the decisions contained in this political agreement for dignified peace in Chiapas and in the region's peace agreement will give sustenance to this demand.

27. To repeal the present Penal Code of the State of Chiapas and elaborate a new one that is oriented towards guaranteeing individual and political rights.

28. A mandate to put an end to the expulsion of indigenous people from their communities will be included in the new Penal Code.

expelled people be returned freely and voluntarily to their lands of origin and that they be compensated for their losses.

29. Indigenous Women's Petition: We, indigenous peasant women, demand the immediate solution to our urgent needs which have long been ignored by the government.

29. To improve the conditions of peasant and indigenous women. To offer support so that women find new space to ensure their well-being and liberty.

a. Childbirth clinics with gynecologists.

b. Child-care facilities in all communities.

c. Sufficient food for all children in rural communities including: milk, cornflour, rice, corn, soy, oil, beans, cheese, eggs, sugar, soup, oats, etc.

d. Fully-equipped popular kitchens for children in the community.

e. Community nixtamal mills and tortillerias depending on the number of families in each community.

f. Poultry, rabbit, sheep, and pig farms.

g. We demand projects for baked goods.

h. Artisan workshops well-equipped with machinery and primary materials.

i. Markets in which to sell our crafts at fair prices.

j. Technical training schools for women.

k. Preschools and maternal schools.

l. Adequate means of transportation.

30. We demand that Patrocinio González Blanco, Absalón Castallenos Domínguez and Elmer Setzer M. be tried politically.

30. To establish agreements that confront the tensions which have generated bitterness and that will include all Chiapanecos in political matters.

31. We demand that the lives of all EZLN members be respected and that no charges will be brought or actions

31. Respect for the lives of all EZLN members and a guarantee that no charges will be brought against

taken against any EZLN members, fighters, sympathizers, or collaborators.

32. That all organizations and commissions for the defense of human rights be independent.

33. That a National Commission for Peace with Justice and Dignity be formed which will oversee the fulfillment and implementation of these accords.

34. That the humanitarian aid for the victims of the conflict be channeled through authentic representatives from the indigenous communities.

32. Increased participation of civil society in the National Human Rights Commission and other new human rights organizations.

33. The government will support the creation of a National Commission for Peace, Justice, and Dignity to oversee the implementation of the agreements contained in this political accord for dignified peace in Chiapas.

34. To channel humanitarian aid to victims of the war through representatives from indigenous communities with the participation of NGO's and government agencies under the terms agreed to by all parties.

Source: *El Financiero,* 3 March 1994.

Archival Abbreviations

ACh	Archivo de Chiapas
AFIM	Archivo Francisco I. Madero
AFLB	Archivo Francisco Léon De la Barra
AGC	Archivo General de Centroamérica
AGN/FIM	Archivo General de la Nación/Fondo Francisco I. Madero
AGN/OC	AGN/Fondo Obregón-Calles
AGN/EPG	AGN/Fondo Emilio Portes Gil
AGN/POR	AGN/Fondo Pascual Ortiz Rubio
AGN/ALR	AGN/Fondo Abelardo L. Rodríguez
AGN/LC	AGN/Fondo Lázaro Cárdenas
AGN/MAC	AGN/Fondo Manuel Ávila Camacho
AGN/MAV	AGN/Fondo Miguel Alemán Valdés
AGN/ARC	AGN/Fondo Adolfo Ruiz Cortines
AGN/CNA	AGN/Ramo de Comisión Nacional Agraria
AGN/Gob	AGN/Fondo Gobernación
AGOM	Archivo General Octavio Magaña
AHCH	Archivo Histórico de Chiapas
AHMR	Archivo Histórico de Matías Romero
ASRE	Archivo de la Secretaría de Relaciones Exteriores
ASRA	Archivo "seis de enero de 1915" de la Secretaría de Reforma Agraria
AVC	Archivo Venustiano Carranza
CGPD	Colección General Porfirio Díaz
LAM	Latin American Manuscripts, Lilly Library

NA/RG 59	National Archives of the United States/Record Group 59: General Records of the Department of State
NA/RG 76	NA/Record Group 76: Records of Boundary and Claims Commissions and Arbitrations
NA/RG 84	NA/Record Group 84: Records of the Foreign Service Posts of the Department of State
NA/RG 165	NA/Record Group 165: Records of the War Department General and Special Staffs
NA/RG 266	NA/Record Group 266: Records of the Office of Strategic Services
PC	Paniagua Collection, Latin American Library, Tulane University
SCh	Serie Chiapas, INAH
SFIM	Serie Francisco I. Madero, INAH

NOTES

PREFACE

1. Vicente Filisola, "Descripción de la provincia de Chiapa," November 28, 1823, Latin American Manuscripts, Lilly Library, Indiana University.

2. Miguel de la Madrid, *31 Experiencias de Desarrollo Regional* (México: Secretaría de Educación Pública, 1985), p. 129.

3. John Womack, Jr., "The Mexican Economy During the Revolution, 1910–1920: Historiography and Analysis," *Marxist Perspectives* I (Winter 1978), p. 104.

4. Hans Werner Tobler, "Conclusion: Peasant Mobilization and the Revolution," in D. A. Brading, ed., *Caudillo and Peasant in the Mexican Revolution* (Cambridge: Cambridge University Press, 1980), p. 252.

5. Paul J. Vanderwood, "Building Blocks But Yet No Building: Regional History and the Mexican Revolution," *Mexican Studies/Estudios Mexicanos* 3 (Summer 1987), p. 432.

6. Stuart Voss, "The Historiography of Nineteenth- and Early Twentieth-Century Mexico" (Paper delivered at the annual meeting of the American Historical Association, New York City, December 1984).

PROLOGUE

1. Vicente Filisola, "Descripción de la provincia de Chiapa," 28 November 1823, Latin American Manuscripts, Lilly Library, Indiana University. This section is also based on the report of Colonel Manuel de Mier y Terán concerning Chiapas written for Filisola: "Instrucciones formadas en Oaxaca por el Coronel don Manuel de Mier y Terán, para el Jefe de la División Auxilar de Guatemala, Brigadier don Vicente Filisola. . . ." reprinted in Rafael Helio doro Valle, ed., *La anexión de Centro América a México (Documentos y escritos de 1821–1822),*

Tomo III (México: Secretaría de Relaciones Exteriores, 1936), pp. 94–109.

2. Jan de Vos, *San Cristóbal ciudad colonial* (México: Instituto Nacional de Antropología e Historia, 1986), p. 7.

3. J. Eric S. Thompson, ed., *Thomas Gage's Travels in the New World* (Norman: University of Oklahoma Press, 1958), p. 138.

4. "Instrucciones formadas en Oaxaca por el Coronel don Manuel de Mier y Terán. . . . ," p. 95.

5. "Instrucciones formadas en Oaxaca por el Coronel don Manuel de Mier y Terán. . . . ," pp. 95–104.

6. Filisola, "Descripción de la provincia de Chiapa." Nearly twenty years earlier Antonio González wrote that his province was backward and decadent, yet "no other province can glory in possessing lands more fertile, than Chiapa by its abundance of streams, woods, valleys." Letter of Antonio González, Ciudad Real, 22 April 1804, Archivo de Chiapas, Tomo II. (Hereafter cited as ACh.)

7. The abuses of the past were described in the "Informe queda el Gover nador e Yntend.te de Chiapa del miserable estado que se hallan a la presente . . . año de 1792," ACh, Tomo I.

8. For the history of colonial Chiapas and Central America see: Kevin Marlin Gosner, "Soldiers of the Virgin: An Ethnohistorical Analysis of the Tzeltal Revolt of 1712 in Highland Chiapas," Ph.D. dissertation, University of Pennsylvania, 1984; Murdo J. MacLeod, *Spanish Central America: A Socio economic History, 1520–1720* (Berkeley: University of California Press, 1973); Miles L. Wortman, *Government and Society in Central America, 1680–1840* (New York: Columbia University Press, 1982); and Robert Wasserstrom, *Class and Society in Central Chiapas* (Berkeley: University of California Press, 1983).

9. Mario Rodríguez, *The Cádiz Experiment in Central America, 1808–1826* (Berkeley: University of California Press, 1978), pp. 31–35.

10. John Lynch, *The Spanish-American Revolutions, 1808–1826* (New York: W.W. Norton, 1973), pp. 318–321.

11. Sala Capitular de Chiapa to Don Pedro Solórzano, 29 October 1821, reprinted in Archivo Histórico del Estado, *Boletín de documentos históricos. No. 12* (Tuxtla Gutiérrez: Chiapas, 1974), pp. 43–48. "Nosotros comparados con nuestros hermanos opulentos de Méjico somos unos pobres; por consiguiente no será prudencia separanos de ellos para pereció; pudiendo disfrutar unido con ellos de sus gran.s riquezas; pues haciendo una sola familia el Gov.no sería como un padre que a los hijos débiles y enfermos les da el mismo sustento que a los robustos y laborios." From "Acta de Independencia," Sala Capitular de Comitán, 25 September 1821, ACh, Tomo III.

12. Miles Wortman, "Government Revenue and Economic Trends in Cen-

tral America, 1787–1819," *Hispanic American Historical Review* 55 (May 1975), pp. 267–268.

13. This desire existed in Mexico, according to John Tutino, where "the leaders of outlying provinces . . . had often supported independence movements, not only to oppose Spanish rule, but also to oppose the dominance of Mexico City." Tutino, *From Insurrection to Revolution in Mexico: Social Bases of Agrarian Violence, 1750–1940* (Princeton: Princeton University Press, 1986), p. 217.

14. Carmelo Saénz de Santa María, "El Proceso Ideológico-Institucional desde la Capitanía general de Guatemala hasta las Provincias Unidas del Centro de América: De Provincias a Estados," *Revista de Indias* XXXVIII (enero–marzo de 1978), pp. 151–152, quoted by Antonio García de León, *Resistencia y utopía: Memorial de agravios y crónicas de revueltas y profecías acaecidas en la provincia de Chiapas durante los últimos quinientos años de su historia,* 2 vol. (México: Ediciones Era, 1985), I, p. 145.

15. Manuel Mier y Terán, Tuxtla en la provincia megicana [sic] de Ciudad Real, to Agustín Iturbide, 24 October 1821, in Valle, ed., *La anexión de Centro América a Mexico,* Tomo I, pp. 59–62.

16. *Memoria sobre la cuestión de limites entre Guatemala y México presentada al Señor Ministro de Relaciones Exteriores por el Jefe de la Comisión Guatemalteca, 1900* (Guatemala: Ministerio de Educación Pública, 1964), p. 60; La Junta General celebrada en Ciudad Real de Chiapa, 8 April 1823. Archivo General de Centroamérica (Guatemala City), B6.2.1., Expediente 2387, Legajo 84, Foleto 1. Also see: Rodric Ai Camp, "La cuestión chiapaneca: revisión de una polémica," *Historia Mexicana* 24 (April–June 1975), pp. 579– 606; and Miles Wortman, "Legitimidad política y regionalismo—El imperio mexicano y centroamérica," *Historia Mexicana* 26 (October–December 1976), pp. 238–262.

17. Luis Chávez Orozco, *Historia de México (1808–1836)* (México: Editorial Patria, 1947), p. 520.

18. Prudencio Moscoso Pastrana, *México y Chiapas. Independencia y federación de la provincia chiapaneca* (Tuxtla Gutiérrez, 1974), pp. 56–63.

19. "Pronunciamiento de Tuxtla," 29 October 1823, reprinted in Matías Romero, "Bosquejo histórico," in Flavio Antonio Paniagua, ed., *Documentos y datos para un diccionario etimológico, histórico y geográfico de Chiapas* (San Cristóbal Las Casas, 1910–11), Vol. II, pp. 139–140.

20. José Manuel López e Iturribarria to Cura, Ixtacomitán, January 1824, quoted by Romero, "Bosquejo histórico," p. 85.

21. Moscoso Pastrana, *México y Chiapas,* pp. 79–93.

22. Ai Camp, "La cuestión chiapaneca," p. 602.

23. "Dictamén de la comisión de padrones de 11 de Setiembre de 1824" and "Sala de la municipalidad de Chiapa, Setiembre [sic] 19 de mil ochocientos

veinticuatro." Both documents are reproduced in Paniagua, ed., *Documentos y datos,* Vol. III, p. 133. The state census of 1827 listed a total population of 138,312. *Memoria del estado actual en que se hallan los ramos de la administración pública de las Chiapas* (San Cristóbal, 1828).

24. Moscoso Pastrana, *México y Chiapas,* p. 127.

25. Soconusco remained independent until 1842. "During this long period," noted a contemporary observer in 1843, "it has experienced all the difficulties of an abandoned country surrendered to rivalries and hatred; without laws, without a plan, without a system and with a purely municipal regime very imperfect, much of which still exists and is leading to anarchy." The lack of security for persons and property contributed to Soconusco's economic ruin. Another observer commented in 1850 that since 1811 "industry, agriculture, and commerce have decayed and are decaying each day more and more." Mexican President Santa Anna ordered the military to occupy the region in 1842, and thereafter it was a department of the State of Chiapas. See Manuel Larrainzar, *Notícia histórica de Soconusco y su incorporación a la república mexicana* (México, 1843), p. 79; Mario García S., *Soconusco en la historia* (México, 1963), p. 171.

26. Manuel Trens, *Historia de Chiapas* (México, 1957), pp. 321–322.

27. Presidencia de la República, *El Gobierno Mexicana,* February 1978.

28. Moscoso Pastrana, *México y Chiapas,* pp. 104–105.

29. Brian R. Hamnett, *Roots of Insurgency: Mexican Regions, 1750–1824* (Cambridge: Cambridge University Press, 1986), p. 178.

30. Tutino, *From Insurrection to Revolution in Mexico,* p. 226.

31. Gilberto Arg;auuello, "El primer medio siglo de vida independiente (1821–1867)," in Enrique Semo, ed., *México: un pueblo en la historia* (México: Editorial Nueva Imagen, 1983), Vol. III, p. 133.

32. Jan Bazant, "Mexico from Independence to 1867," in Leslie Bethell, ed., *The Cambridge History of Latin America. Volume III: From Independence to c. 1870* (Cambridge: Cambridge University Press, 1985), pp. 430–431.

33. For example, see Governor José Mariano Truncoso's exposition of Chiapas's "orden interior" in *Memoria del año de 1829* (San Cristóbal, 1829).

34. Tutino, *From Insurrection to Revolution in Mexico,* p. 244.

35. Robert Wasserstrom, "La evolución de la economia regional en Chiapas, 1528–1975," *America Indígena* 36 (July–September, 1976), pp. 484–86. For a Liberal perspective of the conflicts see "Dictamén y todos los documentos que constan en el espediente sobre traslación de los supremos poderes del Estado de Chiapas," December 1833, ACh, Tomo IV. For a Conservative view see the broadside, "¡Chiapanecos!" 5 June 1854, by Governor Fernando Nicolas Maldonado, ACh, Tomo VI.

36. The movement of people and production to peripheral regions after 1760

and Independence was a general trend in Mexico. See Tutino, *From Insurrection to Revolution in Mexico,* p. 219.

37. Emilio Pineda, "Descripción geográfica del Departamento de Chiapas y Soconusco," *Boletín de la Sociedad Mexicana de Geografía y Estadística,* Tomo III, Num. 7, 1853.

38. Chiapas, *Colección de leyes agrarias y demás disposiciones que se han emitido con relaciones al ramo de tierras* (San Cristóbal Las Casas, 1878), pp. 5–6, 10.

39. A remarkable document found in the national government's agrarian reform archive charts the progressive loss of village lands in the locality of Ocozocoautla (in the Central Valley) during these decades and of church property during the Reform. See "Perito Paleografo: Informe," 10 January 1919, Archivo "seis de enero de 1915" de la Secretaría de Reforma Agraria (ASRA), 23:606 (723.8).

40. Jan Rus, "Whose Caste War? Indians, Ladinos, and the 'Caste War' of 1869," in Murdo J. MacLeod and Robert Wasserstrom, eds., *Spaniards and Indians in Southeastern Mesoamerica: Essays on the History of Ethnic Relations* (Lincoln: University of Nebraska Press, 1983), p. 132.

41. One third of the estates in the district of Comitán, for example, were church properties. "Estado de las haciendas del curato de Comitán. Año de 1803," ACh, Tomo II.

42. "Ley de servicios de 1 de septiembre de 1827," Archivo Histórico de Chiapas (Tuxtla Gutiérrez), Impresos y Manuscritos, Carpeta 1661, Año de 1827. Hereafter cited as AHCH.

43. Wasserstrom, *Class and Society in Central Chiapas,* p. 126.

44. "Atribuciones de los prefectos de Estado de Chiapas," 20 July 1831, ACh, Tomo IV.

45. "Segundo trimestre de los hechos notables de la asemblea departmental de Chiapas," 10 July 1844, Guatemala, ACh, Tomo V.

46. Decree of 9 June 1849, and Decree of 2 May 1851, Archivo General de la Nación (Mexico City), Ramo de Gobernación, Legajo 228. Hereafter cited as AGN.

47. Rus, "Whose Caste War?" p. 135; Trens, *Historia de Chiapas,* pp. 328–31; and Manuel Larrainzar, *Noticia histórica de Soconusco y su incorporación a la república mexicana* (México, 1843), p. 79.

48. The best study of the Mexican Reform is by Richard N. Sinkin, *The Mexican Reform, 1855–1876: A Study in Liberal Nation-Building* (Austin: University of Texas Press, 1979).

49. See Ángel A. Corzo's memoir, *Segunda reseña de sucesos ocurridos en Chiapas desde 1847 a 1867* (México, 1868).

50. From *Alcance al numero 4 de la Voz del Pueblo*, 8 December 1855.

51. "Rematarios de fincas desamortizadas," *La Bandera Constitucional* (Tuxtla Gutiérrez), 19 November, 10 and 17 December 1859; and "Estado demon strativo de las operaciones sobre bienes nacionalizados . . . ," San Cristóbal Las Casas, 1869. AGN, Ramo de Gobernación, Bienes Nacionalizados, 45-170/13. Also see the table, "Cronología del creimiento de las denuncias de tierras," in García de León, *Resistencia y utópia*, pp. 158–164.

52. See *Alcance al numero 8. de la Voz del Pueblo*, 26 January 1856. Numerous articles in this newspaper detailed the oppressive control exercised by Cristobalense landowners, particularly that of the Larrainzar family, over Indian communities. For a discussion of the change in administration, see Rus, "Whose Caste War?," p. 137.

53. García de León, *Resistencia y utopía*, pp. 155–156.

54. "Al público mexicano. Plan de revolución en Chiapas," by D. Juan Ortega and D. José María Chacón, San Cristóbal Las Casas, 22 September 1856, ACh, Tomo VI; and *La Voz del Pueblo*, 10 January 1857.

55. See *Sétima pastoral del Obispo de Chiapa* (Guatemala, 1856) and *Exposición que el Obispo de Chiapa dirige al Supremo Gobierno Gral. de la Nación contra los procedimientos del Sr. Gobierno del Estado* (Guatemala, 1857).

56. San Cristóbal was named San Cristóbal Las Casas in honor of Chiapa's first bishop, Bartolomé de las Casas. Tuxtla was named Tuxtla Gutiérrez in honor of Chiapas's liberal governor of the 1830s, Joaquín Miguel Gutiérrez, by the decree of 31 May 1848. ACh, Tomo V.

57. See *La Bandera Constitucional*, 15 October 1859, and Carlos Cáceres López, *Chiapas y su aportación a la república durante la reforma e intervención francesa, 1858–1864* (México, 1862), p. 27.

58. Manuel B. Trens, *El imperio en Chiapas* (Tuxtla Gutiérrez, 1956), pp. 10–29; Ángel Albino Corzo, *Reseña de varios sucesos acaecidos en el estado de Chiapas durante la intervención francesa en la República* (México, 1867); Gustavo López Gutiérrez, *Chiapas en defensa de la patria: Su participación ante la Intervención Francesa* (México: Sociedad Mexicana de Geografía y Estadística, 1963).

59. Rus, "Whose Caste War?," pp. 140–42.

60. This is the subject of Jan Rus's excellent study, "Whose Caste War?," pp. 140–56. Also see Wasserstrom, *Class and Society*, pp. 147–150.

61. See *Memoria presentado por el C. Secretario Gral. del Gobierno Constitucional del Estado Libre y Soberano de Chiapas* (San Cristóbal Las Casas, 1878); Federico Larrainzar, *La revolución en Chiapas* (San Cristóbal Las Casas, 1878); and Eraclio Zepeda, *Respuesta a la última crisis política en Chiapas de D. Federico Larrainzar* (México, 1878).

62. Stuart F. Voss, *On the Periphery of Nineteenth-Century Mexico: Sonora and Sinaloa, 1810–1877* (Tucson: The University of Arizona Press, 1982), p. 300.

63. Anonymous, "Analisis situación general estado de Chiapas, 1878," Archivo Histórico de Matías Romero (Mexico City), Expediente 28784. Hereafter cited as AHMR.

64. See John H. Coatsworth, "Obstacles to Economic Growth in Nineteenth-Century Mexico," *The American Historical Review*, 83 (February 1978), pp. 99–100; Jan de Vos, "Una legislación de graves consecuencias: El acaparamiento de tierras baldías en México, con el pretexto de colonización, 1821–1910," *Historia Mexicana* XXXIV (julio–septiembre 1984), pp. 76–113.

65. Chiapas, *Memoria que presenta el ciudadano Manuel Carrascosa, como Gobernador Constitucional del Estado Libre y Soberano de Chiapas a la Legislatura* (San Cristóbal Las Casas, 1889).

66. Viviane Brachet, *La población de los estados mexicanos (1824–1895)* (México: Departamento de Investigaciones Históricas, INAH, 1976), pp. 54–55. Most of the immigrant agricultural workers were undoubtedly Guatemalan Indians fleeing from the harsh social conditions in their native land. See "State of Chiapas," *Daily Consular and Trade Reports, September 1886* No. 67 (Washington, D.C.: GPO, 1886), pp. 533–537.

67. Tutino, *From Insurrection to Revolution in Mexico*, pp. 288–290.

68. Friedrich Katz, "Mexico: Restored Republic and Porfiriato, 1867–1910," in Bethell, ed., *The Cambridge History of Latin America*, Volume V, c. 1870–1930 (Cambridge: Cambridge University Press, 1986), p. 55.

69. Alan Knight, "Mexican Peonage: What Was It and Why Was It?" *Journal of Latin American Studies* 18 (1986), p. 52; *La Brújula*, 20 October 1873.

70. Moisés González Navarro, *Historia moderna de México. El porfiriato: la vida social*, Daniel Cosío Villegas, ed. (México: Editorial Hermes, 1957), p. 227, 230.

71. "Resources of Mexico," *Reports from the Consuls of the United States*, XIX, Washington, 1886, quoted in Friedrich Katz, "Labor Conditions on Haciendas in Porfirian Mexico: Some Trends and Tendencies," *Hispanic American Historical Review* (February 1974), p. 38n.

72. Rus, "Whose Caste War?," p. 156.

73. Federico Larrainzar, *Los intereses materiales en Chiapas* (San Cristóbal Las Casas, 1881), p. 8. Also see similar complaints in *El Espíritu del Siglo*, 31 October 1868; *La Brújula*, 20 October 1873; *El Demócrata*, 20 October 1880.

74. Chiapas, *Memoria sobre diversos ramos.* . . . (San Cristóbal Las Casas, 1884), p. 75.

75. See, for example, Decreto 17, 30 December 1879, Serie Chiapas (Mexico

City), Rollo 77, Vol. XXIV, and Decreto 7, 23 December 1883, Rollo 78, Vol. XXVII. Hereafter cited as SCh.

76. Chiapas, *Memoria presentada por el C. Srio. Gral. del Gobierno del Estado Libre y Soberano de Chiapas* (Ciudad de Chiapas de Corzo, 1870); and Decreto 10, 6 December 1881, SCh, Rollo 77, Vol. XXIX.

77. Decreto 5, 6, November 1889, SCh, Rollo 78, Vol. XXVIII; and "Conflictos pecunicarios en Chiapas," *El Universal*, 14 January 1892.

78. Carrascosa to President Díaz, 24 September 1890, Colección General Porfirio Díaz, Rollo 63, Legajo XV, Documento 11897; and Carrascosa to Díaz, 1 October 1890, Rollo 63, Legajo XV, Documento 11898. Hereafter cited as CGPD.

79. Lázaro Pávia, *Los estados y sus gobernantes* (México, 1890), pp. 115–116.

80. Friedrich Katz, "Mexico: Restored Republic and Porfiriato, 1867–1910," pp. 20–21.

81. Rabasa to Romero, 19 January 1879, AHMR, Expediente 28922.

82. Keller to Romero, 18 January 1880, AHMR, Expediente 29746, and Felipe Pineda's complaint of the "pernicious influence" of the Escobar brothers, Pineda to Romero, 19 June 1884, AHMR, Expediente 32079.

83. Merodía to Díaz, 11 July 1888, CGPD, 42, XIII, 7025; also see E. Simón to Díaz, 20 December 1890, CGPD, 64, XV, 14399.

84. Candiani to Díaz, 12 January 1891, CGPD, 65, XVI, 266.

85. Gómez to Díaz, 25 December 1890, CGPD, 64, XV, 14248; also see D. Bejares to Díaz, 22 November 1890, CGPD, 64, XV, 14526.

86. Matías Romero, *Cultivo del café en la costa meridional de Chiapas* (México, 1875); Larrainzar, *Los intereses materiales en Chiapas*, pp. 28–29; *El Centinela de la Frontera* (Comitán), 20 May 1872; *El Demócrata*, 20 October 1880; and Ricardo Jordán to Díaz, 11 January 1885, CGPD, 12, X, 1558.

87. From "La Colonización," *El Caudillo*, 29 April 1888.

CHAPTER I

1. Rabasa to Díaz, 12 August 1892, CGPD, 84, XVII, 12859; *Discurso del Lic. Emilio Rabasa, Gobernador del Estado de Chiapas ante la XVIII Legislatura del mismo* (Tuxtla Gutiérrez, 1893).

2. John H. Coatsworth, "Obstacles to Economic Growth in Nineteenth-Century Mexico," *The American Historical Review*, 83 (February 1978), p. 83.

3. Friederike Baumann, "Terratenientes, campesinos y la expansión de la agricultura capitalista en Chiapas, 1896–1916," *Mesoamérica* 4 (June 1983), pp. 24–25; and Wasserstrom, *Class and Society in Central Chiapas*, pp. 113–115.

4. Albert Brickwood, "Coffee in Soconusco, Chiapas," 26 September 1910, The United States National Archives, Record Group 84, Volume 159 C8.6, Tapachula: Miscellaneous Reports. Hereafter cited as NA.

5. Brickwood, "Lands in Chiapas (Mexico)," 10 August 1910, NA, RG 84, Tapachula: Miscellaneous Reports; and Archivo de la Secretaría de Relaciones Exteriores, "Colonización en Chiapas," Legajo 11-2-141. Hereafter cited as ASRE and identifying information.

6. "Informe sobre el cultivo del café," *La Agricultura*, 15 November 1892; *Chiapas, su estado actual, su riqueza, sus ventas para los negocios* (México: Imprenta de la Escuela Correccional, 1895), p. 8; *Coffee: Extensive Information and Statistics* (Washington, D.C.: International Bureau of the American Republics, 1902), p. 17; and Karl Kaerger, *Landwirtschaft und Kolonisation im Spanischen Amerika*, 2 vols. (Leipsig: Verlag von Duncker und Humbolt, 1901), II, pp. 192–193, 521–525.

7. W. W. Byam, *A Sketch of the State of Chiapas, Mexico* (Los Angeles: Geo. Rice and Sons, 1897), pp. 37, 45–46, 74; J. Figueroa Doimenech, *Guía general descriptiva de la república mexicana, Tomo II: Estados y territorios federales* (México: Ramón Araluce, 1899), p. 91; and *The Mexican Year Book, 1912* (Mexico: Department of Finance, 1912), p. 128.

8. Byam, *A Sketch of the State of Chiapas*, p. 42; Manuel T. Corzo, *Ligeros apuntes geográficos y estadísticos del Estado de Chiapas* (Tuxtla Gutiérrez: Imprenta del Gobierno, 1897), p. 27; *Anuario estadístico de la república mexicana. 1894* (México: Secretaría de Fomento, 1894), p. 611.

9. Emilio Busto, *Estadística de la república mexicana. Estado que guarden la agricultura, industria, minería, y comercio* (México: 1880), I, p. xviii; Datos estadísticos del estado de Chiapas recopilados en el año de 1896 (Tuxtla Gutiérrez: Imprenta del Gobierno, 1898).

10. *El Partido Liberal*, 18 December 1890; *El Universal*, 3 September 1891; *La Juventud Estudiosa*, 1 September 1893; *El Voto de Chiapas*, 1 June 1895; Lázaro Pavia, *Los estados y sus gobernates* (México, 1890), pp. 115–116; and José C. Valadés, *El Porfirismo, historia de un régimen. El crecimiento* (México: Editorial Patria, 1948), I, pp. 288–289.

11. Daniel Cosío Villegas, *Historia moderna de México. El Porfiriato. La vida política interior* (México: Editorial Hermes, 1970), VIII, pp. xxi–xxiii.

12. Marcia Ann Hakala, "Emilio Rabasa, Modern Mexican Novelist," Diss. Indiana University, 1970, pp. 1–2.

13. *Ibid.*, pp. 2–28. Also see: Vicente Llevano, *Lic. Emilio Rabasa* (Tuxtla Gutiérrez: Gobierno Constitucional del Estado, 1946), pp. 8–12; and *El Universal*, 14 July 1891.

14. *El Partido Liberal*, 29 March 1890.

15. "Conflictos pecunicarios en Chiapas," *El Universal,* 14 January 1892.

16. E. Pino, Tonalá, to Porfirio Díaz, 2 November 1890, CGPD, 64, XV, 13828.

17. Díaz to Carrascosa, 9 May 1891, CGPD, 68, XVI, 4666; Valadés, *El Porfirismo,* I, pp. 34–38; and J. Mario García Soto, *Geografía general de Chiapas* (México, 1969), p. 225.

18. *El Monitor Republicano,* 8 January 1892.

19. *El Voto de Chiapas,* 1 June 1895.

20. Rabasa to Díaz, 28 March and 9 April 1892, CGPD, 78, XVIII, 4551, and CGPD, 82, XVIII, 9647.

21. Rabasa to Díaz, 15 June 1892, CGPD, 83, XVII, 11203; Rabasa to Díaz, 12 August 1892, CGPD, 84, XVII, 12859; and Rabasa to Díaz, 23 August 1892, CGPD, 85, XVII, 14543. Also see: Decree 8, 11 August 1892, Governor Emilio Rabasa, SCh, 78, XXVIII; *Traslación de los poderes públicos del estado, de la capital de San Cristóbal Las Casas a la ciudad de Tuxtla Gutiérrez, 1892,* ACh, IX.

22. General S. Escobar, Malacatán, to Díaz, 12 August 1892; Díaz to Rabasa, 12 August 1892 (note written on Escobar's telegram to Díaz); and Rabasa to Díaz, 15 August 1892, CGPD, 323, LI, 6100 and 6122.

23. Alfredo Saavedra, Tuxtla Gutiérrez, to Díaz, 18 August 1894, CGPD, 106, XIX, 11178. There were no federal rural police in Chiapas.

24. M. M. Mijangos, San Cristóbal, to Díaz, 24 June 1892, CGPD, 85, XVII, 14345.

25. "Decreto por el que se nombra a jefes políticos de departamentos para mejorár la administración, 29 de diciembre de 1893," ACh, IX, Ramo de Gobernación; Antonio A. Moguel, *Reseña de las atribuciones y deberes de los jefes políticos de Chiapas formada de acuerdo con la legislación vigente y por disposición del ejecutivo del estado* (Tuxtla Gutiérrez: Imprenta del Gobierno, 1897).

26. Anomino, San Cristóbal, to Secretario de Fomento, México, 8 July 1892, CGPD, 84, XVII, 12856.

27. Joaquín Ortega, San Cristóbal, to Díaz, 18 July 1892; Fortunato Mazarigos, San Cristóbal, to Díaz, 20 June 1892; José Ma. Mijangos, San Cristóbal, to Díaz, 1 July 1892; and C. Morales, San Cristóbal, to Díaz, 20 June 1892, CGPD, 85, XVII, 14386, 14343, 14344, 14342.

28. Rabasa to Díaz, 12 February 1892, CGPD, 77, XVII, 2792; Rabasa to Díaz, 25 March 1892, CGPD, 78, XVIII, 4549; Manuel Figuerro, Tapachula, to Díaz, 11 April 1893, CGPD, 92, XVII; and Rabasa to Díaz, 17 May 1893, CGPD, 92, XVIII, 6224.

29. Rabasa to Díaz, 14 October 1893, CGPD, 98, XVIII, 15335.

30. Teofilo Palacios, Tapachula, to Díaz, 26 November 1893, CGPD, 100, XVIII, 18770; and Rabasa to Díaz, 18 February 1894, CGPD, 101, XIX, 2678.

31. Daniela Spenser, "Soconusco: The Formation of a Coffee Economy in Chiapas," in Thomas Benjamin and William McNellie, eds., *Other Mexicos: Essays on Regional Mexican History, 1876–1911* (Albuquerque: University of New Mexico Press, 1984), p. 132.

32. Julián Grajales, Chiapa de Corzo, to Díaz, 4 January 1892, CGPD, 89, XVIII, 502.

33. Grajales to Díaz, 1 November 1892, CGPD, 86, XVII, 17185.

34. Díaz to Grajales, 25 November 1892, CGPD, 86, XVII, 17186; Grajales to Díaz, 2 August 1894, CGPD, 106, XIX, 11381.

35. *El Partido Liberal,* 10 January 1892.

36. Governor Francisco León, Tuxtla Gutiérrez, to Díaz, 20 December 1898, CGPD, 156, XXIII, 17495.

37. Rabasa to Díaz, 13 January 1894, CGPD, 100, XIX, 300. I uncovered no information regarding actions Rabasa took to bring Pichucalco under the control of the state government.

38. Luis Espinosa, ed., *Chiapas* (Mexico, 1925), n.p. For a similar view see: José Casahonda Castillo, *50 años de revolución en Chiapas* (Tuxtla Gutiérrez: Instituto de Ciencias y Artes de Chiapas, 1974), p. 15.

39. Valadés, *El Porfirismo,* I, p. 124; *Chiapas, su estado actual,* p. 13.

40. "Conflictos pecuniarios en Chiapas," *El Universal,* 14 January 1892; Rabasa to Díaz, 20 January 1892, CGPD, 76, XVII, 1155.

41. Circular 1, Sección de Hacienda, 26 March 1892, and "Dictamen del Comisión," 26 May 1892, SCh, 78, XXVIII; Ramón Rabasa, *El estado de Chiapas: geografía y estadística* (México, 1895), p. 115; *El Universal,* 26 September 1893; Rabasa to Díaz, 4 August 1892, CGPD, 84, XVII, 12862.

42. *Discurso del Lic. Emilio Rabasa* (Tuxtla Gutiérrez: Imprenta del Gobierno, 1892, 1893); Llevano, *Lic. Emilio Rabasa,* pp. 20–21; Alberto Cal y Mayor Redondo, "Evolución política y constitucional del estado de Chiapas," Tesis profesional, Facultad de Derecho, Universidad Nacional Autónoma de México, 1954; and Rabasa to Díaz, 18 July 1893, CGPD, 94, XVIII, 9141.

43. Rabasa to Díaz, 25 March 1892, CGPD, 78, XVIII, 4549.

44. Rabasa to Díaz, 25 March 1894, CGPD, 100, XIX, 300. Also see R. Rabasa, *El estado de Chiapas,* p. 115.

45. Rabasa to Díaz, 23 August 1892, CGPD, 85, XVII, 14543.

46. Fernando Castañón Gamboa, "Panorama histórico de las comunicaciones en Chiapas," *Ateneo Chiapas* 1 (1951), p. 90.

47. Francisco León to Díaz, 15 June 1896, CGPD, 129, XXI, 9371.

48. Rabasa to Díaz, 22 March 1893, CGPD, 92, XXI, 5499; Angel M. Corzo,

Historia de Chiapas (México: Editorial "Protos," 1944), pp. 137–140; Casahonda Castillo, *50 años de revolución,* p. 14.

49. Rabasa to Díaz, 24 April 1892, CGPD, 80, XVII, 6243.

50. *Discurso del Lic. Emilio Rabasa,* 1892, 1983. Also see: Rabasa to Díaz, 24 April 1892, CGPD, 80, XVII, 6243; Rabasa to Díaz, 15 January 1894, CGPD, 100, XX, 300; and Rabasa to Díaz, 5 September 1893, CGPD, 96, XVIII, 12498.

51. See Miguel Mejía Fernández, *Política agraria en México en el siglo XIX* (México: Siglo XXI, 1979), p. 253.

52. *Ley y reglamento para la división y reparto de egidos en el estado de Chiapas* (Tuxtla Gutiérrez: Imprenta del Gobierno, 1893), pp. 1–18.

53. Srio. Gral. Oficina Ejidos to Srio. Gral. Gobierno (*Chiapas*), 23 December 1908, AHCH, Sección de Fomento, 1908, Volume III, expediente 12.

54. *Datos estadísticos del Estado de Chiapas* (1896), p. 1; *Anuario estadístico del Estado de Chiapas, año de 1909* (Tuxtla Gutiérrez: Tipografía del Gobierno, 1911), p. 54.

55. "Oficina General de Ejidos: Copia del inventario general formado por la Oficina Gral. de Ejidos," AHCH, Fomento, 1908, Vol. III, exp. 12.

56. Albert Brickwood, "Tapachula," *Daily Consular and Trade Reports, October 25, 1911* (Washington, D.C.: GPO, 1911), p. 434. Also see: Jean Meyer, *Problemas campesinos y revueltas agrarias, 1821–1910* (México: SepSetentas, 1973), p. 229.

57. Puebla Nuevo Chiapilla, AGN, Comisión Nacional Agraria, Libro 12, Caja 2.

58. Vecinos de Chiapa de Corzo to Díaz, 6 January 1895, CGPD, 112, XX, 936.

59. See "Copia del inventario general formado por la Oficina Gral. de Ejidos," AHCH, 1908, III, 12.

60. Moguel to Díaz, 11 January 1895, CGPD, 112, XX, 936.

61. Rabasa, Mexico City, to Díaz, 21 May 1894, CGPD, 104, XIX, 7417.

62. Emilio Rabasa, *La evolución histórica de México* (México: Editorial Porrua, 1920, 1956), p. 237.

63. Rabasa to Díaz, 15 January 1894, CGPD, 100, XX, 300; and Rabasa to Díaz, 17 December 1892, CGPD, 88, XVII, 19858.

64. *El Universal,* 17 January 1894.

65. "Ley del Director General de Instrucción Pública," 28 December 1892, Decree 8, SCh, 84, Second Series.

66. *El Universal,* 17 January 1894.

67. Elliot S. Glass, *México en las obras de Emilio Rabasa* (México: Editorial Diana, 1975), p. 41; *Discurso del Lic. Emilio Rabasa.*

68. Rabasa, *La evolución histórica*, pp. 222, 224.

69. Castellanos, Comitán, to Díaz, 8 December 1892, CGPD, 90, XVIII, 1802; and Alfonso, Comitán, to Díaz, 28 July 1894, CGPD, 106, XIX, 10114.

70. V. Pineda, San Cristóbal, to Díaz, 8 August 1894, CGPD, 106, XVIII, 11163; B. Topete, San Cristóbal, to Díaz, 15 January 1895, CGPD, 112, XX, 354; and Cal y Mayor R., "Evolución política y constitucional," p. 105.

71. *El Universal*, 27 January 1893 and 9 June 1895; *El Voto de Chiapas*, 1 June 1895; and Ricardo de Marcía y Campos, Administrator de Aduana, Tapachula, to Díaz, 15 November 1894, CGPD, 110, XIX, 17617.

72. Rabasa, *La constitución y la dictadura, estudio sobre la organización política de México* (México: Revista de Revistas, 1912), pp. 305, 316.

73. The Rabasa-Díaz correspondence in the Colección General Porfirio Díaz amply confirms this point.

74. F. Moguel, Tuxtla Gutiérrez, to Díaz, 28 February 1894, CGPD, 102, XIX, 3521.

75. Manuel Lacroix, Tuxtla Gutiérrez, to Díaz, 3 December 1895, CGPD, 123, XX, 18724.

76. Rabasa to Díaz, 13 January 1894, CGPD, 100, XX, 300.

77. Alfonso M. de Lascurian, "Influencia de Don Emilio Rabasa, en la Constitución de 1917," Tesis, UNAM, 1956; Hilario Medina, "Emilio Rabasa y la Constitución de 1917," *Historia Mexicana* 10 (junio–julio 1960), pp. 134–148; Daniel Cosío Villegas, *La constitución de 1857 y sus críticos* (México: Editorial Hermes, 1957). In 1906 Rabasa published *El articulo 14 constitucional* and in 1912 *La constitución y la dictadura*.

78. *El Universal*, 25 May 1956.

79. Albert Brickwood, "Agriculture in the Valley of Cintalapa and Jiquipilas, State of Chiapas, Mexico," 4 October 1910, NA, Record Group 84, Tapachula: Miscellaneous Reports.

CHAPTER 2

1. *El Universal*, 26 May 1899.

2. B. Topete, Tuxtla Gutiérrez, to Díaz, 18 December 1894, CGPD, 111, XIX, 19654; Topete, San Cristóbal, to Díaz, 15 January 1895, CGPD, 112, XX, 354. Also see: Daniel Cosío Villegas, *Historia moderna de México. El Porfiriato. La vida política exterior* (México: Editorial Hermes, 1960), p. 254.

3. León to Díaz, 2 April 1895, CGPD, 116, XX, 6577; Espinosa ed., *Chiapas*, n.p.

4. See, for one example among many, Juan Ángel Peña, San Bartolomé, to Díaz, 27 July 1894, CGPD, 106, XIX, 10113.

5. The precise composition of this group would change over the years. V. Pineda, San Cristóbal, to Díaz, 8 August 1894, CGPD, 106, XIX, 5393; and Pimentel, San Cristóbal, to Díaz, 30 November 1895, CGPD, 103, XX, 5393.

6. After 1900 this group came to be known as "la mano negra." Rafael Pimentel, San Cristóbal, to Díaz, 30 November 1895, CGPD, 122, XX, 18031.

7. Abenamar Evolí, San Cristóbal, to Díaz, 2 April 1895, CGPD, 115, XX, 5948; León to Díaz, 14 December 1895, CGPD, 336, LIV, 7048.

8. Pimentel to Díaz, 30 November 1895, CGPD, 122, XX, 18031.

9. Lacroix to Díaz, 12 December 1895, CGPD, 123, XX, 18685.

10. Pimentel to Díaz, 30 November 1895, CGPD, 122, XX, 18031; Pimentel to Díaz, 31 December 1985, CGPD, 336, LIV, 7434.

11. León to Díaz, 29 April 1897, CGPD, 140, XXII, 5995.

12. *Memoria presentada por el ejecutivo del Estado de Chiapas ...* (Tuxtla Gutiérrez: Imprenta del Gobierno, 1899).

13. *El Partido Liberal,* 27 May 1896.

14. León to Díaz, 26 August 1898, CGPD, 154, XXVII, 12909.

15. "Memorándum que presenta al C. Presidente de la República, el Gobernador de Chiapas," 17 February 1899, CGPD, 158, XXIV, 2339.

16. Quoted in *El Partido Liberal,* 27 May 1896.

17. León to Díaz, 10 June 1896, CGPD, 129, XXI, 9401.

18. Lacroix to Díaz, n.d. (approximately January 1896), CGPD, 124, XXI, 426.

19. Secretaría de Hacienda del Estado de Chiapas, Decreto Num. 8, 28 December 1895, CGPD, 129, XXI, 9439.

20. "Nota de lo recaudado por el Gobierno Federal en el Estado de Chiapas en los años que se indican" and "Lo que ha hecho el Gobierno Federal en beneficio del Estado de Chiapas," January 1899, CGPD, 158, XXIV, 3128 and 3130.

21. Díaz to León, 5 March 1896, CGPD, 300, XLI, 402.

22. *Ibid.*

23. *El Universal,* 16 January 1896; *El Partido Liberal,* 30 September 1896.

24. "Memorándum que presenta al C. Presidente de la República ... ," 1899.

25. "Reglamento de la Inspección General de Salubridad Pública," 31 May 1897, SCh, XXVIII, 78, Second Series.

26. *El Universal,* 1 October 1899.

27. León to Díaz, 9 August 1898, CGPD, 152, XXII, 10721.

28. Gastón García Cantu, *El socialismo en México. Siglo XIX* (México: Ediciones Era, 1969), pp. 239-240, 381-403.

29. The author canvassed all the available issues of Chiapas newspapers for the period 1860 to 1911—more than fifty different periodicals in all.

30. *La Brújula,* 20 October 1878.

31. *El Partido Liberal,* 8 January 1886.

32. For example, see: *El Demócrata*, 10 September 1880; *El Sentimiento Nacional*, 28 December 1883; *El Trabajo*, 10 January 1886; and *El Monitor Republicano*, 26 May 1885.

33. *Documentos relativos al Congreso Agrícola de Chiapas* (Tuxtla Gutiérrez: Imprenta del Gobierno del Estado, 1896), p. 69.

34. Quoted in Diego G. López Rosado, *Historia y pensamiento económico de México*, 6 vols. (México: UNAM, 1969), III, p. 326.

35. *La Agricultura*, 15 January 1893.

36. *Discurso del Lic. Emilio Rabasa*, 1896, n.p. Nearly a year earlier Rabasa had expressed privately to Díaz his reservations regarding the efficiency of indebted servitude. See Rabasa to Díaz, 12 December 1892, CGPD, 88, XVII, 19860.

37. Circular Num. 6, 7 December 1895, SCh, XVIII, 75.

38. León to Díaz, 30 April 1896, CGPD, 128, XXI, 7354.

39. Valadés, *El Porfirismo*, I, p. 274.

40. *Documentos Congreso Agrícola*, pp. 58, 104–105.

41. *Ibid.*, pp. 23, 33, 71. Also see Moisés T. De la Peña, *Chiapas económico*, 4 vols. (Tuxtla Gutiérrez: Departamento de Prensa y Turismo, 1951), II, pp. 357–358.

42. "Cuestionario aprobado por el Congreso Agrícola para su estudio," 9 April 1896, CGPD, 127, XXI, 5536.

43. Díaz to León, March 1896, CGPD, 127, XXI, 7304.

44. León to Díaz, 7 April 1896, CGPD, 127, XXI, 5541.

45. Documentos Congreso Agrícola, pp. 32–33.

46. *Ibid.*, pp. 84–87.

47. *Ibid.*, pp. 63–72.

48. *Ibid.*, p. 91.

49. León to Díaz, 30 April 1896, CGPD, 128, XXI, 7354.

50. Díaz to León, May 1896, CGPD, 128, XXI, 7356.

51. *Documentos Congreso Agrícola*, pp. 131–144.

52. Decreto Num. 8, 24 May 1897, SCh, XXVIII, 78.

53. *Informe del Gobernador de Chiapas, C. Coronel Francisco León* (Tuxtla Gutiérrez: Imprenta del Gobierno, 1897).

54. León to Díaz, 15 June 1896, CGPD, 129, XXI, 9371.

55. Díaz to León, 30 June 1896, CGPD, 129, XXI, 9373.

56. León to Díaz, 20 December 1898, CGPD, 156, XXIII, 17495.

57. Lacroix to Díaz, n.d. (approximately January 1896), CGPD, 124, XXI, 426.

58. Lacroix to Díaz, 31 March 1896, CGPD, 124, XXI, 1863.

59. León to Díaz, 22 November 1898, CGPD, 156, XXIII, 17542.

60. Julián Hornedo, jefe político, Soconusco, to Díaz, 24 March 1896, CGPD, 127, XXI, 5434.

61. General Bravo, San Cristóbal, to Díaz, 23 January 1896, CGPD, 337, LV, 458; Bravo to Díaz, 26 January 1896, CGPD, 124, XXI, 1457.

62. León to Díaz, 26 March 1896, CGPD, 127, XXI, 5584.

63. Díaz to León, 6 April 1896, CGPD, 127, XXI, 5585.

64. Decreto Num. 5, 25 April 1896, AHCH, Hemeroteca, Foleto "San Cristóbal."

65. León to Díaz, 10 April 1896, CGPD, 127, XXI, 5530.

66. León to Díaz, 26 August 1896, CGPD, 154, XVIII, 12906.

67. Utrilla to Díaz, 29 July 1896, CGPD, 338, LV, 4187.

68. León to Díaz, 29 July 1896, CGPD, 338, LV, 4140.

69. León to Díaz, 30 July 1896, CGPD, 132, XXI, 13977.

70. León to Díaz, 30 July 1896, CGPD, 338, LV, 4206.

71. León to Díaz, 17 May 1897, CGPD, 341, LVI, 2026.

72. José Franco, Santos Cristiani, M. Vidal, *et al.,* Pichucalco, to Díaz, 2 April 1899, CGPD, 159, XXIV, 4563; Vecinos de Pichucalco to Díaz, 13 June 1899, CGPD, 346, LVIII, 2267.

73. León to Díaz, 7 July 1897, CGPD, 142, XXII, 9423.

74. J. Antonio Rivera G., David Culebro, Jesús Domínguez, *et al.,* Comitán, to Díaz, 30 May 1899, CGPD, 161, XXIV, 7944.

75. León to Díaz, 19 August 1899, CGPD, 163, XXIV, 11560; José Delegado, Pichucalco, to Díaz, 1 May 1899, CGPD, 160, XXIV, 5841; and *El Universal,* 14 April 1899.

76. *El Universal,* 26 May 1899.

77. León to Díaz, 27 May 1899, CGPD, 346, LVIII, 1994.

78. León to Díaz, 29 May 1899, CGPD, 346, LVIII, 2008. Díaz advised León that he should give "no credit to rumors." See Díaz to León, 30 May 1899, CGPD, 346, LVIII, 2009.

79. *El Universal,* 30 May 1899.

80. León to Díaz, 12 June 1899, CGPD, 346, LVIII, 2247.

81. León to Díaz, 9 July 1899, CGPD, 346, LVIII, 2617; Clemente Robles, San Cristóbal, to Díaz, 10 July 1899, CGPD, 346, LVIII, 2544.

82. *El Universal,* 14 July 1899.

83. Valadés, *El Porfirismo,* II, p. 300; Gustavo López Gutiérrez, *Chiapas y sus epopeyas libertarias,* 3 vols. (Tuxtla Gutiérrez, 1957), II, p. 284.

84. León to Díaz, 15 July 1899, CGPD, 346, LVIII, 2683; León to Díaz, 18 August 1899, CGPD, 163, XXIV, 11709; *El Periódico Oficial del Estado,* 5 August 1899.

85. Mary Lowenthal, "The Elite of San Cristóbal," Harvard Chiapas Project,

1963, pp. 10–11; *Directorio general de la república mexicana, 1893–1894* (Mexico, 1893), pp. 7–10; and *Directorio general de la república mexicana, 1900–1901* (México, 1900), pp. 289–295. Also see Romulo Farrera, Mexico City, to Díaz, 10 August 1899, CGPD, 163, XXIV, 11518.

86. Esposa de Farrera to Díaz, 21 July 1899, CGPD, 346, LVIII, 2814.

87. López to Díaz, 22 August 1899, CGPD, 164, XXIV, 13502.

88. León to Díaz, 17 August 1899, CGPD, 346, LVIII, 3381; Díaz to León, 18 August 1899, CGPD, 346, LVIII, 3381.

89. León to Díaz, 25 August 1899, CGPD, 346, LVIII, 3531. An *amparo* is a writ of protection against the action of a public functionary.

90. León to Díaz, 24 August 1899, CGPD, 164, XXIV, 13502.

91. Díaz to León, 5 September 1899, CGPD, 347, LVIII, 3716; Díaz to León, 7 September 1899, CGPD, 347, LVIII, 3718; and Díaz to Castillo, 6 September 1899, CGPD, 347, LVIII, 3720.

92. León to Díaz, 30 September 1899, CGPD, 347, LVIII, 4215.

93. Díaz to León, 2 October 1899, CGPD, 347, LVIII, 4221; León to Díaz, 2 October 1899, CGPD, 347, LVIII, 4321; Pimentel to Díaz, 16 October 1899, CGPD, 347, LVIII, 4621; Pimentel to Díaz, 30 November 1899, CGPD, 347, LVIII, 5482.

94. López to Díaz, 11 October 1899, CGPD, 165, XXIV, 15048; "Juicio contra presuntos culpables de homicidio frustrado en la persona del Coronel Francisco León, 1900," AHCH, Hemeroteca, Expediente 1673.

CHAPTER 3

1. Diccionario Porrua, 2 vols. (México: Editorial Porrua, 1964), II, pp. 1632–1633.

2. Pimental to Díaz, 30 November 1895, CGPD, 122, XX, 18031.

3. Pimentel to Díaz, 12 September 1904, CGPD, 212, XXIX, 11991; *El Universal*, 3 January 1901.

4. Fred Wilber Powell, *The Railroads of Mexico* (Boston: The Stratford Co., 1921), p. 154; *Moody's Manual of Railroads and Corporation Securities. 1909* (New York: Moody Manual Company, 1909), p. 755. Also see Pimentel to Díaz, 11 April 1909, CGPD, 180, XXVI, 3436.

5. *Revista de Chiapas,* 31 August 1902; Gerente, Banco Orientel de México, Puebla, to Díaz, 21 June 1909, CGPD, 260, XXXIV, 10296.

6. Manuel Cruz, Pichucalco, to Díaz, 30 June 1905, CGPD, 202, XVIII, 20.

7. "Memorándum," Tapachula, 1902, CGPD, 190, XXVII, 5679.

8. *Informe del ciudadano gobernador del estado* (Tuxtla Gutiérrez: Im prente del Gobierno, 1905).

9. *Ibid.;* Pimentel to Díaz, 19 December 1903, CGPD, 205, XVIII, 16346; Sóstenes Esponda, San Cristóbal, to Díaz, 7 March 1904, CGPD, 355, LXII, 760.

10. A. Farrera, "Memorándum sobre el café en Chiapas," 16 March 1899, CGPD, 165, XXIV, 15132. Also see Lic. Agustín Farrera, *Breves apuntes sobre el estado de Chiapas* (México: Libería Madrileña, 1900).

11. Ricardo Pozas, "El trabajo en las plantaciones de café y el cambio sociocultural del indio," *Revista Mexicana de Estudios Antropológicos* XIII (1952), p. 34.

12. Albert Brickwood, "Coffee in Soconusco, Chiapas, México," 26 September 1910, NA, RG 84, Tapachula: Miscellaneous Reports.

13. *El Tiempo,* 15 June 1907.

14. Trinidad Sánchez Santos, "El problema de los indígenas de Chiapas, 1902," manuscript located in the Biblioteca "Fray Bartolomé de Las Casas," San Cristóbal Las Casas.

15. *El Universal,* 15 January 1901; R. Farrera, Tuxtla Gutiérrez, to Díaz, 19 February 1900, CGPD, 170, XXV, 1898; Ramón Rabasa to Díaz, 2 April 1900, CGPD, 170, XXV, 8386.

16. Pimentel to Díaz, 15 January 1901, CGPD, 184, XXVI, 2238.

17. Manuel Cruz, Pichucalco, to Díaz, 30 June 1903, CGPD, 202, XXVIII, 9929.

18. See, for example, Carlos Mason, Simojovel, to Díaz, 17 July 1903, CGPD, 355, LXII, 2436; Jesús Solís, Tuxtla Gutiérrez, to Díaz, 19 October 1903, CGPD, 355, LXII, 3140; and Varios vecinos, Pichucalco, to Díaz, Sep tember 1900, CGPD, 176, XXV, 12052.

19. Pimentel to Díaz, 14 July 1904, CGPD, 210, XXIX, 8254.

20. Pimentel to Díaz, 14 March 1900, CGPD, 170, XXV, 3532.

21. Decreto Num. 2, Sección de Gobernación (Chiapas), 20 September 1905, CGPD, 223, XXX, 13533; Pimentel to Díaz, 3 October 1905, CGPD, 357, LXV, 2127.

22. Pimentel to Díaz, 11 October 1905, CGPD, 233, XXX, 13362.

23. Pimentel to Díaz, 28 September 1905, CGPD, 223, XXX, 13299.

24. Pimentel to Díaz, 11 October 1905, CGPD, 233, XXX, 13362.

25. Emilio Rabasa, "Memorándum," October 1905, CGPD, 233, XXX, 13655.

26. *Ibid.*

27. Pimentel to Díaz, 29 October 1905, CGPD, 244, XXX, 15210.

28. Pimentel to Díaz, 22 December 1905, CGPD, 358, LXIV, 2803; R. Rabasa to Díaz, 27 December 1905, CGPD, 244, XXX, 15849; Miguel Utrilla, Adrián and Gregorio Culebro, J. Espinosa Torres, and others, San Cristóbal,

to Díaz, 21 December 1905, CGPD, 358, LXIV, 2781; José Lazos, Mariano Cruz, Carlos Bonifaz, and twenty-three others, San Cristóbal, to Díaz, 21 December 1905, CGPD, 358, LXIV, 2787.

29. R. Rabasa to Díaz, 5 June 1906, CGPD, 229, XXXI, 7298.

30. Obispo de Chiapas, San Cristóbal, to Díaz, 24 October 1909, CGPD, 262, XXXIV, 5277.

31. R. Rabasa to Díaz, 6 April 1906, CGPD, 235, XXXI, 17893; R. Rabasa to Díaz, 30 May 1908, CGPD, 250, XXXIII, 8218; and R. Rabasa to Díaz, 9 September 1908, CGPD, 252, XXXIII, 12014.

32. R. Farrera to Díaz, 13 May 1906, CGPD, 228, XXXI, 4890; R. Rabasa to Díaz, 3 June 1908, CGPD, 250, XXXIII, 8283; and Emilio Rabasa to Díaz, 26 July 1908, CGPD, 250, XXXIII, 8602. Also see R. Gordillo León, "Informe respeta de la comisión para explorar los lugares por donde puede establecer una vía herrada entre Comitán y Tuxtla Gutiérrez," 10 May 1908, CGPD, 250, XXXIII, 8284; and Romula Farrera, "Se hace necesario un ferrocarril que penetre hasta el interior de Chiapas," *El Tiempo,* 26 October 1910.

33. *Informe rendido por el C. Gobernador del Estado. 1908* (Tuxtla Gutiérrez: Imprenta del Gobierno, 1908).

34. *Anuario estadístico de la república mexicana. 1898* (México: Secretaría de Fomento, 1898), pp. 422–424; *Anuario estadístico. 1904,* p. 238.

35. Virgilio Grajales, for example, became secretary of government, Teofilio H. Orantes was state attorney general, and Abrahám López and later Ausencio Cruz were treasurers.

36. R. Rabasa to Díaz, 27 April 1906, CGPD, 350, LXIV, 826.

37. Martínez Rojas, San Cristóbal, to Díaz, 30 April 1906, CGPD, 228, XXXI, 4341.

38. Martínez Rojas, San Cristóbal, to Governor Rabasa, 29 April 1906, CGPD, 228, XXXI, 4343.

39. *Anuario estadístico del estado de Chiapas, año de 1909,* pp. 273–311; Brickwood, "Political Situation in the State of Chiapas," 19 March 1911, NA/RG 84, Tapachula: Miscellaneous Reports.

40. Vicente Camberos Vizcaino, *Francisco El Grande. Mons. Francisco Orozco y Jiménez, Biografía,* 2 vols. (México: Editorial Jus, 1966), p. 142; Martínez Rojas, San Cristóbal, to Governor Rabasa, 29 April 1906, CGPD, 228, XXXI, 4343.

41. Obispo de Chiapas, Francisco Orozco y Jiménez, San Cristóbal, to Díaz, 24 October 1909, CGPD, 264, XXXIV, 16730.

42. Albert Brickwood, "Rubber in Chiapas (Mexico)," 25 June 1910, NA/RG 84, Tapachula: Miscellaneous Reports; J. L. Hermessen, *India Rubber World* (February 1910), n.p.

43. Brickwood, "Plantations in Palenque, Chiapas, Mexico," 10 October 1910, NA/RG 84, Tapachula: Miscellaneous Reports; *The Mexican Year Book, 1912* (Mexico: Department of Finance, 1912), p. 128.

44. Brickwood, "Annual Industrial and Trade Report for 1909," 1 September 1910, NA/RG 84, Tapachula: Miscellaneous Reports.

45. *Anuario estadístico del estado de Chiapas, año de 1909,* pp. 95–102.

46. *Periódico Oficial del Estado,* 5 September 1908, 14 August 1909, 3 September 1910, 18 February 1911; F. Ruiz, Chiapas de Corzo, to Díaz, 1 November 1910, CGPD, 276, XXXV, 16716; R. Rabasa to Díaz, 17 August 1910, CGPD, 274, XXXV, 14331.

47. *Boletín de la Cámara Agrícola de Chiapas,* 15 June 1909, 8 July 1909, 15 May 1911; Brickwood, "Annual Industrial and Trade Report for 1909."

48. Brickwood, "Soconusco Coffee-Growers Meeting," 1 October 1910, NA/RG 84, Tapachula: Miscellaneous Reports.

49. Brickwood, "Coffee Crop Conditions in Foreign Countries," 1 February 1912, NA/RG 84, Tapachula: Miscellaneous Reports.

50. Brickwood, "Agriculture in the Valleys of Cintalapa and Jiquipilas, State of Chiapas, Mexico," 4 October 1910, NA/RG 84, Tapachula: Miscellaneous Reports.

51. *Ibid.*

52. *Ibid.;* Brickwood, "Agricultural Possibilities in the State of Chiapas, Mexico," 10 June 1910, NA/RG 84, Tapachula: Miscellaneous Reports.

53. *La Voz del Pueblo,* 5 May 1907.

54. Busto, *Estadística de la república mexicana,* I, p. xviii; *Datos estadísticos del estado de Chiapas. 1896* (Tuxtla Gutiérrez: Imprenta del Gobierno, 1897); and *Anuario estadístico Chiapas 1909,* p. 52.

55. Brickwood, "Tapachula," *Daily Consular and Trade Reports, October 25, 1911* No. 250 (Washington, D.C.: GPO, 1911), p. 434.

56. *Anuario estadístico de la república mexicana,* vols. 1894–1907.

57. Valadés, *El Porfirismo,* I, p. 289; R. Rabasa, *El estado de Chiapas,* p. 118; *Chiapas, su estado actual, su riqueza, sus ventas para los negocios* (Mexco: Chiapas Bureau of Information, 1895), pp. 7, 20–21.

58. Brickwood, "Coffee in Soconusco, Chiapas, Mexico."

59. "Claim on Behalf of Chival Planters' Association," National Archives of the United States, Record Group 76, Docket 806, Box 35.

60. Geografe J. Tamborrel, *The Tabasco and Chiapas Land Co. of San Juan Bautista, Mexico* (Mexico, 1901), p. 17.

61. Datos estadísticos 1896, p. 10; *Anuario estadístico Chiapas 1909,* p. 52.

62. Karena Shields, *The Changing Wind* (New York: Thomas Crowell, 1959), p. 40.

63. *Reports of Dr. C. L. G. Anderson, et. al.* (San Francisco, Chiapas Rubber Plantation Company, 1905), pp. 10–12.

64. Brickwood, "Memorandum," August 1911, NA/RG 84, Tapachula Dis patches.

65. See Thomas Benjamin, "El trabajo en las monterías de Tabasco y Chia pas, 1870–1946," *Historia Mexicana* 30 (April–June 1981), pp. 506–529; and Friederike Baumann, "B. Traven's Land des Fruhlings and the Caoba Cycle as a Source for the Study of Agrarian Society," unpublished manuscript.

66. Quoted in Frans Blom and Gertrude Duby, *La selva lacandona*, 2 vols. (México: Editorial Cultura, 1955), I, p. 263. Also see B. Traven's fictional account, *March to the Monteria* (New York: Hill and Wang, 1971).

67. Moisés T. De la Peña, *Chiapas económico*, 4 vols. (Tuxtla Gutiérrez, 1951), II, pp. 675–677, 358; *Estadísticas sociales del Porfiriato, 1877–1910* (México: Dirección General de Estadística, 1956), p. 40; Seminario de Historia Moderna de México, *Estadísticas económicas del Porfiriato: Fuerza de trabajo y actividad económica por sectores* (México: El Colegio de México, 1964), p. 39.

68. Carlos Z. Flores, *Departamento de Las Casas del estado de Chiapas* (San Cristóbal Las Casas, 1909), p. 41; *Anuario estadístico Chiapas 1909*, p. 52.

69. Flores, *Departamento de Las Casas*, pp. 38–39.

70. Sánchez Santos, *El problema de la indígenas* (1902), n.p.

71. Manuel Pineda, *Estudio sobre ejidos* (San Cristóbal: Tipografía Flores, 1910), p. 11.

72. Vecinos de Huistán to Díaz, 12 February 1909, CGPD, 256, XXXIV, 2304.

73. El pueblo de Chapultenango, Pichucalco, to Díaz, July 1909, CGPD, 262, XXXIV, 12506.

74. Quoted in López Rosado, *Historia y pensamiento económico* I, p. 210.

75. Alan Knight, *The Mexican Revolution*, I, pp. 22–23.

76. Bryan R. Roberts, "State and Region in Latin America: The View from Below," in G. A. Banck, R. Buve, and L. Van Vroonhoven, eds., *State and Region in Latin America: A Workshop* (Amsterdam: CEDLA, 1981), p. 20.

77. This is not to say that local and regional (let alone national) government was not used to promote private gain. It was, everywhere.

78. Allen Wells, *Yucatan's Gilded Age: Haciendas, Henequen, and International Harvester, 1860–1915* (Albuquerque: University of New Mexico Press, 1985), p. 38.

79. John Womack, Jr., *Zapata and the Mexican Revolution* (New York: Alfred A. Knopf, 1968), p. 42.

80. Mark Wasserman, *Capitalists, Caciques, and Revolution: The Native Elite and Foreign Enterprise in Chihuahua, Mexico, 1854–1911* (Chapel Hill: The University of North Carolina Press, 1984), p. 70.

81. Frank Tannenbaum, *The Mexican Agrarian Revolution* (New York: The Macmillan Company, 1929), p. 154.

CHAPTER 4

1. Farrera to Francisco León De la Barra, 29 May 1911, Archivo General Octavio Magaña, Caja 8, Expediente F-2, Document 46. Hereafter cited as AGOM and identifying information.

2. Francisco I. Madero, *La sucesión presidencial en 1910. El partido nacional democrático* (San Pedro, Coahuila, 1908), p. 3.

3. Charles C. Cumberland, *Mexican Revolution: Genesis Under Madero* (Austin: University of Texas Press, 1952), pp. 119–151.

4. *Revista Chiapaneca*, 1 May 1910.

5. Knight, *The Mexican Revolution*, 1, pp. 188, 227.

6. *Chiapas y México*, 15 May 1910; J. Antonio Rivera G., México, to Díaz, 5 January 1910, CGPD, 257, XXXV, 73.

7. *Más Allá*, 9 October 1910; *La Voz del Pueblo*, 22 January 1911; and Ramón Rabasa to Díaz, 6 December 1910, CGPD, 277, XXXV, 18289.

8. Manuel Pineda y otros, San Cristóbal, to Díaz, 26 March 1911, CGPD, 370, LXX, 7050.

9. *La Voz del Pueblo*, 20 April 1911.

10. "Bases orgánicas del 'Centro directivo de la libertad del sufragio en Chiapas,' San Cristóbal Las Casas, 3 de abril de 1911," AGOM, 22, 1, 33; and *La Libertad de Sufragio*, 20 April 1911.

11. *El Heraldo de Chiapas*, 14 May, 28 May, 1 June, and 29 June 1911; Consul General, Mexico City, to Secretary of State, 15 May 1911, NA/RG 165, 5761-269; and Consul Brickwood to Secretary of State, 25 May 1911, NA/RG 165, 5761-268.

12. *El Heraldo de Chiapas*, 1 June 1911.

13. T. Flores Ruiz, San Cristóbal, to De la Barra, n.d., AGOM, 22, 1, 44. Also see Luis Espinosa, Tuxtla Gutiérrez, to De la Barra, 4 June 1911, SCh, XXX, 79; *La Libertad del Sufragio*, 22 June 1911.

14. *El Heraldo de Chiapas*, 8, 11, 15, 18 June 1911.

15. *El Heraldo de Chiapas*, 22 June 1911; *La Voz del Pueblo*, 25 February 1912.

16. El Club "Soconusco," to De la Barra, 22 August 1911, AGOM, 18, 5, 287.

17. Gregorio Ponce de León, *El interinato presidencial de 1911* (México: Secretaría de Fomento, 1912), p. 241. Also see *El Heraldo de Chiapas*, 4 June 1911.

18. *El Heraldo de Chiapas*, 22 June 1911.

19. Paul Marina Flores, Chiapas de Corzo, to Madero, 24 June 1911, Archivo Francisco I. Madero, Ms. 21, 2201-2310, Expediente 1/426. Hereafter cited as AFIM and identifying information.

20. Flavio Guillén, "La cuestion de Chiapas," *El Heraldo de Chiapas*, 2 July 1911.

21. *El Heraldo de Chiapas*, 29 June, 2 July 1911.

22. Jesús Martínez Rojas, *Los últimos acontecimientos políticos de Chiapas* (San Cristóbal, 1912), pp. 17–18.

23. Manuel Franco, San Cristóbal, to Madero, 12 October 1911, in Isidro Fabela and Josefina E. de Fabela, comps., *Documentos históricos de la revolución mexicana—Revolución y régimen maderista* (México: Editorial Jus y Fondo de Cultura Económica, 1960–1973), II, Document 350, pp. 152–157.

24. "En la ciudad de San Cristóbal Las Casas," 3 July 1911, AHCH, Sucesos de 1911–1912, Manuscritos y Impresos, Carpeta 1625.

25. Luis Espinosa, *Rastros de sangre. Historia de la revolución en Chiapas* (Tuxtla Gutiérrez: La Colección Ceiba, 1980, edición facsimilar de la primera edición de 1912), p. 25.

26. *El Imparcial*, 6 July 1911.

27. Luis Espinosa, *Rastros de sangre*, p. 7.

28. García de León, *Resistencia y utopia*, II, p. 23.

29. Martínez Rojas, *Los últimos acontecimientos*, p. 18. "The Cristobalense cause is worthy and lofty; it is the pursuit of the great work of Don Francisco I. Madero! Death to caciquismo!" Al pueblo acalteco, Acala, 26 September 1911, AHCH, Carpeta 1625.

30. *El Progreso* (Tapachula), 14 July 1911.

31. R. Gordillo León, Tuxtla Gutiérrez, to De la Barra, 5 July 1911, AGOM, 16, 2, 363.

32. Rovelo Argüello, Tuxtla Gutiérrez, to Senators P. González Mena, Luis G. Curiel, and R. R. Guzmán, 27 September 1911, AHCH, Sección de Guerra, Tomo VII, Exp. 26.

33. "El Policarpo Rueda ha sido designado de acuerdo con los diversos partidos políticos de ese Estado y el Ministerio de Gobernación para Gobernador Interino." See Madero to Manuel Pineda, 4 July 1911, Serie Francisco I. Madero, Roll 20. Hereafter cited as SFIM and identifying information. Also see *El Heraldo de Chiapas*, 22 June 1911.

34. Espinosa, *Rastros de sangre,* p. 29; Martínez Rojas, *Los últimos acon tecimientos,* pp. 20–21; and *El Heraldo de Chiapas,* 10 July 1911.

35. Interview with Dr. Policarpo Rueda in the newspaper *Cuba* (Havana, Cuba), 4 December 1912, in *Documentos históricos de la revolución mexicana,* IV, Doc. 956, pp. 229–233.

36. Martínez Rojas, *Los últimos acontecimientos,* pp. 21–22. This account contains copies of the telegraph exchange between Rivera G. and Rovelo Argüello; see pp. 126–127.

37. Rovelo Argüello to Senators, 26 September 1911.

38. *La Libertad del Sufragio,* 31 August 1911.

39. Rovelo Argüello to De la Barra, 17 September 1911, Archivo Francisco León De la Barra, X-1, Carpeta 2-25, Document 141. Hereafter cited as AFLB and identifying information.

40. T. Flores Ruiz to De la Barra, 30 September 1911, AGOM, 9, F-5, 210.

41. Rovelo Argüello to Senators, 26 September 1911.

42. J. Espinosa Tórres to Secretary General of Government, Tuxtla Gutiérrez, 14 September 1911, AHCH, Legislatura, 1911–1912.

43. *The Mexican Herald,* 26 September 1911.

44. Madero to Espinosa Tórres, 17 September 1911, AHCH, Guerra, VII, 28.

45. "Discurso que pronunció el Sr. Lic. Querido Moheno en la Cámara de Diputados," reprinted in full in Prudencio Moscoso Pastrana, *Jacinto Pérez "Pajarito," último lider chamula* (Tuxtla Gutiérrez: Editorial del Gobierno del Estado de Chiapas, 1972), pp. 111–112; Rovelo Argüello to De la Barra, 19 September 1911, and Rovelo Argüello to De la Barra, 21 September 1911, AFLB, X-1, 2 de 25, 147 and 148.

46. Governor Rovelo Argüello apparently believed San Cristóbal possessed about 1,000 Indian soldiers. García de León gives 5,000 to 8,000 as the figure. Rovelo Argüello to Senators, 26 September 1911; and García de León, *Resistencia y utopia,* II, p. 24.

47. Brickwood to Henry Lane Wilson, 25 September 1911, NA/RG 84, Vol. 148/C8.2; T. Castillo Corzo, Puente Porfirio Díaz, to De la Barra, AFLB, X-1, 2 de 25, 134; Peace Commission to Rovelo Argüello, 15 October 1911, AHCH, Legislatura 1911–1912; *La Patria,* 3 October 1911; *Imparcial,* 21, 25 September 1911.

48. *El Imparcial,* 25 September 1911; Moscoso Pastrana, *Jacinto Pérez "Pajarito";* and García de León, *Resistencia y utopia,* II, pp. 27–28.

49. "Hay datos fundados para creer complicado al Obispo," Rovelo Argüello to Senators, 27 September 1911.

50. *Boletín eclesiástico del Obispado de Chiapas,* 12 December 1911.

51. Espinosa, *Rastros de sangre,* pp. 52–55. The same is true regarding García de León's assertions of the bishop's leadership.

52. Obispo to De la Barra, 17 September 1911, AFLB, X-1, 2 de 25, 139.

53. Obispo to De la Barra, 24 September 1911, AFLB, X-1, 2 de 25, 151.

54. De la Barra to Rovelo Argüello, 15 September 1911, AFLB, X-1, 2 de 25, 133.

55. *El Imparcial,* 25 September 1911.

56. *El Imparcial,* 20 October 1911.

57. De la Barra to Espinosa Tórres, 17 September 1911, AFLB, X-1, 2 de 25, 140.

58. Rovelo Argüello to De la Barra, 5 October 1911, AGOM, 21, 4, 326; *The Mexican Herald,* 2, 4 October 1911.

59. Rovelo Argüello to Senators, 27 September 1911.

60. "Sessión del Senado de la Républica del 6 de Octubre sobre la situación del Estado de Chiapas," in Emilio Rabasa, *Antología de Emilio Rabasa. Bio grafía y selección de Andrés Serra Rojas,* 2 vols. (México: Ediciones Oasis, 1969), pp. 339–341. The volumes of the *Diario de los Debates* for 1911 are missing in the Hemeroteca Nacional.

61. *El Imparcial,* 20 October 1911.

62. *El Imparcial,* 20 October 1911; Moisés Camacho to Rovelo Argüello, 7 October 1911, AHCH, Guerra, VII, 28.

63. Administrador Principal del Timbre, San Cristóbal, to Secretario de Hacienda y Credito Público, 9 October 1911, AGN/Gobernación, Relaciones con los estados, 912(17)5.

64. Brickwood to Henry Lane Wilson, 10 October 1911, NA/RG 84, Vol. 148, Dispatch 131; *El Imparcial,* 11, 13 October 1911; *The Mexican Herald,* 13 October 1911. For details of the military conflict, see AHCH, Impresos y Manuscritos, 1911, Carpeta 1623.

65. General Paz to De la Barra, 12 October 1911, AGOM, 8, P-5, 471.

66. García de León, *Resistencia y utopia,* II, p. 29.

67. "Memorandum of Peace Discussions," 13 October 1911, AHCH, Guerra VII; *The Mexican Herald,* 22, 29 October 1911.

68. General Paz to De la Barra, 12 October 1911, AGOM, 9, P-5, 407; E. Paz, "Al pueblo chiapaneco," October 1911, AGOM, 22, 3, 192.

69. *La Patria,* 23 November 1911; *La Voz del Pueblo,* 3 December 1911.

70. *La Patria,* 15 December 1911.

71. "Retrazos de historia chiapaneca," *Liberación,* 3 February 1935.

72. Madero to Gordillo León, 23 December 1911, *Documentos históricos de la revolución mexicana,* II, Doc. 502, p. 448.

73. Guillén to Madero, 27 January 1912, and 12 February 1912, AGN/

Fondo Francisco I. Madero, 301-1, 13; Rivera G., "Los embrollos políticos del Sr. Madero," *La Tribuna*, 4 February 1912.

74. "Memorandum Sent August, 1911," NA/RG 84, Tapachula Dispatches, Vol. 148.C8.2/105.

75. Brickwood to Henry Lane Wilson, 12 September 1911, NA/RG 84, Tapachula Dispatches; Porash to Henry Lane Wilson, 16 March 1912, NA/RG 84, Consular and Diplomatic Letters Sent.

76. L. A. Osten to Brickwood, 19 August 1911, NA/RG 84, Tapachula Dispatches.

77. Club "Soconusco," Tapachula, to De la Barra, 22 August 1911, AGOM, 18, 5, 287.

78. Vice-Consul Charles Lesher to Henry Lane Wilson, 23 December 1911, NA/RG 84, Tapachula Dispatches.

79. Porash to Henry Lane Wilson, 14 February 1912, NA/RG 84, Consular and Diplomatic Letters Sent. "Llevabamos siete meses poco más o menos de padecer zobras por los perjuicios a causa de lo anormal situación. Desde la llegada del Señor Jefe Político Abelardo Domínguez se ha venido notando el restablecimiento de la tranquilidad." Vecinos de Tapachula to Gobernador de Chiapas, 12 February 1912, AHCH, Gobernación, 1912, VII, 94.

80. Flavio Guillén, "Manifiesto que el Gobierno del Estado dirije a los pueblos de Chiapas," 20 April 1912, AHCH, Carpeta 1623. Tolerance did not extend to Horacio Culebro, tax collector in Ocosingo, the man responsible for cutting off the ears of rebel Chamulas. Guillén's first official act was to fire Culebro. Guillén to Juan Sánchez Azcona, 19 February 1912, AGN, Fondo Francisco I. Madero, Carp. 302-1, Caja 13. Hereafter cited as AGN/FIM and identifying information.

81. *La Libertad del Sufragio*, 23 May 1911. Ciro Farrera died in November 1911.

82. *La Voz del Pueblo*, 28 January 1912.

83. *Manifiesto del Lic. Jesús Martínez Rojas al Pueblo Chiapaneco* (Mexico, 1913), pp. 9–13; *La Voz del Pueblo*, 9 June 1912.

84. *La Voz del Pueblo*, 11 February 1912, 1 September 1912.

85. Guillén to Juan Sánchez Azcona, 19 February 1912, AGN/FIM, 302-1, 3.

86. *Periódico Oficial del Estado*, 30 November, 14 December 1912.

87. "Acuerdo del Sr. Gobernador," 31 March 1912, AHCH, Gobernación, 1914; *Manifiesto del Lic. Jesús Martínez Rojas*, p. 13.

88. Porash to Governor Guillén, 14 March 1912, NA/RG 84, Tehuantepec Post Records, Vol. 150/C8.7; Porash to Secretary of State, 17 February 1912, NA/RG 84, Tapachula Post Records, Vol. 158/C8.4.

89. Secretario General de Gobierno, Tuxtla Gutiérrez, to Jefe Político, Ton alá, 17 September 1913, AHCH, Gobernación, 1913, II, 20.

90. Presidente Municipal Arriaga to Señores Municipes, 25 December 1912, AHCH, Gobernación, 1912, VIII, 95; Jefe Político Palenque to Governor, 8 January 1912, AHCH, Gobernación, 1912, VIII, 100; Angel María Pérez, Tapachula, to Secretario de Gobernación, Mexico, 8 November 1913, Archivo General de la Nación, Fondo Gobernación, Ramo: Relaciones con los Estados, hereafter cited as AGN/Gobernación.

91. *Periódico Oficial del Estado,* 19 March 1910, 24 August 1912.

92. Flavio Guillén, *Dos estudios—Francisco I. Madero y fray Matías de Córdova* (Mexico: Departamento del Distrito Federal, 1974).

93. Decree of 22 February 1913, Governor Gordillo León, SCh, XXX, 79.

94. Gordillo León to Emilio Rabasa, 22 February 1913, AHCH, Gobernación, 1913, VII, 106.

95. "Acuerdo del Gobernador del Estado," 15 March 1913, AHCH, Gobernación, 1913, III, 23. Governor Guillén mentioned the Felicista orientation of Tuxtla Gutiérrez, Tonalá, and Tapachula in 1912; see Guillén to Sánchez Azcona, 13 November 1912, AGN/FIM, 302-1, 13.

96. *La Tribuna,* 4 February 1913; *Manifiesto del Lic. Jesús Martínez Rojas,* p. 8.

97. Asuntos Ayuntamientos, AHCH, Gobernación, 1914, 510.

98. *Periódico Oficial del Estado,* 18 September, 13 November 1913; 30 April 1914.

99. Charles C. Cumberland, *Mexican Revolution: The Constitutionalist Years* (Austin: University of Texas Press, 1974), pp. 23–57.

100. Alfonso Tarecena, *Historia de la revolución en Tabasco* (Villahermosa: Ediciones del Gobierno de Tabasco, 1974), pp. 239–256.

101. Jefe Político, Pichucalco, to Secretary General of Government, 5 August 1914, AHCH, Gobernación, 1914, VII, 30; Governor Palafox to General Huerta, 14 November 1913, AHCH, Gobernación, 1913, X, 143.

102. Governor Palafox to Secretary General of Government, Mexico, 20 June 1913, AHCH, Gobernación, 1913, XI, 146.

103. Blom and Duby, *La selva lacandona,* I, pp. 281–282.

104. Fernando Mijanes, "San Román," to Lindoro Castellanos, Ocosingo, 7 April 1914, AHCH, Gobernación, 1914, VII, 30.

105. Blom and Duby, *La selva lacandona,* I, pp. 281–282.

106. "Dr. Belisario Domínguez (Chiapas), Speech to Senate," 23 September 1913, NA/RG 59, 812.00/9320.

107. Michael C. Meyer, *Huerta: A Political Portrait* (Lincoln: University of Nebraska Press, 1972), pp. 135–136.

108. Jefe Político, Soconusco, to Secretary of General of Government, Tuxtla Gutiérrez, 19 June 1913, AHCH, Gobernación, 1913, XI, 146.

109. Governor Palafox to Secretary of Government, Mexico, 27 September 1913, AHCH, Gobernación, 1913, II, 20.

110. Mauro Calderón, "Tapachula (dos sucesos en el año 1920)," *ICACH*, 1 (June 1959), pp. 50–51.

111. Palafox to Secretary of Government, Mexico, 26 February 1914, AHCH, Gobernación, 1914, VII, 30.

112. See Expediente 30, entitled "Revolución en el Estado," in AHCH, Gobernación, 1914, VII.

113. "Informe de la Secretario de Gobernación," 25 September 1911, AGN/Gobernación, Relaciones con los Estados, 912(17)5.

CHAPTER 5

1. Luis Pola, "Por el honor de Chiapas," *El Sur de México,* 12 April 1945.
2. Knight, *The Mexican Revolution,* II, p. 237.
3. J. M. Marquez, *El Veintiuno. Hombres de la revolución y sus hechos* (Oaxaca, 1916), pp. 65–73.
4. Douglas Richmond, *Venustiano Carranza's Nationalist Struggle, 1893–1920* (Lincoln: University of Nebraska Press, 1983), p. 77.
5. Miguel Ángel Peral, *Diccionario biográfico mexicano* (México: Editorial Pac, 1944), p. 166; Everado Gamiz Olivas, *La revolución en el estado de Durango* (Mexico, 1963), pp. 19–20.
6. Knight, *The Mexican Revolution,* II, p. 239.
7. *Periódico Oficial del Estado,* 23 September 1914.
8. Acuerdo del Gobernador del Estado, 12 October 1914, AHCH, Gobernación, 1914, II, 7; Asuntos Ayuntamientos, 15 October 1914, AHCH, Gobernación, 1914, 351; *Periódico Oficial del Estado,* 23 September, 15 October, 5 December 1914, 16 January, 10 April, 22 May, 28 May 1915.
9. *Periódico Oficial del Estado,* 31 October 1914.
10. Alicia Hernández Chavez, "La Defensa de los Finqueros de Chiapas, 1914–1920," *Historia Mexicana,* XVIII (January-March 1979), p. 356.
11. Friederike Baumann, "Terratenientes, campesinos y la expansión de la agricultura capitalista en Chiapas, 1896–1916," p. 45.
12. Testimony of Mrs. Cora Less Sturgis, in *Investigation of Mexican Affairs. Preliminary Report and Hearings of the Committee on Foreign Relations, United States Senate,* 2 vols. (Washington, D.C.: GPO, 1920), I, pp. 921–922.
13. Hipólito Rébora, *Memorias de un chiapaneco (1895–1982)* (México: Editorial Katun, 1982), p. 93.

14. Santiago Serrano, *Chiapas revolucionario (hombres y hechos)* (Tuxtla Gutiérrez, 1923), p. 9; Moscoso Pastrana, *Jacinto Pérez "Pajarito,"* pp. 98–99; *Periódico Oficial del Estado,* 23 September 1914.

15. Claim on Behalf of Walter A. Quinby, NA/RG 76, Doc. 146, 3024.

16. Spencer, "Soconusco," n.p.

17. J. A. Ross, Consular Agent, Ocós (Guatemala), to William Owen, Consul General, Guatemala City, 2 January 1915, NA/RG 84, Ocós, Guatemala, 1914–15.

18. Marquez, *El veintiuno,* pp. 156–159.

19. Memorandum of Claim, NA/RG 76, Doc. 185, 1649.

20. Baumann, "La expansión de la agricultura capitalista en Chiapas," p. 49.

21. Cumberland, *The Constitutionalist Years,* pp. 151–164. Knight explains the important differences between "nationalist" Carrancismo and "parochial" Villismo: *The Mexican Revolution,* II, pp. 232–233.

22. *Ibid.,* pp. 165–185.

23. The entire document is found in Casahonda Castillo, *50 años de revolución,* p. 49.

24. *Boletín de Información,* 18 December 1914.

25. Informe del Gral. Salvador Alvarado, 20 May 1916, *Documentos históricos de la revolución mexicana,* Vol. 4, Tomo I, Doc. 657, pp. 143–145.

26. Ross to Owen, 10 January 1915, NA/RG 84, Ocós; Ross to Mrs. A. C. Gordon, Seattle, Washington, 5 January 1915, NA/RG 84, Ocós.

27. García de León, *Resistencia y utopia,* II, p. 46.

28. Hipólito Rébora explains that "se denominarón Mapaches, por andar siempre en la noche." *Memorias de un chiapaneco,* p. 94. García de León, on the other hand, relates the story of the maize eaters. A local finquero exclaimed, "Estos no son cristianos, estos son mapachada," in "Lucha de clases y poder político en Chiapas," *Historia y Sociedad* 22 (1979), p. 60.

29. Octavio Gordillo y Ortiz, *Diccionario biográfico de Chiapas* (México: B. Costa-Amic, 1977), pp. 85; Serrano, *Chiapas revolucionario,* p. 11; López Gutiérrez, *Chiapas,* III, p. 261; *Anuario estadístico Chiapas 1909.*

30. Hernández Chavez, "La defensa de los finqueros," pp. 357–358; García de León, *Resistencia y utopia,* II, chap. 4, "La finca en armas," pp. 41–100.

31. Hernández Chavez, "La defensa de los finqueros," pp. 357–358; García de León, *Resistencia y utopia,* II, pp. 62–63.

32. Mario García, *Soconusco en la historia,* pp. 263–265; Spenser, "Soconusco," n.p.

33. V. Carranza to General Castro, 2 February 1915, Archivo Venustiano Carranza, Carpeta 1. Hereafter cited as AVC and identifying information.

"Memorándum—Revolución en Chiapas, 1916," ASRE, Expediente 17-9-101.

34. Gary Gossen, *Chamulas in the World of the Sun: Time and Space in a Maya Oral Tradition* (Cambridge: Harvard University Press, 1974), pp. 271–272.

35. Robert M. Laughlin, *Of Cabbages and Kings: Tales from Zinacantan* (Washington: Smithsonian Institution Press, 1977), p. 129.

36. Lowenthal, "The Elite of San Cristóbal," p. 38.

37. Marquez, *El veintiuno*, p. 85.

38. Cumberland, *The Constitutionalist Years*, pp. 203, 209.

39. "Memorándum—Revolución in Chiapas, 1916."

40. "El 15 de abril de 1916," *El Paladín*, 15 April 1955.

41. Prudencio Moscoso Pastrana, *El pinedismo en Chiapas* (México, 1960), pp. 55–62.

42. "Plan de Compaña contra los rebeldes de Chiapas, 1916," ASRE, 17- 6-10/11.

43. Consul General, Guatemala City, to Department of State, 21 September 1920, NA/RG 84, Correspondence.

44. "Memorándum—Revolución in Chiapas, 1916."

45. Richmond, *Venustiano Carranza's Nationalist Struggle*, p. 215.

46. Alvarado to Carranza, 24 April 1918, AVC, Telegramas, 2.

47. Knight, *The Mexican Revolution*, II, p. 379; Luis Liceaga, *Félix Díaz* (México: Editorial Jus, 1958), p. 394; Peter V. N. Henderson, *Félix Díaz, the Porfirians, and the Mexican Revolution* (Lincoln: University of Nebraska Press, 1981), pp. 127–128.

48. "Memorias del General Juan Andreu Almazán," *El Universal*, 25, 28 May 1958.

49. "Copia del Informe Rendido por el C. General de Brigada Rafael Cal y Mayor al General en Jefe de la Revolución Emiliano Zapata, Año de 1917," Rare Manuscript Collection, Latin American Library, Tulane University. This document has been published; see Thomas Benjamin, "Una historia poco glo riosa: Informe de Rafael Cal y Mayor al General Emiliano Zapata, 1917," *Historia Mexicana* XXXII (April–June, 1983), pp. 597–620. Also see García de León's eloquent treatment of the Zapatistas of Chiapas in *Resistencia y utopia*, chap. 5, "Los zapatistas de Chiapas: una crónica silvestre," pp. 101–133.

50. "Informe que rinde al Senor Ministro de Gobernación, el Gobernador Provisional del estado, General Blas Corral," 27 January 1916, AHCH, Gob ernación, 1915, IV, 23. Social equilibrium, Knight argues, "was central to Constitutionalist thinking, even of a 'radical' kind." *The Mexican Revolution*, II, p. 471.

51. *Ibid.*

52. *Periódico Oficial del Estado,* 19 January 1915; Aviso General, Delegación de la Comisión Nacional Agraria, 27 January 1916, SCh, XXX, 79.

53. "Informe que rinde al Señor Ministro de Gobernación," 27 January 1916.

54. Resoluciones Presidenciales, Archivo General de la Nación, Comisión Nacional Agraria, Libro 2, pp. 81–82; Libro 6, pp. 192–194; Libro 9, pp. 13–14; and Libro 10, pp. 111–112.

55. Visitador de Jefaturas, Comitán, to Secretaría General de Gobierno, Tuxtla Gutiérrez, 15 December 1914, AHCH, Gobernación, 1915, IV, 13.

56. Visitador de Jefaturas, Palenque and Chilón, to Secretaría General de Gobierno, Tuxtla Gutiérrez, 30 December 1914, AHCH, Gobernación, 1914, IV, 13.

57. Delegación Departmental, Palenque, to Secretaría General de Gobierno, Tuxtla Gutiérrez, 24 April 1915, AHCH, Gobernación, 1915, IV, 11; "Informe que rinde al Señor Ministro de Gobernación," 27 January 1916.

58. "Ley de 19 de agosto de 1918," Villanueva, AHCH, Fomento, 1918, IV, 47; "Acuerdo del Gobernador," 31 August 1918, AHCH, Fomento, 1918, IV, 50.

59. De la Peña, *Chiapas económica,* II, p. 377; García de León, "Lucha de clases," p. 69.

60. "Political Conditions in Chiapas, Mexico," 18 March 1919, NA/RG 84, Correspondence, Guatamala City.

61. Vice-Consul, Guatemala City, to Department of State, 18 October 1919, NA/RG 84, Correspondence, Guatemala City.

62. Resoluciones Presidenciales, AGN, CNA, Libro 2, pp. 81–82; Libro 6, pp. 192–194; Libro 9, pp. 13–14.

63. "Political Conditions in Chiapas, Mexico," 18 March 1919.

64. Spenser, "Soconusco," n.p.

65. Juan Dardon y demás to Secretaría General de Gobierno, Tuxtla Gutiérrez, 9 October 1918, AHCH, Fomento, 1918, IV, 50.

66. Knight, *The Mexican Revolution,* II, p. 359.

67. Rafael Pascasio, Tuxtla Gutiérrez, to Secretaría General de Gobierno, 6 February 1918, AHCH, Fomento, 1918, II, 14.

68. For example, see Vecinos de Nicapa, Pichucalco, to Governor of Chiapas, 23 July 1918, AHCH, Gobernación, 1918, XV, 158; Vicinos de Oxchuc to Governor of Chiapas, 15 July 1918, AHCH, Fomento, 1918, II, 19; Vecinos de Zinacantan to Governor of Chiapas, 7 October 1918, AHCH, Gobernación, 1918, XV, 158.

69. Circular, 7 November 1917, AHCH, Gobernación, 1917, V. 117; *Periódico Oficial del Estado,* 22, 29 December 1917.

70. Douglas W. Richmond, "The First Chief and Revolutionary Mexico:

The Presidency of Venustiano Carranza, 1915–1920," Diss. University of Washington, 1976, pp. 233–234.

71. James W. Wilkie, *The Mexican Revolution: Federal Expenditures and Social Change since 1910* (Berkeley: University of California Press, 1970), pp. 246–256.

72. John Womack, Jr., "The Mexican Revolution, 1910–1920," *The Cambridge History of Latin America*, V, p. 131.

73. Villanueva to Carranza, 5 October 1916, AVC, Telegramas, 2; Serrano, *Chiapas revolucionario*, pp. 153–155.

74. López Gutiérrez, *Chiapas*, III, p. 261.

75. *Provincia* (May–June 1949), p. 10.

76. Tuxtlecos to Carranza, 20 September 1916, AVC, Telegramas, 2; Tapachuleños to Carranza, 2 September 1916, AVC, Telegramas, 2.

77. *Diario de los Debates del Congreso Constituyente 1916–1917* (México: Instituto Nacional de Estudios Históricos de la Revolución Mexicana, 1960), II, p. 90. The Chiapas delegation was: Propietarios, Enrique Suárez, Enrique D. Cruz, Cristóbal Ll. Castillo, J. Amilcar Vidal, and Daniel Zepeda; Suplentes, Francisco Rincón, Lisandro López, Amadeo Ruiz, and Daniel Robles.

78. Villanueva to Carranza, 28 October 1916, AVC, Telegramas, 2.

79. Villanueva to Carranza, 10 February 1917, AVC, Telegramas, 2.

80. García de León, *Resistencia y utopia*, II, p. 125.

81. Villanueva to Carranza, 23 September 1916, AVC, Telegramas, 2.

82. Villanueva to Carranza, 7 November 1916, AVC, Telegramas, 2; Serrano, *Chiapas revolucionario*, p. 65.

83. "Statement of Ángel Primo," NA/RG 76, 22, 561.

84. "Statement of William J. McGavock," *Investigation of Mexican Affairs*, I, p. 868.

85. Consul, Salina Cruz, to Secretary of State, 26 February 1917, NA/RG 59, Microcopy 274, 812.00/20571.

86. *Chiapas Nuevo*, 7 June 1917; Serrano, *Chiapas revolucionario*, pp. 100–111.

87. Moscoso Pastrana, *El pinedismo*, p. 113.

88. Moscoso Pastrana, *El pinedismo*, pp. 91–101; Serrano, *Chiapas revolucionario*, p. 113.

89. Serrano, *Chiapas revolucionario*, p. 119; *El Tribuno*, 15 April 1918.

90. *La Patria Chica*, 1 March 1918. Also see Serrano, *Chiapas revolucionario*, p. 120; López Gutiérrez, *Chiapas*, III, p. 202.

91. "Discurso por General Salvador Alvarado al Pueblo de Chiapas," 20 March 1918, AHCH, Gobernación, 1918, I, 14. Also see *Chiapas Nuevo*, 31 March 1918.

92. "Military Activities," Consul, Salina Cruz, to Department of State, 25 July 1918, NA/RG 84, Correspondence, Salina Cruz, Vol. 61.

93. "Informe constitucional del C. Presidente Municipal de Mapastepec, Chiapas, año de 1918," AHCH, Gobernación, 1918, II, 14; *El Obrero,* 10 September 1919.

94. Villanueva to Alvarado, 7 May 1918, AHCH, Fomento, 1918, II, 14.

95. For example, see Secretario General de Gobierno, Tuxtla Gutiérrez, to Jefe del Destacamento Acala, 15 September 1918, AHCH, Gobernación, 1918, V, 42; Decree of 4 June 1918, AHCH, Gobernación, 1918, V, 42.

96. Alvarado to Carranza, 28 April 1918, AVC, Telegramas, 2; Alvarado to Carranza, 6 May 1918, AVC, Telegramas, 2.

97. "Rebel Activities in Chiapas, July 22–September 30, 1918," 7 November 1918, NA/RG 165, Records of the War Department General and Special Staffs and the Military Intelligence Division, 10640-1484 (19); "Rebel Activities in Chiapas, October and November 1918," 19 March 1919, NA/RG 165, 10640-1484 (32).

98. Alvarado to Carranza, 8 October 1918, AVC, Telegramas, 2; Alvarado to Carranza, 12 November 1918, AVC, Telegramas, 2.

99. Serrano, *Chiapas revolucionario,* p. 133.

100. Legación de México en Guatemala to Secretaría de Relaciones Exteriores, 31 October 1918, ASRE, 17-78-28, 23; George Braun, Tuxtla Gutiérrez, to U.S. Consul, Salina Cruz, 17 December 1918, NA/RG 84, Correspondence, Salina Cruz, Vol. 61.

101. Serrano, *Chiapas revolucionario,* p. 145.

102. *Ibid.,* p. 161.

103. "¡Alerta, Chiapanecos!" Tuxtla Gutiérrez, June 1919, AHCH, Carpeta 1625.

104. *El Criterio,* 27 April, 10 August 1919.

105. *El Iris de Chiapas,* 26 February 1920.

106. To get the flavor of local politics, see Club "Radical Chiapaneco," Chiapas de Corzo, to El Gobernador de Chiapas, 27 December 1919; Club "Liberal Soconusense," Tapachula, to Gobernador, October 1919; Club "Liberal de Arriaga," to Gobernador, 26 July 1919, all in AHCH, Gobernación, 1919, III and VI.

107. Juan Santos, Mazatán, to Secretario General de Gobierno, Tuxtla Gutiérrez, 29 May 1918; Vecinos de Niapa de Pichucalco to Gobernador, 23 July 1918, AHCH, Gobernación, 1918, XV, 158.

108. Vecinos de Motozintla to Presidente de la República, 24 July 1919, AHCH, Gobernación, 1919, XII; El Club "Belisario Domínguez" to Presidente, 1 August 1919, AHCH, Gobernación, 1919, III, 21.

109. *El Criterio,* 28 December 1919.

110. The municipal president of Motozintla arrested some of the leaders of the Club "Domínguez" and ordered the dissolution of the party. Presidente Municipal to Ismael Mendoza, 13 December 1919, AHCH, Gobernación, 1919, VI, 20.

111. Juez Mixto, Motozintla, to Gobernador de Chiapas, 31 December 1919, AHCH, Gobernación, 1919, VI, 20.

112. "Acta de constitución del Partido Socialista Chiapaneco, Motozintla, 13 de enero de 1920," in "Expediente relativo al Partido Socialista Chiapaneco fundado en Motozintla, Departamento de Mariscal, Chiapas, 1920," AHCH, Gobernación, 1920, VI, 10.

113. Líbano Avendano, Motozintla, to Gobernador de Chiapas, 21 January 1920, AHCH, Gobernación, 1920, VI, 10.

114. R. A. Paniagua to Gobernador de Chiapas, 27 March 1920, AHCH, Gobernación, 1920, VI, 10.

115. "Bases generales del Partido Socialista Chiapaneco, enero 15, 1920," AHCH, Gobernación, 1920, VI, 10.

116. Juez Mixto Trinidad Marín, Motozintla, to Gobernador de Chiapas, 22 April 1920, AHCH, Gobernación, 1920, VI, 10.

117. Richmond, *Venustiano Carranza's Nationalist Struggle,* p. 231.

118. Knight, *The Mexican Revolution,* II, p. 490.

119. "Bases para la pacificación del Estado," quoted in full in Serrano, *Chiapas revolucionario,* p. 189.

120. "De Facto Government in District," U.S. Consul, Salina Cruz, to Department of State, 22 May 1920, NA/RG 84, Correspondence, Salina Cruz, Vol. 78.

121. *Excelsiór,* 26 May 1920.

122. Knight, *The Mexican Revolution,* II, p. 493.

123. *El Universal,* 7, 24 July 1920; "Public Order in Chiapas State," U.S. Consul, Salina Cruz, to Department of State, 10 September 1920, NA/RG 84, Correspondence, Salina Cruz, Vol. 78.

124. Presidente Colegio Electoral, R. A. Paniagua, to Gobernador del Es tado, 16 December 1920, AHCH, Gobernación, 1921, XVIII, 458.

125. Alcance al numero 28 del *Periódico Oficial,* 20 July 1937.

CHAPTER 6

1. R. A. Paniagua, Motozintla, to Presidente Municipal, San Pedro, Mariscal, 9 December 1920, AHCH, Fomento, 1921, Vol. 133.

2. Claim of the St. Paul Tropical Development Company, NA/RG 76, Doc. 561.

3. Fernández Ruiz to Obregón, 21 March 1921, AGN, Fondo Obregón-Calles, Expediente 816-C-14. Hereafter cited as AGN/OC and identifying in formation.

4. G. W. Knoblauch, "The Railroad Situation in Mexico," n.d., NA/RG 76, File 145, Box 3, Monograph 19; "Descripción de los pueblos y caminos recorridos," AHCH, Fomento, 1926, 417.

5. Fernández Ruiz to Obregón, 15 March 1921, AGN/OC, 816-C-14.

6. Obregón to Finance Secretary, 31 November 1922, and Obregón to Fernández Ruiz, 12 January 1923, AGN/OC, 816-Ch-11 and 816-C-14.

7. El Universal, 7, 11 January 1926; Tannenbaum, The Mexican Agrarian Revolution, pp. 113–114; Tribes and Temples, 2 vols. (New Orleans: Tulane University, 1926), II, p. 331; Carlos Basuri, Tojolabales, Tzeltales, y Mayas (México: Talleres Gráficos de la Nación, 1931), pp. 102–103, 134–135; An omino, "México Desconocido: Las monterías de Chiapas," Universidad de México, I (1931), p. 325.

8. Anuario estadístico, 1923–1924, 2 vols. (México: Talleres Gráficos de la Nación, 1926), I, p. 107; Tannenbaum, The Mexican Agrarian Revolution, pp. 341, 347, 504.

9. Informe de Fernández Ruiz, 1921 and 1922; Periódico Oficial del Estado, 29 June 1921. Volume VIII in the Ramo de Gobernación (AHCH) contains 100 or more individually granted tax dispensations.

10. "Agrarian Law of the State (Chiapas, October 28, 1921)," NA/RG 76, File 146, Binder 15, Box 10.

11. Tannenbaum, The Mexican Agrarian Revolution, pp. 429–450.

12. Eyler N. Simpson, The Ejido: Mexico's Way Out (Chapel Hill: The University of North Carolina Press, 1937), p. 57.

13. Dudley Ankerson, Agrarian Warlord: Saturnino Cedillo and the Mexican Revolution in San Luis Potosi (DeKalb: Northern Illinois University Press, 1984), p. 95.

14. Presidente, Partido Agrarista, to Comisión Nacional Agraria, 30 November 1922, Expediente for Cintalapa, ASRA, 23:589(723.8).

15. Expediente for Cintalapa, 30 November 1922, and Expediente for Huixtla, 3 May 1923, ASRA, 23:589(723.8) and 23:590(723.8).

16. De la Peña, Chiapas económico, II, p. 375.

17. Lopez Gutiérrez, Chiapas, III, p. 269.

18. Gral. Fausto Ruiz to Obregón, 8 November 1922, and F. Ruiz, "Memorándum," 21 December 1922, AGN/OC, 101-R-5.

19. Excelsiór, 6 October 1922.

20. Pineda to Obregón, 10 March 1922, AGN/OC, 816-C-14; De la Peña, Chiapas económico, II, p. 435.

21. Tannenbaum, *The Mexican Agrarian Revolution,* p. 467.

22. The history of the Partido Socialista Chiapaneco is chronicled and an alyzed in the excellent study by Daniela Spenser, "El Partido Socialista Chiapaneco: Rescate y Reconstrucción de su Historia," Tesis para optar por el grado de Maestría, Universidad Nacional Autónoma de México, 1987.

23. G. M. Joseph, *Revolution from Without: Yucatan, Mexico, and the United States, 1880–1924* (Cambridge: Cambridge University Press, 1982), p. 199.

24. Vidal, Mexico City, to Paniagua, Motozintla, 10 November 1920, AHCH, Fomento, 1921, V, 133.

25. Secretario General de Gobierno, Tuxtla Gutiérrez, to General Manuel Mendoza, Jefe de las Operaciones Militares Chiapas, 4 September 1922, AHCH, Gobernación, 1922, XIX, 619.

26. See "Expediente relativo al Partido Socialista Chiapaneco," AHCH, Gobernación, 1920, VI, 10.

27. Paniagua, Motozintla, to Guillermo Kahl, 9 January 1921, AHCH, Fomento, 1921, V, 133; S. Aleleberg, Finca "La Grandeza" (Soconusco), to Amadeo Solís, Motozintla, 16 August 1922, AHCH, Gobernación, 1922, XIX, 619.

28. Acuerdo del Gobierno del Estado, 17 August and 3 September 1921, AHCH, Fomento, 1921, V, 151 and 159.

29. Isabel Nucamendi, El comisionado especial del gobierno, to Fernández Ruiz, 13 April 1921, AHCH, Fomento, 1921, V, 123.

30. "Manifiesto," Tapachula, 7 June 1922, AHCH, Gobernación, 1922, XV, 391.

31. *Ibid.;* "The *mozo* Tomás Morales from today is under the protection of the Partido Socialista Chiapaneco, Julio 20/22," Tarjeta, AHCH, Gober nación, 1922, XIX, 619.

32. Secretaría de Relaciones Exteriores to Gobernador de Chiapas, 19 September 1922, AHCH, Gobernación, 1922, XIX, 618.

33. Gobernador de Chiapas to Departamento de Relaciones Interiores de Gobernación Federal, 27 September 1922, AHCH, Gobernación, 1922, XIX, 618.

34. *La Frontera del Sur,* 22 September 1922.

35. *Tribes and Temples,* II, pp. 327, 356; Henning Silverts, "On Politics and Leadership in Highland Chiapas," in Evon Z. Vogt and Alberto Ruz L., eds., *Desarrollo cultural de los Mayas* (México: UNAM, 1964), pp. 366–367.

36. For example, see Vecinos de Libertad Calera to Obregón, 29 May 1922, ASRA, Libertad Calera, 23:597; Varios ciudadanos de San Pedro Remate to Gobernador, 5 December 1923, AHCH, Gobernación, 1923, 45.

37. Presidente, Partido Agrarista Chiapaneco, to Presidente, Comisión Nacional Agraria, 30 November 1922, ASRA, Cintalapa, 23:589(723.8); Vecinos de Libertad to Obregón, 22 May 1922, ASRA, Libertad Calera, 23:597.

38. M. Marroquín, Tapachula, to Gobernador, 31 July 1922, AHCH, Gobernación, 1922, XV.

39. Tuxtlecos to Calles, 2 December 1924, and López Reyes (San Fernando) to Calles, 12 January 1925, AGN/OC, 428-Ch-8.

40. This judgment is based on a comparison of office holders and political leaders against pre-1910 land registries and commercial directories.

41. For example, Presidente municipal [location not given] to Gobernador de Chiapas, 8 January 1923, AHCH, Gobernación, 1923, 45.

42. Varios ciudadanos conscientes, "Farisaismo. Vidal y su candidatura para Senador por Chiapas," Tuxtla Gutiérrez, 8 May 1922, AHCH, Carpeta 1631; Partido Socialista Chiapaneco to Gobernador de Chiapas, 15 July 1922, AHCH, Gobernación, 1922, XIX, 619.

43. Secretario General de Gobierno, Tuxtla Gutiérrez, to General Manuel Mendoza, Tapachula, 4 September 1922, AHCH, Gobernación, 1922, XIX, 619. General Francisco Serrano, Secretaría de Guerra y Marina, influenced by Vidal, sympathized with the socialists of Chiapas. See Spenser, "El Partido Socialista Chiapaneco," p. 179.

44. A. Rébora to Gobernador Interino Cruz, 29 May 1923, AGN/OC, 428-Ch-8. Rébora was sent to Chiapas to investigate political conditions for President Obregón.

45. Excelsiór, 6 October 1922.

46. Secretario General de Gobierno to Procurador del Estado, 20 June 1922, AHCH, Gobernación, 1922, XIX, 68; Catarino Ramos [et al.] to Gobernador de Chiapas, 18 March 1923, AHCH, Gobernación, 1923, Asuntos Municipales; Rebora to Cruz, 29 May 1923, AGN-OC, 428-Ch-8.

47. U.S. Vice-Consul, Salina Cruz, to Secretary of State, 12 March 1923, NA/RG 84, Salina Cruz, 1924, Vol. 169; Excelsiór, 24 March 1923.

48. Ibid.

49. Presidente Municipal, Motozintla, to Gobernador de Chiapas, 8 January 1923, AHCH, Gobernación, 1923, 45.

50. Paniagua to Obregón, 25 February 1923; Santiago Ramos to Senador Luis Espinosa, 25 February 1923, and Obregón to Fernández Ruiz, 26 February 1923, AGN/OC, 428-Ch-8.

51. Ejercito Reorganizador, Soconusco, to Calles, 28 February 1923, and Fernández Ruiz to Obregón, 28 March 1923, AGN/OC, 428-Ch-8.

52. Rafael Coutiño to Calles, 19 February 1923, AGN/OC, 428-Ch-8.

53. Gobernador Interino Cruz to Obregón, 14 June 1923, AGN/OC, 428-

Ch-8; Randall G. Hansis, "Álvaro Obregón, the Mexican Revolution and the Politics of Consolidation, 1920–1924," Diss. University of New Mexico, 1971, p. 60.

54. Cruz to Obregón, 14 June 1923, AGN/OC, 428-Ch-8; Fernández Ruiz to Obregón, 31 July 1923, and Obregón to Fernández Ruiz, 11 September 1923, AGN/OC, 243-Ch-D-1; U.S. Vice-Consul, Salina Cruz, to Secretary of State, 12 March 1923, NA/RG 84, Correspondence, Salina Cruz, Vol. 169.

55. López Gutiérrez, Chiapas, III, p. 270.

56. Luis Espinosa to Obregón, 29 November 1923, and Fernández Ruiz to Obregón, 3 December 1923, AGN/OC, 408-Ch-8.

57. Excelsiór, 27 November 1923.

58. "Present Executive and Ministry," 10 March 1925, NA/RG 165, 1657-G-547.

59. "Stability of Government: Rebel Activity," 19 December 1923, NA/RG 165, 2657-G-535.

60. López Gutiérrez, Chiapas, III, p. 273–275.

61. Excelsiór, 3 March 1924; Donato Bravo Izquierdo, Lealtad militar. Campaña en el estado de Chiapas é istmo de Tehuantepec (México, 1948), pp. 31, 46, 81.

62. Spenser, "El Partido Socialista Chiapaneco," p. 182.

63. U.S. Vice-Consul, Salina Cruz, to Secretary of State, 26 January 1924, NA/RG 59, 812.00/27048; John W. F. Dulles, Yesterday in Mexico: A Chronicle of the Revolution, 1919–1936 (Austin: University of Texas Press, 1961), pp. 219–220.

64. Obregón to Gobernador de Chiapas, 28 February 1924, AGN/OC, 101-R2-Ch-4.

65. Excelsiór, 3 March 1924; López Gutiérrez, Chiapas, III, pp. 282–283.

66. César Córdova to General Calles, 31 January 1925, AGN/OC, 121-C-Ch-1; Bravo Izquierdo, Lealtad militar, pp. 111, 123–141.

67. Presidente municipal, Chicomuselo, to Gobernador del Estado, 3 September 1925, AHCH, Gobernación, 1925, I.

68. "Al Pueblo Chiapaneco," Partido Politico Estudiantil, 1924, AHCH, Carpeta 1631.

69. López Gutiérrez, Chiapas, III, pp. 299–300.

70. Comité Directivo Electoral, 18 June 1924, AHCH, Gobernación, 1925, I.

71. General Ávila Camacho to Obregón, 9 September 1924, AGN/OC, 428-Ch-9.

72. Quoted in Ernest Gruening, Mexico and its Heritage (New York: The Century Co., 1928), pp. 407–408. A similar complaint came from Vecinos de

San Pedro Remate to Obregón, 28 June 1924, AHCH, Gobernación, 1924, Asuntos Ayuntamientos.

73. PSC to Calles, 9 December 1924; Luis León, CNA, to Calles, 12 December 1924; Proletariado del municipio [unknown] to Calles, 25 January 1925, AGN/OC, 241-A-Ch-17.

74. "Comité directivo de la campaña pro-Vidal, 1924," AGN/OC, 428-T-23; Procurador del Estado to Gobernador, 14 April 1925, AHCH, Gobernación, 1924, I.

75. *La Voz de Chiapas,* 9 February 1928; Diputado Alfredo Marín to Calles, 3 December 1924, AGN/OC, 428-Ch-8.

76. *Diario de los Debates,* 4 September 1924; Gruening, *Mexico and its Heritage,* p. 407.

77. "Comisión revisora de credenciales—Sexta Sección," *Diario de los Debates,* 4 September 1924; Vecinos de Mapastepec to Gobernador del Estado, 24 December 1924, AHCH, Gobernación, 1925, IX; Fernández Ruiz [*et al.*] to Obregón, 9 September 1924, AGN/OC, 428-Ch-9.

78. Hansis, "The Politics of Consolidation," pp. 60–61.

79. Secretario General de Gobierno to Fernández Ruiz, 22 October 1924, and Obregón to Fernández Ruiz, 10 November 1924, AHCH, Gobernación, 1924, XIV.

80. Fernández Ruiz to Obregón, 30 November 1924, and Vidal to Obregón, 30 November 1924, AGN/OC, 428-Ch-8.

81. Obregón to Fernández Ruiz, 6 November 1924, and Obregón to Vidal, 29 November 1924, AGN/OC, 408-Ch-10.

82. Vito Alessio Robles, "Gajos de historia," *Excelsiór,* 28 April 1949; *Excelsiór,* 3, 5, 6, 25 December 1924; *Periódico Oficial del Estado,* 7 January 1925.

83. Córdova to Calles, 7 January 1925, Pascual Córdova to Calles, 7 January 1925, AGN/OC, 428-Ch-8.

84. Ramírez to Calles, 3 March 1925, AGN/OC, 408-Ch-10.

85. *Diario de los Debates,* 15, 27 August, 4, 24 September 1925; Gruening, *Mexico and its Heritage,* p. 409; and Hansis, "The Politics of Consolidation," p. 61.

86. Vidal to Calles, 28 May 1925, AGN/OC, 241-A-Ch-17.

87. *Informe de Carlos Vidal,* 1925; Secretario General, CROM, to Calles, 31 March 1927, AGN/OC, 802-C-29; and García Soto, *Geografía general de Chiapas,* p. 261.

88. *Reconstrucción,* 4 April 1925.

89. Joseph, *Revolution from Without,* p. 101.

90. The term is from Knight, *The Mexican Revolution,* II, p. 500.

91. López Gutiérrez, *Chiapas*, III, pp. 303–304.

92. *Ley reglamentaria del trabajo* (Tuxtla Gutiérrez: Imprenta del Gobierno, 1926).

93. "Ley que establece la junta central de conciliación y arbitraje, las juntas municipales de conciliación y los comisiones especiales del salario mínimo, 15 de enero de 1926," *Periódico Oficial del Estado*, 27 January 1926.

94. "New Labor Law in Chiapas," 9 March 1927, NA/RG 84, Correspond ence, Salina Cruz.

95. "New Law for Expropriation of Lands for Public Use, State of Chiapas," 19 January 1927, NA/RG 76, File 146, Box 10, Binder 15.

96. Circular, AHCH, Fomento, 1927, II.

97. *Anuario de 1930*, p. 375.

98. Vidal to Calles, 21 September 1925, and Calles to Vidal, 6 October 1925, AGN/OC, 816-C-14.

99. Spenser, "Soconusco," ch. 5, p. 10.

100. Spenser, "El Partido Socialista Chiapaneco," pp. 192–193.

101. "Political Conditions, Salina Cruz District," 10 July 1926, NA/RG 84, Correspondence, Salina Cruz.

102. "Conditions Affecting Credits," 4 December 1927, NA/RG 84, Cor respondence, Salina Cruz.

103. Foster to Secretary of State, 12 April 1927, NA/RG 59, 812.512/3368.

104. Spenser, "Soconusco," ch. 5, p. 12.

105. Vice-Consul, Salina Cruz, to Secretary of State, 24 July 1924, NA/RG 59, 812.42/87.

106. *Noticia estadística sobre la educación pública en México correspon diente al año de 1927* (México: SEP, 1929), pp. 62, 162.

107. "Mi labor primordial consistó en conferenciar apliamente con cuanto finquero encontraba a mi paso; haciendole palpar claramente el ideal que persigue nuestro actual gobernante; consistente en desanalfabetizar a los pobres hijos de nuestra queridisima Patria Chica. Son muy contados los Señores Fin queros que se opusierón a los disposiciones de ésta inspección escolar actual mente a mi cargo." Inspector Muñoz to Secretario General de Gobierno, 31 December 1926, AHCH, Instrucción Pública, 1926, X; and *Anuario de 1930*, p. 191.

108. *Informe de Carlos Vidal*, 1926; *Periódico Oficial del Estado*, 16 De cember 1925, 6 January 1926; John Bedwell to U.S. Consul Salina Cruz, 23 June 1926, NA/RG 84, Correspondence, Salina Cruz; and De la Peña, *Chiapas económico*, II, p. 435.

109. R. Ruiz to Gobernador, 18 August 1925; S. Castillejos to Gobernador del Estado, 17 August 1925, AHCH, Gobernación, 1925.

110. Presidente municipal, Tapachula, to Vidal, 12 August 1924; Señores Hind y Cía. to Secretario General de Gobierno, 13 August 1925, AHCH, Gobernación, 1925, VIII.

111. Secretario Municipal, Tuzantán, to Secretario General de Gobierno, 8 December 1926; M. Orduna, Confederación Socialista, to Vidal, 15 December 1926, AHCH, Fomento, 1926.

112. J. Velasez to Vidal, 26 January 1927, AHCH, Fomento, 1927, II. There are numerous examples similar to this one in the Ramo Fomento, 1925–27, of the state archive.

113. Delegado Municipal, El Eden, to Vidal, 1 December 1925, AHCH, Fomento, 1927.

114. Varios ciudadanos de Cancuc to Secretario General de Gobierno, 1 May 1926, AHCH, Gobernación, 1926, XII.

115. J. Martínez to Diputado Paniagua, 17 April 1926, AHCH, Gobernación, 1926, XIV; D. Xetet y otros to Vidal, 28 June 1927, AHCH, Fomento, 1927, II.

116. Circular, "Numero 5," 1 June 1926, AHCH, Fomento, 1926.

117. Quoted in Ralph Miliband, *Marxism and Politics* (Oxford: Oxford University Press, 1977), pp. 155–156.

118. "Local Political Conditions," 30 March 1926, NA/RG 165.

119. Dulles, *Yesterday in Mexico,* ch. 38.

120. Francisco J. Santamaría, *La tragedía de Cuernavaca en 1927 y mi escapatoría célebre* (México, 1939), pp. 23, 27.

121. López Gutiérrez, *Chiapas,* III, pp. 314, 417.

122. Dulles, *Yesterday in Mexico,* p. 338.

123. "Declaraciones de Manuel Zepeda Lara (1935)," and "Declaraciones del Señor Alberto Solís Gamboa y Profesor Epigmenio de León (1935)," in a file entitled "Datos para la historia del vidalismo en Chiapas," AHCH, Carpeta 941.

124. Salvador Martínez Mancera, "Como fué la muerte del General Luis P. Vidal, Gobernador de Chiapas," *El Universal Gráfico,* 8 October 1937.

125. *El Universal,* 9, 10, 11 October 1927; U.S. Consul, Salina Cruz, to Chargé d'Affaires, U.S. Embassy, Mexico City, 15 October 1927; "Political Conditions," 9 October 1927, NA/RG 84, Correspondence, Salina Cruz; U.S. Consul, Frontera, to Secretary of State, 8 October 1927, NA/RG 59, 812.00/29920.

126. U.S. Consul, Salina Cruz, to Chargé d'Affaires, 19 October 1927, NA/RG 84, Correspondence, Salina Cruz, 1927.

127. *Excelsiór,* 5 November 1927.

128. Joseph, *Revolution from Without,* p. 275.

129. Knight, *The Mexican Revolution,* II, p. 496.

130. Raymond Buve, "State governors and peasant mobilization in Tlaxcala," in *Caudillo and Peasant in the Mexican Revolution,* p. 223.

131. Vidal to Morones, 9 June 1927, quoted in full in *La Voz de Chiapas,* 7 June 1928.

CHAPTER 7

1. *La Voz de Chiapas,* 29 December 1927.

2. Partido Agrarista to Calles, 30 December 1927; Enríquez to Club "Laborista" de Margarita, 27 May 1928, AGN/OC, 408-Ch-16.

3. *Ibid.,* 12 January 1928.

4. *Ibid.,* 1 March 1928.

5. Information provided by Daniela Spenser, 1981.

6. Partido Agrarista, Arriaga, to Calles, 30 December 1927, AGN/OC, 408-Ch-16.

7. "Political Conditions," 15 April 1928, NA/RG 84, Correspondence, Salina Cruz.

8. "Dictamen que motivó la destitución del Lic. Federico Martínez Rojas," Mexico, 21 March 1928, AHCH, Carpeta 1616; *La Voz de Chiapas,* 19, 16 April, 10 May 1928.

9. *La Voz de Chiapas,* 24 November, 29 December 1927, 5, 19 January 1928.

10. *Chiapas: Revista Mensual,* 12 October 1928; "Quien es Raymundo Enríquez," *La Vanguardia,* 28 August 1932.

11. "Partido Progresista Chiapaneco Pro-Enríquez al Pueblo Chiapaneco," 26 July 1928, AHCH, Carpeta 1623.

12. Inspector de Correos, Arriaga, to Calles, 22 July 1928, AGN/OC, 217-Ch-18.

13. Presidente Liga Revolucionario Estado de Chiapas to Calles, 1 September 1928, AGN/OC, 408-Ch-16; *La Voz de Chiapas,* 16 September 1928.

14. *Excelsiór,* 7, 8, 27 November, 2 December 1928.

15. Rafael Loyola Díaz, *La crisis obregón-calles y el estado mexicano* (México: Siglo XXI, 1980), pp. 106–107, 112–113.

16. Osorio Marbán, *El partido de la revolución mexicana,* 2 vols. (Mexico, 1970), I, pp. 56–57, 213.

17. Loyola Díaz, *La crisis obregón-calles,* pp. 127–145.

18. *Excelsiór,* 19 December 1928, 2 March 1929.

19. *La Vanguardia,* 24 February, 1 March 1929; El Universal, 1 March 1929.

20. *La Vanguardia,* 12 May, 22 August, 14 September 1929.

21. "Al pueblo chiapaneco," Lic. Amador Coutiño, México D.F., December 1929, ASRA, Huixtla, 25:590(723.8); Enríquez to Portes Gil, 8 October 1929, AGN/Fondo Emilio Portes Gil, 772, 802 (hereafter cited as AGN/EPG and identifying information); *La Vanguardia,* 22 September, 6 October 1929.

22. Joseph, *Revolution from Without,* p. 206.

23. Carlos Martínez Assad, *El laboratorio de la revolución. El Tabasco garridista* (México: Siglo XXI, 1979), pp. 164–165, 170–171; *La Voz de Chiapas,* 9 February, 7 June 1928.

24. Rafael López to Gobernador Martínez Rojas, 10 November 1927, AHCH, Fomento, 1927. Also in the same volume, "Estatutos de la Liga de Resistencia del distrito de Pichucalco."

25. Raymundo E. Enríquez, "Asuntos del Estado de Chiapas—Memorándum," 3 June 1929, AGN/EPG, 722/802 (Caja 22).

26. Martínez Assad, *El laboratorio de la revolución,* p. 129; *La Voz de Chiapas,* 5 January 1928.

27. Lorenzo Meyer, *Historia de la revolución mexicana. El conflicto social y los gobiernos del maximato,* XIII (México: El Colegio de México, 1978), p. 245.

28. Cal y Mayor to Portes Gil, 31 December 1929, ASRA, Cintalapa, 23:589; Liga Central to Cárdenas, 18 July 1936, ASRA, Huixtla, 25:590; Procuraduria de Pueblos to Comisión Nacional Agraria, 20 June 1933, ASRA, Pijijiapám, 23:8237.

29. Ing. Sub-Auxiliar to Agente General de la Secretaría de Agricultura y Fomento, 31 January 1931, ASRA, Cintalapa, 23:589; *Excelsiór,* 31 December 1930.

30. García de León, *Resistencia y utopía,* II, pp. 187–193.

31. Enríquez to Ortiz Rubio, 20 July 1930 and 19 August 1930, AGN/Fondo Pascual Ortiz Rubio, Exp. 24, Año de 1930. Hereafter cited as AGN/POR and identifying information.

32. *La Vanguardia,* 12 October, 9 November 1930; *El Baluarte Chiapaneco,* 20 September 1930.

33. "The Agrarian Movement," February 1931, NA/RG 165; Sub-Delegado Martín de la Peña to Comisión Nacional Agraria, 24 February 1931, ASRA, Ocozocoautla, 23:606; *La Vanguardia,* 8, 15 March, 5 July, 31 August 1931.

34. Jean Meyer, "Mexico: Revolution and Reconstruction in the 1920s," in *The Cambridge History of Latin America,* V, p. 183.

35. Simpson, *The Ejido,* pp. 113–114, 117–118.

36. Robert E. Scott, "Some Aspects of Mexican Federalism, 1917–1948," Diss. University of Wisconsin, 1949, p. 185.

37. *Regiones económico agrícolas de la república mexicana (Memorias*

Descriptivas) (Tacubaya: Secretaría de Agricultura y Fomento, 1936), p. 314.

38. *La Vanguardia,* 28 June 1931.

39. "La reforma agraria y los gobiernos de la Estados," *Excelsiór,* 30 November 1930.

40. Romana Falcón, "El surgimiento del agrarismo cardenista—Una revisión de las tesis populistas," *Historia Mexicana* XXVII (JanuaryMarch 1978), p. 346.

41. Enríquez to Ortiz Rubio, 26 August 1931, AGN/POR, Extractos, Septiembre 1931, Num. 5865.

42. Rodolfo Guzmán, "Al asalto de pueblos indígenas," *Proceso,* 1, 29 January 1977, pp. 6–13.

43. Presidente Comité Ejecutivo Agrario to Presidente de la República, 10 February 1936, ASRA, Simojovel, 23:8073.

44. Matthew Edel, "Zinacantan's Ejido: The Effects of Mexican Land Reform on an Indian Community in Chiapas," unpublished manuscript, 1962, p. 12.

45. Presidente municipal, Tapachula, to Secretario General de Gobierno, 16 April 1929, AHCH, Gobernación, 1929, II. This document lists all major coffee planters and cattle ranchers in Soconusco. Leo Waibel, *La Sierra Madre de Chiapas* (Mexico: Sociedad Mexicana de Geografía y Estadística, 1933), pp. 122–127.

46. Manuel E. Guzmán, *Chiapas: Estudio y resolución de algunos problemas económicas y sociales del estado* (México, 1930), p. 17.

47. *Periódico Oficial del Estado,* 26 February, 19 November, 30 December 1930, 30 December 1931. Taxes on all fincas were annulled for 1927–29. See "Asuntos del Estado de Chiapas—Memorándum," 3 June 1929.

48. *Tribes and Temples,* II, p. 331.

49. Frank Tannenbaum, *Peace by Revolution: An Interpretation of Mexico* (New York: Columbia University Press, 1933), pp. 29–30.

50. *Informe de Raymundo Enríquez,* 1932; Inspector General to Inspector López, 31 January 1931, AHCH, Personal y Cuenta, 1931.

51. *Informe de Raymundo Enríquez,* 1931, 1932; *Excelsiór,* 6 December 1930; *Periódico Oficial del Estado,* 27 May 1931; López, Hernández, y otros to Gobernador del Estado, 20 May 1929, AHCH, Fomento, 1929.

52. *Declaraciones del Gobernador del Estado de Chiapas, Ing. Raymundo E. Enríquez* (Tuxtla Gutiérrez: Imprenta del Gobierno, 1930).

53. *La Vanguardia,* 31 March 1929.

54. Guzmán, *Chiapas: Estudio y resolución,* p. 85. Also, Raymundo E. Enríquez, "Memorándum," [sin fecha] AGN/POR, 2-10815; *La Vanguardia,* 31 March 1929; *UPRECH,* 9 November, 15 December 1928.

55. *La Vanguardia,* 27 December 1931, 3 January, 8 May 1932; Enríquez

to Ortiz Rubio, 6 January 1932, AGN/POR, Exp. 2, Registro 2.

56. *Renovación,* 7, 21 January, 18 February, 4 March 1932; *Excelsiór,* 4, 5 April 1932.

57. Liga Central de Comunidades Agrarias del Estado de Chiapas to Cárdenas, 11 December 1934, AGN/Fondo Lázaro Cárdenas, 542.1/20. Hereafter cited as AGN/LC and identifying information.

58. Gustavo López Gutiérrez, Capitán de Caballería, Tuxtla Gutiérrez, to Cárdenas, 1 January 1935, AGN/LC, 542.1/20; *Renovación,* 2 December 1933.

59. Gutiérrez to Cárdenas, 1 January 1935.

60. *El Nacional,* 6, 13 August 1933; Renovación, 9, 14 August 1933.

61. Meyer, "Mexico: Revolution and Reconstruction in the 1920s," p. 187.

62. *Periódico Oficial del Estado,* 30 January 1935; *Liberación,* 10 February 1935; *La Verdad,* 9 November 1935.

63. *Informe de Victórico Grajales,* 1933.

64. *Anuario de 1930,* p. 428; *Anuario de 1939,* pp. 522–523; *Anuario de 1940;* De la Peña, *Chiapas económico,* II, p. 459.

65. *Liberación,* 27 January 1935; *Periódico Oficial del Estado,* 2 April 1936; De la Peña, *Chiapas económico,* II, p. 366.

66. Renovación, 21 January 1933; *Periódico Oficial del Estado,* 12 February 1936.

67. Informe de Victórico Grajales, 1934; *Periódico Oficial del Estado,* 18 April, 6 June 1934; De la Peña, *Chiapas económico,* I, pp. 299, 319.

68. *La Vanguardia,* 25 August 1929; Gossen, *Chamulas in the World of the Sun,* pp. 269–270.

69. "The Present Church Situation," 12 February 1935, NA/RG 165; Michael Salovesh, "Politics in a Maya Community," Diss. Northern Illinois University, 1972, pp. 123–124. Gustavo Montiel, *Tuxtla Gutiérrez de mis recuerdos* (México: Costa-Amic, 1972), includes photographs in his book of bonfires of religious artifacts.

70. García de León, *Resistencia y utopía,* II, p. 202.

71. *La escuela socialista de Chiapas* (Tuxtla Gutiérrez: Imprenta del Gobierno del Estado, 1935), pp. 33, 37, 59–60; *Periódico Oficial del Estado,* 27 May, 10 June 1936.

72. *Periódico Oficial del Estado,* 28 February 1934. In 1943, by presidential decree, Ciudad Las Casas was renamed San Cristóbal de Las Casas. Vos, *San Cristóbal ciudad colonial,* p. 69.

73. López Gutiérrez, *Chiapas,* III, pp. 449–450.

74. Lucio Mendieta y Nuñez, *La administración pública en México* (México, 1942), pp. 290–291.

75. President Pascual Ortiz Rubio resigned in 1932 following a disagreement

on government policy with "Jefe Máximo" Calles. Some historians maintain Calles "fired" the president. General Abelardo Rodríguez completed the term of Ortiz Rubio.

76. James Wilkie y Edna Monzon de Wilkie, *México visto en el siglo XX: Entrevistas de historia oral* (México: Instituto Mexicano de Investigaciones Económicas, 1969), p. 309.

77. Luis González y González, *Historia de la revolución mexicana: Los artífices del cardenismo*, XVI (México: El Colegio de México, 1979), p. 235.

78. Lyle C. Brown, "Cárdenas: Creating a Campesino Power Base for Presidential Policy," in Wolfskill and Richmond, eds., *Essays on the Mexican Revolution*, p. 105; Meyer, *El conflicto social*, pp. 249–250.

79. Arnaldo Córdova, *En una época de crisis, 1928–1934: La clase obrera en la historia de México* (México: Siglo XXI, 1980), pp. 97–110.

80. *Ibid.*, pp. 154–155, 227.

81. Lyle C. Brown, "General Lázaro Cárdenas and Mexican Presidential Politics, 1933–1940: A Study in the Acquisition and Manipulation of Political Power," Diss. University of Texas, 1964; Expedientes of La Concordia, 12 May 1935, ASRA, La Concordia, 23:8195.

82. Arnaldo Córdova, *La política de masas del cardenismo* (México: Ediciones Era, 1974), p. 54.

83. Antonio García de León, "Lucha de clases," p. 81.

84. Sindicato de Cargadores y Estibadores, Tapachula, to Presidente del Comité de Salud Pública, 27 October 1934, AGN/Fondo Abelardo L. Rodríguez, 525.3, 449. Hereafter cited as AGN/ALR and identifying information.

85. Liga Central de Comunidades Agrarias del Estado de Chiapas to Cárdenas, 11 December 1934, AGN/LC, 542.1, 20.

86. *Ibid.*

87. *Ibid.*

88. "Memorándum: resumen de los cargos que organizaciones campesinos, elementos obreros y políticos hacen al Gobernador del Estado, Coronel Victórico Grajales," El comité de obreros y campesinos, Soconusco, 13 December 1934, AGN/LC, 542.1, 20.

89. Bloc Social Revolucionario Pro-Chiapas to Cárdenas, 11 December 1934, AGN/LC, 542.1, 20.

90. García de León, *Resistencia y utopía*, II, pp. 202–203, gives several examples.

91. Issac Morga, Liga Central, to Cárdenas, 6 July 1935, AGN/LC, 542.1, 299; *Liberación*, 23 June 1935.

92. Trinidad García to Secretario General de Gobierno, Mexico City, 5 April 1934, AGN/LC, 542.1, 299; CCM to Cárdenas, 6 April 1934, AGN/ALR,

516.1, 299; Elisa Vázquez de Gómez, Tuxtla Gutiérrez, to Cárdenas, 10 July 1934, AGN/LC, 525.3, 515-1.

93. Unión de Albaniles to Gobernación Federal, 29 September 1933, AGN/ALR, 516.1, 40-2.

94. Enrique Flores Magón to Rodríguez, 3 April 1934, AGN/ALR, 524, 532; Genero Marín to Jefe de la Guarnición, Tapachula, 1 May 1934, AGN/ALR, 517.1, 43; Cámara de Trabajo, Tapachula, to Cárdenas, 4 January 1934, AGN/ALR, 552.14, 438; Vecinos de Colonia "Salvador Urbina," to Gobernación Federal, 24 February 1934, AGN/ALR, 552.14, 438.

95. Jefe Departamento Agrario to Cárdenas, 4 September 1935, AGN/LC, 551.3, 166.

96. Luis Rodríguez [private secretary of the president] to Grajales, 19 March 1935, AGN/LC, 533, 7.

97. Grajales to Cárdenas, 8 August 1935, AGN/LC, 542.1, 20.

98. Raymundo Enríquez to Rodríguez, 26 July 1933, AGN/ALR, 516.1, 40.

99. *Renovación,* 14 August 1933.

100. Liga Central to Cárdenas, 11 December 1934; Telegrams directed to Governor Grajales, in AGN/ALR, 516.1, 40.

101. Genaro Marín to Jefe de la Guarnición, Tapachula, 1 May 1934, AGN/LC, 517.1, 43; Marín, Carcel Pública Tapachula, to Cárdenas, 2 September 1935, 30 April 1936, AGN/LC, 542.1, 299.

102. Delegado CCM, Tapachula, to Cárdenas, 22 June 1935; Cámara de Trabajo, Tapachula, to Cárdenas, 23 June 1935, AGN/LC, 542.1, 1126. Felipe Galindo, Escuintla, to Cárdenas, 6 October 1936; Francisco Lara, Palenque, to Cárdenas, 1 January 1935, AGN/LC, 544.5, 332 and 371. "Chiapas y sus enemigos," *Liberación,* 6 January 1935; *Excelsiór,* 5 March 1934; *La Prensa,* 23 September 1935.

103. *Excelsiór,* 3 March 1934.

104. "Labor Conditions in Chiapas," 3 March 1936, NA/RG 165.

105. "Commission to Study Labor Problem of Indians in Chiapas," 19 March 1936, NA/RG 165.

106. *Excelsiór,* 5 April 1936; *El Universal,* 5 April 1936.

107. Grupo de partidarios suyos, Las Casas, to Cárdenas, 24 July 1936, AGN/LC, 135.23, 42.

108. *Mexican Labor News,* 20 September 1936.

109. "Social Advancement in Chiapas," 4 December 1936, NA/RG 165.

110. Henri Favre, *Cambio y continuidad entre los mayas de México* (México: Siglo XXI, 1973), p. 75.

111. Alicia Hernández Chavez, *Historia de la revolución mexicana. La mecánica cardenista,* XVI (México: El Colegio de México, 1979), pp. 54–60.

112. "Local Political Conditions," 8 March 1935, NA/RG 165; Ambassador Daniels to Secretary of State, 24 September 1935, NA/RG 59, 812.00/30284; *Excelsiór,* 10 April 1936; *La Prensa,* 23 September 1935.

113. *Diccionario biográfico de México* (Monterrey: Editorial Revesa, 1968), pp. 330–331; *Chiapas Nuevo,* 15 December 1938.

114. *El Universal,* 1 April 1936.

115. Grajales to Cárdenas, 9 March 1936, AGN/LC, 524.1, 20.

116. "Bombing of PNR Offices in Chiapas," 14 March 1936, NA/RG 165; *Excelsiór,* 4, 5 April 1936.

117. *Excelsiór,* 7, 12, 14, 28 April 1936.

118. *Excelsiór,* 5 May 1936.

119. Comité Executivo Nacional, PNR, to Presidente Comité Municipal, 24 June 1936, ASRA, Huixtla, 25:590.

120. *Excelsiór,* 12, 15 May 1936.

121. "Local Political Conditions," 7 July 1936, NA/RG 165.

122. "Local Political Conditions," 21 July, 4 August 1936, NA/RG 165; Ambassador Daniels to Secretary of State, 7 July, 23 September 1936, NA/RG 59, 812.00/30386 and 30409.

123. *Excelsiór,* 23, 24 September 1936.

124. Ankerson, *Agrarian Warlord,* p. 144.

CHAPTER 8

1. Paula Cal y Mayor to Jefe del Departamento Agrario, 12 December 1939, ASRA, Cintalapa, 23:589(723.8).

2. Knight, *The Mexican Revolution,* II, p. 496.

3. Luis Javier Garrido, *El partido de la revolución institucionalizada: la formación del nuevo estado en México (1928–1945)* (México: Siglo XXI, 1982), p. 177.

4. Córdova, *La formación del poder político,* p. 43.

5. Garrido, *El partido de la revolución institucionalizada,* p. 360.

6. Arturo Anguiano, *El estado y la política obrera del cardenismo* (México: Ediciones Era, 1975), pp. 58, 51–65.

7. Gilberto Bosquez, *The National Revolutionary Party of Mexico and the Six-Year Plan* (Mexico: PNR, 1937), p. 312.

8. Moisés González Navarro, *La confederación nacional campesina. Un grupo de presión en la reforma agraria mexicana* (México: Costa-Amic, 1968), pp. 138, 154–155. The ejido was the basic constituent unit of the CNC. Graciano Sánchez, former secretary general of the CCM, was elected secretary general of the CNC.

9. Brown, "General Lázaro Cárdenas and Mexican Presidential Politics," pp. 273–290.

10. Paul Nathan, "México en la época de Cárdenas," *Problemas Agrícolas e Industriales de México* VII (Julio–Septiembre 1955), p. 168.

11. Octavio Ianni, *El estado capitalista en la época de Cárdenas* (México: Ediciones Era, 1977), pp. 44–55.

12. Coutiño to Cárdenas, 1 October 1936, AGN/LC, 542.1, 20.

13. *El Universal,* 7 July 1937.

14. *Chiapas Nuevo,* 30 December 1937.

15. *Chiapas Nuevo,* 26 August 1937.

16. *Periódico Oficial del Estado,* 9 February 1938; *Chiapas Nuevo,* 3 November 1939.

17. Departamento del Trabajo, *Directorio de agrupaciones obreras y patronales de la república* (México: DAPP, 1939), pp. 63–78; *Chiapas Nuevo,* 17 December 1937; *Anuario de 1939,* pp. 322–324.

18. *Mexican Labor News,* 5 January 1939; *Chiapas Nuevo,* 6 April 1939.

19. *Mexican Labor News,* 21 September 1939; *Chiapas Nuevo,* 21 September 1939; Mario Culebro to Gutiérrez, 22 May 1940, ASRA, Cacahoatán, 23:8213.

20. *Informe de Efraín Gutiérrez, 1938.*

21. *Mexico Labor News,* 11, 18 August 1938; Secretario General CNC to Jefe del Departamento Agrario, 4 January 1939, ASRA, Carranza, 23:8142; Secretario, Liga de Comunidades Agrarias, Tapachula, to Jefe, Departamento Agrario, 28 February 1940, ASRA, Unión Juárez, 23:8051.

22. Córdova, *La política de masas,* pp. 197–201.

23. *Estatutos de la H. Cámara Nacional de Comercio e Industria de Tuxtla Gutiérrez, Chiapas* (Tuxtla Gutiérrez, 1938).

24. César Corzo Velasco, *Investigación histórico-político del estado de Chiapas* (México, 1976), pp. 87–101.

25. *Chiapas Nuevo,* 29 September, 20 October 1938.

26. *Chiapas Nuevo,* 7 July, 27 October, 17 November 1938.

27. *Chiapas Nuevo,* 22 June 1939.

28. *Chiapas Nuevo,* 28 December 1939.

29. *Chiapas Nuevo,* 20 February, 27 April 1940; *El Universal,* 5 September 1940.

30. George A. Collier, *Fields of the Tzotzil: The Ecological Bases of Tradition in Highland Chiapas* (Austin: University of Texas Press, 1975), pp. 195–198.

31. *Periódico Oficial del Estado,* 6 January 1937.

32. *Chiapas Nuevo,* 26 August 1936; *Periódico Oficial del Estado,* 28 July 1937.

33. Roger Reed, "Chamula and the Coffee Plantations of Chiapas," AB Thesis, Harvard College, 1973, pp. 84–87.

34. Wasserstrom, *Class and Society in Central Chiapas,* pp. 165–166.

35. García de León, *Resistencia y utopia*, II, pp. 205–209; Wasserstrom, *Class and Society in Central Chiapas*, pp. 166–172; Edel, "Zinacantan's Ejido: The Effects of Mexican Land Reform on an Indian Community in Chiapas," Harvard Chiapas Project, 1962.

36. Ulrich Kohler, *Cambio cultural dirigido en los altos de Chiapas: Un estudio sobre la antropología social aplicada* (México: INI-SEP, 1975), p. 62; Robert Redfield and Alfonso Villa Rojas, *Notes on the Ethnology of Tzeltal Communities of Chiapas* (Washington, D.C.: Carnegie Institution of Wash ington, no. 28, 1939), p. 110.

37. Wasserstrom, "White Fathers and Red Souls," pp. 223–224.

38. Ampliación Ejidos Poblado La Libertad, 29 February 1939, ASRA, La Libertad, 24:8128.

39. *Indigenismo en Acción*, 20 May 1944.

40. "Labor de la Agencia de Colocaciones de Comitán," *Chiapas Nuevo*, 12 January 1939.

41. Gutiérrez to Cárdenas, 24 August 1938, AGN/LC, 533.31, 9.

42. Comité Ejecutivo, Sindicato de Trabajadores Indígenas, San Cristóbal, to Cárdenas, 16 September 1939, AGN/LC, 533.31, 9.

43. Wasserstrom, *Class and Society in Central Chiapas*, p. 169.

44. Communication to author from Jan Rus, 19 January 1988; Asociación Agrícola Local de Cafeticultores de Soconusco, *Ponencias presentadas a la Conferencia de Mesa Redonda* (Tapachula, 1948).

45. *Chiapas Nuevo*, 23 September 1937.

46. "Memorándum que presenta el delegado del SUTICS del Estado de Chiapas, al Sr. Presidente de la República," 19 June 1945, AGN, Fondo Manuel Ávila Camacho, 432, 417. Hereafter cited as AGN/MAC and identifying information.

47. "Political Conditions," 6 April 1927, NA/RG 84, Correspondence, Salina Cruz, 1927.

48. Military Attaché to Secretary of State, 3 November 1939, NA/RG 59, 812.61333/7; "Informe del asemblea de los ciudadanos de Amatenango," 7 May 1936; ASRA, Amatenango, 23:8585(723.1); J. Pineda to Comisión Agraria Mixta, 20 October 1940, ASRA, Benito Juárez, 23:17539.

49. Francisco Isasí, Huixtla, to Cárdenas, 13 August 1938, ASRA, Huixtla, 25:590; *Chiapas Nuevo*, 12 January 1938; *El Universal*, 15 November 1938.

50. Spenser, "Soconusco," N.P.

51. *Chiapas Nuevo*, 16 March 1939.

52. Acta de Posesión, 5 April 1939, ASRA, Cacahoatán, 25:8213(723.8); "Informe del conjunto de Cacahoatán y Unión Juárez, Chiapas," 15 August 1939, ASRA, Unión Juárez, 23:8051(723.1); Gastón de Vilac, *Chiapas bajo el signo de la hoz* (México, 1940), p. 74.

53. Liga de Comunidades Agrarias to Jefe, Departamento Agrario, 28 February 1940, ASRA, Unión Juárez, 23:8051(723.8); *Chiapas Nuevo,* 24 August 1940, 5 October, 9, 23 November 1939; *El Universal,* 18 December 1939.

54. *Excelsiór,* 3, 4, April 1940; William Cameron Townsend, *Lázaro Cárdenas: Mexican Democrat* (Ann Arbor: George Wahr, 1952), pp. 342–343.

55. "Acta de Demarcaciones de las zonas de protección de las propiedades del Sr. Enrique Braun," 7 June 1942, ASRA, Unión Juárez, 23:8051(723.8); Nathaniel and Sylvia Weyl, *The Reconquest of Mexico: The Years of Lázaro Cárdenas* (New York: Oxford University Press, 1939), p. 182.

56. Liga Femenil Revolucionario, Finca "El Retiro," to Ávila Camacho, 20 February 1941, AGN/MAC, 404.1, 380.

57. Salvador Teuffer S., *Resolución y antecedentes del problema agrario en la zona del Soconusco, Chiapas* (Tuxtla Gutiérrez: Liga de Comunidades Agrarias y Sindicatos Campesinos de Chiapas, 1942), pp. 27–28.

58. "Memorándum del Comisariado Ejidal," 21 April 1940, and García Bros, Delegado del Departamento Agrario to Jefe, Departamento, 30 January 1941, ASRA, Cacahoatán, 23:8213.

59. "Memorandum on Coffee Situation in Chiapas, Mexico," 22 May 1946, NA/RG 84, Correspondence, Tapachula, 1946.

60. *Chiapas Nuevo,* 27 July 1937, 11 August 1938, 27 July, 10 August 1939.

61. Comité Agrario, La Concordia, to President Miguel Alemán, 20 May 1947, ASRA, La Concordia, 23:8195; "Manifiesto," 21 November 1937, ASRA, Huixtla, 25:590.

62. De la Peña, *Chiapas económico,* IV, p. 1237.

63. *Chiapas Nuevo,* 20 May 1939; De la Peña, *Chiapas económico,* IV, p. 1241.

64. De la Peña, *Chiapas económico,* IV, p. 1240; *Anuario de 1940,* p. 532.

65. Wasserstrom, *Class and Society in Central Chiapas,* p. 164.

66. Blanca Torres Ramíriez, *Historia de la revolución mexicana: México en la segunda guerra mundial* (México: El Colegio de México, 1979), pp. 81– 95, 106.

67. *La junta de administración y vigilancia de la propiedad extranjera* (México, 1943), pp. 57, 64–65.

68. "Memorandum on Coffee Situation in Chiapas, Mexico," 22 May 1946.

69. Reed, "Chamula and the Coffee Plantations," pp. 86–87; Helbig, *El Soconusco y su zona cafetalera,* pp. 100–101.

70. Manuel Gómez, Confederación de Obreros, Tapachula, to Ávila Camacho, 7 September 1944, AGN/MAC, 546.2, 10.

71. "Restitución de tierras ejidales del poblado de Cacahoatán," 7 December 1943, AGN/MAC, 404.1, 368.

72. Spenser, "Soconusco," N.P.

73. A similar development in the Lagos de Moreno region of Jalisco is discussed by Ann L. Craig, *The First Agraristas: An Oral History of a Mexican Agrarian Reform Movement* (Berkeley: University of California Press, 1983), pp. 241–242.

74. Córdova, *La política de masas*, p. 180.

75. George A. Collier, "Peasant Politics and the Mexican State: Indigenous Compliance in Highland Chiapas," *Mexican Studies/Estudios Mexicanos* 3 (Winter 1987), p. 82.

76. Jean Meyer, "Mexico: Revolution and Reconstruction in the 1920s," p. 190. This is supported by the example of San Luis Potosí in Ankerson, *Agrarian Warlord*, p. 174.

77. El Presidente del Comisariado Ejidal to Cárdenas, 10 February 1938, AGN/LC, 135.23, 42.

78. *Anuario de 1942*, pp. 746–749; *Censo agrícola-ganadero y ejidal 1970*, p. 37.

79. Comisariado Ejidal de Siltepec to Ávila Camacho, 3 April 1943, ASRA, San Isidro Siltepec, 23:642.

80. Los baldíos que vivimos en Tierra Colorado, Municipio Zinacantañ, to Ávila Camacho, 23 March 1944; Presidente Comisariado Ejidal to Jefe, Departamento Agrario, 12 April 1946; Presidente Comisariado Ejidal to Jefe, Departamento Agrario, 2 August 1956, ASRA, Chamula, 23:23232.

81. Salovesch, "Politics in a Maya Community," pp. 128–130, 133–135.

82. Secretario General del Departamento Agrario to Secretario Particular del Presidente, 17 March 1941, AGN/MAC, 404.1, 380.

83. Ejidatarios de Socoltenango to Alemán, 22 March 1948, AGN, Fondo Miguel Alemán Valdés, 402.1-108. Hereafter cited as AGN/MAV and identifying information.

84. Vecinos de Cacahoatán to Ávila Camacho, 15 July 1942, AGN/MAC, 703.4, 238.

85. Secretario General, LCA, to Ávila Camacho, 8 April 1942, AGN/MAC, 703.4, 232.

86. "Carta abierta al C. Presidente de la República por el Comité de Defensa de los Intereses de los Trabajadores Cafeteros del Soconusco," 5 July 1942, AGN/MAC, 703.4, 238.

87. SUTICS, "Memorándum," February 1943, AGN/MAC, 432, 417.

88. SUTICS, Finca "Monte Perla," to Ávila Camacho, February 1943, AGN/MAC, 432, 417.

89. Ramón Mandujano Alfonso, Tapachula, to Ávila Camacho, 9 September 1946, AGN/MAC, 404.1, 368.

90. "Carta Abierta por el Comisariado Ejidal, Cacahoatán, y la Sociedad Local de Credito Ejidal Unión Juárez," 27 August 1942, AGN/MAC, 703.4,

238; Los vecinos de las fincas "La Rioja," "La Argentina," etc., "Labor anti-mexicana en la región de Soconusco, Chiapas," 21 October 1948, AGN/MAV, 546.6, 418.

91. Juan Caracosa Pérez, Tapachula, to Presidente Miguel Alemán, 17 April 1948, AGN/MAV, 544.61, 12.

92. Approximately one third of the state of Chiapas's revenues came from taxes on coffee production and export.

93. Alberto Guzmán, Ex-Secretario local de la Sección Num. 14 de "Numancia," Cacahoatán, to Ávila Camacho, 22 November 1945, AGN/MAC, 432, 262.

94. "Memorándum que presenta el delegado del SUTICS," 19 June 1945.

95. Salvador Durán, Secretario General SUTICS, Tapachula, to Ávila Ca macho, 24 June 1942, AGN/MAC, 703.4, 232.

96. Secretario General, SUTICS, to Ávila Camacho, 19 October 1945, AGN/MAC, 404.1, 380.

97. "Memorándum que presenta el delegado del SUTICS," 19 June 1945.

98. Delegación Migración, Motozintla, to Ávila Camacho, 21 November 1941, AGN/MAC, 546.2, 10.

99. Manuel Gómez, Confederación de Obreros, Tapachula, to Ávila Camacho, 7 September 1944, AGN/MAC, 546.2, 10.

100. "Salen por el norte y entran por el sur," El Universal, 10 March 1950.

101. "Informe del Federación Regional de Trabajadores del Soconusco, CTM," 13 February 1943, AGN/MAC, 432, 520.

102. Reed, "Chamula and the Coffee Plantations," pp. 103–105.

103. Arturo Warman, "We Come to Object": The Peasants of Morelos and the National State (Baltimore: The Johns Hopkins Press, 1980), p. 190.

104. Wasserstrom, "La evolución de la economia regional en Chiapas: 1528–1975," America Indígena XXXVI (Julio–Septiembre 1976), pp. 490–492.

105. García de León, Resistencia y utopia, pp. 155–161; Spenser, "Soconusco," N.P.

106. "Monthly Economic Review," 8 March 1940, NA/RG 84, Correspondence, Tapachula.

107. Wasserstrom, Class and Society in Central Chiapas, p. 178.

108. John Calvin Hotchiss, "The Dynamics of Patronage in Teopisca: A Setting of Integration of Ladinos and Indians in Chiapas, Mexico," Ph.D. Diss., University of Chicago, 1975, pp. 195–199.

109. Warman, "We Come to Object," p. 176.

110. "Economic Effects of the Mexican Agrarian Program," 10 August 1938, NA/RG 59, 812.52, 3102. Also, Albert L. Michaels, "The Crisis of Cardenismo," Journal of Latin American Studies 2 (May 1970), p. 61.

111. Luis Medina, *Historia de la revolución mexicana: Del cardenismo al Ávila camachismo,* XVIII (México: El Colegio de México, 1978), chs. 3–5.

112. *Provincia* (mayo–junio 1949), p. 26; U.S. Consul, Coatzacoalcos, to Secretary of State, 30 November 1941, NA/RG 266, 14986.

113. "Gubernatorial Election of the State of Chiapas, Mexico," 14 July 1944, NA/RG 84, Correspondence, Tapachula 1944.

114. Torres Ramírez, *México en la segunda guerra mundial,* Part IV, "Una economia de paz en tiempos de guerra."

115. Luis Medina, *Historia de la revolución mexicana: Civilismo y modernización del autoritarismo,* XX (México: El Colegio de México, 1979), pp. 62–66.

116. Luis Javier Garrido, *El partido de la revolución institucionalizada (Medio siglo de poder político en México): La formación del nuevo estado (1928–1945)* (México: Siglo XXI, 1982), pp. 341, 301–325.

117. *La Nación,* 21 December 1946; Secretario General, Partido Cívico Tapachulteco, to Alemán, 18 December 1946, AGN/MAV, 544.5, 5; Miguel Ángel Granados Chapa, "La rebelión en la aldea," *Nexos* V, March 1982, p. 24.

118. *Diario de los Debates,* 3 January 1947; Gustavo Sánchez Cano, Tuxtla Gutiérrez, to Alemán, 1 January 1947, AGN/MAV, 544.5, 5.

119. Secretario General, Liga de Comunidades Agrarias y Sindicatos Campesinos del Estado de Chiapas, Comité Regional Campesino, Tapachula, to Presidente Alemán, 28 April 1947, AGN/MAV, 544.5-5.

120. Medina, *Civilismo y modernización,* p. 104; Casahonda Castillo, *50 Años de revolución,* pp. 118–136.

121. Roque Vidal Rojas, Delegado General, Confederación Nacional de la Pequeña Propiedad Agrícola, Delegación en Chiapas, Tuxtla, to President Alemán, 3 November 1949, AGN/MAV, 606.3-32.

122. *Informe que rinde a la XLII Legislatura del Estado de Chiapas el 1 de noviembre de 1949 el C. Gobernador Constitucional del Estado Gral. e Ing. Francisco J. Grajales* (Tuxtla Gutiérrez, 1949).

123. Bernardo Palomeque to Presidente Alemán, 11 December 1951, AGN/MAV, 244.3, 2672.

124. Alexis de Tocqueville, *Democracy in America,* J. P. Mayer edition (New York: Anchor Books, 1969), pp. 677, 692.

EPILOGUE

1. Gustavo Estava, et. al., *La batalla en el México rural* (Mexico: Siglo XXI, 1980), p. 179.

2. Vicente Hernández Méndez, quoted in Francisco Ortíz Pinchetti, "Policía y tropas en Chiapas, al servicio de finqueros y comerciantes," *Proceso,* 21 July

1980, p. 13.

3. Miguel Angel Velázquez y Juan Balboa, "Impera en la selva lacandona la ley del más fuerte," *Uno más Uno*, 18 June 1983.

4. Sebastián Pérez, quoted in Elías Chávez, "Se multiplican los males en Chiapas y Castellanos sólo reprime," *Proceso*, No. 482, 27 January 1986.

5. *Boletín de la Comisión Mexicana de Defensa y Promoción de Derechos Humanos* (México, November 1990), p. 4.

6. *IV Censos agrícola-ganadero y ejidal. 1960. Resumen general* (México, 1965), p. 426; *V Censos agrícola-ganadero y ejidal. 1970. Chiapas* (México, 1975), pp. 221, 371; *La economía del estado de Chiapas* (México: Banco de Comercio, 1968), pp. 23–24; Juan M. Mauricio Leguizamo, Héctor García Juárez, and Rúben Valadares Arjona, *La producción agrícola en Chiapas* (San Cristóbal: Centro de Investigaciones Ecológicas del Sureste, 1982). These figures are not adjusted for inflation or devaluation.

7. *Anuario estadístico 1940*, p. 622; Srio. de la Presidencia, *Monografía del estado de Chiapas* (México: Talleres Gráficos de la Nación, 1975), p. 25; *V Census agrícola-ganadero y ejidal. 1970*, p. 329.

8. Comité Nacional Campesina "Emiliano Zapata" to Presidente Ruiz Cortines, 7 de agosto de 1955, AGN/Fondo Adolfo Ruiz Cortines, 542.1, 921.

9. Juan Balboa, et. al., "La figura de Fidel se reproduce en todo el País, en los multiples caciques de la CTM," *Proceso*, 3 March 1986, p. 17.

10. *La economía del estado de Chiapas*, p. 20.

11. *IV Censos agrícola-ganadero y ejidal. 1960*, pp. 87, 99, 148.

12. Ernesto González Castillo, "Tenencia y explotación de la tierra en Chiapas," *Memoria de la Primera Conferencia Regional de Geografía de Chiapas. 22–24 de mayo de 1972* (México, 1974), pp. 221–224.

13. Paul R. Turner, "Intensive Agriculture among the Highland Tzeltals," *Ethnology*, 16:2 (April 1977), pp, 167–174.

14. María Luisa Acevedo, *Pobreza y riqueza en 378 municipios de México* (México: Centro de Ecodesarrollo, 1984), p. 224.

15. *V Censos agrícola-ganadero y ejidal. 1960*, pp. 17, 23, 99, 462.

16. Steven E. Sanderson, *The Transformation of Mexican Agriculture: International Structure and the Politics of Rural Change* (Princeton: Princeton University Press, 1986), pp. 129–130.

17. *Uno más Uno*, 12 June 1983; Riding, *Distant Neighbors*, p. 212; Pablo E. Muench N., "Las regiones agrícolas de Chiapas," and "La costa de Chiapas," *Revista de Geografía Agrícola*, 2 (January 1982), pp. 57–102, 123–130.

18. *Uno más Uno*, 1 January 1982.

19. Steven E. Sanderson, *Agrarian Populism and the Mexican State: The Struggle for Land in Sonora* (Berkeley: University of California Press, 1981), p. 145.

20. K. Appendini, et. al, *El campesinado en México: dos perspectivas de análisis* (México: El Colegio de México, 1983), p. 179; Ana María Silberman and Eurosía Carraseal Galindo, "Los mames: sus problemas geoeconómicos," and Ernesto González Castillo, "Tenencia y explotación de la tierra en Chiapas," *Memoria de la Primera Conferencia Regional de Geografía de Chiapas*, pp. 111, 223; Ana Bella Pérez Castro, "Movimiento campesino en Simojovel, Chis. 1936–1978: Problema étnica o de clases sociales," *Anales de Antropología*, 19 (1982), pp. 217, 220.

21. Frank Cancian, *Change and Uncertainty in a Peasant Economy: The Maya Corn Farmers of Zinacantan* (Stanford: Stanford University Press, 1972), pp. 16–20, 129–130; Collier, *Fields of the Tzotzil*, pp. 121–122; Gertrude Duby Blom, "Miseria y atraso destruyen a la selva Lacandona," *El Día*, 5 March 1978.

22. Henri Favre, "El cambio socio-cultural y el nuevo indigenismo en Chiapas," *Revista Mexicana de Sociología*, XLVII:3 (July–September 1985), p. 197.

23. Reed, "Chamula and the Coffee Plantations of Chiapas," p. 131.

24. Gertrude Duby Blom, "Pueblos en marcha: La selva reconquistada," *Circulo de Estudios Sociales*, 3 (January–April 1966); Pablo Montañez, *La agonía de la Selva* (Mexico, 1972), p. 28; Debra A. Schumann, "Family Labor Resources and Household Economic Stragegy in a Mexican Ejido," *Research in Economic Anthropology*, 7 (1985), p. 280.

25. Benjamin N. Colby and Pierre L. Van Den Berghe, "Ethnic Relations in Southeastern Mexico," *American Anthropologist*, 63 (1961), p. 778.

26. Margarita Nolasco, *Café y sociedad en México* (México: Centro de Ecodesarrollo, 1985), pp. 182–185.

27. Paul Lamartine Yates, *El desarrollo regional de México* (Mexico: Banco de México, S.A., 1961), pp. 110–127.

28. James W. Wilkie, *The Mexican Revolution: Federal Expenditures and Social Change since 1910* (Berkeley: University of California Press, 1967), pp. 232–236. Also see Manlio Barbosa Cano, "En turno a los factores que detienen el desarrollo en Chiapas, Guerrero y Tabasco," *Anales del Instituto Nacional de Antropología e Historia*, 18 (1965), pp. 195–216.

29. Coordinación General del Plan Nacional de Zonas Deprimidas y Grupos Marginados.

30. Coplamar, *Necesidades esenciales en Mexico: Situación actual y perspectivas al año 2000. Tomo 5. Geografía de la marginación* (Mexico: Siglo XXI, 1982), pp. 48–49. Similar analyses were conducted by Claudio Stern, *Las regiones de Mexico y sus niveles de desarrollo socioeconómico* (Mexico: El Colegio de Mexico, 1973), p. 104; and Enrique Hernández Laos, "La

desigualidad regional en Mexico, 1900–1980," in Rolando Cordera and Carlos Tello, eds., *La desigualdad en Mexico* (Mexico: Siglo XXI, 1984), pp. 155–192. The dramatic rise in per capita income in Chiapas during the 1970s is due entirely to petroleum production in the Reforma fields and does not indicate any significant improvement in the standard of living of most Chiapanecos. See *Sistema de Cuentas Nacionales de Mexico* (Mexico, 1985), p. 530.

31. Wilkie, *The Mexican Revolution*, p. 236.

32. Wasserstrom, *Class and Society in Central Chiapas*, p. 212. This is also the conclusion of Stuart Plattner, "Economic Development and Occupational Change in a Developing Area of Mexico," *The Journal of Developing Areas*, 14 (July 1980), pp. 480–481.

33. Esteva, et. al., *La batalla en el México rural*, p. 179.

34. *Monografía del Estado de Chiapas*, p. 28; "Hydroelectric Development in the Southeast," *Mexican Newsletter*, No. 2, 30 April 1971.

35. George W. Grayson, *The Politics of Mexican Oil* (Pittsburgh: University of Pittsburgh Press, 1980), pp. 57–58, 62; Thomas Sanders, "The Economic Development of Tabasco, Mexico," *Fieldstaff Reports*, No. 8, 1977.

36. Thomas Sanders, "The Plight of Mexican Agriculture," *Fieldstaff Reports*, No. 3, 1979.

37. Favre, "El cambio socio-cultural y el nuevo indigenismo en Chiapas," pp. 182–183. An overview of PRODESCH activities is provided by Frank Cancian, *The Decline of Community in Zinacantan: Economy, Public Life, and Social Stratification, 1960–1987* (Stanford: Stanford University Press, 1992), pp. 38–42.

38. Jesús Agustín Velasco S. and Javier Matus Pacheco, *Chiapas en cifras, 1970–1976* (Tuxtla Gutiérrez: Gobierno del Estado de Chiapas, 1976), p. 180.

39. Miguel Ángel Velázquez, "Transformación de formas de vida en Chiapas por el petroleo," *Uno más Uno*, 18 February 1981; William Chislett, "Mexico's farmers take on the power of Pemex," *Financial Times*, 28 January, 1981.

40. *Excelsior*, 4 July 1983. George A. Collier and Elizabeth Lowery Quaratiello write that "agrarian production was thrown into crisis by energy development in the 1970s." See *Basta! Land and the Zapatista Rebellion in Chiapas* (Oakland, California: A Food First Book, 1994), p. 89.

41. *Diario de México*, 4 October 1975; Leandro Molinar Merár, "Las zonas indígenas, uno de los mayores retos en materia agraria," *El Día*, 16 June 1979; Ricardo del Muro, "Tiene Chiapas atraso de 30 años en materia agraria," *Uno más Uno*, 21 February 1981.

42. Manuel Mejido, *México amargo* (Mexico: Siglo XXI, 1973), pp. 104–110; Moisés González Navarro, *La pobreza en México* (Mexico: El Colegio de Mexico, 1985), p. 385; "Chiapas, el estado rico con habitantes pobres," *Proceso*,

22 September 1980, pp. 18–19; Miguel Angel Velázquez, "Frijoles y 11 tortillas, dieta de privilegiados," *Uno más Uno*, 7 February 1981.

43. Mechthild Rutsch, *La ganadería capitalista en México* (Mexico: Editorial Línea, 1984), pp. 57, 105; René Pietri y Claudio Stern, *Petroleo, agricultura y población en el sureste de México* (México: Centro de Estudios Sociológicos, El Colegio de Mexico, 1985), pp. 103–119; Sanderson, *The Transformation of Mexican Agriculture*, pp. 177–179.

44. Victor Perera and Robert D. Bruce, *The Last Lords of Palenque: The Lacandon Mayas of the Mexican Rain Forest* (Boston: Little, Brown and Company, 1982), pp. 24–25.

45. James D. Nations, "The Lancandones, Gertrude Blom, and the Selva Lacandona," in Alex Harris and Margaret Sartor, eds., *Gertrude Blom—Bearing Witness* (Chapel Hill: The University of North Carolina Press, 1984), p. 31.

46. Luis Ma. Fernández Ortíz and María Tarrío G. de Fernández, "Ganadería, campesinado y producción de granos básicos: competencias por el uso de la tierra en México," *Revista Mexicana de Ciencias Políticas y Sociales*, 26:102 (1980), pp. 242–244. Ronald B. Nigh argues that the expansion of cattle raising has contributed significantly to malnutrition in Chiapas. See "El ambiente nutricional de los grupos mayas de Chiapas," *América Indígena*, XL (January–March 1980), pp. 73–91 and Collier and Quaratiello, *Basta!,* Chapter 2.

47. Juan Balboa, *Uno más Uno*, 12 June 1983; Javier Molina, *Uno más Uno*, 14 July 1983; Balboa, *Uno más Uno*, 15 August 1983.

48. Neil Harvey, "Peasant Strategies and Corporatism in Chiapas," in Joe Foweraker and Ann L. Craig, eds., *Popular Movements and Political Change in Mexico* (Boulder: Lynne Rienner Publishers, 1990), p. 184.

49. Víctor Avilés, "Los problemas con la tenencia de tierra hacen que Chiapas viva una situación difícil," *Uno más Uno*, 2 April 1981.

50. "Las soluciones a conflictos agrarios en Chiapas se han agotado en ocasiones," *Uno más Uno*, 12 November 1980.

51. Virginia Molina, *San Bartolomé de los Llanos* (Mexico: Sep, INAH, 1976), p. 116.

52. Rodolfo Guzmán, "Al asalto de pueblos indígenas," *Proceso*, No. 13, 29 January 1977, pp. 6–13; "Protesta de una comunidad Chiapaneca por la falta de ejecución de una resolución que data de 1965," *Uno más Uno*, 1 July 1980.

53. Gonzalo Alvarez del Villar, "Denuncian el secuestro de tres campesinos en Chiapas," *Uno más Uno*, 12 April 1981; María Moncada, "Movimiento campesino y estructura de poder: Venustiano Carranza, Chiapas," *Textual: Análisis del Medio Rural*, 4 (September 1983), pp. 65–76.

54. By contrast very few agrarian ocupations took place in Chiapas during

the 1950s and 1960s. See Jorge Martínez Ríos, "Las invasiones agrarias en Mexico (o la crisis del modelo de incorporación-participación marginal)," *Revista Mexicana de Sociología*, XXXIV (Ocotber–December de 1972), pp. 764–765.

55. "Response by the Mexican Government to Amnesty International's Memorandum," in *Mexico: Human Rights in Rural Areas. Exchange of Documents with the Mexican Government on Human Rights Violations in Oaxaca and Chiapas* (London: Amnesty International Publications, 1986), p. 113.

56. Esteva, et. al., *La batalla en el México rural*, p. 175.

57. "Presos políticos campesinos," *Punto Crítico*, September 1980, p. 25.

58. *Mexico: Human Rights in Rural Areas*, p. 65.

59. James D. Cockcroft, *Mexico: Class Formation, Capital Accumulation, and the State* (New York: Monthly Review Press, 1983), p. 193.

60. Quoted by Oscar Hinojosa, "Y una corona de flores ciño la frente de Juan Sabines," *Proceso*, No. 192, 7 July 1980, p. 22.

61. Guillermo Correa, "Chiapas, a un paso de la guerrilla, advierte el Episcopado Mexicano," *Proceso*, 12 December 1983, p. 25.

62. Ernesto Reyes, *Proceso*, 28 January 1985, pp. 24–27.

63. Carlos Tello Díaz, "Chiapas y la guerrilla," *Nexos*, April 1995, p. 55. Also see Collier and Quaratiello, *Basta!*, Chapter 3.

64. Ana Bella Pérez Castro, "Estructura agraria y movimientos campesinos en Simojovel, Chiapas," Tesis de Licenciatura, Escuela Nacional de Antropología e Historia, 1981, p. 230.

65. Fernando Alvarez, "Peasant Movements in Chiapas," *Bulletin of Latin American Research*, 7:2 (1988), p. 289.

66. Miguel Angel Velázquez, "Explotación de los ilegales guatemaltecos," *Uno más Uno*, 8 February 1981.

67. Neil Harvey, "Rebellion in Chiapas: Rural Reforms, Campesino Radicalism, and the Limits to Salinismo," in *Transformations of Rural Mexico*, No. 5 (La Jolla, California: Center for U.S.–Mexican Studies, University of California at San Diego, 1994), p. 32.

68. Unión de Uniones Ejidales y grupos campesinos solidarios de Chiapas, "Nuestra Lucha por la Tierra en la Selva Lacandona," Diciembre de 1981, reprinted in *Textual*, 4:13 (September 1983), pp. 151–163; Miguel Angel Velázquez, "40 mil indios, invasores de su propia tierra," *Uno más Uno*, 9 February 1981.

69. Harvey, "Rebellion in Chiapas," p. 32; Guillermo Correa, "En junto con Sabines, los indígenas crean la Unión de Ejidos," *Proceso*, No. 203, 22 September 1980, pp. 15–17.

70. Neil Harvey, "Power and Resistance in Contemporary Chiapas," Paper presented at the Research Workshop on Power and Ethnicity in Guatemala

and Chiapas, University of Texas at Austin, March 27–28, 1992. It is likely that the anti-Orive faction became the core of the EZLN.

71. Pérez Castro, "Movimiento campesino en Simojovel," p. 220.

72. Colectivo, "Lucha laboral y sindicalismo en simojovel," *Textual*, 4:13 (September 1983), pp. 77–80.

73. "El Problema Agrario de Simojovel," *La República en Chiapas*, Tuxtla Gutiérrez, 5 November 1980; Pérez Castro, "Estructura agraria y movimientos campesinos en Simojovel," pp. 230–244.

74. Sindicato de Obreros Agrícolas de Chiapas, "Pliego Petitorio de la Marcha Campesina (October 1983)," reprinted in *Textual*, 4:13 (September 1983), pp. 131–137; Guillermo Correa, "Frente a la represión creciente, la organización independiente cobra fuerza," *Proceso*, No. 360, 26 September 1983, pp. 24–26; Hermenegildo Castro, "Sigue la violencia: Campesinos de Chiapas," *La Jornada*, 19 October 1985; Alvarez, "Peasant Movements in Chiapas," pp. 293–295.

75. Luis López Vázquez, secretary general of CIOAC, reported that campesinos affiliated with CIOAC occupied 109 large fincas in various municipalities. See *La Voz del Sureste*, Tuxtla Gutiérrez, 4 June 1985.

76. Molina, *San Bartolomé de los Llanos* ; María Moncada, "Movimiento campesino y estructura de poder: Venustiano Carranza, Chiapas," *Textual*, 4:13 (September 1983), pp. 65–76.

77. "Protesta de una comunidad chiapaneca por la falta de ejecución de una resolución que data de 1965," *Uno más Uno*, 1 July 1980.

78. Neil Harvey, "Personal Networks and Strategic Choices in the Formation of an Independent Peasant Organization: The OCEZ of Chiapas, Mexico," *Bulletin of Latin American Research*, 7:2 (1988), pp. 299–312.

79. Harvey, "Peasant Strategies and Corporatism in Chiapas," p. 193.

80. Harvey, "The OCEZ of Chiapas, Mexico," pp. 308–310; Joel Solar, "Protesta de la OCEZ por desalojos violentos de campesinos en Chiapas," *Uno más Uno*, 12 July 1984; *La Voz del Sureste*, Tuxtla Gutiérrez, 5 June 1985.

81. Harvey, "Power and Resistance in Contemporary Chiapas," p. 19.

82. Miguel Angel Velázquez, "Impera en la selva lacandona la ley del más fuerte," *Uno más Uno*, 18 June 1983; "Chiapas: atraso y desarrollo para oprimir a los campesinos," *Punto Crítico*, No. 111, September 1980, p. 24.

83. Los firmantes colonos y pequeños propeitarios, "Carta Abierta," *Uno más Uno*, 4 July 1984.

84. Ignacio Ramírez, "Tropas y policías con mandos castrenses se extienden por el país," *Proceso*, 30 March 1987, p. 21. "Chiapas," writes John Bailey, "has at times resembled a military zone." From "Can the PRI be reformed?" in Judith Gentleman, ed., *Mexican Politics in Transition* (Boulder: Westview Press, 1987), p.88(n52).

85. Guillermo Correa, "El gobernador intenta llenar con represión el vacío de poder," *Proceso*, 25 February 1985, p. 22.

86. Quoted by Elías Chávez, "Se multiplican los males en Chiapas y Castellanos sólo reprime," *Proceso*, No. 482, 27 January 1986, p. 23.

87. Daniel C. Levy, "The Implications of Central American Conflicts for Mexican Politics," in Roderic A. Camp, ed., *Mexico's Political Stability: The Next Five Years* (Boulder: Westview Press, 1986), pp. 244–245. Also see Sergio Aguayo, *El éxodo centroamericano: consecuencias de un conflicto* (Mexico: SEP, 1985), pp. 29–38.

88. *El Sol de México*, 18 March 1982.

89. Dennis Volman, "Policies on Central American Issues Change," *The Christian Science Monitor*, 21 October, 1985.

90. *El Sol de México*, 17 November 1984.

91. Carlos Fazio, "Denuncia Sabines más agresiones de Guatemala," *Proceso*, 11 October 1982, p. 33; S. Jeffery K. Wilkerson, "The Usumacinta River: Troubles on a Wild Frontier," *National Geographic*, 168, October 1985, pp. 514–543; Duncan M. Earle, "Mayas Aiding Mayas: Guatemalan Refugees in Chiapas, Mexico," in Robert M. Carmack, ed., *Harvest of Violence: The Maya Indians and the Guatemalan Crisis* (Norman: University of Oklahoma Press, 1988), pp. 256–273.

92. "Cuando ardio el cielo y se quemo la tierra" is the title of a study of the Chichonal tragedy by investigators of the Instituto Nacional Indigenista.

93. Guillermo Correa and Sergio Antonio Reyes, "Sabines y Castellanos completaron la acción destructora del Chichonal," *Proceso*, 19 March 1984, pp. 20–23.

94. Anselmo Estrada Albuquerque, "El Maíz, producto político," *El Universal*, 1 August 1982. The twelve fincas of the Hermanos Castellanos are listed in *Resumen de noticias*, San Cristóbal de Las Casas, Num. 16, December 1987.

95. This makes an interesting contrast with Governor Manuel Velasco Suárez's recommendation in 1974 that the road to a better life for most Chiapanecos lay in the direction of a more just distribution "by those who can and should share their resources." Quoted by González Navarro, *La pobreza en México*, p. 358.

96. *Excelsior*, 4–6 July 1983.

97. Juan Balboa y Guillermo Correa, "El gobernador de Chiapas, vencedor de la renovación moral," *Proceso*, 16 February 1987, pp. 22–25; and Salvador Corro y Oscar Hinojosa, "Los campesinos esperaron 50 años y Cárdenas volvió, reencarnado en su hijo," *Proceso*, 15 February 1988, p. 28.

98. "Plan Chiapas," in *Antología de la Planeación en Mexico, 1917–1985: Tomo 16. Planeación Regional, Estatal y Municipal (1982–1985)* (Mexico:

Secretaria de Programmacion y Presupuesto, 1986), pp. 541–607; Miguel de la Madrid H., "Chiapas: El Plan Chiapas," en *31 Experiencias de Desarrollo Regional* (Mexico: SEP, 1985), pp. 129–135; "A Jab in the Arm for Plan Chiapas: World Bank Ready with the Cash—But Who Will Benefit?" *Mexico and Central America Report*, 3 May 1985, p. 2; *Excelsior*, 19 January 1984; *Notimex*, 1 May 1985.

99. Harvey, "Rebellion in Chiapas," pp. 22–23; *La Voz del Sureste*, Tuxtla Gutierrez, 18 June 1983; Juan Balboa y Guillermo Correa, "El temor alcanza records este sexenio en Chiapas," *Proceso*, 14 December 1987, p. 16.

100. Philip L. Russell, *Mexico under Salinas* (Austin: Mexico Resource Center, 1994), p. 194.

101. Harvey, "Rebellion in Chiapas," p. 9; Anthony DePalma, "In Mexico's Bitter South, Coffee Now Blights Lives," *The New York Times*, 2 February, 1994.

102. Harvey, "Peasant Strategies and Corporatism in Chiapas," p. 191.

103. Carlos C. Zetina, "Está Imposibilitado el Gobierno Para Dotar de Tierras a Todos los Campesinos: SRA," *Excelsior*, 30 November 1984.

104. *La Voz del Sureste*, Tuxtla Gutierrez, 10 November and 3 December 1983.

105. *Ibid.*, 4 June 1985.

106. Quoted by Guillermo Correa, "Chiapas, a un paso de la guerrilla, advierte el Episcopado Mexicano," *Proceso*, 12 December 1983.

107. Alejandro Encinas R., y Fernando Rascón F., *Reporte y cronología del movimiento campesino e indígena*, No. 1–4 (Chapingo: UAC, 1982–83), No. 3, p. 21; Eduardo Aguado López, et. al., "La lucha por la tierra en Mexico (1976–1982)," *Revista Mexicana de Ciencias Políticas y Sociales*, XXVIII: 113–114 (July–December de 1983), p. 58.

108. Quoted by Armando Sepulveda, "Los Campesinos Siempre son Presa Fácil de vivales: Absalón Castellanos," *Excelsior*, 14 January 1983.

109. *La Voz del Sureste*, Tuxtla Gutierrez, 18 June 1983.

110. "Represión y asesinatos solapados por el gobierno," *Así Es*, 10 August 1984; "Represión, crimen y despojos contra los campesinos," *Así Es*, 14 May 1984.

111. Amnesty International, *Mexico: Human Rights in Rural Areas. Exchange of Documents with the Mexican Government on Human Rights Violations in Oaxaca and Chiapas* (London: Amnesty International Publications, 1986); Americas Watch, *Human Rights in Mexico: A Policy of Impunity* (New York: Americas Watch, 1990); Minnesota Advocates for Human Rights, *Civilians at Risk: Military and Police Abuses in the Mexican Countryside* (New York: World Policy Institute, North American Project Special Report 6, 1993).

112. Amnesty International, *Mexico: Human Rights in Rural Areas*, p. 65.

113. AMDH, *Chiapas: cronología de un etnocidio reciente* (México, 1987).

114. Human Rights Watch/Americas, "Human Rights and the Chiapas Rebellion," *Current History*, March 1994, p. 121.

115. Chávez, "Castellanos sólo reprime," p. 22.

116. Guillermo Correa, "Chiapas, a un paso de la guerrilla, advierte el Episcopado Mexicano," *Proceso*, 12 December 1983, p. 20.

117. Rebeca Hernández Marín, "Sur de Chiapas: el Itinerario de la Violencia," *Epoca*, No. 107, 21 June 1993, p. 21.

118. Jessica Kreimerman, "Chiapas, Llegó la Revolución sin que la llamaran," *Reforma*, 21 November 1993.

119. Castañeda quoted by Homero Campa, "Castañeda: A New Threat of Violence," in *World Press Review*, March 1994, p. 17.

120. Russell, *Mexico under Salinas*, p. 284.

121. Harvey, "Rebellion in Chiapas," pp. 17–20; Russell, *Mexico under Salinas*, pp. 281–290.

122. This fear is justified, according to a University of Michigan economist who, despite his support for free trade generally, maintains that the maize farming sector in Mexico, and especially in more remote regions like Chiapas, is the most threatened agricultural sector. Interview of Robert Stern by the author, March 1994.

123. Harvey, "Rebellion in Chiapas," pp. 25–28; Hubert Carton de Grammont, "El campo hacia el fin del milenio," *Nexos*, January 1992, pp. 49–53.

124. Alberto Huerta, "Seeds of a Revolt: All One Needed to do was Listen," *Commonweal*, 28 January 1994, p. 5; Kathleen O'Toole, "Land, economic reforms helped fuel unrest in Mexican state of Chiapas, anthropologist says," *Campus Report* [Stanford University], 5 January 1994, pp. 1, 6.

125. DePalma, "In Mexico's Bitter South, Coffee Now Blights Lives."

126. Andrew Reding, "Chiapas Is Mexico: The Imperative of Political Reform," *World Policy Journal*, XI:1 (Spring 1994), p. 14; Alberto Huerta, "Lawless Roads Still: The 'Red" Bishop of Chiapas," *Commonweal*, 17 December 1993, pp. 12–14.

127. Víctor Guillén Guillén, president de la Unión Regional Fronteriza de la Pequeña Propiedad de Chiapas, quoted by Matilde Pérez U., "Crearán grupos de defensa civil en nueve municipios de Chiapas," *La Jornada*, 30 June 1992.

128. Matilde Pérez, et. al., "Investigan supuestas amenazas contra Samuel Ruiz," *La Jornada*, 1 July 1992; Uniones Ganaderas Regionales de Chiapas, "A La Opinión Pública," *La Jornada*, 2 July 1992.

129. Guillermo Correa, "Hay guerrilleros in Chiapas desde hace ocho años," *Proceso*, No. 880, 13 September 1993, p. 13.

130. Hernández Marín, "Sur de Chiapas," p. 23; Harvey, "Rebellion in Chiapas," pp. 34–35

131. Harvey, "Rebellion in Chiapas," p. 35. Tim Golden writes that "those familiar with the movement have identified its now-dissolved political arm as . . . ANCIEZ." See "The Voice of the Rebels Has Mexicans in His Spell," *The New York Times*, 8 February 1994.

132. Carlos Tello Díaz, "La rebelión de las Cañadas," *Nexos*, January 1995, p. 51.

133. Marcos interviewed by Ann Louise Bardach, "Mexico's Poet Rebel, "*Vanity Fair*, 57:7, July 1994, p. 132.

134. Alma Guillermoprieto, "Zapata's Heirs," *The New Yorker*, 16 May 1994, p. 54.

135. Golden, "The Voice of the Rebels Has Mexicans in His Spell."

136. Luis Hernandez, "The New Mayan War," *NACLA Report on the Americas*, XXVII:5 (March–April 1994), p. 8.

137. Bardach, "Mexico's Poet Rebel," p.132.

138. Marcos has been quoted in two interviews, however, that the timing of the attack was guided less by an astute understanding of political symbolism than was first assumed "Because we weren't ready before." See Guillermoprieto, "Zapata's Heirs," p. 63; Bardach, "Mexico's Poet Rebel," p. 132.

139. Pérez U., "Crearán grupos de defensa civil en nueve municipios de Chiapas."

140. Armando Guzmán y Rodigo Vera, "Militares y sacerdotes se enfrentan por el caso de los dos oficiales asesinados e incinerados en Chiapas," *Proceso*, No. 858, 12 April 1993, pp. 6–9.

141. Hernández Marín, "Sur de Chiapas," pp. 21–23.

142. Bardach, "Mexico's Poet Rebel," p. 132.

143. Hernández Marín, "Sur de Chiapas," p. 23.

144. Correa, "Hay guerrilleros en Chiapas," pp. 12–15.

145. Hernández Marín, "Sur de Chiapas," p. 21.

146. Huerta, "Seeds of a Revolt," p. 5.

147. There are a few good accounts of the rebellion and its development during 1994. See Luis Méndez Asensio and Antonio Cano Gimeno, *La guerra contra el tiempo: Viaje a la selva alzada* (Mexico: Colección Grandes Temas, 1994); John Ross, *Rebellion from the Roots: Indian Uprising in Chiapas* (Monroe, Maine: Common Courage Press, 1995); and Philip L. Russell, *The Chiapas Rebellion* (Austin: Mexico Resource Center, 1995).

148. Alma Guillermoprieto characterizes the agreement as "the most significant, and possibly sincere, proposal for change ever offered [to the poor people of Chiapas] by the State." See Guillermoprieto, "The Shadow War," *The New*

York Review of Books, 2 March 1995, p. 40.

149. Jaime Labastida, "Guerra de Propaganda," *Excelsior*, 20 January 1994. The propaganda war in the United States press is described by David Asman who also argues that the liberal American press has suppressed "the increasing amount of hard evidence indicating at least some degree of outside manipulation of the Chiapas population." See Asman, "Mexican Minefields," *Forbes Media Critic*, Summer 1994, p. 67.

150. Salinas is quoted by Dick J. Reavis, "Chiapas is Mexico," *The Progressive*, May 1994, p. 28.

151. Enrique Krauze, "Zapped: The Roots of the Chiapas Revolt," *The New Republic*, 31 January 1994, p. 9.

152. Octavio Paz, "El nudo de Chiapas," *La Jornada*, 6 January 1994.

153. Castañeda quoted by Campa, "Castañeda: A New Threat of Violence," p. 17.

154. Lorenzo Meyer, "Fallaron las Instituciones," *Excelsior*, 6 January 1994.

155. Lorenzo Meyer, "Realidad Mexicana Color de Rosa," *Excelsior*, 20 January 1994.

156. Marcos quoted by Bardach, "Mexico's Poet Rebel," p. 69.

157. "Urgente Llamado a la paz y la Reconciliación," *Excelsior*, 20 January 1994.

158. Guillermoprieto, "Zapata's Heirs," p. 54; Bardach, "Mexico's Poet Rebel," p. 74; Golden, "The Voice of the Rebels Has Mexicans in His Spell"; "Urgente Llamado a la paz y la Reconciliación."

159. Tim Golden, "Mexican Rebel Leaders Sees No Quick Settlement," *The New York Times*, 20 February 1994.

160. Carmina Danini, "Chiapas uprising apparently inspires demands elsewhere," *Fort Worth Star-Telegram*, 18 February 1994.

161. "Mexican Rebels, Backers Shift Effort Toward Capital," *The Washington Post*, 8 January 1994.

162. "Urgente Llamado a la paz y la Reconciliación."

163. Tim Golden, "'Awakened' Peasant Farmers Overrunning Mexican Towns," *The New York Times*, 9 February 1994.

164. Alberto Navarrete, "Preocupante Situación: Extienden las Invaiones de Tierras," *Excelsior*, 17 April 1994; Gonzalo Egremy, "Dos nuevas invasiones de predios en Chiapas," *El Universal*, 8 May 1994. By the end of the year over 2,000 properties had been invaded.

165. David Clark Scott, "Chiapas Ranchers Vow to Take Law Into Their Own Hands," *The Christian Science Monitor*, 14 April 1994; Scott, "Political Turmoil Roils Mexican Economy," *The Christian Science Monitor*, 19 April 1994.

166. This is also the first Latin American insurrection that has been thor-

oughly reported and documented on the internet. See, for example, Ya Basta! The EZLN Page (http://www.peak.org/~justin/ezln/) and Zapatistas: An Electronic Book. Documents of the New Mexican Revolution (gopher:// lanic.utexas.edu). Also see, Deedee Halleck, "Zapatistas On-Line," *NACLA Report on the Americas*, XXVIII: 2 (September–October 1994), pp. 30–32

167. Guillermo Gómez Peña, "The Subcomandante of Performance," in Elaine Katzenberger, ed., *First World, ha ha ha! The Zapatista Challenge* (San Francisco: City Lights, 1995), p. 90. "The totally unthreatening nature of the insurgency was clear to all by the end of the first week of January 1994," Guillermoprieto, "The Shadow War," p. 35.

168. EZLN. *Documentos y comunicados 1 de enero / 8 de agosto de 1994* (México: Ediciones Era, 1994); *Shadows of Tender Fury: The Letters and Communiques of Subcomandante Marcos and the Zapatista Army of National Liberation* (New York: Monthly Review Press, 1995). For EZLN communiques after August 1994 see Ya Basta! The EZLN Page on the World Wide Web.

169. Guillermoprieto, "The Shadow War," p. 41.

170. The Nacional Democratic Convention is the subject of an excellent documentary film entitled *Viaje al centro de la selva (Memorial zapatista)*, 1994.

171. "Apoyar la mediación, pide Zedillo a la Conai," *La Jornada*, 21 December 1994.

172. Fernando Pérez Correa, "Chiapas: La Hora de la Razon," *Vuelta*, 20 March 1995, pp. 25–29; "Comunicado de la delegación del Ejército Zapatista de Liberación Nacional: San Andrés Sacanichen de Los Pobres, antes San Andrés Larráinzar, 21 April 1995," Ya Basta! The EZLN Page on the World Wide Web.

173. Paul B. Carroll and Craig Torres, "As Elections Approach, the Uprising in Mexico is Shaking Up Politics," *The Wall Street Journal*, 7 February 1994.

GLOSSARY

agrarista	supporter of land reform
alcabala	internal tariff
alcalde	mayor
arrendamiento	rent in cash or produce
arrendatario	renter, tenant farmer, sharecropper
ayuntamiento	town council
baldiaje	system of labor service
baldío	legally vacant land; squatter-sharecropper
bracero	migrant field worker
cabecera	seat of municipal or departmental government
cacicazgo	domain of a cacique
cacique	local or regional political boss
caciquismo	system of boss rule
cafetales	coffee groves
cafetero	laborer on a coffee plantation, coffee planter
cacao	cocoa
camarilla	political clique
campesino	"country person," peasant
caudillo	military chieftain, strongman
Científico	adherent of Positivism and Porfirismo
comisariado ejidal	local committee that administers an ejido
criollo	American-born Spaniard, Creole
Cristobalense	resident of San Cristobal Las Casas
ejidatarios	residents of an ejido who possess land use rights

ejido	village common land; since 1915 communities established through land reform
enganchador	labor contractor
enganche	advance payment to secure labor
estancia	cattle ranch
familia chiapaneca	the landowning elite of Chiapas
finca	"farm," ranch, hacienda, estate
finca rústica	any rural property regardless of size
finquero	farmer, rancher, hacendado, landowner
ganaderización	"cattle-ization," conversion of arable land to cattle pastures
Gobernación	Department of Government, Interior Ministry
gobernador	state governor
guardia blanca	private military force of a landowner
habilitador	labor contractor, enganchador
hacendado	estate owner, finquero
hacienda	rural estate (Mexican term)
hectárea	"hectare," area of land equaling 2.4 acres
indigenismo	movement or philosophy advocating the protection of the Indian and Indian culture
jefatura	prefecture, political district
jefe político	prefect, district political administrator
jornalero	temporary day laborer
ladino	white or mestizo, anyone not an Indian
latifundista	owner of a great estate
latifundio	"latifundium" (pl. "latifundia"), great estate; large landholding
mestizo	person of mixed Spanish-Indian ancestry; ladino
minifundista	owner of a small plot of land for farming
montería	logging camp
municipio	municipality

norteño	northerner; someone from northern Mexico
obrero	worker
partido	political party; political district subordinate to a department
patria chica	"little fatherland," local region
peón	rural laborer, often an indebted laborer, mozo
peonaje	labor system associated with debt
peones acasillados	resident farm laborers
peso	basic unit of Mexican currency
pistolero	thug, gun slinger
político	politician
Porfiriato	age of Porfirio Diaz (1876–1911)
presidente municipal	municipal president, mayor
propietario	property owner; elected official
pueblo	village; "the people"
ranchería	hamlet, village located on hacienda property
ranchero	smallholder, rancher
rancho	small or medium-sized property, homestead, ranch
reparto	distribution of land
sierra	mountain range
sindicato	labor union or federation
sindicato blanco	labor union allied with or created by business or government
tamanes	Indian cargo carriers
terrenos baldíos	legally unoccupied lands belonging to state government
tienda de raya	company store
tierra caliente	"hot country," lowlands
tierra fría	"cold country," highlands
Tuxtleco	resident of Tuxtla Gutierrez
vecino	neighbor, householder, citizen

SELECT BIBLIOGRAPHY

ARCHIVAL SOURCES

Mexico:

Archivo de Chiapas, Departamento de Investigaciones Históricas, Instituto Nacional de Antropología e Historia, Mexico City.
Archivo Francisco I. Madero, Biblioteca Nacional, Mexico City.
Archivo Francisco León De la Barra, Centro de Estudios de Historia de México (CONDUMEX), Mexico City.
Archivo General de Centroamérica, Ramo de Provincia de Chiapas, Guatemala City.
Archivo General de la Nación, Mexico City:
  Ramo de Comisión Nacional Agraria
  Unidad de Presidentes:
    Fondo Francisco I. Madero
    Fondo Obregón-Calles
    Fondo Emilio Portes Gil
    Fondo Pascual Ortiz Rubio
    Fondo Abelardo L. Rodríguez
    Fondo Lázaro Cárdenas
    Fondo Manuel Ávila Camacho
    Fondo Miguel Alemán Valdés
    Fondo Adolfo Ruiz Cortines
Archivo General Octavio Magaña, Archivo Histórico de la Universidad Autónoma de México, Mexico City.
Archivo Histórico de Chiapas, Gobierno del Estado, Tuxtla Gutiérrez, Chiapas.
Archivo Histórico de Matías Romero, Banco de México, Mexico City.
Archivo Histórico de la Secretaría de Relaciones Exteriores, Mexico City.

Archivo "seis de enero de 1915" de la Secretaría de Reforma Agraria, Mexico City.

Archivo Venustiano Carranza, Telegramas, Central de Estudios de Historia de México (CONDUMEX), Mexico City.

Colección General Porfirio Díaz, Universidad de las Américas, Cholula, Puebla.

Fondo de Microfilm, Serie Chiapas and Serie Francisco I. Madero, Instituto Nacional de Antropología e Historia, Mexico City.

United States:

Latin American Manuscripts, Lilly Library, Indiana University, Bloomington, Indiana

National Archives of the United States, Washington, D.C.:

    Record Group 59: General Records of the Department of State

    Record Group 76: Records of Boundary and Claims Commissions

    Record Group 84: Records of the Foreign Service Posts

    Record Group 165: Records of Military Intelligence Division

    Record Group 226: Records of Office of Strategic Services

Paniagua (Chiapas) Collection, Latin American Library, Tulane University, New Orleans, Louisiana.

NEWSPAPER SOURCES

La Agricultura (Tuxtla Gutiérrez, Chiapas)

Boletín de la Cámara Agrícola de Chiapas (Tuxtla Gutiérrez, Chiapas)

Boletín de Información (Tuxtla Gutiérrez, Chiapas)

La Brújula (San Cristóbal Las Casas, Chiapas)

El Caudillo (San Cristóbal Las Casas, Chiapas)

Chiapas Nuevo (Tuxtla Gutiérrez, Chiapas)

Chiapas y México (Mexico City)

El Criterio (San Cristóbal Las Casas, Chiapas)

El Demócrata (San Cristóbal Las Casas, Chiapas)

Diario de los Debates (Cámara de Diputados, Mexico City)

Diario del Hogar (Mexico City)

Excelsiór (Mexico City)

La Frontera del Sur (Tapachula, Chiapas)

El Heraldo de Chiapas (Tuxtla Gutiérrez, Chiapas)

El Imparcial (Mexico City)

El Iris de Chiapas (San Cristóbal Las Casas, Chiapas)

Liberación (Tuxtla Gutiérrez, Chiapas)

La Libertad del Sufragio (San Cristóbal Las Casas, Chiapas)
Más Allá. Revista Católica Dominical Informativa (San Cristóbal Las Casas, Chiapas)
The Mexican Herald (Mexico City)
Mexican Labor News (Mexico City)
El Monitor Republicano (Mexico City)
El Obrero (Comitán, Chiapas)
El Paladín (San Cristóbal Las Casas, Chiapas)
El Partido Liberal (Mexico City)
La Patria Chica (Tuxtla Gutiérrez, Chiapas)
Periódico Oficial del Estado (Tuxtla Gutiérrez, Chiapas)
El Progreso (Tuxtla Gutiérrez, Chiapas)
Reconstrucción (Tuxtla Gutiérrez, Chiapas)
Renovación (Tuxtla Gutiérrez, Chiapas)
Revista Chiapaneca (San Cristóbal Las Casas, Chiapas)
Revista de Chiapas (Tuxtla Gutiérrez, Chiapas)
El Sur de Mexico (Tapachula, Chiapas)
El Universal (Mexico City)
Unomásuno (Mexico City)
La Vangardia (Tuxtla Gutiérrez, Chiapas)
El Voto de Chiapas (Tuxtla Gutiérrez, Chiapas)
La Voz de Chiapas (Tuxtla Gutiérrez, Chiapas)
La Voz del Pueblo (San Cristóbal Las Casas, Chiapas)

PRINTED DOCUMENTS
(and statistical sources)

El Colegio de México. Seminario de Historia Moderna de México. *Estadísticas económicas del Porfiriato: Fuerza de trabajo y actividad económica por sectores.* Mexico City, 1964.
El Colegio de México. Seminario de Historia Moderna de México. *Estadísticas sociales del porfiriato, 1877–1910.* Mexico, 1956.
Chiapas. *Anuario estadístico del estado de Chiapas, año de 1909.* Tuxtla Gutiérrez, 1911.
Chiapas. *Colección de leyes agrarias y demás disposiciones que se han emitido con relaciones al ramo de tierras.* San Cristóbal Las Casas, 1878.
Chiapas. *Confederación de campesinos y obreros del Estado de Chiapas, Estatutos.* Tuxtla Gutiérrez, 1935.
Chiapas. *Datos estadísticos del estado de Chiapas. 1896.* Tuxtla Gutiérrez, 1897.

Chiapas. *Declaraciones del gobernador del estado de Chiapas, Ing. Raymundo E. Enríquez.* Tuxtla Gutiérrez, 1930.

Chiapas. *Discurso del Lic. Emilio Rabasa, gobernador del estado de Chiapas.* . . . Tuxtla Gutiérrez, 1892 and 1893.

Chiapas. *Documentos relativos al congreso agrícola de Chiapas.* Tuxtla Gutiérrez, 1898.

Chiapas. *Informe del gobernador de Chiapas, C. Coronel Francisco León.* . . . Tuxtla Gutiérrez, 1897.

Chiapas. *Informe rendido por el C. gobernador del estado.* . . . Tuxtla Gutiérrez, 1900, 1903, 1904, 1906, 1907, 1908, 1910, 1911, 1920, 1921, 1922, 1924, 1925, 1926, 1929, 1931, 1932, 1933, 1934, 1938, 1939.

Chiapas. *Ing. Efraín A. Gutiérrez. Trayectoria de un gobierno revolucionario: esfuerzo y labor realizados en el estado de Chiapas, 1936–1940.* Mexico City, 1941.

Chiapas. *Ley y reglamento para la división y reparto de egidos en el estado de Chiapas.* Tuxtla Gutiérrez, 1893.

Chiapas. *Ley reglamentaria del trabajo.* Tuxtla Gutiérrez, 1926.

Chiapas. *Memoria del estado en que se hallan los ramos de la administración pública del estado de Chiapas, 1846.* San Cristóbal Las Casas, 1846.

Chiapas. *Memoria sobre diversos ramos de la administración pública del estado de Chiapas.* . . . Chiapas, 1883, 1885, 1889, 1891.

Chiapas. *Reseña de las atribuciones y debates de los jefes políticos de Chiapas.* . . . Tuxtla Gutiérrez, 1897.

Investigation of Mexican Affairs. Preliminary Report and Hearings of the Committee on Foreign Relations, United States Senate. 2 vols. Washington, D.C., 1920.

Mexico, *Antología de la planeación en México, 1917–1985. 16. Planeación regional, estatal y municipal (1982–1985).* Mexico City, 1986.

Mexico. *Anuario estadístico de Chiapas, 1985.* 3 vols. Mexico City, 1986.

Mexico. *Anuario estadístico de la república mexicana.* . . . Mexico City, 1894–98, 1900–07, 1912.

Mexico. *Anuario estadístico, 1923–1924.* 2 vols. Mexico City, 1926.

Mexico. *Anuario estadístico de 1930.* Mexico City, 1932.

Mexico. *Anuario estadístico, 1938.* Mexico City, 1939.

Mexico. *Anuario estadístico de los estados unidos mexicanos.* . . . Mexico City, 1941, 1942, 1948.

Mexico. *. . . censo agrícola, ganadero y ejidal.* Mexico City, 1957, 1965, 1975.

Mexico. *Directorio de agrupaciones obreras y patronales de la república.* Mexico City, 1939.

Mexico. *Estadísticas Históricas de México.* 2 vols. Mexico City, 1985.

Mexico. *Informe de las recursos agrícolas del departamento de Soconusco, en el estado de Chiapas*. Mexico City, 1871.

Mexico. *The Mexican Year Book, 1912*. Mexico City, 1912.

Mexico. *Monografía del estado de Chiapas*. Mexico City, 1975.

Mexico. *Regiones económico agrícolas de la República Mexicana: Memorias descriptivas* (Mexico City: Secretaría de Agricultura y Fomento, 1936).

Mexico. *Sistema de Cuentas Nacionales de México. Estructura Económica Regional Producto Interno Bruto por Entidad Federativa 1970, 1975 y 1980*. Mexico City, 1985.

Valle, Rafael Heliodoro. *La anexión de Centro América a México*. 9 vols. Mexico City, 1924–1949.

CONTEMPORARY BOOKS, PAMPHLETS, AND MEMOIRS

Amram, David W. "Eastern Chiapas," *Geographical Review* XXVII (1937): 19–36.

Basauri, Carlos. *Tojolabales, Tzeltales y Mayas, breves apuntes sobre antropología, etnografía y linguística*. Mexico, 1931.

Blom, Frans y Gertrude Duby. *La selva lacandona*. 2 vols. Mexico, 1955.

Bravo Izquierdo, Carlos. *Lealtad militar—compaña en el estado de Chiapas e istmo de Tehuantepec*. Mexico, 1948.

Byam, W. W. *A Sketch of the State of Chiapas, Mexico*. Los Angeles, 1897.

Chiapas: su estado actual, su riqueza, sus ventas para los negocios. Mexico, 1895.

Coffee: Extensive Information and Statistics. Washington, D.C., 1902.

Corzo, Ángel Albino. *Reseña de varios sucesos acaecidos en el estado de Chiapas durante la intervención francesa en la República*. Mexico, 1867.

———. *Segunda reseña de sucesos occurridos en Chiapas desde 1847 a 1867*. Tuxtla Gutiérrez, 1868, 1964.

Corzo, Manuel T. *Ligeros apuntes geográficos y estadísticos del estado de Chiapas*. Tuxtla Gutiérrez, 1897.

Directorio general de la república mexicana, 1893–1894. Mexico, 1893.

Directorio general de la república mexicana, 1900–1901. Mexico, 1900.

Espinosa, Luis, ed., *Chiapas*. Mexico, 1925.

———. *Rastros de sangre. Historia de la revolución en Chiapas*. Mexico, 1912.

Estatutos de la H. Cámara Nacional de Comercio e Industria de Tuxtla Gutiérrez, Chiapas. Tuxtla Gutiérrez, 1938.

Farrera, Agustín. *Breves apuntes sobre el estado de Chiapas*. Mexico, 1900.

Figueroa, Domenech J. *Guía general descriptiva de la república mexicana. Tomo II: Estados y territorios federales*. Mexico, 1899.

Filisola, General Vicente. *La cooperación de México en la independencia de Centro América (segunda parte)*. Mexico, 1911.

Gris, Carlos. *Sebastián Escobar y el departamento de Soconusco, Estado de Chiapas. Apuntes para la historia*. Mexico, 1885.

Gruening, Ernest. *Mexico and Its Heritage*. New York, 1928.

Guzman, Manuel E. *Chiapas: estudio y resolución de algunos problemas económicas y sociales del estado*. Mexico, 1930.

La junta de administración y vigilancia de la propiedad extranjera. Mexico, 1943.

Kaerger, Karl. *Landwirtschaft und Kolonisation im Spanischen Americka*. 2 vols. Leipsig, 1901.

Larrainzar, Federico. *Los intereses materiales en Chiapas*. San Cristóbal Las Casas, 1891.

―――. *La revolución en Chiapas*. San Cristóbal Las Casas, 1878.

Larrainzar, Manuel. *Noticia histórica de Soconusco y su incorporación a la república mexicana*. Mexico, 1843.

Marquez, J. M. *El veintiuno. hombres de la revolución y sus hechos*. Oaxaca, 1916.

Martínez Rojas, Jesús. *Los últimos acontecimientos políticos de Chiapas*. San Cristóbal Las Casas, 1912.

Montiel, Gustavo. *Tuxtla Gutiérrez de mis recuerdos*. Mexico, 1972.

Paniagua, Flavio Antonio. *Catecismo elemental de historia y estadística de Chiapas*. San Cristóbal Las Casas, 1876.

Pavia, Lazaro. *Los estados y sus gobernates*. Mexico, 1890.

Paz, Ireno. *Los hombres prominetes de México*. Mexico, 1895.

Pineda, Manuel. *Estudio sobre ejidos*. San Cristóbal Las Casas, 1910.

Ponce de León, Gregorio. *El interinato presidencial de 1911*. Mexico, 1912.

Rabasa, Emilio. *Antología de Emilio Rabasa*. 2 vols. Mexico, 1969.

―――. *La constitución y la dictadura, estudio sobre la organización política de México*. Mexico, 1912.

―――. *La evolución histórica de México*. Paris-Mexico, 1921.

Rabasa, Ramón. *El estado de Chiapas: geografía y estadística*. Mexico, 1895.

Rébora, Hipólito. *Memorias de un chiapaneco (1895–1982)*. Mexico, 1982.

Redfield, Robert, and Alfonso Villa Rojas. *Notes on the Ethnology of Tzeltal Communities of Chiapas*. Washington, D.C., 1939.

Rieva, J. *El problema agrario del Soconusco: apuntes y datos estadísticos del agrarismo en el sur de Chiapas*. Mexico, 1935.

Romero, Matías, *Cultivo del café en la costa meridional de Chiapas*. Mexico, 1875.

Sánchez Santos, Trinidad. *El problema de los indígenas de Chiapas.* San Cristóbal Las Casas, 1902.

Santamaría, Francisco L. *La tragedía de Cuernavaca en 1927 y mi escapatoria celebre.* Mexico, 1938.

Sargent, Helen H. *San Antonio Nexapa.* New York, 1952.

Serrano, Santiago. *Chiapas revolucionario (hombres y hechos).* Tuxtla Gutiérrez, 1923.

Shields, Karena. *The Changing Wind.* New York, 1959.

Stevens, John L. *Incidents of Travel in Central America, Chiapas, and Tucatan.* 2 vols. New Brunswick, 1949.

Teuffer S., Salvador. *Resolución y antecedentes del problema agrario en la zona del Soconusco, Chiapas.* Tuxtla Gutiérrez, 1942.

Tribes and Temples: A Record of the Expedition to Middle America Conducted by the Tulane University of Louisiana in 1925. 2 vols. New Orleans, 1927.

Vilac, Gastón de. *Chiapas bajo el signo de la hoz.* Mexico, 1940.

Zepeda, Eraclio. *Respuesta a la última crisis política en Chiapas de D. Federico Larrainzar.* Mexico, 1878.

SECONDARY SOURCES

Aguayo, Sergio. *El éxodo centroamericano: consecuencias de un conflicto.* Mexico, 1985.

Amnesty International. *Mexico: Human Rights in Rural Areas. Exchange of Documents with the Mexican Government on Human Rights Violations in Oaxaca and Chiapas.* London, 1986.

Anguiano, Arturo. *El estado y la política obrera del cardenismo.* Mexico, 1975.

Ankerson, Dudley. *Agrarian Warlord: Saturnino Cedillo and the Mexican Revolution in San Luis Potosí.* DeKalb, Ill. 1984.

Appendini, K., M. Pepin-Lehalleur, T. Rendón, and V. Salles. *El campesinado en México: dos perspectivas de análisis.* Mexico, 1983.

Ashby, Joe C. *Organized Labor and the Mexican Revolution under Lazaro Cardenas.* Chapel Hill, 1963.

Bartra, Armando. *Los herederos de Zapata: Movimientos campesinos posrevolucionarios en México.* Mexico, 1985.

Baumann, Friederike. "Terratenientes, campesinos y la expansión de la agricultura capitalista en Chiapas, 1896–1916." *Mesoamérica* 4 (1983): 8–63.

Benjamin, Thomas, and William McNellie, eds. *Other Mexicos: Essays on Regional Mexican History, 1876–1911.* Albuquerque, 1984.

Bethell, Leslie, ed. *The Cambridge History of Latin America.* Vols. III, IV, and V. Cambridge, England, 1985–86.

Brading, D. A., ed. *Caudillo and Peasant in the Mexican Revolution.* Cambridge, England, 1980.

Cáceres López, Carlos. *Historia general del estado de Chiapas.* 2 vols. Mexico, 1963.

Cancian, Frank. *Change and Uncertainty in a Peasant Economy: The Maya Corn Farmers of Zinacantan.* Stanford, 1972.

Casahonda Castillo, José. *50 años de revolución en Chiapas.* Tuxtla Gutiérrez, 1974.

Castañón Gamboa, Fernando. "Panorama histórico de las comunicaciones en Chiapas," *Ateneo Chiapas* I (1951): 75–127.

Clark, Marjorie Ruth. *Organized Labor in Mexico.* Chapel Hill, 1934.

Cockcroft, James D. *Mexico: Class Formation, Capital Accumulation, and the State.* New York, 1983.

Collier, George A. *Fields of the Tzotzil: The Ecological Bases of Tradition in Highland Chiapas.* Austin, 1975.

———. "Peasant Politics and the Mexican State: Indigenous Compliance in Highland Chiapas," *Mexican Studies/Estudios Mexicanos,* 3 (Winter 1987): 71–98.

Córdova, Arnaldo. *La clase obrera en la historia de México: En una época de crisis, 1928–1934.* Mexico, 1980.

———. *La política de masas del cardenismo.* Mexico, 1974.

Corzo, Ángel M. *Historia de Chiapas.* Mexico, 1944.

Cosío Villegas, Daniel, ed. *Historia moderna de México.* 10 vols. Mexico, 1957–1972.

Craig, Ann L. *The First Agraristas: An Oral History of a Mexican Agrarian Reform Movement.* Berkeley, 1983.

La cuestión de limites entre México y Guatemala. Guatemala, 1964.

Cumberland, Charles C. *Mexican Revolution: The Constitutionalist Years* Austin, 1974.

———. *Mexican Revolution: Genesis under Madero.* Austin, 1952.

———. *Mexico: The Struggle for Modernity.* Oxford, 1968.

De la Peña, Moisés T. *Chiapas económico.* 4 vols. Tuxtla Gutiérrez, 1951.

———. "La potencialidad ganadera de Chiapas," *Ateno Chiapas* I (1951): 43–81.

de Vos, Jan. *San Cristóbal ciudad colonial.* Mexico, 1986.

Dulles, John W. F. *Yesterday in Mexico: A Chronicle of the Revolution, 1919–1936.* Austin, 1961.

Esteva, Gustavo. *La batalla en el México rural.* Mexico, 1980.

Favre, Henri. *Cambio y continuidad entre los mayas de Mexico*. Mexico, 1973.

──────. "El cambio socio-cultural y el nuevo indigenismo en Chiapas," *Revista Mexicana de Sociología* XLVII:3 (julio-septiembre de 1985): 161–196.

García de León, Antonio. "Lucha de clases y poder político en Chiapas," *Historia y Sociedad* 22 (1979): 57–88.

──────. *Resistencia y utopía. Memorial de agravios y crónicas de revueltas y profecías acaecidas en la provincia de Chiapas durante los últimos quinientos años de su historia*. 2 vols. Mexico, 1985.

García S., Mario. *Geografía general de Chiapas*. Mexico, 1969.

──────. *Soconusco en la historia*. Mexico, 1963.

Garrido, Luis Javier. *El partido de la revolución institucionalizada (Medio siglo de poder político en México) La formación del nuevo estado en México (1929–1945)*. Mexico, 1982.

Gilly, Adolfo. *The Mexican Revolution*. London, 1983.

Glass, Elliot S. *México en las obras de Emilio Rabasa*. Mexico, 1975.

González Casanova, Pablo. *Democracy in Mexico*. New York, 1970.

González Calzada, Manuel. *Historia de la revolución mexicana en Tabasco*. Mexico, 1972.

González y González, Luis. *Historia de la revolución mexicana: Los artífices del cardenismo*. Mexico, 1979.

González Navarro, Moisés. *La confederación nacional campesina. Un grupo de presión en la reforma agraria mexicana*. Mexico, 1968.

──────. *La pobreza en México*. Mexico, 1985.

Gossen, Gary. *Chamulas in the World of the Sun: Time and Space in a Maya Oral Tradition*. Cambridge, Mass., 1974.

Grindle, Merilee S. *State and Countryside: Development Policy and Agrarian Politics in Latin America*. Baltimore, 1986.

Helbig, Karl M. *La cuenca superior del Río Grijalva. Un estudio regional de Chiapas, sudeste de México*. Tuxtla Gutiérrez, 1964.

──────. *El Soconusco y su zona cafetelera en Chiapas*. Tuxtla Gutiérrez, 1964.

Henderson, Peter V. N. *Félix Díaz, the Porfirians, and the Mexican Revolution*. Lincoln, 1981.

Hernández Chavez, Alicia. "La defensa de los finqueros en Chiapas, 1914–1920," *Historia Mexicana* XXVIII (enero-marzo 1979): 335–369.

──────. *Historia de la revolución mexicana: La mecánica cardenista*. Mexico, 1979.

Jacobs, Ian. *Ranchero Revolt: The Mexican Revolution in Guerrero*. Austin, 1982.

Joseph, G. M. *Revolution from Without: Yucatan, Mexico, and the United States, 1880–1924*. Cambridge, England, 1982.

Katz, Friedrich. "Labor Conditions on Haciendas in Porfirian Mexico: Some Trends and Tendencies," *Hispanic American Historical Review* LIV (1974): 1–47.

———. *The Secret War in Mexico: Europe, the United States, and the Mexican Revolution.* Chicago, 1981.

———. *La servidumbre agraria en México en la época porfiriana.* Mexico, 1980.

Kohler, Ulrich. *Cambio cultural dirigido en los altos de Chiapas: Una estudio sobre antropología social aplicada.* Mexico, 1975.

Knight, Alan. "Mexican Peonage: What Was It and Why Was It?" *Journal of Latin American Studies* 18 (1986): 41–74.

———. *The Mexican Revolution.* 2 vols. Cambridge, England, 1986.

———. "The Mexican Revolution: Bourgeois? Nationalist? Or just a 'Great Rebellion'?" *Bulletin of Latin American Research* 4:2 (1985): 1–37.

Knowlton, Robert J. *Church Property and the Mexican Reform, 1856–1910.* DeKalb, Ill., 1976.

Laughlin, Robert M. *Of Cabbages and Kings: Tales from Zinacantan.* Washington, D.C., 1977.

Liceaga, Luis. *Félix Díaz.* Mexico, 1958.

Llevano, Vicente. *Lic. Emilio Rabasa.* Tuxtla Gutiérrez, 1946.

López Gutiérrez, Gustavo. *Chiapas y sus epopeyas libertarias.* 3 vols. Tuxtla Gutiérrez, 1932.

López Monjardín, Adriana. *La lucha por los ayuntamientos: una utopia viable.* Mexico, 1986.

López Rosado, Diego G. *Historia y pensamiento económico de México.* 4 vols. Mexico, 1968.

Loyola Díaz, Rafael. *La crisis obregón-calles y el estado mexicano.* Mexico, 1980.

Lynch, John. *The Spanish-American Revolutions, 1808–1826.* New York, 1973.

MacLeod, Murdo J. *Spanish Central America: A Socioeconomic History, 1520–1720.* Berkeley, 1973.

Macleod, Murdo J., and Robert Wasserstrom, eds. *Spaniards and Indians in Southeastern Mesoamerica: Essays on the History of Ethnic Relations.* Lincoln, 1983.

Marbán, Osorio. *El partido de la revolución mexicana.* 2 vols. Mexico, 1970.

Martínez Assad, Carlos. *El laboratorio de la revolución. El tabasco garridista.* Mexico, 1979.

McQuown, Norman A., and Julian Pitt-Rivers, eds. *Ensayos de antropología en la zona central de Chiapas.* Mexico, 1970.

Medina, Hilario. "Emilio Rabasa y la constitución de 1917," *Historia Mexicana* X (junio-julio 1960): 134–148.

Medina, Luis. *Historia de la revolución mexicana: Civilismo y modernización del autoritarismo.* Mexico, 1979.

———. *Historia de la revolución mexicana: Del cardenismo al avilacamachismo.* Mexico, 1978.

Mejía Fernández, Miguel. *Política agraria en México en el siglo XIX.* Mexico, 1979.

Mejía Pineros, María Consuelo, and Sergio Sarmiento Silva, *La lucha indígena: un reto a la ortodoxia.* Mexico, 1987.

Memoria sobre la cuestión de limites entre Guatemala y México. Guatemala, 1964.

Meyer, Jean. *Problemas campesinas y revueltos agrarios (1821–1910).* Mexico, 1975.

———. *La revolución mejicana, 1910–1940.* Barcelona, 1973.

Meyer, Lorenzo. "El estado mexicano contemporáneo," *Historia Mexicana* XXIII (abril-junio 1974): 722–752.

———. *Historia de la revolución mexicana: El conflicto social y los gobiernos del maximato.* Mexico, 1978.

Meyer, Michael C. *Huerta: A Political Portrait.* Lincoln, 1972.

Molina, Virginia. *San Bartolomé de los Llanos: Una urbanización frenada.* Mexico, 1976.

Montagu, Roberta. "Chicago Mimeographs." Books 1–13. n.d.

Morales Avendano, Juan María. *Evolución y tenencia de la tierra en San Bartolomé de los Llanos.* Venustiano Carranza, Chiapas, 1977.

Moscoso Pastrana, Prudencio. *Jacinto Pérez "Pajarito," último lider chamula.* Tuxtla Gutiérrez, 1972.

———. *México y Chiapas: Independencia y federación de la provincia chiapaneca. Bosquejo Histórico.* Tuxtla Gutiérrez, 1974.

———. *El pinedismo en Chiapas.* Mexico, 1960.

Paniagua, Alicia. "Chiapas en la coyuntura centroamericano," *Cuadernos Políticos* (octubre-diciembre 1983): 48–52.

Perera, Víctor, and Robert D. Bruce. *The Last Lords of Palenque: The Lacandon Mayas of the Mexican Rain Forest.* Boston, 1982.

Pérez Castro, Ana Bella. "Estructura agraria y movimientos campesinos en Simojovel, Chiapas," Tesis, Escuela Nacional de Antropología e Historia, 1981.

———. "Movimiento campesino en Simojovel, Chis. 1936–1978. Problema étnico o de clases sociales," *Anales de Antropología* 19 (1982): 207–229.

Pozas, Ricardo. *Chamula.* 2 vols. Mexico, 1977.

————. "El trabajo en las plantaciones de café y el cambio sociocultural del indio," *Revista Mexicana de Estudios Antropológicos* XIII (1952): 31–65.

Richmond, Douglas. *Venustiano Carranza's Nationalist Struggle, 1893–1920.* Lincoln, 1983.

Riding, Alan. *Distant Neighbors: A Portrait of the Mexicans.* New York, 1985.

Rincón Coutiño, Valentín. *Chiapas entre Guatemala y México.* Mexico, 1964.

Rodríguez, Mario. *The Cadiz Experiment in Central America, 1808–1826.* Berkeley, 1978.

Ross, Stanley R. *Francisco I. Madero: Apostle of Mexican Democracy.* New York, 1970.

Ruiz, Ramon Eduardo. *The Great Rebellion: Mexico, 1905–1924.* New York, 1980.

Salamini, Heather Fowler. *Agrarian Radicalism in Veracruz, 1920–1928.* Lincoln, 1978.

Sanderson, Steven E. *Agrarian Populism and the Mexican State: The Struggle for Land in Sonora.* Berkeley, 1981.

————. *The Transformation of Mexican Agriculture: International Structure and the Politics of Rural Change.* Princeton, 1986.

Sepulveda, César. "Historia y problemas de los limites de México. La frontera sur," *Historia Mexicana* VIII (octubre-diciembre 1958): 145–174.

Simpson, Eyler N. *The Ejido: Mexico's Way Out.* Chapel Hill, 1937.

Sinkin, Richard N. *The Mexican Reform, 1855–1876: A Study in Liberal Nation-Building.* Austin, 1979.

Spenser, Daniela. "El movimiento campesino y la reforma agraria en Soconusco." Unpublished manuscript, 1983.

————. "El Partido Socialista Chiapaneco: Rescate y reconstrucción de su historia," Tesis, Grado de Maestria, Facultad de Ciencias Políticas y Sociales de la Universidad Nacional Autónoma de México, 1987.

Stern, Claudio. *Las regiones de México y sus niveles de desarrollo socioeconómico.* Mexico, 1973.

Svendsen, Kirsten A. "El trabajo asalariado en las comunidades indígenas." Tesis, Licenciado en Economía, Universidad Nacional Autónoma de México, 1967.

Tannenbaum, Frank. *The Mexican Agrarian Revolution.* Washington, D.C., 1929.

————. *Peace by Revolution: An Interpretation of Mexico.* New York, 1933.

Tórres Ramírez, Blanca. *Historia de la revolución mexicana: México en la segunda guerra mundial.* Mexico, 1979.

Trens, Manuel. *El imperio en Chiapas, 1863–1864.* Tuxtla Gutiérrez, 1956.

———. *Historia de Chiapas*. Mexico, 1942.

Tutino, John. *From Insurrection to Revolution in Mexico: Social Bases of Agrarian Violence, 1750–1940*. Princeton, 1986.

Valadés, José C. *El porfirismo, historia de un régimen*. 2 vols. Mexico, 1948.

Voss, Stuart F. *On the Periphery of Nineteenth-Century Mexico: Sonora and Sinaloa, 1810–1877*. Tucson, 1982.

Waibel, Leo. *La sierra madre de Chiapas*. Mexico, 1953.

Warman, Arturo. *"We Come to Object": The Peasants of Morelos and the National State*. Baltimore, 1980.

Wasserman, Mark. *Capitalists, Caciques, and Revolution: The Native Elite and Foreign Enterprise in Chihuahua, Mexico, 1854–1911*. Chapel Hill, 1984.

Wasserstrom, Robert. "A Caste War that Never Was: The Tzeltal Conspiracy of 1848," *Peasant Studies* 7 (1978): 73–85.

———. *Class and Society in Central Chiapas*. Berkeley, 1983.

———. "La evolución de la economía regional en Chiapas: 1528–1975," *América Indígena* (1976): 478–498.

———. "Population Growth and Economic Development in Chiapas, 1524–1975," *Human Ecology* 6 (1978): 127–143.

Wells, Alan. *Yucatan's Gilded Age: Haciendas, Henequen, and International Harvester, 1860–1915*. Albuquerque, 1985.

Whetten, Nathan L. *Rural Mexico*. Chicago, 1948.

Wilkie, James W. *The Mexican Revolution: Federal Expenditure and Social Change since 1910*. Berkeley, 1967.

Wilkie, James W., and Edna Monzón de Wilkie. *México visto en el siglo XX: entrevistas de historia oral*. Mexico, 1969.

Wolfskill, George, and Douglas Richmond, eds. *Essays on the Mexican Revolution: Revisionist Views of the Leaders*. Austin, 1979.

Woodward, Jr., Ralph Lee. "Economic and Social Origins of the Guatemalan Political Parties," *Hispanic American Historical Review* 45 (1965): 544–566.

Wortman, Miles. "Government Revenue and Economic Trends in Central America, 1787–1819," *Hispanic American Historical Review* 55 (1975): 251–286.

———. *Government and Society in Central America, 1680–1840*. New York, 1982.

———. "Legitimidad política y regionalismo—El Imperio Mexicana y Centroamérica," *Historia Mexicana* 26 (1976): 238–262.

Yates, Paul Lamartine. *El desarrollo regional de México*. Mexico, 1961.

INDEX

Note: Page numbers in italics refer to tables on those pages.

Department of Agrarian Affairs and
Colonization, 232
Department of Agrarian Reform, 234
Department of Agriculture and Animal
Husbandry, 221
Department of Education, 165
Department of Indigenous Affairs,
191–92
Department of Labor, Proletarian
Defense, and Social Welfare, 180
Department of Public Works, 239
Department of Rural Education and
Indigenous Protection, 202
Department of Social Action, Culture,
and Indigenous Protection, 184–85,
202
deportation, of rebellious Indians, 89
desaparición de los poderes, 109–10
development, economic, 34, 48;
federally funded, 229–30; and
government, 33; impact of, 84–90;
industrial, 184; and Liberal power,
13; program of, 241–43; state
promotion of, 30; Vidalista, 166
Díaz, Félix, 114–15, 128
Díaz, Porfirio, 19, 33, 40; and aid to
Chiapas, 58–59; and caciques, 30;
and conflict with Guatemala, 56;
and control of elections, 56; and
Farrera trial, 71–72; and forced
labor, 89; and indebted servitude,
62; loyalty to, 52; overthrow of, 95,
99–100; political stability of, 53;
power of, 39–40; and Rafael
Pimentel, 75; rebellion of, 21; and
reelection of Francisco León, 70;
and use of tamanes, 65–66. *See also*
Porfiriato
Dirección General de Caminos, 166
Division of Ejidal Promotion, 206
División Veintiuno, 134
divorce, 121
Domínguez, Abelardo, 112
Domínguez, Belisario, 108, 113, 130;
and opposition to Huerta regime,
116
Domínguez, José Pantaleón, 19–21

Domínguez, Luis Felipe, 115
Dominican Order, 18; property of, 14
Durán Pérez, Salvador, 224–25

Echeverría, Luis, 229, 234
economy; crisis of 1907–11, 83–84;
expansion of, 24–25, 27, 38, 223–
27; national, 37; North Atlantic, 24;
peasant, 218; recovery of, 214–18,
regional, 30, 60–61, 64, 85, 214;
regional devastation of, 136–37;
regional, modernization of, xvii, 34,
149. *See also* development, economic
education, 45, 131, 222; agricultural,
84; federal intervention in, 165–66;
freedom of, 17; Indian, 202, 227;
need for, 239; and Rafael Pimentel,
6–77; primary, 81, 181; public, 34,
50–51, 132; rural, 181, 192;
socialist, 186; state government
support of, 54, 57–58
"ejército reorganizador," 157
ejidos, 13, 69; breakup of, 206;
conflict between, 197, 211; creation
of, 165, 205; division of, 57;
enlargement of, 15; political
incorporation of, 203; privatization
of, 39, 48–50; revival of, 202
El Baluarte Chiapaneco, 177
El Demócrata, 141
El Economista Mexicana, 60
elections, 154–56, 161; as concession,
142; general, 99–100, 219;
gubernatorial, 69–70, 110, *111*,
133, 138, 161–62, 172–73;
municipal, 139, 161, 221, 236; and
PRM, 200; state, 105–6, 113, 190–
94; union, 224–25; and violence,
220
Electoral Law (1945), 220–21
electoral reform, 197
electricity, production of, 38, 229–30
El Imparcial, 104
elite, regional, 55; rebellion against,
100. *See also* familia chiapaneca
El Monitor Republicano, 41